T0089710

SACRED
LIBERTY

SACRED LIBERTY

—

America's Long, Bloody, and Ongoing

Struggle for Religious Freedom

Steven Waldman

HarperOne
An Imprint of HarperCollinsPublishers

HarperOne

SACRED LIBERTY. Copyright © 2019 by Steven Waldman. All rights reserved.
Printed in the United States of America. No part of this book may be used or reproduced
in any manner whatsoever without written permission except in the
case of brief quotations embodied in critical articles and reviews. For information,
address HarperCollins Publishers, 195 Broadway, New York, NY 10007.

HarperCollins books may be purchased for educational, business, or sales
promotional use. For information, please email the Special Markets Department
at SPsales@harpercollins.com.

FIRST HARPERCOLLINS PAPERBACK EDITION PUBLISHED IN 2020

Library of Congress Cataloging-in-Publication Data is available upon request.

ISBN 978-0-06-274315-2

20 21 22 23 24   LSC   10 9 8 7 6 5 4 3 2 1

To my parents

Contents

INTRODUCTION

The long march to religious freedom.

The Reverend John Waller was preaching in Caroline County, Virginia, in 1771 when an Anglican minister strode up to the pulpit and jammed the butt end of a horse whip into his mouth. Waller was dragged outside, where a local sheriff beat him bloody.[1] He spent 113 days in jail—for the crime of being a Baptist preacher.[2] When the Reverend James Ireland was jailed in nearby Culpeper County, he continued to preach through his cell's barred windows. To stop him, Anglican church leaders galloped horses through the crowd, and hecklers urinated in his face.[3] The Reverend David Thomas's services were disrupted by protesters who hurled live snakes and a hornet's nest into the room.[4]

These were among 150 major attacks against Baptists in Virginia between 1760 and 1778, many of them carried out by leaders of local Anglican churches—and, significantly, many of them within a horse ride of a young James Madison.

"This vexes me the most of any thing," Madison, then twenty-three, complained to his friend William Bradford in 1774. He told Bradford that five or six "well-meaning" Baptist ministers were at that moment imprisoned in neighboring Culpeper County for what he considered an absurd charge—preaching the gospel and "publishing their religious Sentiments." In the two years since Madison returned home from college in New Jersey, he had "squabbled and scolded" about the abuse of the Baptists but to little avail: "That diabolical, Hell-conceived principle of persecution rages."[5]

As alien as these kinds of attacks seem today—Anglican ministers brutalizing Baptist ministers on the eve of the American Revolution?—they were much more common in our history than we like to admit. Those who demand religious rights have too often been mocked and murdered, tarred and feathered. The same nation that boasts of its commitment to religious liberty also allowed for the following injustices.

-   In the seventeenth century, Massachusetts hanged people for being Quakers.

-   When the Declaration of Independence was signed, nine of the thirteen colonies barred Catholics and Jews from holding office.

-   In 1838, the governor of Missouri issued Executive Order 44, calling for the "extermination" of the Mormons.

-   Protestant mobs burned convents, sacked churches, and collected the teeth of deceased nuns as souvenirs during anti-Catholic riots in the 1830s—just one of the many spasms of "anti-papism" that roiled America from the colonial era until well into the twentieth century.

-   Hundreds of thousands of Africans were stripped of not only their liberty but also their religions when they were brought to America, in what one historian called "a spiritual holocaust."

-   After the Civil War, the United States government banned many Native American spiritual practices while coercing indigenous children to convert to Christianity.

-   Before and during World War II, Jehovah's Witnesses were imprisoned, beaten, and even castrated for refusing, as a matter of conscience, to salute the American flag.

Yet today we enjoy such robust religious freedom that this litany of persecutions is horrifying. Proof of how far we have come was on display in 2016 when the United States Supreme Court began its session by seating six Catholics and three Jews as justices. Men and women who would not have been allowed to hold office in early America would pass judgment on paramount questions of state, including religious liberty. Progress can also be seen each time Congress convenes, with invocations offered by every flavor of Christian clergy as well as by Muslim imams, Hindu priests, and Jewish rabbis.

Or consider the story of Parley Pratt, one of the original "twelve apostles" who helped found the Church of Jesus Christ of Latter-day Saints. Pratt was imprisoned in 1838 with Mormonism's founder, Joseph Smith, and driven out of Missouri by mobs of angry Protestants. Pratt had twelve wives and was later murdered by the estranged former husband of one of them.[6] His relatives fled to Mexico to avoid prosecution for polygamy. Yet in 2012, the Republican Party—which had earlier led the drive to ban Mormonism—chose as its nominee Parley Pratt's great-great-grandson Mitt Romney.[7]

More recently we saw a grassroots demonstration of the American love of religious freedom when thousands of people of different faiths flooded airports in 2017 to protest President Donald Trump's plan to ban Muslim immigrants. After Trump floated the idea of creating a national registry of Muslims, Jonathan Greenblatt, chief executive officer of the Anti-Defamation League, the leading group fighting anti-Semitism in the United States, offered a poetically effective response: "Because I am committed to the fight against anti-Semitism ... if one day Muslim-Americans are forced to register their identities, that is the day this proud Jew will register as Muslim."[8]

The strength of America's approach may be judged not just in the relative absence of persecution but in the nation's spiritual vibrancy—three hundred sixty thousand houses of worship, from Adventist to Zoroastrian, from urban storefront churches that seat a dozen to Christian mega-churches that hold forty thousand.[9] Spiritual practice thrives even more in the privacy of our homes: 76 percent of Americans pray regularly.[10] Notably, affluence has not dampened our religiosity as it has in other countries. The Pew Research Center recently mapped the relationship between wealth and religious practice. On the upper left of the chart is a cluster of countries that are religious but poor—Afghanistan, Nigeria, Djibouti and Guatemala. On the lower right are wealthy but secular nations including Norway, Switzerland, Ireland and Germany. Way off by itself on the right edge of the chart is a single stray dot, the United States—wealthy *and* religious.[11] America has reduced religious persecution without subduing religious passion.

This accomplishment is rare in world history. For millennia, societies have puzzled over how to have both religion and freedom. Government efforts to promote a single faith often had short-term benefits—the favored religion would gain influence, wealth, and security—but they levied tragic costs as well: wars against heretics, persecution of religious minorities, and corruption of the faith itself. Thomas Jefferson complained that the quest for doctrinal orthodoxy had "made of Christendom a slaughter house, and at this day divides it into Casts of inextinguishable hatred to one another."[12] Religion often has been a powerful source for good, yet there's no denying the frequency with which it devolves into crusades, inquisitions, holy wars, jihads, genocides, pogroms, civil wars, and terrorism. The problem is not religion per se; atheism's historical track record has been no better. Joseph Stalin, Mao Zedong, Adolf Hitler, and Pol Pot all attempted to destroy or suppress religion, and in fifty years they killed more people than had died in all the religious wars of the previous millennia.[13] Rather, the troubles arise because majority groups have invariably expected their faith to dominate, usually at the expense of religious minorities.

Today, most nations still have not found the right balance. More than three-quarters of the world's population lives in countries with limited religious freedom.[14] Most countries still have an official or government-preferred religion.[15] Varieties of oppression have flowered: Eastern Orthodox Christians harass Protestants (Russia); Muslims persecute Coptic Christians (Egypt); Buddhists attack Muslims (Myanmar); Muslims assail Protestants (Somalia); Protestants clash with Catholics (Northern Ireland); and Hindus agitate against Pentecostals (India). Even Western nations committed to *liberté* have stumbled—for example, in 2016 when French policemen forced female Muslim beachgoers to strip off their head scarves and burkinis because of the disrespect their religiously mandated clothing ostensibly showed to secularism.[16]

The more successful American paradigm has emerged over many years, shaped through civil disobedience, elections, lawsuits, coalition building, and bloodshed. Won through great struggle, religious freedom achieved an exalted status as a core element of our national identity. In allowing Americans to follow their souls' yearnings, religious freedom has become a sacred liberty. While this book describes America's little-known history of religious persecution, it is ultimately about how the nation moved forward. It is no exaggeration to say that America's unique approach to religious freedom is one of its greatest inventions.[17]

Ratification of the First Amendment to the United States Constitution—"Congress shall make no law respecting the establishment of religion, or prohibiting the free exercise thereof"—was, of course, extremely important. But that did not by itself produce full religious liberty, any more than the Declaration of Independence gave African Americans civil rights. The struggle to make religious freedom real in America has been long and tempestuous.

As with civil rights, the journey began with a set of ideas. The most significant visionary—and the most effective activist for religious freedom—was Madison, who wrote the seminal treatise "Memorial and Remonstrance Against Religious Assessments" and engineered the passage of the Virginia Statute for Religious Freedom before then guiding the creation of both the Constitution and its First Amendment. More than anyone else, this underappreciated founder devised the ingenious, counterintuitive, and often-misunderstood blueprint for the religious liberty we enjoy today.

First, he argued that the best way to promote religion was to leave it alone. This was revolutionary. In all of previous human history, those who wanted to encourage religion had enlisted the government's help. Madison believed that the state should neither constrain *nor* coddle religion and, above all, that it should not favor one faith over another. Even well-intentioned efforts would backfire, he insisted, sapping religion of its strength. His thinking was highly influenced by his interactions with Virginia's much-persecuted Baptists, the first of many times when evangelical Christians would play a central role in advancing religious liberty.[18] Like the evangelicals, Madison ardently supported the separation of church and state—not because he wanted to secularize society but, to the contrary, because he believed that it was the only way to ensure that religion would flourish.

Second, he wanted checks and balances—*for religion*. He was skeptical about the efficacy of what he referred to as "parchment barriers"— the lofty declarations of rights found in constitutions. He believed that the surest path to religious liberty would come from a "multiplicity of sects," a diversity of different denominations all jostling for followers. In a free marketplace of faiths, no one religion would dominate. Spiritual innovation would spread. New styles, denominations, and religions would continually emerge, creating still larger constituencies for religious freedom. Madison approached religion the way an early twentieth-century progressive approached capitalism: he wanted open competition but also rules to keep the big players from undermining the upstarts. This second concept, far less understood than the first, has proven to be essential.

Over time, in addition to creating the conditions for a spiritual free market, we have coalesced around a few core principles. The phrase "separation of church and state" does not adequately describe the creed, which today includes these ideas:

Religious freedom is a right, not a favor granted to a minority by a benevolent ruler or an indulgent majority.

The "state" must not favor one religion over another. That's true whether the government body in question is the US Congress or the local school board.

The majority religion does not get to regulate or push around minority religions.

People define for themselves what a religion is and whether it speaks to them. Religions are largely left to govern themselves.

Religious expressions by public officials in public places are welcomed but must be inclusive.

Our society must often make special accommodations for the religious—meaning we allow believers to sidestep certain laws that would force them to violate their conscience. We bend over backward to allow spiritual journeys to proceed unimpeded.

Progress has been largely driven by regular Americans—unheralded religious pioneers and, in some cases, martyrs. Mary Dyer decided to challenge "the bloody law" that made it illegal to be a Quaker in Massachusetts in 1659, and she paid with her life. Robert Fischer, a Jehovah's Witness, refused to kiss the American flag—and had his head smashed against a flag-draped car hood each time he demurred. In the chapters that follow, we will meet many others—including quite a few courageous children—who helped move religious freedom forward: Catholic elementary school students who refused to read from what they considered to be the Protestant Bible; Native Americans who persisted in performing their sacred dances under the threat of starvation; evangelical Protestant preachers arrested for speaking against slavery; Mormon leaders who went to jail rather than give up their religiously sanctioned practice of polygamy; Zilpha Elaw, a free African American woman who risked enslavement so she could preach to audiences in Maryland and Virginia, including Robert E. Lee's wife; and the Muslim American women who have fought off anti-Muslim attacks from the right while simultaneously challenging traditional Islamic leaders to accept a more pluralistic, American style of Islam.

The bravery of ordinary Americans occasionally has been complemented by the wisdom of the country's leaders. As commander of the

Continental Army, George Washington created a cohesive national institution out of a mix of soldiers practicing different religions. (First rule: don't burn effigies of the pope when we're trying to make alliances with Catholic countries.) After the Civil War, an evangelical congressman named John Bingham wrote the Fourteenth Amendment to the Constitution—which had profound implications for religious freedom— in part as a way of fulfilling what he saw as a divine plan. The three presidents of the World War II era—Franklin Roosevelt, Harry Truman, and Dwight Eisenhower—united the nation by casting religious tolerance as a weapon against fascism and communism. And by making sharp distinctions between Muslim terrorists and patriotic American Muslims after the attacks of September 11, 2001, George W. Bush strengthened liberty during a moment of great peril.

Why does religious freedom matter? For most Americans, the pursuit of happiness requires a pursuit of meaning. That manifests differently for each of us: the perfect ritual, polished through a thousand years of use, to help us grieve; a small prayer that makes us feel significant by connecting us to something far greater than ourselves; a moral code, or battle plan, that guides our behavior; an inspiration to live.

Beyond that, religious freedom has helped create a more perfect Union. Faith has fueled our most significant social movements, including the efforts to ban slavery, gain women the vote, and combat poverty, as well as more controversial efforts to advance same-sex marriage and limit alcohol use and abortion.[19] The civil rights movement of the 1950s and 1960s was fundamentally a religious crusade, made possible in part because African Americans, who had been denied so many rights, mostly held on to one: the ability to gather in churches, read scripture, and imagine the Exodus story brought forward into modern times. We may also be unconscious of how religion has shaped our civic culture. Imagine America without the likes of Alcoholics Anonymous, the YMCA, Boys & Girls Clubs of America, Habitat for Humanity, and so many other faith-based, communitarian institutions.

Madison also believed that religious liberty led to economic and cultural vitality. A few hundred years later, academics looked at global data and concluded that his intuition had been correct: nations that restrict religious freedom tend to have weaker economies.[20] The American approach to religion also minimizes violent conflicts and improves social comity. Of special relevance now, scholars believe that the relative scarcity of Islamic radicalism in the United States stems at least in part from our model of religious pluralism, which gives Muslims here more freedom to practice their faith than they might have in many Muslim nations. Finally, for atheists and agnostics, the system that gives the right to believe also guarantees the right not to believe. All of these benefits will no doubt become more important, not less, as the planet grows smaller. In the future, part of what will make America exceptional will be our ability to teach the rest of the world how people of different faiths can coexist and thrive.

———————

Although we have come a long way, religious freedom in America now faces some serious threats. As a presidential candidate in 2016, Donald Trump proposed banning Muslim immigrants and creating a special registry for American Muslims—both unprecedented assaults on religious liberty. A powerful new combination of social media and partisan television amplified verbal attacks on American Muslims. Public opinion shifted ominously. In one poll, only half of Republicans were willing to declare that Islam should be legal in America. Communities around the country attempted to block the construction of mosques and cemeteries.

Toward the end of this book, we will explore the nature of the assault on American Muslims, as well as the deep concerns of American Christians that their own faith is being persecuted. But it's important to view these challenges in the context of the full history of religious freedom. The attacks on liberty through the years often have had common characteristics. They were frequently triggered by immigration. They grew especially severe when the majority denomination felt its demographic dominance slipping away. Irresponsible news media often made matters worse. In several different generations (including our own, unfortunately), those opposed to religious freedom have made the same audacious claim: that a particular minority faith didn't deserve protection because it wasn't a legitimate religion. In the early twentieth century, Mormonism was deemed an "immoral and quasi criminal conspiracy," as the *Kalamazoo Telegraph* put it.[21] Some have used similar language about Islam in the twenty-first century. "Islam is a political ideology.... It definitely hides behind being a religion," said Michael Flynn, President Trump's first national security advisor. In case there was any ambiguity about why this distinction was important, Lieutenant General William G. "Jerry" Boykin, an anti-Muslim activist and former Pentagon official, explained that since Islam is "a totalitarian way of life," it "should not be protected under the First Amendment."[22]

As the cofounder (in 1999) of the multifaith website Beliefnet, I observed a digital version of the Madisonian ideal—people finding their own spiritual path in the context of a freewheeling, diverse community. This prompted me to write, in 2007, *Founding Faith*, an examination of the Founding Fathers' views on religion. But in subsequent years I came to realize that while the founders started us down the path, we also owe our freedoms to later heroines and heroes who are much less well known. Each generation has done its part, and now, today, it's time for contemporary Americans to do theirs. In the final chapter, I offer some suggestions for how we might strengthen this system. But the first step is to learn why we came to have religious freedom in the first place.

In an antiquated but still compelling analogy, Lewis Peyton Little, the author of an early history of Virginia's Baptists, compared religious liberty to "a sharp sword in a shop window."

> Men look upon it and admire its beauty and usefulness, but do not stop to think of the fires and painstaking processes through which it had to pass before its present shape was accomplished.[23]

This book is about the fires that forged religious liberty. If we want to preserve this great legacy, we need to understand how it was painstakingly built.

The execution of Mary Dyer

Chapter One

FAILED EXPERIMENTS

For more than two hundred years, the American colonies try traditional approaches to religious tolerance. It does not go well.

In the beginning, America pretty much rejected religious liberty. While believers in the seventeenth and eighteenth centuries sometimes came here from other lands to flee restrictions on their faith, real religious liberty rarely existed on our continent, at least in the modern sense of the term.

Mary Dyer discovered this in the early 1600s. By modern standards, Dyer was no groovy freethinker. Like many of the other Puritans who came to America seeking religious sustenance, she was a serious Bible-following Christian (how else to explain her naming her son Mahershalalhashbaz, after a line in Isaiah 8:1?). But at twenty-five, she fell in with a troublesome crowd in Boston. She attended meetings at Anne Hutchinson's house, where the women had the audacity to critique the weekly sermons of the local minister, accusing him of favoring the heretical doctrine of salvation by works. By 1636, Hutchinson and Dyer had been marked by the Puritan elders as dangerous radicals.

The local leaders believed they had another clear piece of evidence that Dyer was in the devil's orbit: she gave birth to a horribly deformed still-born baby. When officials heard the news, they had the baby exhumed so they could catalog its features. ("It had no forehead, but over the eyes four horns, hard and sharp . . . all over the breast and back full of sharp pricks and scales. . . . It had on each foot three claws, like a young fowl, with sharp talons.")[1] A history book from that time concluded that the "Lord had pointed directly to their sinne" by having Mary Dyer bring forth "a very fearfull Monster."[2]

Alas, this was just the first chapter in the remarkable story of Mary Dyer, one of the first great American religious martyrs. She fled Massachusetts and eventually went to England, where she met George Fox, founder of the Society of Friends, or the Quakers. She was drawn to the Quaker teaching that one could find the light of God within oneself and (therefore) need not rely on clergy or prescribed ritual.

In Massachusetts, being a Quaker was not just frowned upon—it was illegal. Puritans despised Quakers for reasons of theology (they heretically believed they could have a direct relationship with God), power (they refused to pay taxes to support the Congregational Church), and manners (the zealous Quakers sometimes interrupted church services and banged pots and pans in the streets). The punishment for being a Quaker was whipping on the first offense, having an ear cut off after the second, and execution on the third. The authorities enforced the law with sadistic enthusiasm. One elderly Quaker, William Brend, was whipped 117 times with rope "so that his flesh was beaten black and as into a jelly, and under his arms the bruised flesh and blood hung down."[3]

The first time Dyer returned to Massachusetts, in the fall of 1657, she was arrested and expelled. A few years later she returned to Boston to declare solidarity with two imprisoned Quaker friends, William Robinson and Marmaduke Stephenson, and to challenge the system—or, as she put it, to "try the bloody law." For this act of civil disobedience, she was sentenced to death.

Governor John Endecott puzzled over the persistence of Dyer and her friends. "We have made many laws and endeavored in several ways to keep you from among us, but neither whipping nor imprisonment, nor cutting off ears, nor banishment upon pain of death, will keep you from among us," he declared.[4]

On October 27, 1659, the three were brought to the Boston Common to be hanged. The colonial masters performed the executions sequentially rather than simultaneously, so Dyer could watch as her friends' necks snapped.

Suddenly, someone in the crowd yelled, "Stop, for she is reprieved!" This was no act of last-minute mercy. The whole drama had been orchestrated by the Massachusetts court so Dyer would witness the deaths as a lesson and then be freed. She left the area for a time, but on May 21, 1660, she was spotted walking the streets of Boston and was again sentenced to death. On June 1, wearing a plain gray dress, cloak, and bonnet, she walked from the prison to the Boston Common.[5] A row of drummers played to drown out any words of encouragement that might be offered her or that she might speak to the crowd. When the commander of the military declared that she had brought this on herself by defying the law, she responded, "I came to keep blood-guiltiness from you, desiring you to repeal the unrighteous and unjust law."[6]

A rope was tied to a large elm tree and a ladder propped against it. After she climbed it, the noose was placed around her neck and her arms and feet were bound together. The ladder was removed, and Mary Dyer was executed by the Holy Commonwealth of Massachusetts for the crime of attempting to practice her faith.

Purity

As pilgrims, profiteers, missionaries, and explorers moored their boats off the northeastern and southern coasts of North America, almost none of them wanted their new home to treat all religions equally.

John Cotton, one of the first Puritan ministers in New England, explained that they had come to America so they could follow the proper rules of their faith—"not of some ordinances of God, but of all, and in all purity."[7] They did come to the New World to avoid harassment in Europe, but their main critique was that the Church of England had been corrupted, in large part because it had retained too many of the trappings of Catholicism. "Kneeling at the Sacrament, bowing to the Altar to the name of Jesus, Popish holy days, Holiness of places, Organs and Cathedral Musick. . . . They are nothing else but the reliques of Popery, and remnants of Baal," wrote one prominent Puritan.[8]

The Puritans brought their antipathy to Catholicism and Paganism with them to America. Here, among other things, those devout Christians launched the first war on Christmas. The Bible did not sanction the holiday, which in their eyes was both papist (invented by Catholics, they believed) and pagan (in that it co-opted the winter solstice festivities of pre-Christians).[9] And people tended to get excessively, well, merry. The drinking, gift giving and lovemaking that accompanied the holiday's "Saturnalian jollities," in the words of Puritan leader Cotton Mather, seemed quite the opposite of what God intended. "Men dishonoured the Lord Jesus Christ more in the twelve days of Christmas" than during the rest of the year, he declared.[10] So in 1659, the Puritans made Christmas illegal.[11] Eventually the ban was lifted, but until the mid-nineteenth century, New England children did not get a day off from school on Christmas.[12] The rules were similarly strict during the rest of the year. Failure to observe the Sabbath and blasphemy were both serious crimes. And the Puritans' requirements for modesty would fit neatly into modern-day Saudi Arabia. Women could not expose their arms or necks. Their sleeves had to go down to their wrists, and their gowns had to be closed around the throat.[13]

This yen for purity flowed from the Puritans' theology, which obliged them, as "God's chosen people," to build a kingdom of God on Earth, a "City upon a Hill." The purpose of the church was not to turn regular folk into good Christians but to identify those "visible saints" who were already selected by God to receive saving grace—and eject the rest. As the Reverend Thomas Shepard of Cambridge explained, "one man or woman secretly vile, which the church hath not used all means to discover, may defile the whole church."[14] The Puritans rejected the modern notions of tolerance that were already in the air. "The Toleration of all Religions and Perswasions," wrote Increase Mather, "is the way to have no Religion at all."[15] Their persecution of the Quakers was deemed necessary to preserve "liberty of conscience"—that is, the freedom to have their own consciences unbothered by the intrusions of other beliefs.[16]

It made great sense, then, to fuse church and state so the combined entity could enforce pious behavior. The church comprised the godly, and the government comprised the church's members. "Theocracy, or to make the Lord God our governor, is the best form of government in a Christian commonwealth," explained John Cotton.[17]

Lest we see the Puritans as ogres through and through, we should acknowledge just how much we owe them. The American character was shaped in part by the Puritans' commitment to hard work, thrift, and personal devotion to God. Their conviction that they were players in a divine drama helped them survive those horribly grueling first years in the New World. They created institutions and traditions assisting middle-class families, advancing universal literacy and education. Alas, an appreciation of religious freedom was not among their positive attributes.

They were not alone. While the settlement in Jamestown, Virginia, in 1607 was partly a commercial venture, King James's charter also declared the goal of promoting Christianity to those living "in darkness and miserable ignorance of the true knowledge and worship of God," a.k.a. the Native Americans. In 1611, during a time of mass starvation, the Virginia Company instituted the "Lawes Divine, Morall and Martiall," which attempted to bring discipline, and perhaps divine support, through forced religiosity. Failure to observe the Sabbath three times drew the death penalty. Blasphemy—including taking God's name in vain—could be punished by having an iron plunged through the tongue.[18]

Over time, the colonies' religious rules became more civilized. Mary Dyer's pleas were heard; apostates would no longer be hanged.[19] But the laws rarely resembled the religious liberty we treasure today. In most colonies, residents designated a particular church to be the official religion and then paid taxes to support the clergy. Special parcels of land called glebes were often set aside to provide them income.[20] Anglicanism, the official religion of the Church of England, was "established" as the religion of several southern colonies. New England colonies gave preference to the Congregational Church, the religion of the Puritans. Pennsylvania, New York, and Rhode Island did not have establishments (more on them shortly).

In Connecticut, taxpayers subsidized the salaries of Congregational ministers; Baptists or members of another minority church had to apply for special exemptions from the tax. Only Congregational ministers could perform marriages. The church controlled the school systems, both primary and collegiate (e.g., Yale University), and helped run the government.[21] The Reverend Lyman Beecher, a nationally prominent minister throughout the first half of the nineteenth century, fondly recalled those days:

> On election day they had a festival. All the clergy used to go, walk in procession, smoke pipes, and drink. And, fact is, when they got together, they would talk over who should be governor, and who lieutenant governor, and who in the Upper House, and their counsels would prevail.[22]

These colonies also limited who could be an elected official or vote. In most, it was illegal for Jews or Catholics to hold office.

These systems did not promote "Judeo-Christian" values in general but rather Protestantism, as in the religion invented to protest Catholicism. As they say in the twenty-first-century technology world, anti-Catholicism was not a bug but a feature of the American project. Remember, the first English settlers arrived in North America just sixty years after the death of Martin Luther. The war between Protestants and Catholics still raged in Europe, and both sides viewed the New World as a battlefield. What's more, the Protestants who landed in America feared they were already losing. In 1503, more than a hundred years before Jamestown, the Spanish Catholics had planted their flag in Florida, which included parts of modern-day Alabama, Mississippi, South Carolina, Georgia, and Louisiana.

The seventeenth-century laws took direct aim at Catholics. Virginia banned all Catholics in 1642, and Massachusetts banned priests in 1647.[23] Georgia's charter provided full religious freedom, except for "Papists." Maryland, initially chartered as a refuge for Catholics, was eventually taken over by Protestants. In 1700, the colony prevented Catholics from inheriting or purchasing land and banned priests; in 1704, it banned Catholic worship; in 1715, it decreed that children of a Catholic mother and a Protestant father could be removed from the mother if the father died.[24] The antagonism to Catholics persisted right up until the Revolutionary War. At the time of independence, five colonies prohibited Catholics from voting.[25] Catholic schools were banned in all colonies except Pennsylvania.[26]

Quite a few of our freedom-loving Founding Fathers could not suppress their disgust with what they considered a regressive, backward religion. John Adams believed that "the Monster" of Catholicism worked to keep its subjects in "sordid Ignorance and staring Timidity"[27] and that "a free government and the Roman Catholick religion can never exist together in any nation or Country."[28] Influenced by the previous few hundred years of European history—in which the Roman Catholic Church *did* often side with tyrants, torturers, and crusaders—Enlightenment thinkers associated the Church with inquisitions, hostility to science, and superstition. After visiting St. Mary's Catholic Church in Philadelphia, Adams mocked "the poor Wretches, fingering their Beads, chanting Latin, not a Word of which they understood."[29] Samuel Adams referred to the Church as "the Whore of Babylon" (a reference to a villain in the Book of Revelations), while Roger Sherman, a member of the Continental Congress, wanted to prohibit Catholics from serving in the Continental Army. Colonists

routinely celebrated Pope Day, also known as Guy Fawkes Day, by burning effigies of the pontiff.

Of course, the Spanish Catholics who lived in the Americas were no
more enlightened. One of America's earliest recorded religious atrocities
occurred in 1565, when the Spanish in St. Augustine, Florida, demanded
that more than one hundred French Protestant soldiers convert to Catholicism. When they refused, they were massacred. More often, the Spanish
focused their religious cruelty on the Native Americans. When the Spanish landed in Tampa Bay, they read aloud, in Spanish, the *requerimiento*
that the Native Americans convert to Catholicism:

> If you do so, you will do well . . . [and we] shall receive you in
> all love and charity, and shall leave you, your wives, and your
> children, and your lands, free without servitude.

Then came the "or else." If they didn't convert:

> With the help of God, we shall powerfully enter into your country,
> and shall make war against you in all ways and manners that we
> can, and shall subject you to the yoke and obedience of the Church
> and of their Highnesses; we shall take you and your wives and
> your children, and shall make slaves of them, and as such shall sell
> and dispose of them as their Highnesses may command; and we
> shall take away your goods, and shall do you all the mischief and
> damage that we can.[30]

They meant it. The Spanish leader Pánfilo de Narváez invited area Indians to a peace negotiation and then cut off the chief's ears and threw his
mother to dogs.[31] The fusion of Spanish sadism and Catholic expansion-
ism did not improve the Church's reputation among other Americans.

Experiments Holy and Livelie

A few colonies did experiment with religious freedom. New York, North
Carolina, and especially Rhode Island and Pennsylvania provided alternative models for the founders to consider, while also showing how hard it
was to get religious freedom right.

Roger Williams came to the colonies in 1630, in the wake of the first
wave of Puritan settlers. He already had a reputation as a leading thinker

when he arrived, but he quickly became an irritant, in part because of his suggestion that his fellow Puritans had not separated sufficiently from the Church of England (i.e., the Puritans weren't pure enough). But his disagreements went further, reminding us that in any period some remarkable men and women are able to pull themselves out of context and think in shockingly modern ways. He opposed slavery.[32] He criticized the Church of Plymouth for using land taken from the Native Americans. In 1635, the Massachusetts Bay Colony banished him. He went to present-day Rhode Island, purchased land from the Indian leader Massasoit, and established the First Baptist Church.

In 1644, Williams published his most influential work, *The Bloudy Tenent of Persecution for Cause of Conscience*, in which he argued that state efforts to advance any particular religious ideas constitute "soule rape" which "stinks in God's nostrils." He declared that religious liberty should be afforded even to religious minorities that barely existed in the colonies, such as "the most paganish, Jewish, Turkish or antichristian consciences."[33] And to help us understand that state involvement with religion ended up harming it, he offered a novel new metaphor: there needed to be a "wall of separation" between "the garden of the church and the wilderness of the world." This separation of church and state, he argued, would benefit both, though he emphasized especially how the wall would protect religion from the pollution of secular society. Rhode Island, which Williams called a "Livelie Experiment" in "absolute Soul-Freedom," did attract an unusual diversity of believers—Quakers, Baptists, Seventh-Day Baptists, and even Jews.[34]

New York, parts of which were controlled by the Dutch, also offered somewhat more religious freedom than did New England or the southern colonies. Lady Deborah Moody was an Anabaptist who was driven out of Salem, Massachusetts, for believing that infants should not be baptized. Massachusetts governor John Winthrop sighed, "With the exception of her troubling the church with her religious opinions, she appears to have been a lady of great worth."[35] Instead of going to Rhode Island, Moody in 1645 sailed across the Long Island Sound to New Amsterdam, where she created Gravesend, now part of Brooklyn, the first New World settlement founded by a woman.[36] She was granted a patent for the land, which included the provision that settlers were "to have and injoye the free libertie of conscience according to the costome and manner of Holland."[37] But even in the Dutch areas, tolerance was defined narrowly, especially when it came to the ever-irksome Quakers. In 1657, the director general of the colony, Peter Stuyvesant, tried to block Quaker immigration in nearby Vlissingen (now Flushing, Queens), prompting objections from the non-Quaker residents, including some followers of Moody who had moved there from Gravesend.[38] They issued the Flushing Remonstrance, one of the first communal articulations of a more universal conception of religious liberty in the New World. They defiantly rejected Stuyvesant's rules—a shocking bit of civil disobedience—and proclaimed tolerance not only of Quakers and Baptists but even of Presbyterians, "Jews, Turks and Egyptians" because Jesus had instructed all "to doe unto all men as we desire all men should doe unto us, which is the true law both of Church and State." Note they did not include Catholics in their list of protected faiths. In any event, Stuyvesant's response to the eloquent appeal was to arrest some of its authors.[39]

The most influential experiment was in Pennsylvania. The founder of Pennsylvania, William Penn, decreed that it too would be a "Holy Experiment" in toleration. Philadelphia had the colonies' only Catholic church that was protected by the authorities.[40] "Sects of every belief are tolerated," commented one visitor. "You meet here Lutherans, Reformed, Catholics, Quakers, Mennonites, Herrenhuter or Moravian Brethren, Seventh-Day Baptists, Dunkers, Presbyterians, the New Born, Free Masons, Separatists, Free Thinkers, Negroes and Indians."[41] Benjamin Franklin and others raised money to build a nondenominational church. The architectural design would be neutral so it would work "even if the Mufti of Constantinople were to send a missionary to preach."[42] James Madison wrote to his friend William Bradford asking for materials about Pennsylvania, which he and other founders viewed as a model for religious freedom and social organization. This town of Philadelphia had not only a variety of churches but also libraries, museums, and businesses. Religious freedom seemed somehow connected to civic, cultural, and economic health.

While Pennsylvania's Quakers avoided the most egregious mistakes of other colonies—stripping and whipping heretical women, driving hot irons through tongues, favoring one religion over another—they tripped over one of their core beliefs: pacifism. In 1755, Indians near present-day Reading murdered fifteen settlers and scalped three children. Furious that the Quaker-led legislature had failed to protect them, eighteen hundred angry German immigrants who lived in the area drove four hundred wagons into Philadelphia, where they displayed the mutilated, blackened bodies of the victims in front of the governor's mansion. The legislature increased the military presence on the frontier, marking the end of the Quakers' theological control. The moral of the story is that when a government is run by and for a religious group—even a formerly oppressed one, even one that is highly sensitized to the rights of religious minorities—its policies will be seen as religiously biased.

The Revolution Begins

The colonists' distasteful behaviors ought not to be seen strictly through our modern eyes. The fusion of churches and states was the norm throughout most of world history. Societies that valued religion enlisted their governments to support it. The idea that people possessed by error—if not by the devil—should be left alone to follow their bliss was considered absurd. So the colonies mostly tried more theocratic approaches.

Yet by the time the US Constitution was written, there was a wide consensus that the colonies must not apply those old models to the new nation. For one thing, the breakaway colonists then saw the Church of England as more an instrument of the tyrannical Crown than a beloved mother church. If you asked John Adams about the cause of the rebellion, he would not say what we've all been taught in school, that it was a reaction to taxation. For him, British *religious* meddling contributed "as much as any other cause, to arouse the attention not only of the inquiring mind but of the common people." This was "a fact as certain as any in the history of North America."[43]

One of the early flash points occurred in 1761, when the Church of England made moves to station a bishop in America. The church saw this as a solution to a practical problem, eliminating the need for ministers to travel to Great Britain to be ordained. But the church did not sell the idea deftly. The Reverend East Apthorp, a candidate to be a bishop, insulted New Englanders by writing that Anglicans had "manifestly improved" the conditions left by those sourpuss Puritans of earlier times. "Religion no longer wears among us that savage and gloomy appearance."[44] Patriot-leaning clergy expertly demagogued the issue. Commenting on rumors that a large new house in Cambridge was being set aside for a bishop, the Congregationalist minister Jonathan Mayhew wailed: "Will they never let us rest in peace, except where all the weary are at rest? Is it not enough that they persecuted us out of the old world? Will they pursue us into the new to convert us here?"[45] Activists suggested that the bishops would live lavishly, which would require higher taxes. Proving that exaggeration about religious persecution has as long a history as religious persecution itself, Samuel Adams warned that if the bishop landed, the colonies could suffer "the utter loss of those religious rights" that "our good forefathers" had sought "when they explored and settled this new world."[46]

Back then, an easy way to smear England was to suggest that it was soft on Catholicism. When Parliament passed the Quebec Act in 1774, which protected the Catholic Church in Canada, colonists warned that England had just empowered an engine of religious tyranny on their border. "Your lives, your property, your religion, are all at stake," Alexander Hamilton hyperbolized.[47] The *Pennsylvania Gazette* predicted that "these dogs of Hell" would now invade, while the *Boston Evening Post* reported that four thousand Canadian Catholics were readying an attack.[48] Patriot clergy fueled the terror. Connecticut minister Joseph Perry said that if residents did not fight "the barbarity, trumpery and superstition of popery," then they should prepare to "burn at the stake, or submit to the tortures of the inquisition."[49] The British were baffled by the patriots' propagandistic use of religion. An aide to Britain's Admiral Lord Howe reported to his superiors that "at Boston the war is very much a religious war."[50] In all, the fight against the Scepter became a fight against the Miter—two forms of tyranny that had to be overthrown together.

By the time of the war, America had also become more religiously diverse. Before 1690, 90 percent of churches were affiliated with either the Anglican or the Congregational denomination. By the 1770s, only 35 percent were. One cause was immigration. From 1776 to 1820, roughly 250,000 Europeans arrived in America, especially from Scotland, Germany, Ireland, and Canada. Even more important, an earlier explosion of what we would now call evangelical fervor, known as the Great Awakening, increased religious variety and had a residual political impact at the time of the Revolution. In the 1740s, the arrival of the English preacher George Whitefield had gripped the colonies. Church attendance soared. Baptists and other new denominations grew. Religiously grounded universities sprang up, including Princeton, Brown, Rutgers, and Dartmouth. These proto-evangelicals challenged the dominant religious hierarchies, often refusing to abide by rules requiring preachers to have licenses or limit their ministries to particular geographic areas. The evangelical message that God's grace could reach the humblest colonist helped teach them to be small-*d* democrats. (When Benedict Arnold led an expedition to Quebec, he and his troops stopped off at the grave of Whitefield, exhumed the body, and took away a bit of the long-resting preacher's clothing to inspire their work.) This evangelical movement taught a generation how to defy authority. "This spirit—a frank expression of popular democracy and the sharpest attack yet on inherited privilege in colonial America—probably had much to do with the rise of the similar spirit in politics later on," wrote historian Mark Noll.[51]

Although it is rarely mentioned, this early American diversity also included the nonreligious. The attention given to the Puritans and others makes colonial America seem like a land of regular churchgoers, but by the time of the Revolution, a huge percentage of the population was not practicing. The religious adherence rate was only 17 percent in 1776, by one estimate.[52] So while most of the founders believed religion to be essential to this great new project, they also were aware that their passion for piety was not shared by many of their compatriots.

Most important, the war necessitated the creation of the would-be Union's first national institution—the Continental Army—which had to manage and harness the religious diversity represented by the thirteen pseudo-nations. There were Baptists from Rhode Island, Dutch Reformed from New York, Presbyterians from New Jersey, Congregationalists from Connecticut, and Catholics from Maryland. George Washington was well aware that Catholic soldiers were shedding blood for the cause, with the Maryland militia helping to thwart British raids from the south. Stephen Moylan, a Catholic from Pennsylvania, organized a group of volunteers in March 1776 who rushed to Boston when it came under siege. Washington would eventually make Moylan muster-master general of the army, brigadier general, commander of a cavalry unit, and his personal secretary.

Washington also focused on a strategic consideration: he needed the military help of France, a Catholic nation, as well as the French Canadians in Quebec. He therefore attempted to stamp out anti-Catholic behavior in the army. He banned the troops from burning effigies of the pope, appalled that they would pursue the "ridiculous and childish custom" while they were seeking support from Canadian Catholics. "To be insulting their Religion . . . is so monstrous, as not to be suffered or excused," he fumed. When the expedition to Quebec set off, Washington advised his officers to proceed "without insulting them" for their "errors." "While we are contending for our own Liberty," Washington wrote, "we should be very cautious of violating the Rights of Conscience of others, ever considering that God alone is the Judge of the Hearts of men, and to him only in this Case, they are answerable."[53] Washington also confronted the challenges of religious pluralism when appointing military chaplains. The Rhode Island brigade had named John Murray, a founder of American

Universalism, as its chaplain. As Universalism denied the reality of Hell, orthodox Protestant clergy protested. Washington stood his ground.

The war also led the Continental Congress to slowly shed biases. In 1775, it allowed Quakers to avoid military service as conscientious objectors.[54] It encouraged Hessian mercenaries who were fighting for the British to defect by distributing a special message on the backs of tobacco wrappers promising fifty acres of land and "the free exercise of their prospective religions" if they would lay down their arms.[55] After earlier lambasting the Catholics in Quebec, the congress reversed course and assured them that they "perceived the fate of the Protestant and Catholic colonies to be strongly linked together." The previously anti-Catholic John Adams began to change his views. After attending a Catholic Mass in Brussels, he wrote to his wife, Abigail, that perhaps he had been "rash and unreasonable" in earlier "cursing the knavery of the priesthood and the brutal ignorance of the people."[56] When a Catholic Spanish agent died, a number of members of the congress attended his funeral Mass, causing one member, Ebenezer Hazard, to gush that he'd witnessed "the minds of people so unfettered with the shackles of bigotry."[57]

By the end of the war, many of the Founding Fathers had come to realize that when it came to religious freedom, the approaches tried by the founding grandfathers had mostly failed.

And they could now see a better way.

James Madison, 1783

Chapter Two

MADISON'S MODEL

James Madison helps craft the Constitution,
the First Amendment, and an ingeniously
counterintuitive theory of religious freedom.

The man who worked his whole life to advance religious liberty was not fervently religious. This unusual combination—being passionately pro-religion but without much religious passion—manifested itself throughout James Madison's adulthood. He attended church regularly but declined to kneel in prayer.[1] He praised the "innate excellence" of Christianity while declining to be confirmed. He thought religion essential to society but described his own spirituality in highly intellectualized terms, as when he explained that the "mind prefers" the idea of a "self-existing cause to that of an infinite series of cause and effect."

Why did he care so much about religious liberty? Intellectual historians persuasively suggest that the deeply learned Madison was influenced by John Locke and David Hume, who both advocated for "toleration." Biographer Lynne Cheney speculates that his health problems made him rebel against religious dogmatism. Madison, we have learned, suffered from partial epilepsy and would periodically have minor, but immobilizing, seizures. Cheney suggests that having epilepsy at a time when religious leaders explained the ailment as a sign of demonic influence may have turned him against the strictures of religion.[2]

But what likely influenced Madison's thinking most was his relationship with Virginia's Baptists. Though born in the Anglican church (his father was a vestryman), he attended the College of New Jersey (later known as Princeton) when evangelicalism was common among its faculty and students.[3] Madison was prim but had classmates who followed the fervent New Light approach to Christianity and later traveled the South preaching. After college, Madison returned home to find his classmates' spiritual cousins being dragged through the mud and hurled into jail. By one estimate, half of all the Baptist preachers in Virginia had been arrested by the time of the American Revolution.[4] There is evidence that Madison became personally involved in some of the cases. He wrote that he had "spared no exertion to save them from imprisonment & to promote their release from it."[5] He told William Bradford that he had "squabbled and scolded abused and ridiculed so long about it."[6] A popular encyclopedia written in the nineteenth century claimed that Madison had been "repeatedly appearing in the court of his own county to defend the Baptist nonconformists."[7]

Through close exposure to the Baptists' cause, he arrived at a nuanced understanding of their persecution. Yes, it was violent, but it also was bureaucratic. Baptists could be lashed by the law as well as the whip. The most common charges were preaching without a license or disturbing the peace. For instance, authorities imprisoned four preachers in Orange County, where Madison lived, for being "Vagrant and Itinerant Persons and for Assembling themselves unlawfully at Sundry Times and Places Under the Denomination of Anabaptists and for Teaching & Preaching Schismatick Doctrines."[8] The process of obtaining a license was humiliating. A Baptist minister had to secure permission from Virginia's General Court, which sat just twice a year in Williamsburg, and then from panels of Anglican clergy and laymen, who held the dissenting religions in disdain. If successful, the Baptist minister received a license to preach only in a particular building. Anglican leaders could use any standard. In one case, the General Court refused to approve a Baptist meetinghouse in Richmond because the Presbyterians already had a church in the city. The imbalance of power could be seen not only in the haughty pronouncements of the Anglicans but also in the poignantly subservient pleas of the Baptists. Through gritted teeth, Baptists in Amelia County did "humbly submit the consideration to your worships, hoping you will in mercy grant the same." The response written on the back expressed no such deference: "Dissenters petition called Baptist, Rejected."[9]

Virginia's Anglicans—a group that generally included the property-owning gentry—believed that Baptist theology undermined morality and social order. Adult baptism, it was thought, provided criminals and other reprobates with a "get out of hell free" card. "Having been once dipped in your happy Waters," wrote one critic, the Baptists could then "let loose to commit upon us Murders, and every Species of Injury."[10] Worse, the Baptists preached to slaves and appealed to the lower classes. They tended to be less educated than the Anglicans, and their style—emotional and emphatic—was seen as gauche. "Bauling as you Do to Be heard for half a mile Round . . . in my opinion is nothing but ostentation," said one magistrate.[11] Madison reported that their "enthusiasms" rendered them "obnoxious to sober opinion."[12]

Such persecutions were fresh in Madison's mind when, at twenty-five, he made his debut in civic life at a special convention of Virginia's leaders called in 1776 to craft a new Declaration of Rights. Just five foot four, "Little Jemmy," as he was called, cut a wispy figure amid such towering leaders as Patrick Henry and George Mason. The first draft of the declaration seemed to strike a blow for religious freedom. "All men should enjoy the fullest toleration in the exercise of religion," stated the provision, written by Mason. This kind of toleration meant "the mutual duty of all to practice Christian forbearance, love, and charity toward each other."

But Madison had seen firsthand how easily the majority's "Christian forbearance" could be withdrawn. Rights conferred by the powerful were counterfeit. Madison successfully proposed a simpler, more radical position: that "all men are equally entitled to enjoy the free exercise of religion, according to the dictates of conscience, unpunished and unrestrained by the magistrate."[13] He made religious liberty a natural right, which, like other natural rights being championed at the time, did not depend on the whims of rulers. They just *existed*—as something to which all men were "entitled." They were, as Jefferson put it later, "endowed by our Creator."

By 1784, the idealism of those early days of revolution had been dampened by some serious practical problems. The war had destroyed many churches in Virginia. Attendance was down, and clergy struggled to survive. A friend wrote to Jefferson that one preacher he knew "has been almost starved," and another had given up the work to avoid perishing.[14] Patrick Henry, then a leading member of the legislature, proposed a solution: instead of supporting just Episcopalian ministers, taxpayers would help pay the salaries of *all* Christian ministers. Voters would designate which denomination or Christian church would get their tax dollars.[15] This "Bill Establishing a Provision for Teachers of the Christian Religion" drew broad support. Richard Henry Lee suggested that without such a system of taxpayer support, "avarice is accomplishing the destruction of religion."[16] George Washington backed the plan, as did John Marshall, the future chief justice of the Supreme Court.

Madison detested the idea—and decided to lead a fight against it. The odds were very much against him. The charismatic Henry was one of the great orators of his time. Though Madison impressed with his intellect almost immediately, his style was dry and lawyerly. No record exists of Henry's comments to the legislature, but he likely argued that promoting religion was essential, since Republican government required a virtuous public.

The crib sheet from which Madison spoke has been preserved, and it provides clues as to how he responded when he stood on November 11, 1784:

> *What edition, Hebrew, Septuagint, or vulgate? What copy—what translation. . . . What books canonical, what apochryphal? The papists holding to be the former what protestants the latter*[17]

If the state supported the teaching of the Bible, which one would be used? Madison was teaching a lesson that Americans would learn and forget repeatedly over the coming years: it is nearly impossible for government to aid "Christianity" because the differences *within* the religion are so profound. Help one denomination or school of thought and others will feel slighted or subjugated. Madison was also channeling a theological point made by many dissenting Protestants—that individuals should have the right to interpret the Bible for themselves.[18]

> *True question not—Is Rel. neccs.? Are Rellis. Estabts. Neccsy. For Religion? No*

This bit of shorthand hints at the core argument. For most of history, communities that considered religion important had used the tools of the state to support it. Madison argued that religion must now, at long last, be viewed differently. An establishment—by which he meant tax dollars supporting churches and paying ministers' salaries—was not necessary for religion to flourish.

> *Experience shows Relig. Corrupted by Estabt.*

He took the argument further. Not only is taxpayer support not necessary; it is harmful.

> *Case of primitive Christianity*

As proof, he suggested that the earliest Christianity, the "primitive" form, was the best. Once Constantine embraced the faith—providing the church with money, protection, and power—it became corrupted.

Prevent immigration = into it as asylum

Freedom attracts talent, and Virginia would become a backwater if it lost the ability to draw a wide range of people. In contrast, Madison had seen with his own eyes how the religious liberty of Pennsylvania had allowed it to become culturally and economically rich.

Probably defects of Bill dishonor Christianity.

For all these reasons, this bill would violate the principles of Christianity.

Henry and his allies won the first round. The legislature voted 47 to 32 that citizens "ought to pay a moderate tax or contribution annually for the support of the Christian religion."[19] Madison maneuvered for a delay in the final vote and conferred by mail with his friend Jefferson, who was in France, on how to defeat Henry. Jefferson's first idea was not terribly practical: "What we have to do I think is *devoutly to pray* for *his death.*"[20]

Madison had a more cunning plan. Henry was winning in part because the other major religious minority, the Presbyterians, had backed the bill. This "shameful" position created a powerful alliance between them and the Episcopalians. In a crafty bit of legislative jiujitsu, Madison publicly endorsed a piece of legislation he privately opposed—providing legal incorporation to the Episcopal church. This alarmed the Presbyterians, who began to see that once the government started exerting power on behalf of religion, the dominant players—the Episcopalians—would have the upper hand. "The mutual hatred of these sects has been much inflamed," Madison proudly reported to Jefferson. "I am far from being sorry for it as a coalition between them could alone endanger our religious rights."[21]

Then Madison quietly mobilized the grass roots. The favored tactic of the day was writing a petition. His "Memorial and Remonstrance Against Religious Assessments" is considered one of the most important documents in the history of religious freedom (though he didn't acknowledge his authorship of it until years later). Madison was not nearly as gifted as Jefferson with a turn of phrase, but his arguments were brilliantly positioned to synthesize different views and bind the growing population of evangelicals into a coalition with Enlightenment-oriented gentry men. It stated: "The religion then of every man must be left to the conviction and conscience of every man."[22]

That seems noncontroversial. But now behold how Madison imagined the role of government: "Religion is wholly exempt from its cognizance."

Exempt from its *cognizance*. A remarkable word choice. He was not merely inveighing against the state restraining or oppressing religion. He was arguing that government should not even be aware of religion. It should neither harm nor help religion or even think about it.

He then moved on to more practical arguments. A tax would drive people away from Virginia and discourage those of other faiths from moving there and experiencing the "light of Christianity." Small impositions that violate big principles could open the door to greater persecutions, leading inevitably to "the Inquisition from which it differs only in degree." In assisting religion, government would necessarily acquire the power to regulate it. "Who does not see that the same authority which can establish Christianity, in exclusion of all other religions, may establish with the same ease any particular sect of Christians, in exclusion of all other sects?" What's more, efforts to help Christianity had backfired throughout history. "During almost fifteen centuries has the legal establishment of Christianity been on trial. What have been its fruits? More or less in all places, pride and indolence in the Clergy, ignorance and servility in the laity, in both, superstition, bigotry and persecution."

Madison believed that the yearning for government validation revealed a profound lack of confidence among Christians. Modern religious conservatives often argue that excluding, say, the Bible from public schools weakens Christianity. Madison believed that healthy Christianity wouldn't need such help. The assessment bill, he wrote, shows "an ignoble and unchristian timidity" that attempts to guard against "error" through law rather than an open quest for God. He had no doubt that in a real free market of ideas, we would see "the victorious progress of Truth."

This attempt to misuse the power of the state was an affront to God. The reason: faith coerced is not real. "If this freedom be abused, it is an offense against God, not against man." America, Madison declared, had shown the possibility of a new approach—one that would correct the ills of the world's previous attempts to force religious uniformity.

> Torrents of blood have been spilt in the old world, by the vain attempts of the secular arm to extinguish Religious discord, by proscribing all difference in religious opinion.
> Time has at length revealed the true remedy. Every relaxation of narrow and rigorous policy, wherever it has been tried, has been

found to assuage the disease. The American Theatre has exhibited proofs, that equal and compleat liberty, if it does not wholly eradicate it, sufficiently destroys its malignant influence on the health and prosperity of the state.

This "true remedy" on display in the American Theatre involved a counterintuitive idea: eliminate the toxicity of conflict by allowing diverse beliefs to flourish. It encouraged religious peace by allowing religious competition. It promoted faith by telling the government to stop helping ministers and churches. A cacophony of religious voices can blend together harmoniously, while, ironically, efforts to force the use of the same hymnal will lead to discord, oppression, and bad religion.

The thirteen copies of Madison's "Memorial" that circulated around the state attracted 1,552 signatures ("It has been sent thro' the medium of confidential persons," Madison wrote Jefferson).[23] Its mix of theological, practical, and political arguments appealed to Enlightenment thinkers who deplored government restraints, to westerners who abhorred tax increases, and, most important, to evangelicals who feared persecution.

The Baptists weighed in with their own petitions, which provided arguments quite similar to Madison's and attracted even more signatures. Elder Jeremiah Walker, one of the imprisoned preachers, opposed the assessment even though his church would have been one of its beneficiaries. Echoing Madison's view of Christian history, he said that with the arrival of Constantine, the church was soon "Over run with Error and Immorality." He too rejected the panicky idea that government had to intervene to block the spread of erroneous theologies, like Deism. "Let their Doctrines be scriptural and their lives Holy, then shall Religion beam forth as the sun and Deism shall be put to open shame."[24]

A Baptist group at Dupuy's Meetinghouse in Powhatan County explained how the well-intended idea of government support would lead inevitably to government interference: "Sheriffs, County Courts and public Treasury all to be employed in the management of money levied for the express purpose of supporting Teachers of the Christian religion." In all, the Baptists argued, the bill to help Christians was anti-Christian because it conflicted with Jesus's injunction that his followers should render unto Caesar the things that are Caesar's—that the civil and religious spheres should remain separate. The Baptists of Orange County declared that the idea that government should support religion was "founded neither in scripture, on Reason, on Sound Policy; but it is repugnant to each of them."[25]

Madison understood the political math. While the Episcopalians were the largest group, if you added up all the other "dissenting" sects, they now outnumbered the historically dominant denomination. United, the minorities were a majority. The Quakers and the Methodists came out against the bill. The Presbyterians of Rockbridge County argued that the measure was "best calculated to destroy Religion" because it would sustain low-quality ministers who couldn't earn support through their own talents. Soon, they predicted, the state would be "swarming with Fools, Sots and Gamblers."[26]

In the battle of the memorials, Madison and his Enlightenment-evangelical coalition won. Anti-assessment petitions garnered ten thousand signatures, while supporters got only twelve hundred. Patrick Henry's bill died.

Fresh off that victory, Madison moved to solidify religious freedom. He reached into the pile of moribund proposals previously considered by the legislature and pulled out Bill Number 82—the Virginia Statute for Religious Freedom. Thomas Jefferson had written the bill five years earlier. He later considered it such an important accomplishment that he had it chiseled on his tombstone. But the bill had languished after Jefferson went off to Paris to be America's new ambassador. Madison revived it and engineered its passage. The legislation eliminated the possibility of future religious establishments by banning use of tax dollars to support religion. It also elaborated on the idea that a free market of religion would encourage good theology: "Truth is great and will prevail if left to herself." During the deliberations, a proposal was offered to make reference to Jesus Christ instead of the phrase Jefferson had used, the "holy author of our religion." The change was rejected. Jefferson later explained that he had wanted the statute to protect "the Jew and the Gentile, Christian and Mahometan, the Hindoo and infidel of every denomination."

Madison had a somewhat different explanation for why he opposed the Jesus reference. Referring to Christianity in the law, he said, would "profane it by making it a topic of legislative discussion," especially given "His own declaration that His Kingdom was not of this world."[27]

The Constitution

Those who want to identify a divine inspiration for the United States Constitution point to a dramatic moment involving Benjamin Franklin. On June 28, 1778, when the Constitutional Convention appeared to be hopelessly deadlocked, the revered eighty-one-year-old suggested that they join in collective prayer. Congress had asked for divine help daily during the Revolution, he noted. "Our prayers, Sir, were heard, and they were graciously answered." How else to explain how the underequipped little army could have defeated Great Britain? "All of us who were engaged in the struggle must have observed frequent instances of a Superintending providence in our favor." And then the man who represented the scientific Enlightenment more than any other man said to the convention's chairman, George Washington, "I have lived, Sir, a long time and the longer I live, the more convincing proofs I see of this truth—that God governs in the affairs of men. And if a sparrow cannot fall to the ground without his notice, is it probable that an empire can rise without his aid?"[28]

There's one small problem with using this speech as an example of divine intervention—the convention declined to approve Franklin's motion. Most likely they figured that the process of drafting such a prayer, or finding a clergyman to lead it, would prove too difficult, perhaps even stirring more discord rather than ending it. The delegates belonged to eight different Christian denominations.

When it came to deciding the Constitution's approach to religious freedom, the convention faced two realities. First, the nation had become more religiously diverse. We moderns may not think of a land that was 98 percent Protestant as diverse, but the divisions among Protestant sects and between Protestants and Catholics were intense. Second, they were quite aware that the attempts to establish, promote, or suppress religion over the previous 150 years had not gone well.

This helps explain why the document that emerged from the convention was so strikingly devoid of religious language. Given the almost universal practice of invoking God in state charters, constitutions, and proclamations, the absence of a religious preamble was stunning.

The Constitution's only overt reference to religion related to the qualifications for public office. Article VI, Clause 3, declares that "no religious Test shall ever be required as a Qualification to any Office." This important protection was almost not included. Charles Pinckney of South Carolina proposed the idea, but it was sent to committee and ignored. Ten days later he raised it again before the full convention, and this time it passed.[29] The religious test ban is rarely mentioned in modern debates because, unlike the First Amendment, it seems noncontroversial today. But at the time, eleven of the thirteen states did have religious tests, stipulating that only Christians, or in some cases Protestants, could hold office. The convention forbade the national government from doing what it allowed state governments to do. It's not clear whether the convention opposed religious tests on principle or figured it would be impossible to reach a consensus on who precisely the test should exclude.

Another phrase was pregnant with religious meaning, despite its secular appearance. In Articles II and VI, the Constitution requires the president and members of Congress to be bound by "Oath or Affirmation." The affirmation was a direct accommodation for Quakers, who regard swearing an oath to God as sacrilegious.

James Madison, of course, was also a central player at the Constitutional Convention. As schoolchildren, we learn that Madison drove the idea of government checks and balances, and it's tempting to believe that his views about politics shaped his views about religious freedom. In fact, it appears to have been the other way around. He arrived in Philadelphia just a little more than a year after the Virginia fight over religious taxes. While arguing the merits of the Constitution in *The Federalist Papers*, he explained his views about the preservation of political rights as follows:

> In a free government the security for civil rights must be the same as that for religious rights. It consists in the one case in the multiplicity of interests, and in the other in the multiplicity of sects. The degree of security in both cases will depend on the number of interests and sects.

Having "multiplicity of sects," he believed, was crucial to advancing religious freedom. And when, also in *Federalist*, no. 10, he made the (short-lived) case against "faction," one of his examples was again religion: "A religious sect may degenerate into a political faction in a part of the Confederacy." The solution was to have a "variety of sects dispersed over the entire face" of the nation. Madison's experience in Virginia convinced him that declarations of rights could be best safeguarded when no one religion could dominate. After all, the Anglicans were defeated in part because the Baptists and the Presbyterians had teamed up.

The relative silence of the Constitution on religion has been interpreted by some as proof that the founders wanted a secular society. Hardly. They mostly believed that America could survive only if religion flourished. While it did not establish a national religion, the Constitution left states free to promote and regulate religion as they liked. This was not Madison's intention. He had proposed that Congress be able to veto state laws, but the idea was soundly rejected. At the time of the ratification, few states actually had religious neutrality or liberty.

Of course, the Constitution also allowed states that were inclined toward religious liberty to pursue it with gusto. After Pennsylvania ratified the convention, Philadelphians witnessed a celebratory parade featuring a rabbi and two ministers marching arm in arm. Benjamin Rush remarked, "There could not have been a more happy emblem contrived of that section of the new constitution, which opens all its power and office alike, not only to every sect of Christians, but to worthy men of every religion."[30]

The Constitution's "God"-lessness did not go over well with everyone. At the state conventions called to ratify the document, some objected to what one critic called its "cold indifference toward religion."[31] Another warned that God would notice the omission and punish us, citing the fate of the Bible's King Saul: "Because thou hast rejected the word of the Lord, he hath also rejected thee."[32] Some feared that the ban on religious tests would make it possible for an infidel to attain high office. Surely, Luther Martin of Maryland suggested, they could "hold out some distinction between the professor of Christianity and downright infidelity or paganism." A delegate from Western Massachusetts complained that religious freedom was not sufficiently protected and then, with no sense of irony, complained that through the religious test ban, "there is a door opened for the Jews, Turks and Heathens to enter into publick office."[33] And it would allow Catholics to gain power. A Massachusetts delegate attacked the Constitution because "Popery and the Inquisition may be established in America." In one widely published article, a writer offered a vivid, full-spectrum prediction of horrors.

ist. Quakers who will make the blacks saucy, and at the same time deprive us of the means of defense.
—2dly. Mahometans, who ridicule the doctrine of the Trinity
—3dly. Deists, abominable wretches
—4thly. Negroes, the seed of Cain
—5thly. Beggars who when set on horseback will ride to the devil
—6thly Jews etc. etc.[34]

But more significant were the questions that came from the other side, from the religious minorities who wondered whether the Constitution protected them enough. Shouldn't there be an explicit declaration of rights? Madison believed that the silent treatment worked best. Congress had only those powers granted to it in the Constitution. No power to regulate religion was mentioned, so the legislature had no such authority.[35]

Many were not convinced. Several states had enumerated rights in their constitutions. In fact, the lack of a Bill of Rights became a rallying cry for those who wanted to block ratification of the Constitution entirely. Virginia again became a key battleground—with Madison once again in the middle. His allies, the Baptists, supported the Constitution but believed that they would be vulnerable without an explicit guarantee of religious freedom.

One of the most popular local Baptist preachers was a charming transplant from Massachusetts named John Leland.[36] "What is clearest of all— Religious Liberty, is not sufficiently secured," wrote Leland about the new constitution. "If a Majority of Congress with the President favour one System more than another, they may oblige all others to pay to support their System as much as they please." He opposed Madison's election to the ratification convention. So Madison stopped off at Leland's home outside of Orange on his way back from New York. Neither man wrote about what transpired, but Madison likely argued that once the Constitution was ratified it could be amended, but to do so now would doom its chances. Leland did change his mind, revealing his shift at a gathering of voters that took place close to the election. Standing atop a large wood barrel used to ship tobacco, Madison calmly spoke and answered questions for two hours. "Though Mr. Madison was not particularly a pleasing or elegant speaker, the people listened with respectful attention," Leland recalled later. Then Leland rose—and announced he would switch sides and support Madison as delegate to the convention.[37] The 168 assembled residents voted by a margin of just 10 votes to send Madison.[38]

At the conclave, his primary antagonist was once again Patrick Henry. In a series of thirty-two speeches,[39] Henry maintained that the Constitution gave the national government too much power. But his main point of attack was the lack of a Bill of Rights. "The rights of conscience, trial by jury, liberty of the press, all your immunities and franchises, all pretensions to human rights and privileges, are rendered insecure, if not lost." He mocked Madison's legalistic argument that rights are safer if they're not mentioned. "This sacred right ought not to depend on constructive, logical reasoning."[40] Ever the showman, Henry suggested that God Himself opposed ratification of the Constitution. "I see the awful immensity of the dangers with which it is pregnant. I see it—I feel it," he declared. "I see *beings* of a higher order anxious concerning our decision." As if at his command, the skies grew dark and a thunderstorm erupted.[41]

Madison, in contrast, addressed the convention in a voice so soft that the official scribe often couldn't make out what he was saying. He went clause by clause. The balance of powers, he argued, would safeguard freedom far better than the mere "parchment barriers" of delineated rights. After all, Virginia had a Declaration of Rights and yet Henry had nearly passed his bloody tax assessment. The best guarantor of freedom was a "multiplicity of sects," such that "there cannot be a majority of any one sect to oppress and persecute the rest." Finally, he reiterated that even without a Bill of Rights, the Constitution—through its silence on religion—had offered the greatest protection of all. "There is not a shadow of right in the general government to intermeddle with religion," he declared.[42] Again, we see the expansiveness of Madison's approach: The Constitution did not merely prohibit the creation of a national religion. It provided "not a shadow of right" to even "intermeddle" with religion.

But Madison also let it be known that he might be open to amendments after ratification, and he thereby got the support of the Baptists and other dissenters. In the end, the convention voted narrowly, 89 to 79, to ratify, also recommending that Congress add a Bill of Rights.

In correspondence with Thomas Jefferson—who supported the addition of a Bill of Rights—Madison revealed some anxieties he had not expressed publicly. Vagueness, he confided, may be our best friend. Once we start to define the specific nature of these rights, we should not take it for granted that our liberal views will win the day. After all, look how the reactionaries responded to the ban on religious tests. "I am sure that the rights of Conscience in particular, if submitted to public definition would be narrowed much more than they are likely ever to be by an assumed power."[43] But Jefferson was unpersuaded, arguing that an explicit guarantee was required "without the aid of sophism." (Ouch.) "A bill of rights is what the people are entitled to against every government on earth, general or particular & what no just government should refuse or rest on inference."[44] Jefferson had his own secret worry. He suspected that Americans' current love of freedom might be a passing fad. The War of Independence had instilled an unusual sense of tolerance in the nation, which could well fade. "The time for fixing every essential right on a legal basis is while our rulers are honest, and ourselves, united," he wrote later. "From the conclusion of this war we shall be going down hill."[45]

The Campaign Promise

In 1788, after the Constitution was ratified, Madison campaigned to serve in the first House of Representatives. But he had a tough race. His nemesis, Patrick Henry, now Virginia's governor, plotted to thwart Madison, whose victory, he warned, would produce "rivulets of blood throughout the land." Henry intentionally shaped the congressional district to include many voters who opposed the Constitution with which Madison was so closely associated. To run against Madison, Henry recruited a war hero, James Monroe, the tall, dark, and handsome future president who had crossed the Delaware with Washington and still carried bits of musket ball in his shoulder from the Battle of Trenton.

At first, Monroe outcampaigned Madison. While the colonel traveled the state meeting would-be constituents, Madison was stuck doing legislative business for the Continental Congress in New York. He didn't much like campaigning, once losing an election over his refusal to provide "spirituous liquors" to the voters.[46] The frail Madison balked at coming home to Virginia for another reason: hemorrhoids. We know this because he complained about them to George Washington. Apparently, no problem was too intimate or inflammatory for the Father of our Country.[47]

But Madison's biggest political problem was the Baptists. Monroe's allies had spread word that Madison had "ceased to be a friend to the rights of Conscience" and refused to make any changes to the Constitution.[48]

Because Madison needed their votes, he made perhaps the most consequential campaign promise in American history. In a letter to the Reverend George Eve, pastor of the Rapidan Baptist Church in Culpeper County, Virginia, he wrote that "circumstances are now changed." With the Constitution now ratified, he supported amending it.

> It is my sincere opinion that the constitution ought to be revised, and that the First Congress . . . ought to prepare and recommend to the States for ratification the most satisfactory provisions for all essential rights, particularly the rights of Conscience in the fullest latitude, the freedom of the press, trials by jury, security against general warrents.[49]

Madison's assurances worked. In a political meeting in Culpeper—at a church whose ministers had a decade earlier been arrested for preaching without permission—an Anti-Federalist resident criticized Madison for thinking that the Constitution "had no defects." George Eve came to Madison's defense, explaining Madison's new position and reminding them of his long history of fighting for Baptists.[50]

By Election Day, February 2, 1789, a storm had dropped ten inches of snow on the Virginia countryside. Men had to ride on horseback, sometimes for hours, to cast their votes. Madison earned lopsided majorities in the heavily Baptist areas of Culpeper and Orange Counties. The final tally: Madison 1,308, Monroe 972. The evangelicals had delivered for Madison.[51]

On June 8, 1789, Congressman James Madison went to the floor of the House of Representatives in New York City and kept his campaign pledge, proposing the series of amendments that would, after considerable negotiation, become the Bill of Rights.

Founding Fathers at War

Anytime someone says, "The Founding Fathers believed . . . ," the rest of the sentence is almost certainly untrue. There was no unitary Founding Fathers position. They had diverse views and motivations. So, while we have focused so far on James Madison, we should be clear: Madison did not alone invent the general concept of religious freedom. Rather, he put forward his own ideas, borrowed others' ideas, and built consequential coalitions for action. As we consider the drafting of the First Amendment, it's important to understand how his views compared with those of the rest of the founders.

On one end of the spectrum can be found those who most emphasized rational thought—the Enlightenment caucus. This group included Thomas Jefferson, Benjamin Franklin, Thomas Paine, and others who rejected biblical literalism and distrusted the clerical class. Jefferson's Virginia Statute for Religious Freedom declared, "Almighty God hath created the mind free, and manifested his supreme will that free it shall remain by making it altogether insusceptible of restraint." God's greatest gift, in effect, is not the prospect of eternal salvation—it is human intelligence.

Unlike Madison, Jefferson exhibited a deep hostility to organized religion, both its modern and ancient varieties. In Jefferson's view, Christianity was ruined almost from the start. "But a short time elapsed after the death of the great reformer of the Jewish religion, before his principles were departed from by those who professed to be his special servants, and perverted into an engine for enslaving mankind, and aggrandizing their oppressors in church and state," he wrote.[52] The authors of the canonical Gospels laid "a groundwork of vulgar ignorance, of things impossible, of superstitions, fanaticisms and fabrications."[53] The apostle Paul made matters worse. "Of this band of dupes and imposters, Paul was the great Coryphaeus, and first corrupter of the doctrines of Jesus."[54] The doctrine of the Trinity was the "mere Abracadabra of the mountebanks calling themselves the priests of Jesus"[55] and the "hocus-pocus phantasm of a god like another Cerberus, with one body and three heads."⁵⁶ The Immaculate Conception, he wrote, would someday be "classed with the fable of the generation of Minerva in the brain of Jupiter."⁵⁷

The Protestant Reformation did not reform much, according to Jefferson. John Calvin's idea of predestination—that God chose some to be saved and that their actions couldn't alter their fate—disgusted him. By detaching salvation from behavior, it undermined morality. "Calvinism has introduced into the Christian religion more new absurdities than its leader [Jesus] had purged it of old ones," he explained.⁵⁸ Driven by the conviction that history had obscured the moral teachings of Jesus, Jefferson created his own Bible by literally cutting out all the miracles, including Jesus's divine birth and resurrection, rescuing the "diamonds" of Jesus's true teachings from the "dung" that littered its pages.⁵⁹

Compared with Madison's, Jefferson's approach to religious freedom was narrow and outside the mainstream. For Jefferson, spirituality was primarily an individual quest, while Madison believed that organized religion was valuable and must, for the sake of the republic, be purified and strengthened. Jefferson wanted religious freedom in order to end persecution and remove limitations on intellectual creativity; Madison believed that liberty would lead to religious vibrancy. Jefferson emphasized the freedom to think; Madison, in effect, the freedom to pray. Jefferson also seemed angrier. On the wall of the Jefferson Memorial are the eloquent words "I have sworn upon the altar of God eternal hostility against every form of tyranny over the mind of man." The marble chiselers left off the first part of the quote, which referred to Jefferson's plans to get back at the Congregationalist ministers who had attacked him during the 1800 presidential campaign. "They believe that any portion of power confided to me, will be exerted in opposition to their schemes. And they believe rightly."⁶⁰ Jefferson's and Madison's views were not incompatible. But Madison's were expansive enough to appeal to both rationalists and believers.

A second group consisted of dissenting Protestants, such as the Baptists, who were deeply religious but antagonistic to government involvement. They had the same practical agenda as the Enlightenment group, but in terms of culture, practice, and theology, they couldn't have been more different. They believed the Bible was the revealed word of God. These Dissenters were driven not just by self-preservation but also by their belief in the ability of individuals to interpret the Bible and commune with God without interference.⁶¹

In the middle of the spectrum were leaders such as John Adams. This third group—let's call them the Religious Freedom Centrists—wanted protection from egregious types of religious oppression but also believed that the state should be "cognizant" of religion. Adams had veered from the faith of his youth, eventually becoming a Unitarian. He loathed the Church of England, which he viewed as complicit with royal tyranny. But he still considered himself to be a Christian, a religion founded by the "benevolent, all powerful and all merciful Creator, Preserver and Father of the Universe, the first good, first perfect, and first fair."[62] Like Madison, Adams believed that without religion there could be no virtue.

But unlike Madison, Adams was open to state support for religion. For a long time, he defended the Massachusetts approach, in which taxpayers supported Congregational churches. When confronted by Baptists seeking greater freedom in his state, Adams responded petulantly. "We might as soon expect a change in the solar system" as to expect Massachusetts to give up its official state religion.[63] As president, he overtly invoked Christianity in his rhetoric. In his inaugural address, he expressed "a veneration for the religion of a people who profess and call themselves Christians" and a belief that "Christianity [was] among the best recommendations for the public service."[64] In the nasty election of 1800, his supporters in New England challenged whether Jefferson was devout enough. The Federalist *Gazette of the United States* declared, "The only question to be asked by every American, laying his hand on his heart, is, 'Shall I continue in allegiance to God and a religious president; or impiously declare for Jefferson and no God!!!'"[65] Adams supported religious freedom in theory but hadn't fully awakened to its implications. (Jefferson's supporters, in turn, falsely accused Adams of wanting to establish a national religion.)

George Washington also believed that religion was essential to the health of the new Republic. "Of all the dispositions and habits which lead to political prosperity, religion and morality are indispensable supports," he declared.[66] He regularly drafted God into his wartime missives and believed that God had intervened to protect him during the Revolution. But he also rebelled against tradition. For instance, he refused to take Communion in the Episcopal church, on some days waiting in the carriage while Martha took the Holy Sacrament.[67]

Finally, on the far end of the spectrum, were those who wanted full government support for religion and sometimes for particular denominations. By the time of the Constitution, few argued that there should be a national religion, but many argued that there should be state religions. Let's call this last group the Traditionalists.

To be clear, almost all of the founders believed that religion was important to the health of the Republic. Empowering citizens to control the levers of power requires a *demos* with an *ethos*—a population that is guided by a deep sense of morality, enforced through a system of heavenly rewards and punishments that incentivize good behavior. Religion was also thought to undergird the justice system, because those who don't believe in God may lie under oath on the witness stand.

But while each of these four groups agreed that religion was essential, they differed over how to ensure its vitality. That they split into these four rough groups—Enlighteneds, Dissenters, Centrists, and Traditionalists—helps explain why public pronouncements about religion during the American Revolution and its immediate aftermath sound contradictory or ambivalent. The Declaration of Independence was itself a product of linguistic compromise.[68] Like the Bible, it includes the voices of two different gods. Jefferson originally wrote that our rights were provided by "the Laws of Nature and of Nature's god" and by "their Creator."[69] This was the god of the Enlightenment. But Congress added another god, "appealing to the Supreme Judge of the world." We do not know who asked for those more biblical phrases to be inserted, but the Declaration entered the room with a Deist coloration and left with a simultaneous appeal to the Old Testament god of judgment.[70]

Throughout the religious freedom battles in Virginia, Madison had managed to assemble a coalition of strange bedfellows (Enlighteneds, Centrists, and Dissenters) while neutralizing the Traditionalists. He did so by fusing the evangelical desire for an unobstructed individual path to God with the Enlightenment demand for freedom of thought.

Once the Constitution was ratified, his coalition-building skills faced their most consequential test.

The First Amendment Compromise

On June 8, 1789, Congressman Madison went to the floor of the House of Representatives and proposed a series of amendments, including one that would insert into the body of the Constitution these words:

> The civil rights of none shall be abridged on account of religious
> belief or worship, nor shall any national religion be established, nor

shall the full and equal rights of conscience be in any manner, or any pretext, infringed.[71]

As we can see, Madison's original proposal was quite different from what ended up in the Bill of Rights. ("Congress shall make no law respecting an establishment of religion, or prohibiting the free exercise thereof.") He put forth religious freedom as a universal right—something to which all Americans were entitled. In contrast, the First Amendment that ultimately passed was merely a limitation on the powers of Congress.

Less well known, Madison also proposed that religious freedom rights be required at the state level too—"No State shall violate the equal rights of conscience, or the freedom of the press, or the trial by jury in criminal cases." His experiences in Virginia had convinced him that the greatest threats to religious liberty would likely come from the states.

The House of Representatives created a special committee to consider the language that would ultimately become the First Amendment. They discarded Madison's version and suggested instead: "No religion shall be established by law, nor shall the equal rights of conscience be infringed."

The full House debated the language on August 15.[72] They did not discuss the phrase "rights of conscience," which would morph into the "free exercise" clause. That apparently was noncontroversial, which, given the lack of such a free exercise reality in America, is remarkable. The debate instead centered on what we now refer to as the Establishment Clause, the part limiting the government's ability to support a particular religion or religion in general, that is, the separation of church and state.

Lawmakers focused on how the amendment could affect the states. Peter Sylvester of New York, for instance, "feared it might be thought to have a tendency to abolish religion altogether."[73] Abolish religion altogether? How could the amendment designed to provide the ultimate protection for religion end up abolishing it? What Sylvester probably meant was that, in its newfound opposition to religious establishments, Congress could feel empowered to abolish the *state* religious establishments.

Congressman Benjamin Huntington of Connecticut raised the same concern. This new amendment could "be extremely harmful to the cause of religion," he warned. At the time of this debate, Connecticut taxpayers funded the salaries of Congregational ministers, and only Christians could hold public office.[74] Huntington wondered what would happen if a Connecticut taxpayer refused to pay taxes to support the local establishment because the national constitution deemed such things void. Congress would, he said, end up helping "those who professed no religion at all."[75]

Madison tried to convince Huntington and Sylvester that he intended no such thing. He suggested inserting the word "national" into the sentence to clarify that only a national establishment of religion would be forbidden. Samuel Livermore of New Hampshire had a better idea: let's curtail Congress's powers even more dramatically. He proposed:

> Congress shall make no laws touching religion, or infringing the rights of conscience.

No *touching*.

In modern times, we tend to focus on whether someone supports more separation of church and state or less. But Livermore had been the president of the New Hampshire convention, which authorized the state to collect taxes to support "protestant teachers of piety, religion and morality."[76] He wanted more separation of church and state at the national level *and* less at the state level.

Madison allowed himself to be thrown into that briar patch, accepting Livermore's version. It not only assuaged the concerns about autonomy of the states but also curtailed Congress's powers in a more Madisonian way by preventing it from even "touching" religion.

Alas, the legislative sausage factory was just gearing up. On August 20, Fisher Ames of Massachusetts submitted a new version that zigged back a bit toward allowing Congress to take *some* steps supporting religion. Touching would be allowed, in effect, as long as Congress didn't go too far.[77]

On September 3 through 9, the Senate took up the issue.[78] After rejecting several versions, they settled on one that invited considerable congressional involvement in religion and less separation of church and state. Congress, they decreed, could "make no law establishing articles of faith or a mode of worship."[79]

Madison was furious. This language was far too narrow. By delineating just these few types of congressional action as verboten, every other intervention was fair game. The national government could legislate on a wide range of religious matters, just so long as it didn't create "articles of faith or a mode of worship." Madison said that he'd rather have no amendment than this one.[80] Others seemed to agree. An Anti-Federalist senator wrote to Patrick Henry that the Senate had "so mutilated and gutted" the amendments that they were now "good for nothing, and . . . will do more harm than benefit."[81]

Led by Madison, the House rejected the Senate's proposal.

A conference committee formed to resolve the major differences between the Senate and House positions. Apparently, they engaged in some legislative horse-trading. The Senate agreed to accept the House's language on freedom of religion, speech, and press if the House accepted the Senate's language on sixteen other amendments.[82] The House approved the language on September 24; the Senate, the next day. When Congress repackaged the changes into the format of amendments, they presented what we now know as the First Amendment:

> Congress shall make no law respecting an establishment of
> religion, or prohibiting the free exercise thereof. . . .

Congress considered two other Madison amendments related to religion. His proposal for what would later become the Second Amendment stated that "no person religiously scrupulous of bearing arms shall be compelled to render military service in person." This provision, aimed at accommodating Pennsylvania's Quakers, puzzled later historians because it seemed to cut against Madison's belief that government should not be "cognizant" of religion. But in the case of conscientious objection to military service, Madison consistently made an exception. Congress later dropped this clause from the Second Amendment.[83]

Congress also took up Madison's proposal that "No State shall violate the equal rights of conscience." In an extraordinary disquisition about the danger of majority power, Madison declared:

> The prescriptions in favor of liberty ought to be leveled against that
> quarter where the greatest danger lies. . . . But this is not found in
> either the executive or the legislative departments of Government,
> but in the body of the people, operating by the majority against the
> minority.[84]

In other words, in the states. When some resisted the amendment, Madison insisted that this was "the most valuable amendment on the whole list." Think about that: the "whole list" included what we now call the Bill of Rights, Amendments 1–10. Yet Madison was saying that more important than any of those was this proposal requiring that the states also provide equal rights of conscience, as well as freedom of press.

Remarkably, the House voted overwhelmingly for the amendment. But with little debate, and no record, the Senate then rejected it. Presumably the senators, who were appointed by the legislatures, did not wish

Congress to limit the rights of states. On the issue he cared about the most, Madison had lost—and his position would not prevail until after the Civil War, with the passage of the Fourteenth Amendment.

Original Intents

When asking what "the founders" believed about this or that, most people really mean, what did the famous founders think? Rarely do culture warriors call forth the inspiring words of Peter Sylvester, Benjamin Huntington, or Samuel Livermore. Yet in Congress their views mattered. In order to get this amendment passed, Madison needed their votes.

The men involved in crafting the First Amendment had a variety of motives. Consider Representative Livermore's proposed language to prevent the national government from "touching" religion. Madison no doubt liked it because it entailed the most separation of church and state. But Livermore seemed to want it for the *opposite* reason: it would allow for less separation, at least at the state level, which he cared about the most. This should not be shocking, as it happens in the legislative process all the time. But we've come to think of the founders as operating in a realm of immaculate legislation, in which coherent ideas become historic charters in the National Archives without being soiled by politics. Alas, the First Amendment was not a verse of scripture but a political compromise. Separationists such as Madison won limits on the national government's ability to "intermeddle" with religion, but to do so they had to give the states free rein, even if that meant rampant local violations of religious liberty.

Madison did secure limits on the *national* government. What were they? Madison would say that the First Amendment required a separation of church and national government. Some modern religious conservatives have claimed that the concept of separation of church and state was actually invented in 1947 by an activist US Supreme Court. This notion is flat wrong. Madison spent his career defining and advocating for separation. In Virginia, he asserted that the state should not have even a "cognizance" of religion. During the ratification convention, he said that government should not have even "a shadow of right" to "intermeddle" with religion. When he railed against establishments, he did not mean merely an official state religion. He had opposed Patrick Henry's liberal efforts to support all Christian ministers. Later, he opposed the appointments of congressional and military chaplains, on the grounds that using tax dollars to pay ministers was creating a religious establishment.[85] He objected when Presidents Washington and Adams issued prayer proclamations because they "seem to imply and certainly nourish the errionious idea of a *national* religion."[86] He argued that the first census should not attempt to count the number of ministers, as that would show government cognizance of religion.[87] As president, Madison continued to insist on strict separation. In 1811, Congress passed a law establishing a church in the District of Columbia. Madison vetoed the bill on the grounds that it violated the First Amendment. That same year he opposed giving land to a church because appropriating government funds "for the use and support of religious societies" was contrary to the First Amendment.[88]

So, no, the idea of separation of church and state was not a twentieth-century concoction. The Founding Father who had more to do with the crafting of the First Amendment than anyone else was crystal clear: because government should not pay attention to religion, it was best to keep them far apart.

But Madison—father of the Constitution, champion of the First Amendment, master philosopher of religious freedom—had precisely one vote. To build a winning coalition, he had to draw support from people who did not agree with his interpretation.

Can we conclude anything about how Congress as a collective wanted the national government to behave? First, debates over religious "establishments" went beyond the question of an "official religion." Most interpreted the phrase to at least include taxpayer support for clergy, churches, and religious institutions. We can infer a broad resistance to letting the national government use its power—especially the power to tax—to subsidize or support a particular religion, including Christianity.

But, when they had the opportunity to embrace the most pro-separation phrasing, they balked. The resulting compromise gave states great leeway. Since many of these congressmen came from states where the government did do plenty of "touching," Madison's separationist purity likely seemed a bit much. It's therefore not surprising that the same Congress that passed the First Amendment also opened sessions with prayers.[89]

Madison and his coalition put forward some important but opaque principles. There was a spirit of liberty in the air, but others would have to determine how this would manifest in practice. Indeed, at the point of its ratification, it was an open question whether the First Amendment would really achieve much of anything.

Revival meeting

Chapter Three

THE STARTUP BOOM

*The state religious establishments collapse
and religious fervor erupts.*

In 1832, more than three decades after the passage of the First Amendment, James Madison assessed whether the separation of church and state had worked well. Unsurprisingly, he offered a positive verdict, but the nature of his evidence was revealing. He pointed not to the decline in religious persecution but to the rise in enthusiasm. In a letter to a Federalist writer, Robert Walsh Jr., Madison explained:

> On a general comparison of the present & former times, the balance is certainly & vastly on the side of the present, as to the number of religious teachers, the zeal which actuates them, the purity of their lives, and the attendance of the people on their instructions. . . .
>
> The number, the industry, and the morality of the priesthood & the devotion of the people have been manifestly increased by the total separation of the Church from the State.[1]

Madison connected two important phenomena of that era: the decline of state religious establishments and the rise of "the zeal," or what historians refer to as the Second Great Awakening. In a virtuous circle, the new freedoms had helped unleash religious revivals, which in turn had fueled the further collapse of the old religious order.

In the coming-of-age story of religious freedom, this period, from 1791 to the Civil War, was its adolescence. The body was changing. Religion was growing; freedom was breaking out. But emotions ran high, inconsistencies abounded, and when it came to religious liberty, the nation was still struggling to figure out who it wanted to be.

The Rise of the Ruff-Scuff

January 2, 1802, is a date that should loom large in the history of both religious freedom and dairy. On that day two monumental things happened in the nation's capital:

A 1,235-pound cheese—made by nine hundred pro-Jefferson cows in Massachusetts—was delivered to President Thomas Jefferson at the executive mansion in Washington, DC. It was emblazoned with a pro–religious liberty slogan: Rebellion to Tyrants Is Obedience to God.

And . . .

Jefferson wrote his famous letter to the Danbury Baptist Association of Connecticut, praising America for ratifying the First Amendment to the Constitution and "thus building a wall of separation between Church & State."

As we shall see, the cheese and the letter were very much related. Both were emblems of the convulsive period after the ratification of the First Amendment, when the states moved to change their laws and constitutions to make them friendlier to religious liberty.

One of the most acrimonious battles was fought in Connecticut, where the Congregational Church—the descendants of the Puritans—had been in control for more than a century. In 1784, the Connecticut legislature loosened its laws: denominations that were properly certified by the state would no longer have to pay taxes to support the Congregational Church.[2] But the evangelical Baptists kept protesting. Having to apply for state exemptions still meant they were being tolerated, not treated equally. "Religious liberty is a *right*, not a *favor*," wrote the Reverend John Leland, in the colorfully titled treatise *The Rights of Conscience Inalienable, and Therefore Religious Opinions Not Cognizable by Law or, the High-Flying Churchman Stripped of His Legal Robes Appears a Yahoo.*[3] (After working as an itinerant preacher in Virginia—where he prodded Madison to add a

Bill of Rights—Leland had moved back to New England, where he had been born.[4])

In 1801, an association of Baptists based in Danbury, Connecticut, organized a petition drive asking the legislature to repeal the law requiring that dissenting religions be certified. They had not made much progress, but in November 1800 they figured the tide might now turn: Jefferson—hero of religious freedom and villain to Congregational ministers—had been elected president in a polarizing election in which his iconoclastic views of religion had been an issue. On October 7, 1801, the Danbury Baptists wrote to the new president and asked for his help. Given that Jefferson had been condemned as an atheist and infidel, it's not clear whether the Baptists were being cheeky or earnest when they began their letter by declaring that "America's God has raised you up" to be president. They then complained that in Connecticut they must beg for their freedoms: "What religious privileges we enjoy (as a minor part of the State) we enjoy as favors granted, and not as inalienable rights."

While acknowledging that Jefferson couldn't personally abolish the Connecticut laws, they wondered if he might issue forth some of those powerful Jeffersonian phrases that, "like the radiant beams of the Sun, will shine & prevail through all these States and all the world till Hierarchy and tyranny be destroyed from the Earth."[5] Jefferson's response merits dissection. In a narrow sense, he rejected their request. He did not inveigh against the Congregationalist establishment in Connecticut. But he gave them something better: the metaphor to end all metaphors. He praised America for ratifying the First Amendment, "thus building a wall of separation between Church & State."

This new phrase, more than any other, would come to define the American approach to religious liberty.[6] In 1879 and again in 1947, the Supreme Court would deploy it as a simple exhortation for government to stay away from religion—whether that was tax support for a church, a crèche on the city hall lawn, or prayer in school.

What did Jefferson mean by this "wall"? We can do more than make educated guesses. As it turns out, Jefferson did not treat the letter from the Danbury Baptists as a routine constituent service matter but invested considerable thought in his reply. He asked his attorney general, Levi Lincoln, who was from Connecticut, to look over an early draft. Lincoln told him to delete some language that would alienate Traditionalists, and he did. What language? We actually know, thanks to help from . . . the FBI. In

1998, the Federal Bureau of Investigation was asked to use the latest foren-sic tools to uncover the words that Jefferson had inked out. According to historian James Hutson, Jefferson had originally intended to use the letter to needle his Federalist predecessors. He'd vowed not to issue presidential prayer proclamations, as Washington and Adams had, or carry out "even occasional performances of devotion." Hauling out the most biting insult he could muster, Jefferson noted that such displays would be like those of the British.

"Be assured," Jefferson wrote in his original draft, "that your religious rights shall never be infringed by any act of mine."[7]

Viewing both the edited and unedited versions, it becomes clear: Jefferson was just as hard-line as ever on separation. That wall? He was thinking it should be pretty high.

But he also believed in states' rights and that the First Amendment re-stricted only Congress. So, neither Congress nor the president could ne-gate the wishes of Connecticut. Changes would have to happen on the ground through persuasion and protest, not via an edict from the national government or even the new Constitution. "I shall see with sincere satis-faction the progress of those sentiments which tend to restore man all his natural rights," Jefferson concluded.[8]

That "progress" would happen slowly. The state religious establish-ment in Connecticut would remain for another sixteen years. It finally fell, in part because the demographics changed. While there were just nine Baptist churches and 450 adherents in Connecticut in 1760, by 1810 there were fifty-five churches with 5,700 members.[9]

When the establishment finally ended in 1818, the Traditionalists thought religion itself had been wounded by irresponsible minorities. The Rever-end Lyman Beecher railed against the lowlifes that were responsible. "So the democracy, as it rose, included nearly all the minor sects, besides the Sabbath-breakers, rum-selling tippling folks, infidels, and ruff-scuff gen-eral, and made a dead set at us of the standing order," he grumbled. When the "cause of Christ" was defeated, Beecher lamented, "it was as dark a day as ever I saw."[10]

Now, back to the cheese, born in Cheshire, Massachusetts.

Massachusetts's leaders boasted of their support for religious liberty. The state's 1780 Declaration of Rights, written in large part by John Adams, proclaimed that "no subject shall be hurt, molested, or restrained, in his person, liberty or estate, for worshipping GOD in the manner and season most agreeable to the dictates of his own conscience."[11] Strong language. Yet the state's constitution also required that Massachusetts residents pay taxes to subsidize the salaries of local Protestant ministers, usually members of the Congregational Church, which had preferred status. Minority sects had to apply for exemptions. Approval wasn't automatic. For instance, an itinerant Baptist preacher in Hampshire County in 1797 was rejected on the grounds that he was not "a settled minister."[12] In 1802, a Methodist church was taxed to pay for building repairs for the Congregational Church. Catholics had it even worse. When a Catholic brought a suit objecting to paying taxes to support Protestant ministers, the Supreme Court of Massachusetts coldly explained:

> The Constitution obliges everyone to contribute to the support
> of Protestant ministers and them alone. Papists are only tolerated,
> and as long as their ministers behave well, we shall not disturb
> them.[13]

Supporters of this system of "multiple establishments" argued that religion, made robust by the state, would ensure a more moral populace. "Full liberty of conscience does not imply in it, that men shall have liberty to have no conscience at all," the Reverend Samuel West explained, "or that they may be as obstinately wicked as they please."[14]

The dissenting religions opposed this system, and once again a key player was the Reverend John Leland, now living in Cheshire. His attacks on the New England laws echoed Jefferson in their insistence that only God, not the state, had the power to "certify" a religion.

> Government has no more to do with the religious opinions of
> men than it has with the principles of the mathematicks. Let every
> man speak freely without fear—maintain the principles that he
> believes—worship according to his own faith, either one God,
> three gods, no God, or twenty Gods; and let government protect
> him in so doing.

He cleverly noted that "Jesus never forced any man to pay him for his preaching, and we must imitate him."[15]

Leland, who gave about eight thousand sermons in his lifetime, was known for eschewing theological jargon in favor of humor and storytelling. To get attention for their cause and give support to their hero, Thomas Jefferson, Leland and his church organized an ambitious public relations gambit—making a mammoth cheese for the president. On July 20, 1801, farmers from all over Cheshire brought their own cheese curds to a central location, where they were placed into a single cheese hoop, seasoned, and pressed.[16] As the resulting cheese traveled to Washington, DC, it generated press coverage. Some ridiculed Leland and his gift. The *Stockbridge Western Star* mocked the "cheesen God,"[17] while the *Boston Mercury* published a snarky poem.

> Then Elder J—with lifted eyes,
> In musing posture stood,
> Invoked a blessing from the skies,
> To save from vermin, mites and flies
> And keep the bounty good.[18]

President Jefferson gave the cheese an enthusiastic welcome, with a special reception in the East Room of the Executive Mansion. Leland presented a statement from the town elders that really was (I'm so sorry about this) quite cheesy. Outdoing the Danbury Baptists in over-the-top obsequiousness, he declared, "We believe the supreme Ruler of the Universe, who raises up men to achieve great events, has raised up a Jefferson at this critical day, to defend Republicanism and to battle the arts of Aristocracy." He praised the US Constitution, including "the prohibition of religious tests." Finally, Leland noted that no slaves were involved in the making of this cheese.[19]

Jefferson thanked Leland and offered his own remarks, which utterly lacked any sense of humor about the nature of the gift. He declared that the cheese did "present an extraordinary proof of the skill with which those domestic arts contribute so much to our daily comfort" and praised the use of "freeborn farmers, employed personally in the useful labors of life."[20] And, believing that the president should not profit from gifts, Jefferson insisted on paying for the cheese.

Though a clever stunt, the cheese did not much affect the fight over the establishment in Massachusetts, which remained intact until 1834. Yes, a full fifty-eight years after the American Revolution, Massachusetts still taxed its citizens to pay for its churches.

In truth, Massachusetts and Connecticut were among the slowest states to fully embrace religious freedom. Other states moved faster but still with stops and starts. The First Amendment was adopted in 1791. North Carolina and New York had already eliminated their establishments in

1776, and Virginia, Maryland, and South Carolina had eliminated theirs in 1779, 1785, and 1790, respectively. Georgia followed in 1798 and then Vermont (1807), Connecticut (1818), New Hampshire (1819), Maine (1820), and Massachusetts (1832–33).[21] Rhode Island, Delaware, New Jersey, and Pennsylvania never had establishments.

The First Amendment did not require that the states make these changes, but the ideas of religious liberty were contagious. "Yield to the mighty current of American freedom," urged the Reverend William Tennent of South Carolina during the debates over the state's religious freedom laws.[22]

Although the states generally moved in the direction of religious freedom, they preserved some contradictions. For instance, New Jersey's declaration of religious principles in 1776 triumphantly declared that no resident "shall be denied the enjoyment of any civil right, merely on account of his religious principles"—as long as they were Protestant.[23] The ban on Catholic and Jewish officeholders remained until 1844.[24]

New Hampshire's 1776 constitution stipulated that "liberty of conscience shall be allowed unto Protestants" and banned Catholics from some public offices.[25] The state's constitutional convention of 1791 considered an amendment exempting dissenters from church taxes. It failed, 3993 to 994.[26] When a Universalist challenged the policy, the state's supreme court ruled that his religion was not a legitimate "sect, persuasion or denomination."[27] New Hampshire dissenters got relief in 1816, but until 1852 only Protestants could be elected to Congress.[28]

Maryland's constitution required that an office holder be Christian.[29] In 1818, a lawmaker named Thomas Kennedy campaigned for the "Jew bill," allowing Jews to hold office (despite his never having met one). Called an "enemy of Christianity" and "Judas Iscariot," he was voted out of office.[30] Kennedy and the tiny Jewish community persisted and in 1826[31] got full political rights (as long as they professed "the existence of God").[32]

The Delaware Constitution of 1776 required would-be office holders to swear allegiance to "God the Father and in Jesus Christ His only Son, and the Holy Ghost, one God, blessed for evermore." In 1792, it liberalized, allowing Jews to hold office.[33]

South Carolina's 1778 constitution established "the Christian Protestant religion" as the official faith, banning Catholics and Jews from holding office.[34] The state's 1788 constitution provided religious freedom "without distinction or preference," yet in 1813, the legislature gifted state land to the Presbyterian and Episcopal Churches (and not other denominations) to help them build new schools and churches.[35]

Pennsylvania's otherwise liberal constitution banned Jews from holding office until 1790, when they were accepted as long as they believed in "a future state of rewards and punishments," essential, it was believed, to being a moral person.[36] In 1794, Pennsylvania made it a crime to "profanely swear or curse by the name of God, Jesus Christ, or the Holy Ghost."[37]

New York had wide religious liberty, but in 1811 a man was sentenced to three months in jail for saying in public, "Jesus Christ was a bastard, and his mother must be a whore." This blasphemy was, the New York Supreme Court ruled, "an abuse of that right" to religious freedom.[38] The state also appropriated money for church-run schools.[39]

In one sense, the speed of the move toward religious liberty in the states was impressive. Historian Steven K. Green notes:

> The reversal of events was truly phenomenal: in 1775, nine of thirteen colonies had maintained religious establishments with assessment systems and legal preferences based on religious affiliation. Only fifteen years later, a majority of states (eleven of fourteen) had either abolished religious assessments or failed to adopt legal mechanisms necessary for their operation, causing the practice to die out.[40]

On the other hand, while there was a strong impulse toward religious freedom, the states were just beginning to wrestle with how to preserve liberty while maintaining religion's role as a guarantor of civic morality. They started by dispensing with the most egregious form of government meddling—the designation of a particular religion as the official faith of the state. Whether this happened immediately or took forty-three years often depended on the local demographics. States that already had strong or numerous dissenting groups aborted their establishments faster than those in which a particular denomination constituted an overwhelming majority, proving Madison's idea that diversity would improve the politics of religious freedom.

Quite a few states assumed that religious freedom could be achieved by providing exemptions to minority religions. But dissenting religions, along with religious skeptics, argued that the majority was missing the bigger point. Since rights came from Our Creator, it was not up to state governments to offer toleration. It also turned out to be quite difficult to benignly help religion in general. If the state donates land to one denomination, doesn't it have to donate an equal parcel to the others? Eventually, the states stopped taxing citizens to support churches.

But disagreements persisted about whether religious freedom meant equal treatment for non-Protestants. At first, few saw a conflict in praising religious liberty while, say, banning Catholics or Jews from holding office. This reflected a common view, sometimes stated, sometimes merely implied, that Protestantism *was* religion, and religion was Protestantism. Eventually, most came to see that real religious liberty meant nondiscrimination against people of other faiths.

Many stumbled over the counterintuitive idea, pushed especially hard by the evangelical Baptists, that helping religion hurts religion. Government assistance, the Baptists believed, undermines the clergy's motivation and the faith's credibility. As Leland put it, "These establishments metamorphose the church into a creature, and religion into a principle of state, which has a natural tendency to make men conclude that Bible religion is nothing but a trick of state."[41]

James Madison certainly agreed. That's why, as he watched the activity in the states as a senior citizen, he argued that religious freedom meant far more than not preferring one denomination over another. It meant that government—even if well-intentioned—needed to just *stay away*. In 1822, he wrote to Edward Livingston that each successful example of "a perfect separation" was important because it would lead both government and religion to "exist in greater purity."[42]

Madison was quite confident on this point because, he believed, the proof was all around him.

Second Great Awakening

From 1800 to 1850, the nation experienced a tidal wave of religiosity that historians call the Second Great Awakening. From 1770 to 1860, the number of churches per capita grew by 1,470 percent, while the number of Christian ministers increased at three times the rate of the population.[43] Mark Noll, the foremost historian of the period, argues that this "Protestant surge" resulted in large part from the collapse of the religious establishments that occurred in the years after the passage of the First Amendment and the "creative exploitation" of that disestablishment by religious leaders.[44] Under this new system—referred to as the "voluntary" approach—America's piety doubled. That's not hyperbole—from 1775 to 1845, the percentage of the population that was actively involved with a church rose from 17 percent to 34 percent.[45]

Lyman Beecher, who had earlier described the elimination of state support for churches as a "dark day," later admitted that it was "the best thing that ever happened to the State of Connecticut." The reason:

> It cut the churches loose from dependence on state support. It threw them wholly on their own resources and on God. . . . They say ministers have lost their influence; the fact is, they have gained. By voluntary efforts, societies, missions, and revivals, they exert a deeper influence than ever they could by queues, and shoe-buckles, and cocked hats, and gold-headed canes.[46]

The Madisonian model produced religion with a very un-Madisonian worship style. By 1860, the majority of Christians in America were evangelical,[47] which is to say they believed that the Bible was both accessible and central to their faith, that Jesus was their savior, and that they had a personal relationship with God.[48] The biggest winners in this new free market of religion were Methodists and Baptists. The number of Methodist churches grew from 65 in 1776 to 13,302 in 1850,[49] while Baptist churches increased from 471 in 1784 to 7,920 in 1848.[50]

In effect, the two denominations succeeded by making a series of product and marketing innovations. First, they encouraged the rise of itinerant preachers. This allowed them to cover more ground, reach underserved areas, and poach new members from other congregations. Under the old system, no polite minister would encroach on the territory of another. When Methodist preacher Peter Cartwright went into a new community, a local Presbyterian minister asked him to avoid forming a church within the "bounds of his congregation." It doesn't work that way anymore, Cartwright politely informed him. People could decide for themselves whom they wanted to hear. The Presbyterian retaliated by sermonizing against the Methodists, which only helped advertise Cartwright's arrival.[51]

The new religions also allowed the less educated to preach. Of the 2,000 Baptist ministers in 1823, only about 100 had more than a grade school education, and only 50 of the 4,282 Methodist ministers did.[52] In contrast, some 95 percent of Congregational ministers had college degrees.[53] This proved to be a selling point for Baptists; apparently many Southerners felt

condescended to by their Episcopalian clergy.[54] While the Congregationalists and Episcopalians begged for state support, the Baptists and Methodists operated with low overhead—in part because they didn't pay their
ministers, who usually had second jobs as farmers or artisans.

Another product innovation was the revival meeting. Imagine a multi-
stage rock concert with preachers instead of guitarists. Revival meetings
could be set up anywhere with a few months' planning. An eyewitness to
a revival in Cane Ridge, Kentucky, in 1802 painted a vivid picture.

> The noise was like the roar of Niagara. The vast sea of human
> beings seemed to be agitated as if by a storm. I counted seven
> ministers, all preaching at one time, some on stumps, others on
> wagons. . . . Some of the people were singing, others praying,
> some crying for mercy. A peculiarly strange sensation came over
> me. My heart beat tumultuously, my knees trembled, my lips
> quivered, and I felt as though I must fall to the ground.[55]

The style was energizing and the message hopeful. Through a simple act
of faith, anyone could change his or her life.

The preachers finished what the legislative reformers began. The established churches collapsed. In 1776, Congregationalists and Episcopalians had claimed 35 percent of all church members. By 1850, they had just
6.5 percent.[56] During that same period, the Methodist and Baptist share
rose from 23 percent to 54.7 percent.[57] "As free market conditions increasingly prevailed in the religious economy," explained historians Roger
Finke and Rodney Stark, "the old mainline denominations failed to meet
the competitive challenges and eventually abandoned the marketplace to
the upstarts."[58] The evangelical influence became tremendous. Noll notes
that by 1850, evangelical churches were maintaining twice as many facilities and employing nearly double the personnel of the US Post Office,
while taking in three times its revenue. In 1840, Americans received on average about three letters and two and one-half newspapers—but listened
to some twenty sermons.[59]

The Protestant surge also led to the creation of numerous important
nondenominational service groups. The American Sunday School Union
formed in 1824 to accelerate the creation of Sunday schools,[60] and the
number of people attending Sunday classes jumped from 127,000 in 1828
to 1 million by 1835.[61] The American Bible Society and the American Tract
Society formed to distribute religious materials around the country.[62]

Missionaries created colleges at a rapid clip, including Western Reserve Academy in Ohio, Knox College in Illinois, Ripon College in Wisconsin, DePauw University in Indiana, and Ohio Wesleyan University.[63]

With the spirit flowing and the structural impediments falling, moral crusades erupted. The American Temperance Society attracted 1.5 million members within just twelve years.[64] Charles Finney's evangelical writings inspired George Williams to start the Young Men's Christian Association[65] and William and Catherine Booth to start the Salvation Army,[66] two institutions that would go on to improve millions of lives. Most important, the Second Great Awakening energized abolitionism and helped sustain the slaves themselves. One of the leading abolitionists, Theodore Weld, whose book *American Slavery as It Is* supplied Harriet Beecher Stowe with much of the background for *Uncle Tom's Cabin*, was converted at a Charles Finney revival.[67] Abolitionist Methodist preachers—possessed by the spirit of God and liberated by newfound notions of religious freedom— regularly sermonized in the South.

In this new climate, women took on more powerful roles. The Freewill Baptists, the northern Methodists, the African Methodists, the Christian Connection, and the Millerites (precursors of the Seventh-day Adventists) all allowed women to take the pulpit. More than one hundred evangelical women preached at revival meetings across the country. The most famous of the lot, Harriet Livermore, spoke before Congress four times. These women did not advocate feminist positions and were not usually embraced by suffragists; most adhered to biblical teachings about female subservience. But their mere presence on the stump was revolutionary.[68]

The most courageous was probably Zilpha Elaw, a black woman, who put her liberty at risk by traveling to Maryland and Virginia to preach to slaves as well as white audiences.[69] One of twenty-three children born to a free Quaker family in Philadelphia, she had an intense conversion experience after a Methodist revival.[70] In 1825, she began preaching.[71] "When I arrived in the slave states," she wrote in her autobiography, "Satan much worried and distressed my soul with the fear of being arrested and sold for a slave, which their laws would have warranted, on account of my complexion and features."[72] Each time she became terrified, she said, she blamed Satan, asked for God's help, and soldiered on. On one two-month trip to Virginia, she preached to the wife of General Robert E. Lee.

> This formed a topic of lively interest with many of the slave
> holders, who thought it surpassingly strange that a person (and

a female) belonging to the same family stock with their poor debased, uneducated, coloured slaves, should come into their territories and teach the enlightened proprietors the knowledge of God.[73]

The spirit of revivalism even fertilized the ground for entirely new denominations and religions. The Church of Jesus Christ of Latter-day Saints (Mormonism), Seventh-day Adventism, Christian Universalism, Transcendentalism, and the African Methodist Episcopal Church all arose between 1800 and the Civil War.

It was through the Second Great Awakening that Protestantism gave its second great gift to the American experiment. The first was the idea that rights come from God; since all human beings are made in God's image, we are owed these rights equally. The second gift was creative religious destruction. Evangelicals helped to take down the old system—which relied on government support for its nourishment—and showed what could emerge in its place. Americans could see with their own eyes and hear with their own ears, and maybe even feel with their own souls, that religion flourishes when left untouched by government.

None of this could have happened without the new set of rules that Madison and his fellow travelers in the states had put into place. No believer should have to beg for a license from another religious official or from the government. No preacher should be blocked from spreading his or her message to receptive ears in any field or town. No denomination should be propped up by taxpayer dollars. Removing these obstacles unleashed spiritual creativity on a colossal scale. Americans' understanding of religious liberty was still crude—most thought of themselves as citizens of a Protestant nation and expected to see that reflected in public institutions. But having tasted freedom, the religious upstarts would work to ensure that their newly won liberty wouldn't be snatched away.

Great Excitements

Thomas Jefferson despised scriptural literalism and revelation, so on one level, he was no doubt turned off by evangelical Bible-thumping. But he and Madison viewed the religious upstarts as their political allies and constituents. The evangelicals had gotten Madison elected to Congress and had helped lift Jefferson to the White House. In 1820, Jefferson praised Virginia's Methodists and Baptists not for their spiritual ingenuity but for their political loyalty ("the Baptists are sound republicans and zealous supporters of their government. The Methodists are republicans mostly, satisfied with the government").[74]

It must have been quite the scene when President Jefferson, the champion of rationalism, invited a special guest to speak before the House of Representatives on January 3, 1801. It was none other than the Reverend John Leland, still in town after having delivered his cheese. The political and social gulfs between established and newfangled religionists leap out in this description by a thoroughly appalled Reverend Manasseh Cutler, who was both a Federalist congressman and a Congregationalist minister from Massachusetts:

> Last Sunday, Leland, the cheesemonger, a poor, ignorant, illiterate, clownish preacher (who was the conductor of the monument of human weakness and folly to the place of its destination), was introduced as the preacher to both Houses of Congress. . . . Such a performance I never heard before, and I hope never shall again. The text was, "And behold a greater than Solomon is here [Matt. 12:42; Luke 11:31]."
>
> The design of the preacher was principally to apply the allusion, not to the person intended in the text, but to *him* who was then present [Jefferson]. Such a farrago, bawled with stunning voice, horrid tone, frightfull grimaces, and extravagant gesture, I believe, was never heard by any decent auditory before. Shame or laughter appeared in every countenance. Such an outrage upon religion, the Sabbath, and common decency, was extremely painful to every sober, thinking person present.[75]

Madison, even more prim than Jefferson, referred to some of the evangelical activity as the "great excitements." But he was more personally acquainted with evangelical personalities than Jefferson was, having worked directly with the Baptists in Virginia and having attended college with evangelicals. Some feared that these movements could slide toward what Madison called "extravagances injurious both to Religion and to social order."

Don't worry, he said. First, what's the alternative? Government intervention to reduce their influence? That would make it worse. More important, this new religion was at least *pure*. If it wasn't the staid Episcopalianism practiced by the gentry of northern Virginia, it was at least a product of uncoerced choices. The "zeal" provided powerful proof that disentangling religion and government was good for both—evidenced by "the greater purity & industry of the Pastors and in the greater devotion of their flocks."[76]

And if religious extremists ever got too popular, well, there was a check on that too. "Reason," Madison wrote optimistically, "will gradually regain its ascendancy."[77]

He was wrong.

Destruction of the Ursuline Convent

Chapter Four

THE ROMISH
THREAT

America confronts a flammable question:
Should religious freedom apply to Catholics?

There were rumors. Sinister things were happening behind the walls of the Ursuline Convent in Charlestown, Massachusetts, in August 1832. The Catholic school housed there had become popular with affluent Boston Protestants and Unitarians, but word had spread that a "mystery" woman was being held there against her will. On the morning of August 10, posters appeared around Charlestown.

> To arms!! To arms! Ye brave and free, the avenging sword shield us!! Leave not one stone upon another of that curst nunnery that prostitutes female virtue and liberty under the garb of holy religion.[1]

That night, about two miles away in Boston proper, the Reverend Lyman Beecher delivered a sermon on a similar topic—the Catholic threat to America. The renowned New England minister had gone to Cincinnati to run a seminary and returned with a warning: the American West would become a new battlefield between Protestants and the "Romish Church." In sermons and writings, Beecher warned that Catholics were a "dark-minded, vicious populace—a poor, uneducated mass of infuriated animalism."[2] The corrupt Catholic Church, he said, was working to "subvert our free institutions."

The next day, a few thousand people gathered around the Ursuline Convent. Most were working-class, many were drunk, and some were disguised as Indians, as was the fashion among the anti-immigrant nativists of the day. About fifty girls between the ages of six and fourteen were inside the building. Finally, a few hundred of the men busted through the convent gate, chanting, "Down with the pope! Down with the convent!" The Mother Superior hurried the nuns and the students out the back and over the wall that surrounded the convent. The men rampaged, destroying Bibles, the nuns' belongings, and musical instruments. After taking Eucharist wafers, one rioter said, laughing, "Now I have God's body in my pocket."[3]

Some descended to the convent's crypt, opened the coffins of deceased sisters, and grabbed their teeth as souvenirs. Then they burned the convent to the ground while a fire company stood by and watched.

It is unclear whether Lyman Beecher's sermon incited the riot (there's evidence on both sides), but at a minimum there was something in the air that fed both his own overheated rhetoric and the mob's violence. Intellectuals and workingmen alike had become obsessed with the dangers of Catholicism and the supposed depravities of priests and nuns. In 1834, a hoax "memoir"—*Awful Disclosures of the Hotel Dieu Nunnery of Montreal*—became a sensation. Although it was later revealed that Protestant ministers wrote the book, it was published as a true confession of a former nun, Maria Monk, who described how priests would creep into her Montreal convent at night through secret passages so they could rape the Sisters.[4] The Mother Superior, the book claimed, forced the women to perform sexual acts: "Things were done worse than the entire exposure of the person, though this was occasionally required of several at once, in the presence of priests."[5] Some nuns became pregnant. After their babies were born, they would be baptized, murdered, thrown into a pit in the cellar, and covered with lime.[6] *Awful Disclosures* likely sold more copies in the United States than any other book published between 1800 and 1852.[7]

The riots, the popularity of anti-Catholic literature, the sermonizing by popular Protestant preachers—these were just a few elements of the anti-Catholic wave of the 1830s, 1840s, and 1850s. In the twenty-first century—now that the Catholic share of the US population has surpassed 20 percent;

now that we've had a Catholic president, Nobel Prize winners, astronauts, pop stars, and Supreme Court justices; now that millions of Americans cheer for the Fighting Irish of Notre Dame; now that a sarcastic way to criticize someone's generosity is to say, "Well, she ain't Mother Teresa"— it's hard to fathom how broad-based and commonplace was America's hatred of Catholics and Catholicism.

This chapter traces the battles in the first half of the nineteenth century over which religion would dominate the American West and whose Bible should or should not be taught in the public schools. In the Madisonian marketplace of religion, Protestants perceived a new competitor. They didn't like it one bit, and they attempted to write the rules of religious freedom to preserve their own preeminence.

Ultimately, these Protestant-Catholic conflicts forced Americans to confront and redefine their ideas about religious tolerance and the separation of church and state. This period also illustrated how immigration can strengthen religious freedom; the waves of new Americans from Catholic countries broke the Protestant monopoly, enabling a healthy system of spiritual checks and balances to develop.

The Cloven Foot

Less than 1 percent of Americans were Catholic at the turn of the nineteenth century, so the Catholic threat had been largely symbolic.[8] But as a result of immigration from Ireland, the Catholic population surged from 663,000 in 1841 to 3.1 million in 1860,[9] from 4.6 percent of the population to 11.5 percent.[10] Foreign-born people made up more than 45 percent of the populations of New York, Chicago, Milwaukee, St. Louis, Cincinnati, Buffalo, and Detroit.[11] While early Catholic immigrants tended to be skilled workers, later arrivals were mostly poor and uneducated, many driven from Ireland by the potato famine between 1845 and 1852. Preachers, politicians, and editors sounded a clarion: America was in grave danger.

One prominent New Yorker got a great deal of attention for his nationalist tirades. A celebrity who used his fame in the commercial sector to launch a political career, he argued that a foreign country was intentionally sending us "their criminals" because America did not have sufficient "walls" and "gates" to keep them out.[12] While acknowledging that some immigrants might be good, he said, "we must of necessity suspect them all."[13] What's more, he advocated restricting the entry of those immigrants practicing one particular religion that was, he said, associated with violence and tyranny.

The man was Samuel Morse, an inventor of the telegraph and the Morse code. The religion he assailed, of course, was not Islam but "Popery." The nation he warned about was not Mexico, or even Ireland, but rather Austria, because he believed that an organization based there had hatched a plan to finance the immigration of hundreds of thousands of Catholics. And while Morse did not win his election (for mayorship of New York City), he had a significant influence on the popular culture through the two books he published in 1835, *Foreign Conspiracy Against the Liberties of the United States* and *Imminent Dangers to the Free Institutions of the United States Through Foreign Immigration and the Present State of the Naturalization Laws.*

The Catholic immigrants were decrepit—"halt, and blind, and naked"—and easy to manipulate, Morse wrote. With their "darkened intellects," they "obey their priests as demigods." The Europeans could deploy these "senseless machines" to seize power in America, Morse and other anti-Catholic activists said, through our electoral system. The Vatican controlled the priests, who then controlled the voters.[14] Morse pointed to local elections, in which Catholics were already having an impact. A Jesuit priest had been elected to Congress from Michigan, where the Catholics used color ballots to help enforce voting discipline. "The cloven foot has already shown itself," Morse said, via this "truly Jesuitical mode of espionage."[15] "Up! Up! I beseech you. . . . Shut your gates," Morse urged.[16]

Lyman Beecher was just as alarmist. The immigration deluge meant "half a million of unprincipled, reckless voters, in the hands of demagogues."[17] How could someone like Beecher—father of abolitionist icons Harriet Beecher Stowe and Henry Ward Beecher—have not seen the irony of championing liberty while attacking Catholics? First, these anti-Catholic activists believed Catholicism was not a legitimate religion, or at least not a genuine form of Christianity (a tendency that would reappear later in the treatment of Mormons and Muslims). That's why they used the terms "Romish," "popery," and "the Whore of Babylon." The publication *Home Missionary* declared:

> The great battle is to be fought between truth and error, between law and anarchy, between Christianity with her Sabbaths, her ministry and her schools on the one hand, and the combined forces of Infidelity and Popery on the other.[18]

Second, they viewed Catholicism as a tool of foreign powers. Beecher explained the intentions of the European tyrants. By "emptying upon our shores" so many paupers—"the sweepings of the streets"—they would impose heavy burdens on our government and society.[19] The result would be "multiplying tumults and violence, filling our prisons, and crowding our poor-houses, and quadrupling our taxation." The American Patriot organization called for "sending back Foreign Paupers and Criminals."[20]

Third, Catholicism was not worthy of freedom because it opposed democracy, they believed. "Popery is a Political system, despotic in its organization, anti-democratic and anti-republican, and cannot therefore coexist with American republicanism," Morse said.[21] To save religious freedom in America, Catholicism would have to be defeated.

Some formerly persecuted groups joined in the attacks. The publication of the American Baptist Home Mission Society in 1832 declared of Roman Catholicism, "Its outward form is chameleon, and with Jesuitical cunning and adroitness, adopts itself to all changes of circumstances."[22]

While the Protestant attacks reeked of bigotry, the Catholic Church gave them plenty of ammunition. The Church at various moments of world history *had* opposed freedom and democracy in Europe and other parts of the world. But what anti-Catholic activists left out was any evidence that *American* Catholics had rejected the democratic system. After all, the primary means through which Catholics attempted to reshape America was by setting up schools and charities. And the way they were hoping to gain power was through elections.

Bible Riots

When Pennsylvania created its public school system in 1834, the legislature required that it use the Bible to teach morality. By "Bible," it meant the King James Version. The problem was that, for several hundred years, Catholics had rejected the King James Version in favor of the Douay-Rheims Version. The Catholic Bible included numerous annotations, in keeping with the Catholic tradition that the Bible is best understood with help from priestly experts. It also kept eight books of what Protestants called Apocrypha that the King James Version had purged, including the books of Tobit, Judith, Wisdom, Sirach, Baruch, 1 and 2 Maccabees, and parts of Esther and Daniel. Catholics also used a different version of the Ten Commandments. For Protestants, the third Commandment was

"Thou shalt not make unto thee any graven image, or any likeness of any-thing that is in heaven above." Catholics had a long tradition of creating literal depictions of Jesus on the cross and icons of the saints.

Philadelphia's Catholic bishop, Francis Kenrick, objected to Catholic children being forced to read the King James Bible. Born in Dublin, he had immigrated in 1821 after receiving his doctorate, and he now managed a fast-growing diocese.[23] "THE READING OF THE PROTESTANT VERSION OF THE BIBLE IS UNLAWFUL AND NO CATHOLIC PARENT CAN PERMIT HIS CHILDREN TO USE IT AS A SCHOOLBOOK OR OTHERWISE," he wrote in the *Catholic Herald* in 1841. The rule violated "the rights of conscience," which were supposed to be "inviolable."[24] Many Catholic parents instructed their children to re-fuse to read the "mutilated work," as they called the King James Version.[25]

Kenrick suggested that schools continue to use the Protestant Bible but that Catholic students be allowed to read from the Catholic Bible and be excused from singing Protestant hymns. He did *not* propose that the Bible be removed from the schools or that Protestant children be kept from reading the King James Version.

The members of the Board of Controllers, which managed the school system, were mostly Protestants, but they knew that the Catholic pop-ulation had risen from 21 percent in 1808 to 39 percent in 1832.[26] So they crafted what they thought was a Solomonic compromise. Catholic stu-dents should not be forced to read a Bible to which they were "conscien-tiously opposed." But while they could bring in a Bible of their own, it had to be one "without note or comment," which ruled out the Catholic Bible.[27] Their Liberty of Conscience resolution,[28] as they called it, angered everyone. Protestant leaders thought the board had capitulated to evil, falsely asserting that the Catholics wanted to exclude the Bible from the schools. The Catholics were perfectly free to leave the common schools if they didn't like them, they argued. "Protestants founded these schools, and they have always been in a majority," explained an article in the *Pres-byterian*. "Why then should the minority who have come in afterwards for the benefits of these schools" get to change the rules?[29] The *Protes-tant Banner* warned that acceding to the Catholic position would mean, in effect, "erecting the cross of the antichrist over our common school houses."[30]

Philadelphia's Protestants organized, with more than eighty ministers of various Protestant denominations setting aside their own differences in 1842 to form the American Protestant Association. They maintained that

"Romanism . . . under a foreign priesthood" was aggressively trying "to destroy the religious character and influence of public Protestant education."[31] The American Republican Association, a nativist group, urged that naturalized citizens—those not born in the United States—be excluded from public office.[32]

The next year, a teacher in the Kensington district falsely claimed that her principal had told her to stop teaching from the Bible. A school official then told an audience at a Methodist church that the principal, who was Catholic, was acting under "Popish dictations" and that it was time to "resist such attempts 'to kick the bible from the Public Schools.'" The *Episcopal Recorder* asked:

> Are we to yield our personal liberty, our inherited rights, our very Bibles, the special, blessed gift of God to our country, to the will, the ignorance or the wickedness of these hordes of foreigners, subjects of a foreign despot. . . . ?[33]

On March 4, 1844, a crowd of more than six thousand gathered across from Independence Hall to "save the Bible." In response to the agitation, Kenrick hardened his line. While before he'd asked that Catholic students be excused from reading from the King James Version, he now asked that they be allowed to recite from the Douay-Rheims Version. And if that wasn't possible, the schools should just avoid Bible readings altogether.[34]

Tensions reached a dangerous level. On May 3, a Protestant group tried to hold a protest meeting in the Catholic area of Kensington, but club-wielding Irish Catholics drove them out. Three days later, more than two thousand Protestants returned. Fists flew, a scuffle broke out at a nearby market, a shot was fired, and an eighteen-year-old Protestant boy named George Shiffler was killed. The nativist press demanded revenge. "We write at this moment with our garments stained and sprinkled with the blood of victims to Native American rights—the rights of conscience," the *Daily Sun* declared. Allowing Catholics to read their own Bible amounted to an assault on Protestant freedoms, the *Native American* declared. It was time "to arm," since "the bloody hand of the Pope has stretched itself forth to our destruction."[35]

In the ensuing riot, lasting from May 6 to May 8, about thirty Catholic homes were burned down. Some Protestants took a page from Exodus and adorned the doors of their homes with signs saying "native American" to ensure that the rioters passed them over. The Sisters of Charity convent was destroyed,[36] as was St. Augustine's Church, including its library of five thousand books.[37] The crowd gave a great cheer when the cross atop St. Augustine's fell to the ground.[38] Hundreds of Catholic families loaded their possessions into wagons and fled to safety. The governor sent in thousands of soldiers to guard the churches and restore order.[39]

After a few months of calm, nativists organized a major show of strength during a July 4 parade. A float depicting an open Bible traveled the route. One banner read, "Our Fathers gave us the Bible—we will not yield it to a Foreign hand." Another depicted an American eagle grasping the good book in its claws.[40] The next day, it was discovered that, with the permission of the government, muskets were being stored in the basement of the St. Philip Neri Catholic Church. A nativist mob descended upon the church to demand the removal of the weapons and exchanged gunfire with the local militia. In all, between the May and July riots, about thirty people were killed.[41] A telling footnote to the episode: one nativist leader, Lewis Levin, the next year became the first Jew elected to Congress, proving that being part of a persecuted group does not necessarily bring sensitivity to the plight of other religious minorities.

Similar battles played out in the 1840s and 1850s in Kentucky, Maryland, Michigan, Massachusetts, and New York.[42] In Boston, a ten-year-old named Thomas Whall was commanded to recite the Protestant Ten Commandments. When he refused, an assistant to the principal beat the boy's hands for thirty minutes with a rattan stick until they bled. The teacher told those unwilling to recite to leave, and a hundred did. The next day, three hundred more Catholic students were dismissed. When Catholic students brought their own Bibles to school a week later, they too were sent home.[43] The incident helped prompt the creation of parochial schools in Boston.

The Western Front

Americans once ignorantly believed that the land we now call the United States went from being uninhabited to being settled by Protestants. In more recent years, we've been reminded that Native Americans were already here. But that revised image isn't quite right, either. If we look at a map of the modern continental United States, more than half of its square footage is in states that had actually belonged to *Catholic* countries. Texas,

New Mexico, Arizona, Utah, Nevada, Colorado, Wyoming, Idaho, and California were part of Mexico, which had Catholicism as its official religion. Modern-day Oklahoma, Kansas, Nebraska, South Dakota, North Dakota, Louisiana, and Montana were part of Catholic France. And Florida was a part of Catholic Spain. The United States has deep Catholic roots. San Francisco was named after Saint Francis of Assisi, Des Moines originally meant "River of the Monks," and Sacramento refers to the Catholic Eucharist. At least fifty-seven American cities are named after Catholic saints.

When Protestant leaders looked west in the 1830s, they saw not an empty expanse but a land where Catholics had a head start. Lyman Beecher's book *A Plea for the West* warned of catastrophe if Protestants didn't move aggressively and creatively: "The conflict which is to decide the destiny of the West, will be a conflict of institutions for the education of her sons, for purposes of superstition, or evangelical light; of despotism, or liberty." Many Protestants believed they were being outhustled. A Vermont minister, George Campbell, was haunted by the spectacle of "crowds of Catholics, of priests and bishops, sent out by the Pope and emptied upon our shores, their institutions of learning—their monasteries and nunneries—their churches and cathedrals scattered over the land."[44]

In fact, American Catholicism had a great awakening of its own during the first half of the nineteenth century. The number of nuns in the United States exploded from 270 in 1820 to 5,090 by 1860, while the number of priests rose from 150 to 2,235.[45] Western bishops worked with the railroads to attract Catholic homesteaders and missionaries.[46] Father Francis X. Weninger traveled two hundred thousand miles to preach to more than eight hundred Catholic missions.[47] Catholic settlements sprang up in Minnesota, Iowa, Nebraska, Kansas, and the Dakotas. They emphasized education, starting Xavier University in Cincinnati, the University of Notre Dame, Santa Clara College (now University) in California, St. Mary's Institute (now University) in Texas, and the University of San Francisco.[48]

As Madison predicted, religious factions are wont to compete. In the sixteenth, seventeenth, and eighteenth centuries, Catholic missions had been established by Mexico, France, and Spain. In the nineteenth century, European Catholics created the Society for the Propagation of the Faith to subsidize new missions. Donors would commit to offering a prayer and five cents per month to help support the missionaries.[49] In response, Protestant missionaries intensified their efforts. The American Home

Missionary Society was created in 1826 to spread the word in the West. The Missouri chapter reported with bitter admiration that popery had turned St. Louis into its "commanding citadel of the West."

> She has occupied [the West], and in all the chief places of
> concourse—on every bluff, along the banks of the mighty
> rivers . . . and on its blooming prairies, spread out like the ocean,
> inexhaustible in their fertility—she has erected her banner, and
> bids defiance to Protestantism—to free intelligence, equal rights,
> and a pure evangelical piety. And shall this fair land be abandoned,
> without a struggle, to the undisputed and perpetual dominion of
> the Man of Sin?[50]

Another Protestant group, the Society for the Promotion of Collegiate and Theological Education at the West, focused on higher education. As a speaker at one of the society's conferences in 1845 put it:

> The Jesuits are willing, nay, longing, nay, plotting and toiling, to
> become the educators of America. Let them have the privilege of
> possessing the seats of education in the west, and of moulding the
> leading minds of the millions that are to inhabit there, and we may
> give up all our efforts to produce in the west what Puritanism has
> produced here.[51]

Military metaphors abounded, although the chief weapons were books and schools. "America is a field on which the open, manly, Christian discipline of a Protestant College must annihilate the rival system of Jesuitical instruction," the Reverend E. N. Kirk sermonized.[52] "The Papists have laid out the West with the experienced eye of generals."[53]

For Protestant leaders, the question of how to plant religion in the West became more complicated—and more exciting—when the United States went to war with Mexico in 1846. Most of the debate over entry into the war had centered on the implications for slavery. Northerners feared and Southerners hoped that annexing some of Mexico would bring more pro-slavery states into the Republic. But religion was an important factor as well. The Mexican-American War was fueled and stoked by anti-Catholic sentiment.

For Protestant leaders, the massive tracts of land owned by Mexico at the time—present-day Texas, Arizona, New Mexico, Colorado, Utah, and California—posed both a threat and an opportunity. Absorbing those areas into the United States would mean adding hundreds of thousands of Catholics to the population. They would become voters: a terrifying thought. On the other hand, they could be converted. This could be a war of liberation—of Catholics from the bondage of their Church. Methodist leaders recalled that Great Britain's Opium Wars had opened "heathen" China to evangelical efforts. They imagined a vast new mission field.[54] America had a duty to "civilize, humanize, and reclaim vanquished savages," argued Representative Charles J. Ingersoll of Philadelphia, be they Indians or Mexican Catholics.[55]

Abolitionists felt conflicted. They tended to oppose the war out of fear it would further entrench slavery. But they also saw its value as an opportunity to weaken Catholicism. As Arthur Tappan, a noted abolitionist, put it, "the only consolation for us in this matter is, that with the spread of our race is secured the spread of liberty, civilization and Christianity." Note that Catholicism was not deemed to be Christian. Tappan's paper, the *New York Journal of Commerce*, argued that "this unhappy war" could at least provide Mexicans with "liberty of Conscience."

After all, the publication explained, "one nation is full of Christians, the other is full of Catholics."[56]

Once the war began, some who'd opposed it allowed that it would be a pity if something good didn't come out of it. Presbyterian leaders declared that "now is the time to strike" with an assault wave of missionaries. The Reverend William Buck, editor of the *Baptist Banner and Western Pioneer*, gushed that with the commencement of hostilities, a "door opened for the Bible and the missionary of the cross, to the vast multitudes of Priest-ridden Mexicans and benighted Indians, who sit in that region of the shadow of death."[57]

With a sales pitch that came to be known as the myth of the "Golden Jesus," army recruiters summoned images of a Catholicism grown fat off the labors of Mexican peasants, enticing would-be soldiers with "hyperbolic tales of gold crucifixes, statues with gemstone eyes and studded garments, and gilded altar rails" in churches that were ripe for looting, in the words of historian John Pinheiro. "The Song of Volunteers," a recruitment jingle set to the tune of "Yankee Doodle," declared:

> We're the boys for Mexico
> Sing Yankee Doodle Dandy,
> Gold and silver images,

Plentiful and fancy.
Churches grand, with altars rich,
Saints with diamond collars,
(That's the talk to understand,)
With lots of new bright dollars.[58]

There was one other advantage to the war. Protestants figured that American soldiers would report back on the horrors of Catholicism. Letters from soldiers that mocked the rituals of Mexican Catholics were reprinted in anti-Catholic or gullible newspapers back home. Want evidence that Catholicism suffocates thought and breeds poverty? Look at the poverty of Mexico. Need proof that it is in conflict with Republican principles of government? See how politically unstable the Mexican political system is.[59] Some propaganda was invented out of whole cloth. In the book *Adventures in Mexico*, author Corydon Donnavan claimed that a nun invited two American soldiers to her cell, where she showed them the body of a monk, an unfortunate former lover. Pulling a gun, she demanded that the Americans help dispose of the corpse. The fake report, adapted from a fictional account that was originally set in Spain, was reprinted by a number of Protestant newspapers.[60]

Antagonism to Catholics hit a wartime high point when a group of Irish Catholic soldiers known as the Saint Patrick's Battalion deserted and fought with the Mexicans. Though most of the nine thousand men who deserted during the war were Protestants, these Catholic defections drew much attention. Twenty-seven were hanged. Some scholars maintain that they rebelled because they were abused by their superiors; it's also possible that the Mexican leadership had tried to drive a wedge between Catholic American soldiers and the rest of the army. Mexican general Antonio López de Santa Anna cheekily declared, "Can you fight by the side of those who put fire to your temples in Boston and Philadelphia?"[61]

Notably, the American government did not stir anti-Catholic sentiment. President James Polk, a Democrat, had won the election narrowly, in part by taking New York and Pennsylvania, where the Catholic vote was growing rapidly and nativist activity was associated with the Whig Party. By one estimate, 95 percent of New York's Irish voted for Polk.[62] His Whig opponents grumbled that his close victory was enabled in part by the foreign vote, or, as John Quincy Adams put it, "the Pope of Rome."[63] Moreover, Polk and his generals had concluded that it made no sense to antagonize the Catholic Church in Mexico or regular Mexicans who often disliked their own government. So, setting the myth of the Golden Jesus to rest, he directed the troops to respect the holy places.[64] Though we hardly think of Polk as a paragon of enlightenment, he, like George Washington during the American Revolution, viewed religious tolerance as a tactical necessity.

But the war certainly helped fuel anti-Catholic sentiment back home, further energizing the nativist movement. In 1851, a priest in Ellsworth, Maine, was tarred and feathered after he criticized a requirement that Catholics read from the Protestant Bible.[65] Around 1852, these ad hoc nativist uprisings congealed into a more overt political movement called the Know-Nothings. Know-Nothing candidates won the mayoralties of Washington, DC; Chicago; Philadelphia; and other cities. A new national political party, the American Party, enrolled 1 million members.[66] In 1854 and 1855, it elected seven governors, eight senators, and between fifty and one hundred congressmen (including the Speaker of the House of Representatives, Nathaniel Banks).[67] In 1856, its candidate for the White House, former president Millard Fillmore, won 20 percent of the vote. Nativist gangs, such as the Black Snakes and the Rough Skins, attempted to intimidate Catholic voters, often leading to Election Day violence. In Baltimore, officials mounted a cannon at one polling place.[68] Substantively, the Know-Nothings focused on preventing foreign-born residents from holding office or becoming citizens. In Massachusetts, the legislature blocked state courts from processing citizenship applications, prohibited immigrants from holding state jobs, and instituted compulsory daily reading of the King James Version of the Bible. The legislature tried unsuccessfully to restrict voting to people who had lived in the state for at least twenty-one years. Violence broke out in many places. Anti-Catholic riots in Louisville, Kentucky, killed twenty-two; ten died in St. Louis and four in New Orleans.

Even the Washington Monument became caught up in religious conflict. As of 1852, for reasons of politics and incompetence, the monument still had not been completed. In January, Pope Pius IX let it be known that, as a sign of respect, the Vatican would contribute a large stone taken from the ancient Temple of Peace in Rome. Three feet long, eighteen inches high, and ten inches thick, it carried the inscription "Rome to America." Nativists were appalled. Some suggested that they produce a "protest block" to be placed "on top of the objectionable stone."[69] As activist John

Weishampel of Baltimore put it, "We as a people believe that God raised up our Washington to lead us out of bondage," unlike the pope, who planned no doubt to "burn our Bibles, bind our consciences, make slaves of us, and put us to the stake, the rack, or the dungeon."[70] On March 6, 1854, a group of nativists broke into the construction site where the Roman stone was stored, hoisted it onto a barge, and dumped it into the Potomac River.[71]

The assaults on Catholicism finally receded with the arrival of the Civil War. For one thing, the war put an end to most immigration. Also, just as the prospect of Maryland's Catholics fighting in the Continental Army had led to a greater appreciation of religious diversity, Northerners could not help but notice that a huge part of the Union Army was Catholic. Some five hundred thousand immigrants wore the blue uniform, making attacks on them seem suddenly un-American.[72]

Harbingers

The anti-Catholic wave of the 1830s, 1840s, and 1850s offers several lessons worth keeping in mind as we consider other religious conflicts.

First, immigration played a critical role. Anxiety about religious freedom often intensifies when new people with new spiritual proclivities and political allegiances arrive. But the surge of immigration in the first half of the nineteenth century shattered Protestant dominance, paving the way for expansive religious freedom.

Leadership mattered. Passionate people often push too far, but throughout this period, some leaders tried to see the big picture. The mayor of Boston preached brotherhood to a crowd of Protestants at Faneuil Hall. The governor of Pennsylvania sent in the militia to defend Catholics during the Bible riots. President Polk attempted to damp down anti-Catholic sentiment during the Mexican-American war. A few Protestants saw that religious freedom meant nothing if it didn't include tolerance for Catholics. "The guarantee of the rights of conscience, as found in our Constitution, is most sacred and inviolable, and one that belongs, no less to the Catholic, than to the Protestant," said Illinois state legislator Abraham Lincoln in 1844.[73]

The press often made matters worse. Run by religious denominations and political parties, the newspapers of that era were far from objective. The false story of Maria Monk's convent was reprinted by numerous Protestant publications. In Philadelphia, the Protestant papers spread the lie that Catholics wanted to remove the Bible from public schools.[74] Protestant newspapers engaged in fearmongering about a papal takeover of the West and circulated horror stories about Mexican Catholicism before and during the war.

The availability of land in America was an important factor too. The open frontier fueled antagonistic competition, but it also provided a pressure valve. Evangelicals put their energy into the more peaceful task of planting schools and churches out west. And while Catholics did the same, the spaces were wide enough that religious conflict could sometimes be dispersed.

Efforts to create a nondenominational "public religion" proved difficult. Throughout the colonial period, the most enlightened advocates of religious freedom had tried to stake out a common linguistic ground, such as appreciation of the Creator. But few elements of religion proved to be truly universal. Even the Ten Commandments drove a wedge between Protestants and Catholics.

It turns out that having been the object of religious persecution does not make one more courageous, clearheaded, or empathetic when others are in the line of fire. Baptists, for instance, had been brutally harassed in the 1740s, but in the 1840s they attacked the pope as "the man of sin" and Catholicism as destructive of American democracy. The term "religious freedom" proved malleable. With their majority status now at risk, many Protestants defined it as the freedom to practice their faith as it was meant to be—vibrant, imbued with the Holy Spirit . . . and utterly dominant.

Colored engraving by unknown artist

Chapter Five

THE RELIGIOUS FREEDOM OF SLAVES

*African spirituality and Islam are purged,
creating a "spiritual holocaust."*

D iscussions of religious liberty before the Civil War rarely consider the status of African Americans for an understandable but perverse reason: their subjugation was so thorough that the loss of their religious freedom seemed to be the least of their problems. But if anything, depriving them of their faith as they tried to endure slavery was especially cruel. While Americans have held up religious liberty as sacred, we have repeatedly declined to offer it to those we viewed as subhuman. The slave experience also showed that when other freedoms are curtailed, religious liberty suffocates as well.

In all, about 455,000 Africans were brought to the United States as slaves, 388,000 directly from Africa and the rest via the Caribbean. Historians debate the extent to which slaves in America were discouraged from practicing Christianity—but that question skips a step. The vast majority had practiced indigenous African religions or Islam, not Christianity, before they were kidnapped. Traces of African religion have persisted through the generations via African American music, dance, and other cultural practices. But while African spirituality partly survived as culture, it mostly did not survive as religion. Between the 1680s and 1860, slaves "experienced a spiritual holocaust that effectively destroyed traditional African religious systems," wrote historian Jon Butler.[1] Albert Raboteau, one of the preeminent scholars of slave religion, noted that African traditions persisted more successfully in Cuba, Haiti, Brazil, and other countries with large slave populations. "In the United States," he wrote, "the gods of Africa died."[2]

The first thing to understand about African religion is that it existed. Slaves in America were often thought to have no religion or an ad hoc collection of superstitions. But while they did come from different regions and tribes, there were shared elements. They tended to believe in a High God, a Supreme Creator who was removed from day-to-day earthly doings, which were controlled by lesser gods and ancestor spirits.[3] They believed in reincarnation and revered the elderly in part because they helped preserve the memory of the dead. Music, dance, and medicine cured the soul as well as the body. "The religious background of the slaves was a complex system of belief," wrote Raboteau, "and in the life of an African community there was a close relationship between the supernatural, the secular and the sacred."[4]

By breaking up families, slavery thwarted the preservation of their religion. Young men were taken from the mothers and grandmothers, who had been the primary keepers of ancestral memory and traditions. Slave purchasers often avoided taking African spiritual leaders, who would be troublemakers and poor laborers.[5] Masters usually prevented five or more slaves from gathering at a time, making religious rituals difficult to sustain except in secret. Slaves were forbidden from speaking African languages. After the end of slave importation in 1808, the slave population in America grew mostly through reproduction. With each generation, knowledge and commitment to African traditions faded. By the way, there is no evidence that James Madison, the foremost champion of religious freedom, sought such rights for his own slaves.

This in no way diminishes the importance of Christianity in sustaining African Americans during the slave period. Moreover, had slavery never existed, many might well have voluntarily chosen Christianity in Africa. But most Africans had no such choice. To better fathom the consequences, consider this thought experiment. More than 30 million living African Americans are descended from slaves. If their ancestors had been able to maintain the faith of their ancestors, and those traditions had been passed

down, African religions—the spirituality of the Akan, Ashanti, Daho-
mean, Ibo, and Yoruba societies—would be as significant in the United
States today as Judaism, Islam, Buddhism, and Hinduism combined.

Muslim American Slaves

About 10 percent of the slaves—hundreds of thousands of people—were
Muslims,[6] meaning that at the time of the country's founding, there were
probably more Muslims in America than Jews or Catholics.[7]

The first Muslims to live in America were brought as slaves in the
seventeenth century by the Spanish Catholics. But most came later as
part of the slave trade with West Africa, including the Sokoto Caliphate[8]
in modern-day Nigeria and Cameroon and an area called Senegambia in
modern-day Senegal and Gambia[9] (Gambia today is 90 percent Muslim).[10]

Many historical fragments confirm the presence of practicing Muslim slaves in the United States. An advertisement in Savannah, Georgia,
sought the return of some runaway slaves with Muslim names,[11] while
an ad in the *Charleston Courier* described a runaway named Sambo "who
writes the Arabic language."[12] George Washington in 1784 listed in his
ledger the names "Fatimer" and "Little Fatimer," a mother and daughter
almost certainly named after Muhammad's daughter Fatima.[13] Interviews
with slave descendants in Georgia in the 1930s turned up several descriptions of Muslim prayer practices. Rosa Grant described her grandmother
Ryna: "Every morning at sun-up she kneel on the floor in a room and bow
over and touch her head to the floor three time. Then she say a prayer. . . .
When she finish praying, she say, 'Ameen, ameen, ameen.'"[14] A slave, Bilali
Mohamed, had daughters named Medina and Margaret. Margaret would,
according to her granddaughter, pray on a special "little mat to kneel
on."[15] She "was very particular about the time they pray and they were
very regular about the hour; [they prayed] when the sun come up, when it
straight over the head, and when it set."[16] Ed Thorpe remembered that his
grandmother, Patience Spalding, would "bow her head down three times
and say 'Ameen, Ameen, Ameen.'"[17]

In a few unusual cases, Muslim slaves became celebrities of sorts, usually because they converted to Christianity or seemed unusually learned.
One named Abd al-Rahman had apparently owned two thousand slaves
as a nobleman in Africa before he became a slave himself in the United
States. John Quincy Adams and others championed his case because he'd
supposedly become Christian.[18] Others pretended to embrace Christianity

while secretly maintaining their religion. Omar ibn Said, a slave in North Carolina, was said to have converted in 1819, yet his autobiography, written in 1831, begins "In the name of God, the merciful, the compassionate. May God bless our Lord Mohammad."[19] In some cases, the blending of faiths was not trickery as much as syncretism, an organic mixing of traditions. A priest commented that "the Mohammedan African" slaves had been known to accommodate Christianity to Islam: "God, say they, is Allah, and Jesus Christ is *Mohammed*—the religion is the *same*."[20]

The disappearance of Islam happened through some combination of coercion, pressure, and voluntary spiritual choices. A Muslim slave in Mississippi noted to a merchant, "in terms of bitter regret, that his situation as a slave in America, prevents him from obeying the dictates of his religion. He is under the necessity of eating pork, but denies ever tasting any kinds of spirits."[21] The normal means for passing Islam from one generation to the next—Quranic schools, mosques, and regular readings from the Quran—were not allowed. Families were routinely broken up, so "the chances for a Muslim man to find a Muslim spouse, have children, and keep them long enough to pass on the religion were indeed slim," wrote historian Sylviane A. Diouf in *Servants of Allah*.[22] Finally, to the extent that slaves were allowed to have religion, it needed to be Christianity. In fact, a Virginia law required that slaves—"whether Negroes, Moors, Mollattoes or Indians . . . shall be converted to the Christian faith."[23]

"Glad Tidings to the Poor Bondman"

After 1800, the Second Great Awakening energized Christianity among slaves. The evangelical emphasis on a personal conversion experience and having a direct relationship with God made the Bible more accessible to illiterate slaves. One former slave explained its appeal.

> It brought glad tidings to the poor bondman; it bound up the broken-hearted; it opened the prison doors to them that were bound, and let the captive go free. As soon as it got among the slaves, it spread from plantation to plantation, until it reached ours, where there were but few who did not experience religion.[24]

Some of the religious activity happened in recognized churches. Converting slaves on plantations became a cause for outside missionaries and pious Christians throughout the South. Some whites believed that Christianity would make slaves more obedient. Others hoped that it would give a noble aura to the institution of slavery itself, as it could be seen as a way of elevating the hapless African. Many slaves attended the churches of their masters, but some independent black churches survived too. A few grew so strong that they could raise money to buy members' freedom.[25] From 1846 to 1861, the Methodist Episcopal Church saw its black membership rise from 118,904 to 209,836.[26] Black Baptists, by one estimate, grew from 40,000 in 1813[27] to 200,000 in 1846 to 400,000 in 1860.[28]

But because the preaching in approved churches was geared toward the teaching of obedience, slaves often came to resent it. Underground religion developed. They would gather secretly in "hush harbors" in the woods—"singing and praying while huddled behind quilts and rags, which had been thoroughly wetted 'to keep the sound of their voices from penetrating the air,'" as one former slave recalled.[29] At these secret revivals and prayer meetings, "the slave forgets all his sufferings," a slave recalled, "except to remind others of the trials during the past week, exclaiming, 'Thank God, I shall not live here always!'"[30] Some religious services offered the promise that they or their children would see freedom ("I know that some day we'll be free and if we die before that time, our children will live to see it," as one slave put it).[31] Others emphasized the freedom awaiting them in the next life.[32] When describing how an overseer had set vicious dogs on his mother, a slave explained, "She died soon after, and was freed from her tormentors, at rest from her labors, and rejoicing in heaven."[33]

Since slave masters feared the insurrectionist potential of religion, the very act of worshipping was a form of rebellion. "The white folks would come in when the colored people would have a prayer meeting, and whip every one of them," recalled one slave.[34] A black preacher named G. W. Offley liked to tell the story of a slave he called "Praying Jacob." This man prayed in the fields three times a day. His master said that if he did it again he'd blow his brains out. Jacob told him to shoot away.

> Your loss will be my gain. I have two masters, one on earth and one in heaven—master Jesus in heaven, and master Saunders on earth.
> I have a soul and a body; the body belongs to you, master Saunders, and the soul to Jesus.[35]

When the charismatic Reverend Turner first began preaching in the fields of Southampton County, Virginia, he urged the slaves to obey their masters, assuring them that their liberation would come in the hereafter. But that changed after he had apocalyptic visions. In 1825, he saw "white spirits and black spirits engaged in battle, and the sun was darkened—the thunder rolled in the Heavens, and blood flowed in streams." A few years later, he "heard a loud voice in the heavens, and the Spirit instantly appeared to me and said the Serpent was loosened, and Christ had laid down the yoke he had borne for the sins of men, and that I should take it and fight against the serpent." His interpretation: the serpent was slavery, and it must be destroyed. "The time was fast approaching," he said, "when the first should be last and the last should be first."[36]

And so, on August 21, 1831, the Reverend Nat Turner led sixty fellow slaves in a rebellion, killing more than fifty-five whites, including twenty-five children.[37] The white population's long-standing fears of a slave insurrection had finally come true. Why had it happened? What could be done to prevent it from ever happening again? John Floyd, the governor of Virginia, knew where to lay the blame: the Yankees who came South and made the slaves religious,

> telling the blacks [that] God was no respecter of persons—the black man was as good as the white man—that all men were born free and equal—that they cannot serve two masters—that the white people rebelled against England to obtain freedom, so have the blacks a right to do.

In Floyd's view, Southern whites—both "our females and the most respectable"—came to think that piety required teaching the Negroes to read and write so they could absorb scripture. Before long, these naïve do-gooders were passing out incendiary pamphlets "from the New York Tract Society." Finally, the black preachers, both freed and slave, read abolitionist tracts from the pulpit. "The Northern incendiaries, tracts, Sunday Schools, religion and reading and writing has accomplished this end," Floyd explained.[38]

Southerners knew this wasn't the first time that religion had been implicated in a slave uprising. Denmark Vesey, who ostensibly plotted a rebellion in Charleston, South Carolina, in 1822, had recruited most of his comrades from the Emanuel African Methodist Episcopal Church, which had been created by the small community of freed blacks.[39] After the incident, the church was burned to the ground and nineteen of its members were arrested.[40] (Hauntingly, it was at that same church, rebuilt, that a white supremacist gunman named Dylann Roof massacred black parishioners in June 2015.) In 1800, a slave named Gabriel near Richmond, Virginia, organized a plot among thousands of slaves, using religious meetings to coordinate and Bible passages to motivate.[41]

So, when the Nat Turner rebellion occurred, Southern governors did not hesitate to attack the religious freedom of slaves. South Carolina banned black churches.[42] Virginia forbade slaves and free blacks from conducting religious meetings. They could attend only gatherings led by white preachers, during the day, after getting permission from their masters.[43] North Carolina decreed that free Negroes could not preach. Alabama prohibited any assembly of five or more blacks and required that they could preach only if five "respectable slave-holders" were present.[44] In Louisiana, an earlier law provided the death sentence for ministers who used their pulpits to "produce discontent" among slaves or free blacks.[45] As a teenage slave in Maryland, Frederick Douglass had been asked to help teach "Sabbath School" to other slaves. But after word spread, several slave owners stormed the meeting and declared that Douglass apparently "wanted to be another Nat. Turner, and that, if I did not look out, I should get as many balls in me as Nat. did into him. Thus ended the Sabbath-school."[46]

Religious rights, it became clear, do not exist in isolation. Eliminating other basic liberties—especially freedom of expression, speech, assembly, and press—invariably undercuts religious freedom too. Attacks on one right will degrade others. Dehumanization was the predicate to regulation. If slaves weren't people, then masters could avoid the cognitive dissonance of being God-fearing Christians who prevent slaves from worshipping God. Douglass noted the irony: "Think of a body of men thanking God every Sabbath-day that they live in a country where there is civil and religious freedom . . . [even while] there are three millions of people herded together in a state of concubinage, denied the right to learn to read the name of the God that made them."[47]

Of course, the slaves had no way to fight back against these additional infringements. But some abolitionists were noticing this aspect of slave subjugation, and after the Civil War they had an opportunity to do something about it.

Hon. John Bingham

Chapter Six

THE DIVINE PLAN

*Real religious freedom exists
because of the Fourteenth Amendment,
which exists because of Representative
John Bingham, a devout Christian
on a special mission.*

I n the tiny frontier town of Cadiz, Ohio, annual revival meetings "broke the monotony of the winter nights."[1] But religion had a deadly serious purpose in Cadiz too. The area was a bastion of "evangelical abolitionists,"[2] and on the day in 1859 that anti-slavery radical John Brown was executed, its church bells tolled for two hours.[3]

The most consequential action the people of Cadiz took for the cause of civil rights was sending John Armor Bingham—now considered by scholars to be among America's "second Founding Fathers"—to the United States Congress. He's called that because he was the primary author of the Fourteenth Amendment to the United States Constitution, which decrees that the Bill of Rights protects Americans from oppressive actions not only of the federal government but also of state and local lawmakers. Passed in the wake of the Civil War, it fundamentally altered the nature of the Constitution, making our rights inviolable in every nook and cranny of America.

Before the passage of the Fourteenth Amendment, it was assumed that the states could regulate religion as they liked. In case there was any doubt about the matter, the US Supreme Court made it crystal clear in 1845. A New Orleans law prohibited open-casket funerals, a clear attack on the Roman Catholic approach to mourning the dead. When a priest was fined for offering prayers over a body in an open casket, the Supreme Court said there was nothing it could do to help. "The Constitution," the justices shrugged, "makes no provision for protecting the citizens of the respective states in their religious liberties."[4]

Thanks to the Fourteenth Amendment, the courts would eventually apply the First Amendment's religion clauses to stop attacks by state and local governments. State bureaucrats can no longer draft official prayers and require children to recite them. Cities cannot use zoning rules to block the construction of undesired churches, synagogues, or mosques. Indeed, it is because of the Fourteenth Amendment that most of our religious freedoms exist. As we'll see later, it was not until deep into the twentieth century that its slow-motion impact would be fully felt. But in hindsight we can see that what Bingham and his colleagues did in 1866 was a pivotal moment in the history of religious freedom.

Less well understood is the fact that religion played an indirect but significant role in the *crafting* of the Fourteenth Amendment. Religious freedom both caused and resulted from the rise of evangelicalism, which in turn helped fuel abolitionism. Bingham grew up in a devout, anti-slavery family.[5] He attended Franklin College, described as "the fountain-head of the abolition sentiment of eastern Ohio."[6] Not surprisingly, he used highly religious language to describe the Fourteenth Amendment's origins. "It surged from my understanding of the Divine Plan for people," he said.[7]

Bingham and his colleagues recognized the connection between religious liberty and other rights, including freedom of expression and the press. Earlier in his career, Kansas had passed a law criminalizing writings that might induce slaves to escape. Bingham argued that the law violated the rights of people "to know, to argue freely, and to utter freely, according to conscience."[8]

He also discerned something else. Because abolitionism was largely a religious movement, a statutory assault on the anti-slavery cause would often manifest as an attack on religion.[9]

Indeed, those defending slavery before the Civil War did often target ministers. The Reverend Daniel Worth of South Carolina, a sixty-four-year-old preacher, was convicted of giving out copies of an anti-slavery book. While Worth was in jail, the local newspaper mused, "We still think that Worth when arrested, should have been taken in hand by the populace and swung to the nearest tree."[10] The Reverend Jesse McBride, a Methodist preacher from Ohio, was arrested in South Carolina for giving a young white girl a pamphlet on the Ten Commandments that suggested slaveholders were violating God's laws.[11] The Reverend Jacob Gruber, a Methodist minister in Maryland, was arrested for giving a sermon that some feared might lead slaves to revolt.[12]

Bingham laid out the case for the Fourteenth Amendment during a campaign speech in the small town of Bowerston, Ohio, in 1863. He started by reading to the crowd the amendment's basic demand for "equal protection of the law."

"That's right!" someone shouted.

"Yes, it is right," responded Bingham. "It is the spirit of Christianity embodied in your legislation."

Equal rights should never be denied any person, he continued, "no matter whence he comes, or how poor, how weak, how simple—no matter how friendless." He then challenged the crowd. "If there be any man here who objects to a proposition so just as that, I would like him to rise in his place and let his neighbors look at him and see what manner of man he is."

No one stood.

"He isn't here, I guess," someone yelled.

Bingham then offered one specific example of a right that was endangered. "The Americans cannot have peace," he said, if "states are permitted to take away the freedom of speech, and to condemn men, as felons, to the penitentiary for teaching their fellow men that there is a hereafter."[13]

Bingham was not the only one who saw the strong connections between religious freedom, the Fourteenth Amendment, and other civil liberties. One of its strongest advocates was Representative Owen Lovejoy, who knew well that oppression sometimes comes from mobs, not governments. His brother, the Reverend Elijah Lovejoy, had been murdered in 1837 by pro-slavery residents in Illinois for publishing abolitionist literature. Representative Lyman Trumbull of Illinois, coauthor of the Thirteenth Amendment, which abolished slavery, noted that Southern laws prevented blacks from "exercising the functions of a minister of the Gospel,"[14] and Congressman Cydnor Tompkins of Ohio declared that the states' laws "condemn as a felon the man who dares proclaim the precepts of our holy religion." They also neutered religiously motivated white abolitionists. They have "silenced every free pulpit within its control," Representative James M. Ashley of Ohio declared.[15]

Privileges and Immunities

When Congress began considering the Fourteenth Amendment in December 1865, the Civil War's cannons had only recently cooled. Lincoln had been assassinated earlier that year. The bodies of the Union Army dead had not yet been transported north to national cemeteries. And the Southern states were still fighting. In an attempt to retain the power dynamics of slavery, new "black codes" had been passed. For example, Louisiana made it a crime to encourage anyone "who leaves his or her employer."[16] In 1866, President Andrew Johnson, a racist Democrat,[17] vetoed a major civil rights act. The Republicans in Congress became convinced that the Constitution must be amended to preserve the rights of blacks.

By this point, Bingham had earned a reputation as one of the stars of the House of Representatives. His legal and oratorical skills were such that his colleagues chose him to lead the prosecution of John Wilkes Booth's conspirators and, later, the impeachment of President Johnson. He was usually described as whip-smart and often persuasive, if occasionally verbose. During one congressional debate, the *New York Times* offered this baroque word picture:

> John A. Bingham . . . suddenly electrified the House by the
> first thoroughgoing pronunciamento we have had of Abolition
> principles. Bingham is a sandy-haired middle aged man, rather tall,
> vigorously built, with a broad and commanding forehead; very
> deep set, but full sized, greenish eyes; a long and rather curved
> nose drooping over a straight, thin mouth; little patches of rusty-

red whiskers placed in front of each ear, and a complexion rather
inclined to be sallow across the eyes, especially; the forehead
is broad and mathematical, and on the whole the expression of
the face conveys, the idea of a strong will inclined to extreme
convictions, an intellect practiced in the guerilla-support of every
opinion, and a temperament which is inclined to antagonize on
every possible occasion with all, or any, who do not think precisely
in the same channel.[18]

Like the First Amendment, the Fourteenth went through multiple
drafts. Bingham's first effort stipulated that *Congress* should have the
power to overturn oppressive state laws. But it was pointed out that this
left individual rights subject to the whims of elected officials. On February 13, 1866, the amendment was tabled. Bingham was upset, but he
reasoned that eventually, "acting in harmony with the Divine Plan, my
proposal will be crowned with triumph."[19] When, two weeks later, it was
further postponed, he fumed that "true justice in conformity with the
Divine Plan cannot and will not be stopped."[20]

He soon had another opportunity to push forward an amendment,
and this time he offered the phrasing that would become the Fourteenth
Amendment:

No State shall make or enforce any law which shall abridge the
privileges or immunities of citizens of the United States; nor shall
any State deprive any person of life, liberty, or property, without
due process of law; nor deny to any person within its jurisdiction
the equal protection of the laws.

At the time, this version was deemed weaker than his original, but in
hindsight it was probably stronger. Rather than relying on Congress to
police states' misbehavior, it decreed that these were natural rights, immune from attack. This gave citizens recourse not only through Congress
but in the courts.[21] On June 8, 1866, the Senate approved the Fourteenth
Amendment, and five days later the House did as well.

In later years, there was some debate about whether Bingham and his
colleagues really intended to limit state regulation of the rights listed in the
first ten amendments. What "privileges" was the Fourteenth Amendment

referring to? Bingham was quite clear that he intended the amendment to apply the Bill of Rights throughout the land. Lest there be any doubt that religious liberty was included, he said during a campaign speech that "freedom of conscience is one of the privileges of citizens of the United States, and men are not to be put to torture, sent to the dungeon, [made to] walk the narrow steps of the scaffold, for teaching their children the holy principles of our Lord and Master."[22]

Bingham repeatedly cast the Fourteenth Amendment in religious terms. To one friend, he said his purpose was "to crown the rights of persons made in the image of the Almighty."[23] To Titus Basfield, an African American classmate from Franklin College, he explained that the amendment fit into "the Divine Plan for the Sacred Union."[24] Perhaps most striking, in a letter to Dr. John W. Comly, Bingham described the effort in profoundly evangelical terms. The civil rights included

> privileges and immunities bestowed upon human beings by the Supreme Power. These are natural rights. The Deity moved his plan through the Christian Republic, the United States of America.[25]

Bingham's story reveals how the Madisonian model could create a virtuous circle that leads to the expansion of religious freedom. The disestablishment of state religions in the early nineteenth century both was caused by and resulted from the Second Great Awakening, which, in turn, fueled evangelicalism in places such as Cadiz, Ohio. Out of that milieu came John Bingham, who then demanded that the religious liberty rights be further strengthened.

Bingham has appropriately been called the Fourteenth Amendment's James Madison. Beyond their mutual conviction that rights were as likely to be trampled by local governments as by national rulers, the two men shared something else: neither would live to see his vision fully implemented. Madison died thirty years before the Constitution, through ratification of the Fourteenth Amendment, finally confronted the potential tyranny of local governments. Bingham would not see the Fourteenth Amendment properly implemented. For six decades after its passage, the Supreme Court, dominated by conservative states' rights justices, insisted that the amendment did not protect Americans from state violation of

religious liberty, again illustrating Madison's wisdom about the impo-
tence of "parchment barriers" alone.

Regular citizens—including those with some deeply unpopular beliefs—
would have to demand their rights before Bingham's words would have
real power.

Imprisoned Mormons

Chapter Seven

THE MORMON CHALLENGE

*The astonishing American war on
Mormonism reveals the shallowness of
the nineteenth-century commitment
to religious freedom.*

A t one point in 2012, both the Democratic leader of the United States
Senate and the Republican presidential nominee were Mormons.
So were five other senators and eight congressmen.[1] Globally,
in 2018 the Church of Jesus Christ of Latter-day Saints, often called the
LDS Church, was the faith of some 16 million people, including 163,000
in Nigeria, 765,000 in the Philippines, 1.4 million in Mexico, and 151,000
in Australia.[2] Mormonism is a significant world religion, slightly bigger
than Judaism.

It might seem embarrassing for America, then, that Joseph Smith, the
founder of this respectable world religion, was murdered by a mob in
Carthage, Illinois. Local residents passed a formal resolution in 1844 stating that if "the prophet and his miscreant adherents" did not surrender, "a
war of extermination should be waged to the entire destruction, if necessary for our protection, of his adherents."[3]

They kept their word. As Smith sat in Carthage's jail on June 27, 1844, about 125 men emerged single file from the woods. Several broke down the door and shot Smith's brother Hyrum in the face. As Joseph Smith scrambled away, they shot him in the back, causing him to fall out of a nearby window. He landed on the ground in front of a crowd of bayonet-wielding militiamen whose faces were smeared with mud. Seeing that he was still alive, one of them propped him up against a wall. His colleagues then fired several more rounds into his chest.[4]

Those accused (but acquitted) of Smith's murder included a newspaper publisher, a state senator, the captain of a local militia, a future member of Congress, and a respected Baptist minister.[5] The killing took place with the possible acquiescence of the governor of Illinois (who had pledged to protect Smith), less than six years after the governor of Missouri had threatened to exterminate the Mormons and had succeeded in driving them from his state.

It is hard today to fathom how loathed Mormons were by mainstream Christians. They were regarded as foreign (many were immigrants), heretical (they crafted an entirely new version of the Bible), threatening (they grew rapidly and asserted themselves aggressively), and, in most American minds, perverted (they practiced polygamy). The early days of the LDS Church include some of the most brutal religious persecution in American history. Church members were massacred, attacked by the United States Army, and spurned by the United States Supreme Court.

To be clear, theirs is not a morally tidy story of a humble community of believers wanting nothing more than to be peaceably accepted into the American mainstream. The Mormons often refused to accept certain American values, such as monogamous marriage, private property, and the separation of church and state. But their brave defiance challenged eighteenth-century notions of religious freedom.

This chapter describes the rise of this entrepreneurial new religion, its breathtaking persecution, its adaptation, and its ultimate acceptance by the mainstream. The Mormon story demonstrates both the ability of the American system to cultivate piety and innovation and the extent to which the country hadn't yet bought into the founders' vision. When confronted with an unapologetically out-of-the-mainstream sect, Americans revealed a relatively shallow commitment to religious liberty. In the end, however, the conflicts with the Mormons did advance freedom as their rising political clout—and their courage—forced the Protestant majority to recalibrate their approaches to minority religions.

An American Faith Rises

Mormonism began in 1820 in the woods outside Palmyra, New York, some twenty-five miles east of Rochester. As he later told the story, the fourteen-year-old Joseph Smith was walking near his home, pondering his own "wickedness and abominations" as well as "the darkness which pervaded all mankind." Suddenly a pillar of brilliant light came down from the sky and he saw God and Jesus.[6] Smith asked which religious sect he should follow, and Jesus responded that he "must join none of them, for they were all wrong."[7]

About three years later, in 1823, Smith was visited by another spirit, who called himself Moroni. He told Smith that a sacred book inscribed on gold plates, which had been buried, told a very different story about Jesus and a lost tribe of Israel from what was in the gospels. Three years after that, Smith dug up the plates near his home in Manchester, New York, and in 1829 he translated them into the Book of Mormon. Over the course of the next fifteen years, two things happened: Smith attracted followers at an amazing pace, locally and from around the world. And Smith and his growing flock were driven out of town after town as they made their way west.

The religious startup boom that was the Second Great Awakening didn't just spawn new Protestant denominations: entirely new religions were born. At first, Smith, who had attended revival meetings in upstate New York, described his new belief system as a sort of turbocharged Methodism. Smith believed that Jesus was the Messiah, that he died for our sins, and that he was resurrected in body and spirit. But Smith's vision went much further, amounting, most religious scholars agree, to the first major new religion that the world had seen in hundreds of years.

Smith made his followers feel that they were part of an ongoing biblical drama that was every bit as real as the one the ancients had experienced. God still offered revelations (through Smith); the Holy Spirit still touched people directly (as evidenced by spiritual "gifts" such as talking in tongues); and the return of Christ was imminent. But the United States, not the Middle East, was the locus of the drama that was about to unfold. God would soon establish the New Jerusalem in America. For those struggling to make their way on the dangerous and uncertain frontier, Mormonism seemed spiritually rich, relevant, and thrilling.

The Book of Mormon told the story of Jesus's activities in America. A lost tribe of Israel had traveled to the Americas around 600 BC. Soon after Jesus was crucified (so soon that the wound in his side was still open and the holes the nails had left could be seen in his hands), he appeared in America, where he spent several days visiting, praying, healing, and teaching. Before he left, he made three apostles impervious to attack. When evil men pushed them into furnaces or dens with wild animals, they survived—and continued to preach the gospel. One of those righteous leaders, Mormon, created and buried the golden plates so someone could later revive the teachings that Christ had brought to America.

Mormonism's appeal went beyond its theology. Smith established communities where economic activity was strongly coordinated, which was appealing given the fragile nature of life on the frontier. Eventually, he required Mormons to donate their goods to a common pool, with the church using the funds to build temples and subsidize the poor. Mormons felt spiritually and economically nourished, part of a growing, protective family. By 1840, Smith had thirty thousand followers.[8]

Residents of Ohio, Illinois, and Missouri found the Mormons to be terrifying. In 1842, Jonathan B. Turner, a professor at Illinois College, wrote that the Mormons were the "most dangerous and virulent enemies to our political and religious purity, and our social and civil peace, that now exist in the Union." The threat, he wrote, was not so much that people would believe the Book of Mormon but that, presented with two books of miracles, they would decide neither was true and thus become atheists.[9] Some believed the Mormons bastardized Christianity. In his 1842 pamphlet *Mormonism Exposed and Refuted*, the abolitionist minister La Roy Sunderland argued that the Mormons were ignorant of scripture and could not "perceive the vast, the momentous difference between the miracles recorded in the Bible, and the juggling tricks of Smith."[10]

Others feared Mormon economic and political power. By 1833, Mormons already made up one-third of Jackson County, Missouri.[11] A year later, Smith survived being tarred and feathered. A Protestant minister who participated in the attack said that he wanted to "get rid of" the Mormons because he feared they would take his property.[12] This fear was stoked by Smith's revelation that Independence, Missouri, would be the site of the New Kingdom of God when Christ returned. The Gentiles, as Mormons called nonbelievers, figured they could lose their land in the new millennium.[13]

Smith merged church, state, and commerce. When the Mormons bought the town of Commerce, Illinois, and changed its name to Nauvoo, he named himself mayor, lieutenant general of the Nauvoo Legion, and treasurer of the church. Later, he would be appointed by church elders as "King, Priest and Ruler over Israel on the Earth."[14] He controlled all land sales to Mormon members and orchestrated the creation of mills and factories. He even claimed that God had ordered the Mormons to build a hotel. ("And let it be a delightful habitation for man, and a resting-place for the weary traveler. . . . And they shall not receive less than fifty dollars for a share of stock in that house.")[15]

Many towns had their own militias, but in Nauvoo the Mormons went all out. Smith wore a uniform with gold braid and a hat topped with ostrich feathers. A US artillery officer who witnessed a parade of the Nauvoo Legion shared his misgivings in the *New York Herald*: "Why this exact discipline of the Mormon corps? Do they intend to conquer Missouri, Illinois, Mexico?"[16] Smith thought that the Kingdom of God could be best approximated when righteous religious leaders also held the levers of government power. His need for control was no doubt reinforced by government officials' refusal to defend the Mormons against attack. Convinced that the presidential candidates in 1844 were not taking the plight of Mormons seriously, he ran for the presidency himself, urging religious freedom for all Americans. He certainly did not believe that religious liberty required a separation of church and state.[17] He stated that he sought to establish a "theodemocracy, where God and the people hold the power to conduct the affairs of men in righteousness."[18] Yet, according to recently released minutes of early LDS deliberations, he adamantly urged tolerance of other religions.[19] He lectured the LDS leaders that every person must have the right "of choosing for himself voluntarily his God, and what he pleases for his religion."[20] One eyewitness recorded Smith as saying to a gathering in Nauvoo "that if he were the emperor of the world and had control over the whole human family he would sustain every man, woman and child in the enjoyment of their religion."[21]

Extermination

When the citizens of Jackson County, Missouri, demanded that the Mormons leave, they offered this as the reason:

> They were of the very dregs of that society from which they came, lazy, idle, and vicious. . . . They brought into our country little or

no property with them and left less behind them, and we infer that those only yoke themselves to the "Mormon" car who had nothing earthly or heavenly to lose by change.[22]

An editorial in the *Missouri Commercial Appeal* declared, "Their manners, customs, religion and all, are more obnoxious to our citizens than those of the Indians, and they can never live among us in peace. The rifle will settle the quarrel."[23]

The Mormons actively encouraged immigration, luring thousands of low-income, uneducated foreigners from right across the porous border. Missourians feared crime would rise and jobs would be lost because of these undocumented . . . Canadians. On September 12, 1838, the non-Mormons of Daviess County, Missouri, pleaded with the governor to help them "get rid of those Cannadian Refugees and Emmissaries of the prince of Darkness."[24] An anti-Mormon group in Carroll County complained that too many Mormons came from other parts of the world.[25] "It is impossible that the two communities can long live together," wrote the *Signal*. "They can *never* assimilate."[26]

Locals feared that Mormons would act as a unified voting bloc and then subjugate their political rivals. On Election Day, August 6, 1838, Mormons and non-Mormons scuffled in a town square. When one Mormon attempted to vote, a settler blocked him and declared, "Daviess County don't allow Mormons to vote no more than niggers."[27] A riot ensued.

The Mormons were suspected of being anti-slavery themselves. Smith was no abolitionist and believed slaveholders had every right to keep their slaves. But most Mormon converts were from Northern states and therefore mistrusted. In July 1833, W. W. Phelps, a New Yorker who had become the editor of the pro-Mormon newspaper in Missouri, went rogue and advocated that slaves convert to Mormonism.[28] Furious local civic leaders called for the expulsion of Mormons from the county.[29] Phelps quickly retracted the article, but five hundred settlers met, broke into the office of the newspaper, destroyed the printing press, and tarred and feathered two Mormon leaders.[30] The Gentiles also feared that Mormons had overly cozy relations with the Indians.[31]

After residents of Clay County, Missouri, asked the Mormons to leave, the governor decided not to defend them. With stunning cowardice, he summarized the problem: "Your neighbors accuse your people of holding illicit communication with the Indians, and of being opposed to slavery. You deny. Whether the charge or the denial is true I cannot tell. The fact exists and your neighbors seem to believe it is true; and whether true or false, the consequences will be the same." He urged them to convince neighbors of their innocence: "If you cannot do this, all I can say to you is that in this Republic the *vox populi* is the *vox Dei*."[32]

Historian Juanita Brooks describes how mobs of Missourians terrorized Mormons:

> Bands of armed bandits scoured the country, driving off stock, breaking windows and furniture, driving out women and children then shooting to frighten them further as they ran for shelter into the fields.
>
> Then began the burnings. A mob would ride up to a farmhouse, order the family out, give them a generous few minutes in which to salvage such necessities as they could and allow them to watch the glow of their burning home against the sky, or to compare its blaze with that of the granary and haystack. If the owners resented it or had too much to say, it was sometimes fun to enliven the party by giving the father a taste of blacksnake [whip] in full view of his terrified children or by stripping him and smearing his body with tar.[33]

Mormons began to arm themselves, but the lieutenant governor, Lilburn Boggs, promised that if they disarmed he would protect them. After word spread that the Mormons had given up their guns, a mob sacked Mormon homes and drove them from Jackson County.[34] Smith tried to negotiate a settlement that would recapture some of their lands, but his offer was rejected, prompting the editor of the *Liberty Enquirer* to write, "The citizens of Jackson are determined to dispute every inch of ground, burn every blade of grass, and suffer their bones to bleach on the hills, rather than the Mormons should return to Jackson County."[35]

With his people under attack, Smith militarized the Mormons. They created a secret society known as the Danites, and some Mormon leaders became infected with martial fervor. Sampson Avard instructed his men to go to non-Mormon settlements and take what they needed: "For it is written, the riches of the Gentiles shall be consecrated to my people, the house of Israel; and thus you will waste away the Gentiles by robbing and plundering them of their property; and in this way we will build up the kingdom of God."[36] On July 4, 1838, Sidney Rigdon went even further, declaring, fatefully, "From this day and hour we will suffer it no more. . . .

And that mob that comes on us to disturb us, it shall be between us and them a war of extermination; for we will follow them till the last drop of their blood is spilled, or else they will have to exterminate us."[37]

Smith himself used an analogy with modern resonances. According to the testimony of one apostate Mormon leader, Smith reacted to a spate of incidents in which Mormons were beaten unconscious by comparing himself to Muhammad. "Like Mohammed, whose motto in treating for peace was 'the Alcoran [the Quran] or the Sword.' So shall it eventually be with us—'Joseph Smith or the Sword!'"[38]

The similarities between Smith and Muhammad were noticed by others. In a glowing dispatch from the *New York Herald*—"Wonderful progress of Joe Smith, the modern Mahomet"—the correspondent recounted the arrival of new religions throughout world history. "But a new age has come—a fresh infusion of faith is required. . . . May not this wonderful Mormon movement be the signal for a new religious movement? Is not Joe Smith its master spirit?"[39]

Mormon soldiers clashed on a few occasions with non-Mormon settlers in what came to be known as the Mormon War. Most encounters were minor, but rumors and fabrications proliferated. In the fall of 1838, Lilburn Boggs, now governor, was told—falsely—that Mormons had massacred a group of Missouri militia members.[40] He soon issued one of the most infamous documents in the history of religious liberty: Missouri Executive Order 44. Writing to his military commander, General John B. Clark, on October 27, Boggs declared that Mormons had adopted "the attitude of an open and avowed defiance of the laws, and of having made war upon the people of this State." Therefore, he wrote,

> the Mormons must be treated as enemies, and must be exterminated or driven from the State if necessary for the public peace.[41]

To implement what came to be known as the "extermination order," the general was instructed to increase his forces "to any extent you may consider necessary."

Three days after the order was issued, on October 30, 1838, the biggest religiously motivated massacre in American history occurred. About two hundred fifty Missourians, including a state senator, arrived at Haun's Mill, a small Mormon community. They rode their horses forward, assembled in a line, and, when they were about seventy-five yards away, opened fire. Children and women screamed and ran for cover.[42] Some retreated to the blacksmith shop, built of loose-fitting logs. After raining bullets on it for a while, the militia members entered the building. A ten-year-old boy, Sardius Smith, was still alive, having crawled under the bellows for protection. He pleaded for his life. One soldier put his gun to the boy's head and, according to an eyewitness, "literally blew off the upper part of it, leaving the skull empty and dry while the brains and hair of the murdered boy were scattered around and on the walls." When one of the other militia men suggested that his actions were excessive, the gunman replied, "Nits make lice."

The attackers chased down a white-haired seventy-eight-year-old Mormon, Thomas McBride, who had fought under Horatio Gates and George Washington in the Revolutionary War. They demanded his gun, which he gave them. They then took a corn knife, a scythe used for cutting stalks, and chopped up McBride's face. The soldiers stripped the dead of their boots and clothing and told the survivors that if they didn't leave by the next day, they too would die.

In all, seventeen Mormons were killed and fifteen wounded. Fearful that the soldiers would desecrate the bodies, the survivors quickly dumped them in an unfinished well. "All through the night we heard the groans of the dying," one recalled.[43] Soon after, the Mormons left Missouri for Illinois, where they built the town of Nauvoo. A year later, a mob murdered Joseph Smith.

Exodus

After the persecutions, the massacres, and the assassination of their founder, the Mormons decided to leave America. The LDS Church's new leader, Brigham Young, explained: "The exodus of the nation of the only true Israel from these United States to a far distant region of the West, where bigotry, intolerance and insatiable oppression lose their power over them—forms a new epoch."[44]

On February 10, 1848, the Mormons left the United States for the territory of Utah. Alas, though Utah was a part of Mexico when they started their journey, within a year it had been transferred to the United States. Still, the Saints lived in peace there for almost a decade. Undeterred by the attacks on Mormonism, new adherents poured in from around the world in response to recruitment missions. Soon, some forty thousand Mormons had settled in the new homeland.[45]

But the Mormons came under attack again—this time by the US Army. On July 18, 1857, President James Buchanan dispatched the Tenth Infantry

Regiment from Fort Leavenworth, soon to be joined by the Fifth Infantry, 1,200 American soldiers. "This is the first rebellion which has existed in our Territories; and humanity itself requires that we should put it down in such a manner that it shall be the last," Buchanan declared. "We ought to go there with such an imposing force as to convince these deluded people that resistance would be vain, and thus spare the effusion of blood." He exaggerated in calling the circumstance a "rebellion," but it is true that Brigham Young was both the head of the church and the governor of the territory, and the church had been routinely undercutting the authority of the territorial courts and administrators.[46]

Buchanan had decided to install a new governor. Since he assumed that Young wouldn't step down voluntarily, he'd sent the new governor in with the massive military escort to deal with the "frenzied fanaticism as exists among the Mormons."

When Mormon leaders got wind of what was happening, they were, not surprisingly, alarmed, especially given their past experiences with government militias. "An army has been sent by the United States to make war upon us for the sole purpose of destroying The Church of Jesus Christ of Latter-day Saints," declared future church president Wilford Woodruff.[47] Fortunately, a full military confrontation was forestalled. The army paused on the outskirts of Salt Lake City, and the Mormon leadership sent thousands of residents on an "exodus" to Provo, Utah, and safety.

But the episode illustrated that the United States had little idea how to deal with the rapidly growing non-Protestant religion. For the next fifty years, the LDS Church and the Gentiles would fight, both citing the Constitution as their guidepost. Some of the flash points from the first half of the nineteenth century were revisited: the concern that the Mormons fused church and state; their passion for drawing in new immigrants; their militarism; their heavy-handed treatment of Gentiles. But the explosive new element that enraged the rest of the nation was the Mormon practice of polygamy.

The doctrine of "plural marriage" or "celestial marriage" came directly from Joseph Smith. Rumors had swirled for years that Smith had married multiple women, but he denied them and attacked his accusers. But by the mid-1840s, the truth could no longer be suppressed. On August 12, 1843, the Prophet told church leaders that he'd received a revelation from God that having multiple wives not only was allowed but was a requirement for priesthood. He cited the polygamous marriages in the Old Testament, including those of Abraham, David, Jacob, and Solomon (who had at least seven hundred wives) and the system's effectiveness at fulfilling God's injunction to be fruitful and multiply. Smith was particularly taken by Jacob's belief that if a man slept with a woman, he had an *obligation* to make her one of his wives ("And if a man entice a maid that is not betrothed, and lie with her, he shall surely endow her to be his wife").[48]

Polygamy was consistent with the Mormon desire to embrace a literally biblical way of life, a "restitution of all things." In the Mormons' larger cosmology, spirits live on after death. Only those in families could be "sealed" and achieve full "exaltation" in the afterlife. By marrying a woman, a Mormon man was ensuring the afterlife of his wife. And only those men who practiced plural marriage could achieve the highest level of priesthood during the forthcoming reign of Christ. In addition, polygamy encouraged the birth of many children, crucial because there was a surplus of pre-mortal spirits awaiting bodily vessels. Eventually, Smith had approximately twenty-seven wives, scholars believe. At least twelve were women who were already married. One wife was fifteen years old, another sixteen. There were two mother-daughter pairs.[49]

Smith's revelation did not go over well with many Mormon leaders, not to mention his first wife, Emma. William Law was disgusted by the doctrine, even more so after Smith hit on his wife. Law bolted from the church and set up a dissident newspaper, the *Nauvoo Expositor*, in which he described Smith's polygamy to the rest of the world. Smith, then the mayor of Nauvoo, instructed the city council to destroy the *Expositor*'s printing press.

Over time, almost all of the Mormon leaders took multiple wives. Brigham Young had fifty-five. As the years went on, they continued to explain polygamy as a significant religious doctrine. They also strongly believed it solved a variety of social problems. Orson Pratt, a leader of the church and Mitt Romney's great-great-grand-uncle, suggested it was a time-tested way to wipe out prostitution—"in the way the Lord devised in ancient times; that is, by giving to his faithful servants a plurality of wives."[50] They mocked monogamists who hailed the sanctity of marriage while having mistresses on the side. "Our crime has been: we married women instead of seducing them," said apostle George Q. Cannon. "We reared children instead of destroying them; we desire to exclude from the land prostitution, bastardy and infanticide."

To counter the argument that polygamy enslaved women, Mormon wives testified by the hundreds in support of the tradition. "Our enemies pretend that in Utah, woman is held in a state of vassalage—that she does not act from choice, but by coercion—that we would even prefer life elsewhere, were it possible for us to make our escape," Eliza Snow declared. "What nonsense!"[51] Martha Hughes Cannon advanced a decidedly feminist argument. Sharing the burden of matrimony with other women, she said, freed up time so she could become both a physician and a state senator. "A plural wife is not half as much a slave as a single wife," she said.[52]

To strengthen their feminist credibility (and increase the size of their voting population), in 1870 the Mormons took the bold step of allowing women to vote, more than four decades before the Nineteenth Amendment granted women suffrage nationally. But the rest of the nation remained disgusted, and maybe a bit titillated, by polygamy, which was linked to a more general sense that Mormon culture was depraved. The book that introduced Sherlock Holmes to the world in 1887, Arthur Conan Doyle's *Study in Scarlet*, depicted Mormons as murderous kidnappers.[53] Hundreds of popular novels and magazine articles offered tales of Mormon depravity. Alfreda Eva Bell, author of a popular anti-Mormon novel of the era, wrote that women in Utah "are in fact white slaves; are required to do the most servile drudgery; are painfully impressed with their utter inferiority."[54]

In 1856, the brand-new Republican Party explicitly linked polygamy and slavery as "twin relics of barbarism." Harriett Beecher Stowe, author of *Uncle Tom's Cabin*, suggested that action against slavery could create a precedent for the abolition of polygamy.[55] Indeed, polygamy was less popular than slavery, which at least had the support of the Southern aristocracy.[56] Polygamy would, its critics declared, lead to the decline of civilization. "Point me to a nation where polygamy is practiced, and I will point you to heathens and barbarians," said Caleb Lyon, the governor of Idaho.[57]

Mormons were creating an "Asiatic" race, according to some opponents.[58] In a presentation at the New Orleans Academy of Sciences in 1861, military doctor Robert Bartholow described a typical polygamist: "yellow, sunken, cadaverous visage; the greenish-colored eye; the thick, protuberant lips, the low forehead; the light, yellowish hair, and the lank, angular person, constitute an appearance so characteristic of the new race, the production of polygamy, as to distinguish them at a glance."[59] This context explains the otherwise perplexing comment from Mormon leader Heber Kimball that "we are not accounted as white people."[60]

Polygamy was just a gross secular practice being given a religious justification, other critics argued, doubting that it was even a sincerely espoused component of the Mormons' theology. "We are told," Vermont representative Justin Morrill declared, "that we must tamely submit to any burlesque, outrage, or indecency which artful men may seek to hide under the name of religion!"[61] Schuyler Colfax, vice president under Ulysses S. Grant, challenged the third president of the church, John Taylor: "I do not concede that the institution [of polygamy] you have established here, and which is condemned by the law, is a question of religion."[62]

"With us it is 'Celestial Marriage,'" Taylor responded. "Take this from us and you rob us of our hopes and associations in the resurrection of the just."[63]

Polygamy was not the only issue in the battle for public opinion. The Mormons were in some ways premillennialists.[64] They believed that Christ would soon return to rule Earth but that they needed to start the creation of that kingdom right away, not merely wait for Jesus to do all the work. The LDS Church needed to run society. The Mormons' electoral system thus relied on a non-secret ballot, which allowed the church leadership greater control. The legislature gave the local probate courts—controlled by the church—broad authority, reducing the influence of the federal courts. Creating a godly kingdom also meant an economic organization that (and this is no exaggeration) approximated Communism. The goal, never fully achieved, was to have land be communally owned and then lent back out to individuals. The church in Utah limited the ability of non-Mormons to own property,[65] resisted federal surveyors' attempts to inspect their land,[66] and discouraged Mormons from trading with non-Mormons.[67]

Perhaps most problematic, the Mormon leadership became increasingly militarized and separationist. "In regard to those who have persecuted this people and driven them to the mountains, I intend to meet them on their own grounds," Brigham Young thundered. "We could take the same law they have taken, viz., mobocracy, and if any miserable scoundrels come here, cut their throats."[68] Not without some justification, they feared future massacres and annihilation. The Missouri "extermination order" was recent history; they viewed "American" hostility as potentially lethal. On the eve of the 1856 conflict with the US Army, one Mormon leader, Isaac C. Haight, stated:

> The [Missourians] drove us out to starve. When we pled for mercy, Haun's Mill was our answer, and when we asked for bread they gave us a stone. We left the confines of civilization and came far

into the wilderness where we could worship God according to the dictates of our own conscience without annoyance to our neighbors. We resolved that if they would leave us alone we would never trouble them.

But the Gentiles will not leave us alone. They have followed us and hounded us. They come among us asking us to trade with them, and in the name of humanity to feed them. All of these we have done and now they are sending an army to exterminate us.

So far as I am concerned I have been driven from my home for the last time. I am prepared to feed to the Gentiles the same bread they fed to us. God being my helper I will give the last ounce of strength and if need be my last drop of blood in defense of Zion.[69]

That truculent spirit may have contributed to one of the most tragic episodes in Mormon history—a moment that helped cement the public perception of Mormons as violent and prone to terrorism. In 1857, a wagon train of western settlers from Arkansas, the Baker-Fancher party, was passing through an area called Mountain Meadows in the Salt Lake region. A group of more than fifty Mormons, under the leadership of the regional Mormon militia, attacked. After several days of fighting, the Mormons announced that they would let the emigrants go if they surrendered some of their cattle. After they did, each male settler was paired with an LDS Church member and told to walk in a single file. As they did, there came a cry: "Halt!" That was the signal for the Mormons to kill the men. Members of a local Indian tribe who were coconspirators emerged from the bushes to kill the women and children. In all, 120 were murdered, including 50 children. The dead were thrown into a ravine and covered with dirt. Seventeen children who were deemed too young to describe what had happened were spared and taken to live in Mormon households. A grotesque cover-up ensued, with the church initially blaming the local Indians who had participated. But an army investigation concluded that Mormons were involved.

In the eyes of their critics, all of these factors—the theocratic nature of Mormon governance, the violent incidents, the secrecy—meant that Mormonism was not so much a religion as a political system, or, as the *Kalamazoo Telegraph* put it, an "immoral and quasi criminal conspiracy."[70] It would not be enough to eliminate polygamy; they would have to destroy the entire machine.

For most of the second half of the nineteenth century, the US government waged an unprecedented war against both plural marriage and Mormonism more broadly. In 1862, the Republican Congress passed the Morrill Anti-Bigamy Act, which outlawed polygamy, annulled the incorporation of the Mormon Church, and forbade the church from owning real estate valued at more than $50,000. The law was designed to break the religion.[71] Hostile to Republican government, Mormonism sought to "maintain and perpetuate, a Mohammedan barbarism," claimed Representative Morrill.[72] In 1871, Brigham Young himself was indicted for practicing polygamy.[73]

Wasn't the law a blatant violation of the First Amendment? After all, it attempted to destroy the church. That was certainly the view of the Mormons, and in 1879 they challenged the law before the US Supreme Court. The test case, one of the first on religious freedom, involved George Reynolds, a secretary to a number of Mormon leaders. He was young (thereby countering the images of skeevy old Mormon men with their harems of young wives) and he had just two wives, making it easier to imagine their loving relationships. The Mormons argued that since polygamy was not only a belief but also a religious duty, it was protected by the First Amendment's Free Exercise Clause.

On January 6, 1879, the Court ruled, unanimously, against the Mormon Church. *Reynolds v. United States* upheld all of the anti-Mormon legislation. Chief Justice Morrison Waite acknowledged that the First Amendment protected religious beliefs, even making reference to Thomas Jefferson's letter to the Danbury Baptists and the separation of church and state. But the First Amendment protects only religious *beliefs*, he stipulated, not religious *behavior*. "Laws are made for the government of actions, and while they cannot interfere with mere religious belief and opinions, they may with practices," Waite wrote. To rule otherwise, he said, would enable groups to justify all manner of abominable behavior on religious grounds. "Suppose one believed that human sacrifices were a necessary part of religious worship; would it be seriously contended that the civil government under which he lived could not interfere to prevent a sacrifice? Or if a wife religiously believed it was her duty to burn herself upon the funeral pyre of her dead husband; would it be beyond the power of the civil government to prevent her carrying her belief into practice?" He offered a narrow but clear-cut rationale for why religious freedom should not protect religiously motivated behavior. "To permit this would be to make the professed doctrines of religious belief superior to the law of the land," he wrote. That would "permit every citizen to become a law unto himself."[74]

While championing the freedom to believe, the Court cast religious freedom narrowly—leaving citizens and future generations of judges to grapple with the deeper question: Is it really religious freedom if we can't live our lives according to our faith?

The Court also seemed to accept the assumption of the law's sponsor, Justin Morrill, that polygamy wasn't *really* a spiritually justified practice. The government could not accept "the pretense that, as religious beliefs, their supporters could be protected" by the Constitution.[75] The ruling echoed the idea that polygamy was the emblem of primitive nonwhite peoples. "Polygamy has always been odious among the northern and western nations of Europe, and, until the establishment of the Mormon Church, was almost exclusively a feature of the life of Asiatic and of African people."

Mormon leaders were surprised and devastated. "Now Latter-day Saints, what are we going to do under the circumstances?" asked Wilford Woodruff. "God says 'we shall be damned if we do not obey the law.' Congress says 'we shall be damned if we do'. . . . Now who shall we obey? God or man? My voice is that we will obey God."[76]

They were on legal thin ice. They had managed to avoid local enforcement of the Morrill Anti-Bigamy Act in Utah, but after the *Reynolds* decision, Congress followed up with legislation designed to obliterate polygamy and the church. In 1882, it passed the Edmunds Anti-Polygamy Act, which banned "unlawful cohabitation," since it was easier to prove than marriage. Those guilty of cohabitation or polygamy could not vote, hold public office, or serve on juries.

In 1887, Congress approved the Edmunds-Tucker Act, which disincorporated the LDS Church and suggested that confiscated church property be sold off, with the proceeds used to fund public education. The law nullified the Perpetual Emigrating Fund Company, which had financed Mormon immigration. It required jurors and voters to take an anti-polygamy oath. It required Mormon wives to testify against their husbands in polygamy cases. It replaced local judges—who tended to avoid ruling against Mormons—with federal judges in polygamy cases. And, after years of claiming that Mormonism abused women, Congress revoked voting rights for Utah's women.

The neighboring state of Idaho went the furthest of all, denying the right to vote not just to polygamists but to anyone who was part of an "organization" that allowed such a practice. In other words, it stripped the right to vote from Mormons. Amazingly, the Supreme Court affirmed these laws too. In *Davis v. Beason*, the Court unanimously upheld the Idaho law, with Justice Stephen Johnson Field echoing the distinction between the protections of beliefs and actions. The Bill of Rights really meant only to allow an American to have his own "relations to his Creator" and to protect his "modes of worship." Polygamy was not a mode of worship or, for that matter, a real religious doctrine: "A crime is nonetheless so, nor less odious, because sanctioned by what any particular sect may designate as religion."

The Raid

From 1882 to 1896, in a period that came to be known as "The Raid," scores of federal officials scoured the territory for polygamous marriages. Bounties were offered for information leading to the capture of a suspect. Mormon men had to be ready to flee at a moment's notice. One mother told her children to respond to questions by saying they didn't know the names of their parents or where they lived.[77] A polygamist wife described the feeling of desperation:

> It is difficult to picture the unsettled conditions in Utah and Idaho during the raid against polygamists. Homes were broken up and families scattered among relatives or friends. . . . Some had secret hiding places in their own homes; others trained the children to watch for the Deputy Marshall, and to evade or deceive when asked questions by strangers or deputies about family relations. If people were at any public gatherings and the federal marshal entered the town, there was a scattering of local Church authorities. . . . Mothers ran with their babies to the neighbors; old men took to the fields.[78]

From 1882 to 1896, there were fourteen hundred indictments under the anti-polygamy acts.[79] Nearly one thousand Mormons were jailed, most in the Utah Territorial Penitentiary. George Q. Cannon, the representative of Utah to Congress, was imprisoned—and defiantly posed in a stunning photo of a few dozen Mormons in striped prison uniforms. By sticking to their principles and refusing to denounce their own family structures, Mormons had engaged in a massive act of civil disobedience.

The situation pained Mormon leaders. They declared their intent to fight for God's word, but they knew that the members of the church could not live on the run forever. They had some difficult decisions to make. Should they keep defending polygamy? Should they keep believing that polygamy is a central religious obligation? The Mormon leaders knew they had lost—in Congress, in the Supreme Court, and in the media. They had thought they had the protection of the Bill of Rights, but they were wrong. Now, many in Congress wanted to go further and destroy the religion itself.

The Mormon leaders bitterly resented being put in the position of having to choose between their survival and their beliefs, but they were forced to ask: Was it worth it? In answering that question, they balanced the defense of their religious doctrine with something more temporal: their yearning for statehood. Utah leaders since 1849 had petitioned to have the territory become a state. They knew that they would actually have more freedom and autonomy as a state, which had stipulated rights under the Constitution, than as a territory. "We are now, politically speaking, a dependency or ward of the United States," Wilford Woodruff, now the LDS Church president, cannily explained. "But in a State capacity we would be freed from such dependency, and would possess the power and independence of a sovereign State, with authority to make and execute our own laws."[80]

And Woodruff knew something else. While Congress had repeatedly rejected Utah's statehood applications, circumstances had changed. More and more politicians were warming to the idea of Utah becoming a state, if Mormons would only eliminate polygamy. What was different? Politics and demographics—the balance of power was shifting from east to west. In just the previous decade, the US Senate and the electoral college had added the states of Wyoming, Idaho, Washington, Montana, South Dakota, and North Dakota to their membership. Mormons now represented a sizable number of votes beyond Utah. From 1876 to 1879, more than one hundred Mormon settlements had been established in Arizona, Nevada, Wyoming, Colorado, and other states.[81] Membership in the church had reached around two hundred thousand,[82] more than the combined populations of Nevada, Idaho, and Wyoming.

Both political parties now curried favor with Mormons.[83] Money played a role as well. The railroad corporations wanted to build through Utah and made a secret deal with Mormon leaders to aid their statehood claims in exchange for help with the construction plans. Railroad interests had blocked earlier anti-polygamy legislation "to preserve anticipated profits in Mormon country," wrote historian J. Spencer Fluhman.[84] Now they were helping to normalize the Mormons.

But for Mormons, eliminating polygamy wasn't just a matter of deleting a clause from a contract. For sixty years they had insisted that the practice was mandated by God. How could they change this policy without making rank-and-file Mormons think the leadership had been disingenuous all along? The church leaders could not simply shift their position.

But God could. On September 18, 1890, Woodruff met with a group of top church leaders. He revealed that he had been "struggling all night with the Lord" and had news: the church should no longer countenance polygamy. He didn't so much denounce the practice as diminish its importance relative to the commitment to obey the laws of the land.

> Inasmuch as laws have been enacted by Congress forbidding plural marriages, which laws have been pronounced constitutional by the court of last resort, I hereby declare my intention to submit to those laws, and to use my influence with the members of the Church over which I preside to have them do likewise.

At first, the apostles were furious. Several rose from their seats and, holding back tears, declared that they were willing to suffer persecution or death rather than violate their covenants with their wives. But Woodruff had the ultimate rebuttal: "the Holy Spirit had revealed that it was necessary."[85] The new doctrine became known as "the Manifesto." That was all Congress needed. In January 1896, Utah became a state.

There is one final chapter to this story. Many in Congress suspected that the Mormons had only *said* they opposed polygamy in order to get statehood and that once they had the grand prize, they would resume the practice. Sure enough, it came to be known that some Mormon leaders continued to practice polygamy. This so enraged members of Congress that, from 1903 to 1907, some tried to expel Utah's new Mormon senator, Reed Smoot. In hearings stretching over four years, one hundred witnesses testified. The Reverend Charles L. Thompson, leader of the General Assembly of the Presbyterian Church, did not mince his words: "[Mormonism] is not to be educated, not to be civilized, not to be reformed—it must be crushed. . . . Beware the Octopus. There is one moment in which to seize it, says Victor Hugo. It is when it thrusts forth its head. It has done it. Its high priest claims a senator's chair in Washington. Now is the time to strike."[86] One commentator predicted that "the Smoot case will abolish Mormonism without war . . . cleansing the country of one of the barbarous relics."[87] Previously compared to Muslims, the Mormons were now also compared to Catholics. A senator warned his colleagues to beware "the fine Italian hand of the Mormon apostles."[88]

But in this final battle, we begin to hear a motif that would recur in future debates over religious liberty. Some senators began to identify with the plight of the Mormons, recognizing that successful attacks on the LDS Church could make their own faiths vulnerable. Former Idaho senator William J. McConnell wrote, "If we close the doors of the Senate today against Smoot why not against the members of the Catholic Church next session?"[89] Senator John Lourie Beveridge of Illinois noted that the attacks on Mormonism sounded similar to earlier attacks on Methodism.[90] Ultimately, the senators began to believe they were throwing stones from a glass house. Senator Boies Penrose of Pennsylvania reportedly said, "I think the Senate should prefer a polygamist who doesn't 'polyg' to a monogamist who doesn't 'monog.'"[91]

The Senate voted to allow Smoot to stay. In the words of historian Kathleen Flake, the vote "marked the beginning of the nation's acceptance of the Latter-day Saints on the same denominational terms as other American religions: obedience, loyalty, and tolerance defined in political, not religious terms."[92] She also suggests that the growing acceptance of Mormons reflected another change in American politics, one that would be brought to the fore as the Progressive Era continued. In the economic sphere, progressives sought to create a set of rules that would ensure fair competition. They applied the same principles to religion. Mormonism could be tolerated as long as the LDS Church was willing to play by the same rules as other faiths did. This echoed the founders' free market of faith. It worked well, as long as pro-competition policies kept one denomination from disadvantaging another.

In several ways, the clash with Mormons resembled the Protestant-Catholic conflict. Like Catholics, Mormons were described as hostile to American values of democracy. They were cast as alien, Asiatic, nonwhite, and perverse. Immigration fueled both the sect's rapid growth and the backlash against it. The churches' growth stirred a sometimes justifiable fear that their members would exert political power.

Whatever incipient notions of universal religious liberty existed in this period could not accommodate a faith that was this far outside the mainstream. Americans had not sufficiently imbibed the all-for-one, one-for-all notion that destroying one faith's liberty would ultimately harm everyone's. Leaders of other religions rarely defended Mormons and often led the attacks against them. Some of them would pay dearly for their myopia. The *Reynolds v. United States* and *Davis v. Beason* decisions stood for more than eighty-five years. While the US Supreme Court allowed Americans to believe whatever they wished, it didn't protect their right to practice their faiths or to live their lives in accordance with their religious scruples.

But the Mormon episode also showed how the religious freedom model could grow slowly stronger. After years of attacking the LDS Church, Congress ultimately welcomed Utah as a state and, with it, its dominant religion. In this case, it was the political system more than the legal system that worked. The Mormons' presence in key states gave them added clout. But they could use it only if they made a massive theological compromise. The Mormons made that choice, and it allowed them to enter the mainstream. Not all groups were offered such a choice.

Timber Yellow Robe, Henry Standing Bear, and Wounded Yellow Robe

Chapter Eight

KILL THE INDIAN, CHRISTIANIZE THE MAN

The efforts to help Native Americans include the campaign to ban their spiritual practices and convert their children to Christianity.

In 1866, the "good guys" were the Christians who merely wanted to annihilate the Native Americans' religion. It was a strange turning point in white America's relationship with the Indians. The Native Americans had been pushed farther west. Disease and war had dramatically reduced their numbers. The buffalo population had been so decimated that the Indian economic system had collapsed in many areas. They were cornered.

Some argued that they should be exterminated. "The more we can kill this year, the less will have to be killed the next war," explained General William T. Sherman. "For the more I see of these Indians the more convinced I am that they all have to be killed or be maintained as a species of paupers."[1]

But Sherman's views were increasingly in the minority. In his State of the Union address in 1863, Abraham Lincoln urged "constant attention" to the Indians' well-being and a commitment to the "moral training which under the blessing of Divine Providence will confer upon them the elevated and sanctifying influences, the hopes and consolations, of the Christian faith."

Many of those who would come to be known as "the reformers"—most of them religious Christians—believed that the Indians had just as much intelligence and skill as whites but were held back by their depraved culture. Richard Henry Pratt, a leading educator of Indians, declared: "A great general has said that the only good Indian is a dead one. . . . In a sense, I agree with the sentiment, but only in this: that all the Indian there is in the race should be dead. Kill the Indian in him, and save the man."[2] Or, as Carl Schurz, the secretary of the interior, put it, "If the Indians are to live at all, they must learn to live as white men!"[3]

This chapter explores a little-known episode in American history: the movement, intensifying after the Civil War, to Christianize Native Americans. The United States government banned Indian religious dances, seized land with deep spiritual significance, eliminated Indian spiritual leaders, and stripped Indian children of their religion. Many Christians still believed that religious liberty meant their own freedom to promote the one true faith. Some strange side fights erupted, as when Protestants and Catholics clashed over who got to convert the Indians. Some of them had good intentions. But the Madisonian architecture for religious freedom became useless when those in power denied, ignored, or misconstrued another group's spirituality. Notably, those misunderstandings were exacerbated by an irresponsible media, a phenomenon that would recur in future conflicts.

Reformers

Ulysses S. Grant believed that "the whole Indian race would be harmless and peaceable if they were not put upon by the whites."[4] As an army officer, he seemed saddened by their decline: "This poor remnant of a once powerful tribe is fast wasting away before those blessings of 'civilization,' whisky and small pox."[5] In his inaugural address in 1868, he called for citizenship for the "original occupants of this land."

Rejecting the advice of Sherman and his other Civil War comrades, Grant proposed instead a "Peace Policy." Over the next few decades, the US government launched a number of "reforms," often with the support of private activists, many of whom were former abolitionists. Some efforts focused on land reform; others, on teaching English and farming.

But throughout the decades there was a common theme: civilizing the Indians meant "Christianizing" them.

Grant's first step was to bring in religious leaders who he figured would be more humane stewards. He created a Board of Indian Commissioners, which matched Christian denominations to tribes. For example, the Baptists were asked to manage the Cherokees. The Presbyterians got the Omahas in Nebraska and the Ottawas in Michigan. The Pueblos in New Mexico went to the Disciples of Christ. All in all, the Methodists oversaw fourteen Indian "agencies"; the Presbyterians, nine; and the Episcopalians, eight. The Quakers, the Baptists, and the Dutch Reformed each got five; the Congregationalists, three; the Unitarians, two; and the Lutherans, one. Even the Catholics got eight, though that wasn't as many as they wanted.[6] Needless to say, none of the commissioners were Indians.

Not everyone welcomed the involvement of the religious agencies. Newspapers on the frontier, where Indians continued to attack settlers and vice versa, felt that East Coast naïveté was putting their families at risk. "If more men are to be scalped and their hearts boiled," declared the *Leavenworth Bulletin*, "we hope to God that it may be some of our Quaker Indian agents."[7] The *Junction City Weekly Union* seethed, "Many plans have been tried to produce peace on the border; but one alternative remains—EXTERMINATION."[8]

Nonetheless, the policy proceeded, with a mission of erasing the existing Indian culture and substituting something far better. "As we break up these iniquitous masses of savagery," explained Merrill Gates, chairman of the Board of Indian Commissioners (and former president of Amherst College), "as we draw them out from their old associations and immerse them in the strong currents of Christian life and Christian citizenship, as we send the sanctifying stream of Christian life and Christian work among them, they feel the pulsing life-tide of Christ's life."[9]

There seemed to be only the dimmest recognition that the Indians already had religions of their own. Occasionally the reformers would refer to their "heathenism" and "superstition," but there certainly was no sense that the Indians had a coherent, deeply embedded religious order, let alone one that might be providing them health, morality, inspiration, or meaning.

What were the religions that the reformers tried to repeal and replace? It's hard to generalize, as there were hundreds of Native American religions, each different. But they shared a common belief that there was no clear separation between the spiritual and physical worlds. Spirits inhabited animals, land, the sun and the moon, and in some cultures these spirits were associated with a larger deity, such as the Lakota's Wakan-Tanka, or the "Great Mysterious."[10] They often practiced life cycle rituals that combined religious and ceremonial elements. During vision quests they communicated directly with the supernatural, sometimes in the form of an animal. They taught their children myths, songs, dances, and rituals, each pregnant with spiritual meaning. "In the life of the Indian there was only one inevitable duty—the duty of prayer—the daily recognition of the Unseen and Eternal," wrote Charles Eastman, a Native American physician and author. "His daily devotions were more necessary to him than daily food."[11] Scholar David Wallace Adams summarized:

> Traditional Indian cultures were so thoroughly infused with the spiritual that native languages generally had no single word to denote the concept of religion. It would have been incomprehensible to isolate religion as a separate sphere of cultural existence. For the Kiowa, Hopi, or Lakota, religion explained the cosmological order, defined reality, and penetrated all areas of tribal life—kinship relations, subsistence activities, child raising, even artistic and architectural expression.[12]

That all had to be purged, along with other elements of culture, if the Indians were to prosper. The assimilation efforts were, US Commissioner of Indian Affairs Francis Leupp proudly explained, "a mighty pulverizing engine for breaking up [the last vestiges of] the tribal mass."[13]

"Take Their Children Away"

Education became one of the key arenas for conflict with Native Americans, as it would be in the future with Catholics, Jehovah's Witnesses, and Jews. The idealistic reformers of the post–Civil War era viewed schools as the heart of the "pulverizing engine" that would help the Indians. One needed to remove the children from their parents, the pollutions of tribal life, and their religion. "Education cuts the cord that binds [Indians] to a Pagan life, places the Bible in their hands, substitutes the true God for the false one, Christianity in place of idolatry . . . cleanliness in place of filth, industry in place of idleness, self-respect in place of servility, and, in a word, an elevated humanity in place of abject degradation," read an 1887 report from agents overseeing the Dakota reservations.[14] They tried to get the children young. "All those concerned with the school agree that the smaller the children are taken in the better and faster they learn," reported Father Bandini of the St. Xavier Mission Boarding School on the Crow Reservation in Montana.[15]

What evolved during this period was a multilayered system that included day schools and boarding schools on reservations and boarding schools far from home. Some were run by religious groups and some by the government. By 1890, 75 percent of Indian children in school were in immersion programs, according to Jon Reyhner and Jeanne Eder in *American Indian Education.*[16] Senator George G. Vest explained that "it is impossible to do anything for these people, or to advance them one single degree until you take their children away."[17]

The most acclaimed was the Carlisle Indian Industrial School in Pennsylvania, a government-backed boarding school created by General Richard Henry Pratt. When it came to his educational philosophy, he explained, he was like a Baptist: "I believe in immersing the Indians in our civilization and, when we get them under, holding them there until they are thoroughly soaked."[18] On the plus side, the boarding schools taught the Native American children to read and write, gave them some employable skills, and offered them cultural opportunities, such as playing musical instruments or participating in sports. Olympian Jim Thorpe came out of the Carlisle football team.

But the approach of Carlisle and other similar schools left many scars. The children were taught to hate their culture. First, their hair would be cut off. The Sioux writer Zitkála-Šá recalled hiding under a bed. "I remember being dragged out, though I resisted by kicking and scratching wildly. In spite of myself, I was carried downstairs and tied fast in a chair. I cried aloud, shaking my head all the while, until I felt the cold blades of the scissors against my neck, and heard them gnaw off one of my thick braids. Then I lost my spirit."[19] Luther Standing Bear, a Sioux who went to Carlisle, remembered crying after his hair was cut: "I felt that I was no more Indian but would be an imitation of a white man."[20]

Then the schools changed the children's names. They emerged with names like Mary, Joseph, Aloysius, Francis Xavier, Hildegarde Fischer,[21] Julius Caesar, and Henry Ward Beecher.[22]

Discipline was more like that in the military, or in some cases prison, than a school. A Hopi woman recalled being whipped after she and her friends left the school's grounds to pick apples nearby.[23] A Lakota woman recounted a tale from her grandmother about a punishment she received for not paying attention in church.

Instead of praying she was playing jacks. As punishment they took her to one of those little cubicles where she stayed in darkness because the windows had been boarded up. They left her there for a whole week with only bread and water for nourishment. After she came out she promptly ran away together with three other girls. They were found and brought back. The nuns stripped them naked and whipped them. . . . Then she was put back into the attic—for two weeks.[24]

Schools severely punished "deserters," as they were known. The Chilocco Indian Agricultural School in Oklahoma had eighty escapes in three months in 1925.[25] Keams Canyon Elementary School, in modern-day Arizona, padlocked the dormitory's doors at night to prevent escape. Some Hopi boys protested by defecating on the floors.[26] At the Chilocco School, the head of the school responded to word that students were planning to run away. "Telling them to undress, he handed each one a blanket, transported them ten miles out into the prairie and left them."[27] At the Williams Lake School in British Columbia, nine children attempted suicide by eating water hemlock after receiving severe beatings.[28] The most amazing runaway story happened at Fort Mohave in Arizona: a group of *kindergartners* took a large log and used it as a battering ram to break down the jail door, releasing the students who were being punished there.[29]

Indian parents had mixed feelings. Many had concluded that, sadly, the Indian way of life was dying and that to succeed, their children would need to learn the ways of the whites. The father of Charles Eastman, who would go on to become a doctor, praised the white man's emphasis on the written word. "I think the way of the white man is better than ours, because he is able to preserve on paper the things he does not want to forget."[30]

But as shocking stories came back from the schools, many parents changed their mind. The most terrifying news: the children were dying at alarming rates. Often cramped and unhygienic, the schools were breeding grounds for disease. Of the 640 students who attended Hampton Normal and Agricultural Institute over thirteen years, 110 died.[31] In 1890, sixty-eight children died of scarlet fever.[32] The agent at Fort Apache, Arizona, C. W. Crouse, reported that the deaths of several children had prompted a rebellion among parents: "I was compelled to resort to force, and every pupil was returned to the school by the police."[33] A Spokane tribe saw sixteen of the twenty-one children they'd sent to eastern schools die in 1891.

The chief complained that the schools didn't have the decency to send the bodies back. "If I had white people's children I would have put their bodies in a coffin and sent them home so they could see them. . . . They treated my people as if they were dogs."[34] Each boarding school had a cemetery for the children.

The government required the students to be in these schools and sent Indian police out to round up truants. The agent to the Mescalero Apache, in what is now New Mexico, in 1886 wrote:

> Everything in the way of persuasion and argument having failed, it became necessary to visit the camps unexpectedly with a detachment of police, and seize such children as were proper and take them away to school, willing or unwilling. Some hurried their children off to the mountains or hid them away in camp, and the police had to chase and capture them like so many wild rabbits.
> This unusual proceeding created quite an outcry. The men were sullen and muttering, the women loud in their lamentations, and the children almost out of their wits with fright.[35]

S. J. Fisher, the agent in modern-day Idaho, reported that he'd had "to choke a so-called chief into subjection" to get his children.[36] A group of Hopi Indians were sent to military prison on Alcatraz in part for refusing to surrender their children.[37] The annual report of the US Department of the Interior in 1901 cheerfully detailed the government's good work.

> Gathered from the cabin, the wikiup, and the tepee, partly by cajolery and partly by threats; partly by bribery and partly by force, they were induced to leave their kindred to enter these schools and take upon themselves the outward appearance of civilized life.[38]

In 1893, Congress authorized the agents to deny food rations to families that resisted sending their kids to school. Indian parents resisted in part because they realized that the schools were converting their children. Spotted Tail, a leader of the Brulé Lakota at the Rosebud Indian Reservation in South Dakota, sent four of his children to Carlisle. A year later, he saw his kids shorn of their hair and learned that they'd been baptized. Appalled, the Brulé parents pulled all thirty-four children out of the school.[39] Albert Kneale, who worked as principal of a boarding school, reported frankly that students "were taught to despise every custom of their forefathers, including religion."[40]

Although all of the schools banned expressions of Indian religions, they differed in their approaches to teaching Christianity. The schools run by religious missions instilled Christianity throughout the day. At the St. Xavier Mission Boarding School on the Crow reservation, the Catholic instruction was pervasive. The kids stayed year-round; parents could visit on Sundays for one hour.[41] The children had daily morning Mass at 6:30 a.m. They were taught academic, vocational, and religious subjects during the day and also had time to learn to play the organ, violin, and other instruments. At 8:00 p.m. they had prayer time. Throughout the day, the kids at St. Xavier—like the children at most of the schools—did unpaid menial labor, such as washing clothes, to help run the school.[42] On Sunday there was a full Mass. They also celebrated Ash Wednesday, Good Friday, Easter, Pentecost, and Christmas.

The teachers struggled to sell the Crow on certain elements of Catholic theology.

Scholar Karen Watembach describes how the Jesuit missionaries who ran St. Xavier first had to convince the Crow that there was such a thing as "sin," which was not a concept in the Crow religion, for "unless the Crow people had heard of sin they would have no need of a redeemer."[43] The Crow believed that bad behavior was to be expected from humans but that the person was "not condemned unless an act had brought disgrace to the whole family. Then the person was shunned." They were confused by the idea that God would make people in his own image and then have them be steeped in sin.[44] Teachers also had to convince the Crow about the existence of hell. One day, the priest, Father Prando, drew a picture to show where the Indians had gone before the missionaries had arrived— two small circles for heaven and hell and a large one for purgatory. A Crow leader, Plenty Coups, who had invited the Jesuits to the reservation, pointed to the large circle and said, "That's where I want to go, where most of my people are."[45]

Zitkála-Šá recalled being introduced to the concept of the devil. The Sioux taught about bad spirits, she wrote, but there was no "insolent chieftain" attempting to organize the evil spirits against God. "Then I heard the paleface woman say that this terrible creature roamed loose in the world, and that little girls who disobeyed school regulations were to be tortured by him." One night, she dreamed that a yellow-eyed devil had invaded her home. The next morning, she opened her *Stories of the Bible* to the picture of the devil and scratched out his eyes.[46]

The Crow discovered that their method of prayer, which was personal and improvisational, was all wrong. They needed to recite the Catholic prayers word for word, they were told. Bible stories supplanted the "superstitious" Crow tales.[47] For example, the story of how Old Man Coyote created the earth from a lump of clay at the bottom of a pond was replaced with the "true" Genesis story of God creating the heavens and the earth and then making a woman out of Adam's rib. Mary Crow Dog, a Lakota writer, recalled that as a girl at a Catholic boarding school, "I learned quickly that I would be beaten if I failed in my devotions or, God forbid, prayed the wrong way, especially prayed in Indian to Wakan Tanka, the Indian Creator."[48]

The government schools—the ones not run directly by religious organizations—had a somewhat different approach. They emphasized religion on the weekends rather than during the week. There was a sermon each Sabbath, Sunday school, and a weekly prayer meeting conducted by students.[49] They used the Protestant Bible and hymns. Protestant youth organizations such as the Young Men's Christian Association were active. The "non-sectarian schools," wrote scholar Francis Paul Prucha, "were in fact Protestant schools." An 1899 report from the superintendent of Indian schools offered assessments of the religious instruction at the schools she visited.[50] "Religious exercises are conducted regularly," "religious training is carefully given," "the religious welfare of the children is carefully looked after," and "at each school there is a force of faithful, Christian teachers," she reported.[51]

Reformers routinely advocated "Christian civilization." That wasn't just a religious term but included cultural elements such as speaking English, wearing proper white-man clothes, and abandoning hunting as a vocation. Indian schools were required to celebrate the "discovery" of the New World each Columbus Day. When, in 1892, Richard Henry Pratt brought 322 of his students to march in a Columbus Day parade in New York City, the banner they carried read "Into Civilization and Citizenship." A similar parade in Chicago prompted the *Springfield Union* to note that "the students of Carlisle PA, Indian school represented the savages Columbus found. But instead of appearing as savages, they marched in their present character as intelligent, well-dressed and well-bred young men."[52] They also celebrated Thanksgiving and Christmas.

When children died at boarding schools, they were given Christian burials. Pratt seemed to think he was comforting a parent, Chief White Thunder, when he informed him that his child, Ernest, had died but assured him that he would be given a "white" burial.

I had them make a good coffin and he was dressed in his uniform
with a white shirt and nice collar and necktie. . . . And the minister
read from the good book and told all the teachers and the boys
and girls that some time they would have to die too. He told them
they must think a great deal about it and they must be ready to
die too. . . . He explained that they emphasized the Bible because
"it is that book which makes the white people know so much as
they do."[53]

The policy of having the government fund religious schools ended in
the late 1890s for reasons that were in some ways darkly comical. Conflict
arose over matters of religious tolerance. No, members of Congress did
not suddenly realize that forcing Indian children to attend government-
financed Christian schools violated their religious freedom. Rather, a
fight broke out between Protestants and Catholics over how to best Christianize the Indians. The Catholics complained that Indian children were
being assigned to schools run by the Protestant denominations. The First
Amendment, they said, guaranteed the parents' right to choose . . . between Christian religions. "The Indians have a right, under the Constitution, as much as any other person in the Republic, to the full enjoyment
of liberty of conscience," declared a statement from the Catholic leaders of
Oregon.

"Accordingly, they have the right to choose whatever Christian belief
they wish, without interference from the government."[54]

At first, the Protestant denominations enthusiastically supported the
government's funding. But then a funny thing happened. Over time, more
and more of the money went to Catholic organizations, in part because
they had been doing extensive missionary work with Indians for much
longer than the Protestants and were more adept at setting up schools.
By 1889, 75 percent of the funds for the fifty religious schools was going
to Catholic institutions.[55] Catholics also raised money privately to open
more schools, seeing them as weapons in a missionary battle, in which
their rivals were not the Indians but the Protestants. "If we do this, we do
an immense deal of good, get the Indians into our hands and thus make
them Catholics," wrote the director of the Bureau of Catholic Indian Missions, which coordinated these efforts. "If we neglect it any longer, the
Government and the Protestants will build ahead of us schools in all the
agencies and crowd us completely out and the Indians are lost."[56]

With the Catholics ascendant, the Protestant organizations began pulling out of the program and decrying the system of government-funded religious schools as—wait for it—a violation of the separation of church and state.[57] As during the battles over the Bible in schools, they decided they'd rather go secular than have the Catholics be the ones to teach about God. Thomas Jefferson Morgan, the commissioner of Indian affairs, in 1889 proposed a system of universal "non-sectarian" government-run schools, which would effectively reduce the role of the churches. He attacked the Catholic schools as "un-American, unpatriotic and a menace to our liberties . . . a corrupt ecclesiastical-political machine masquerading as a church." Morgan, a Baptist minister, referred to the Catholic Church as "an alien transplant from the Tiber . . . recruiting her ranks by myriads from the slums of Europe."[58]

The Catholics rightly interpreted the effort to support only nonsectarian schools as an attack on them. "[The] sole aim and purpose is to drive the Catholic Church out of the Indian educational and missionary field," wrote Joseph A. Stephan of the Bureau of Catholic Indian Missions in 1893.[59] And the Protestants had a lot of nerve, given their own shoddy record of teaching good values. "Morals are said to be very low in that school," wrote Father J. B. Boulet to the editor of *Catholic News* when students were slotted to be transferred from a Catholic school to the government-run Chemawa Indian School in Salem, Oregon. "Too much freedom among the sexes and followed by many breaches against chastity. Graduates of this school are generally proud, haughty—polished heathens."[60]

Some Catholics even wondered whether it might be better to let the Indians languish in their heathenism than to have Protestant teachers draw them away from the Catholic Church's schools. "Is it possible that we have labored so long and so diligently among Indians only to bring up them and their children a greater damnation? I fear it might have been better for them never to have known the truth, than after having been incorporated in the Church to be perverted and corrupted."[61]

This issue became part of the 1892 presidential election, the first in which a candidate, Democrat Grover Cleveland, openly campaigned to gain the support of Catholic voters. Catholic missionary groups charged the Indian commissioner and the sitting president, Republican Benjamin Harrison, with being anti-Catholic. The *Catholic Herald* declared that the Republicans, "led by bigots," had "robbed the Catholic Indians of their only treasure, their faith." By "their faith," of course, they meant their newfound Catholicism, not the Indian spiritual practices that the Catholicism had erased.[62] Nonetheless, Congress gradually moved away from the highly religious mission-led schools to the somewhat religious "government schools." In 1897, Congress ended the appropriations for religious schools.[63]

Not all Indians disliked these schools. Many said that becoming Christian changed their lives for the better, especially given the poverty on the Indian reservations, devastated as they had been by disease, war, and the disappearance of the buffalo. "This was my great good fortune," said Jason Betzines, who had gone to the Carlisle school, "to make something of myself, to lift myself to a more useful life than the old pitiful existence to which I had been born."[64] Thomas Alford had been told by tribal elders to learn skills and English but resist the efforts to purge him of his religion: "Then came the conviction of truth, the dawn of knowledge, when I knew deep in my soul that Jesus Christ was my savior."[65] Thousands of other students who converted to Christianity gained great sustenance from it. And it's impossible to know how many of those conversions would have happened anyway through voluntary exposure.

But while the schools' leaders viewed those conversions as a triumph, the students' parents mostly viewed them as an assault. Their growing resistance was fueled, wrote historian David Wallace Adams, by their realization that the schools expected their children not only to sever their bonds with their families but also to "abandon their ancestral gods and ceremonies."[66]

The Ban on Sacred Dances

In 1883, the commissioner of Indian affairs, Hiram Price, issued what amounted to a full-scale attack on Native American religion. First, the government banned a variety of Indian dances, including the Sun Dance, the Scalp Dance, the War Dance, and "all other so-called feasts assimilating thereto." Those guilty of the crime of unlawful dancing would lose rations for ten days. On the second offense, they could lose rations for thirty days. The third time, they could go to prison for ten to thirty days.[67]

Second, it criminalized the role of "medicine men," who acted as spiritual leaders in most tribes.

Third, it banned an Indian mourning ritual in which families would destroy property of the deceased.

All of these measures were justified in nonreligious terms (as attacks on Mormonism had been, and attacks on Jehovah's Witnesses would be, decades later). But as we'll see, each policy attempted to uproot important elements of religious (as well as cultural) practice for most Indians. The Christian majority had great difficulty understanding how dances or the mumbo jumbo of medicine men could be viewed as akin to worshipping in church or taking sacraments. Ignorance about the nature of unfamiliar spirituality blinded them to the notion that they were guilty of an assault on religious freedom.

Let's start with the mourning ritual. Grieving Indian families in the Dakota Territory traditionally gave away some of the deceased's property "to prove their deep sorrow."[68] The Indians believed that spirits sometimes linger, and giving away property would ensure that they moved on. They used other life milestones as occasions to give away belongings as well. This disgusted government officials and missionaries who worried that without a sufficient appreciation of private property, the Indians would never advance from their barbaric hunter-gatherer state. A poster that missionaries gave to Indians to put on their walls offered this bit of advice: "Believe that property and wealth are signs of divine approval."[69] But to the Indians, the devaluation of property was the whole point. "It was our belief that the love of possessions is a weakness to be overcome," Charles Eastman wrote. "Its appeal is to the material part, and if allowed its way it will in time disturb the spiritual balance of the man."[70]

The government's efforts largely succeeded. "This pernicious custom is almost wholly broken up," the authorities reported.[71]

As for the ban on medicine men, one must remember that in Indian culture they were at once clergy, prophets, and health-care workers. They frequently mixed prayers, herbs, predictions, and psychotherapy. Imagine if the government today were to issue a ruling banning the "the usual practices of so-called ministers or pastoral counselors." Medicine men were highly influential and therefore viewed as obstacles to the program of civilizing and Christianizing the Indians.[72] The new rules required that any person who practiced "the arts of the conjurer to prevent the Indians from abandoning their heathenish rites and customs" should be imprisoned for at least ten days "or until such time" as he "will forever abandon" his practices.

Perhaps the most consequential element of the crackdown was the ban on dances. Though dances varied by tribe, they were invariably an important part of their spiritual practice, a way of deploying the spirits for essential purposes and creating tribal cohesion.

The Sun Dance, for instance, was used to summon spiritual help for those going on hunts or into battle or to beseech the Great Spirit for a good harvest. The preparation involved fasts, property giveaways, songs, and other elements over several days. Its most controversial feature was self-torture. The dancers sometimes cut themselves, and in some tribes the practice became gruesome—slits were cut into the skin, and straps were passed through them. The pain and loss of blood made it more likely that they would have visions. The government banned the dance, which had a particularly demoralizing effect on the Sioux, according to historian Robert Utley.

> No longer could they appeal directly to Wi [the Sun] for personal power and assistance. No longer could they experience the pervading sense of religious security that came only from the Sun Dance. . . . The Sioux had been dealt a shattering emotional blow, and their lives began to seem like a great void.[73]

Throughout America, police were told to break up the dances. In 1885, James McLaughlin, the agent at Standing Rock Indian Reservation in modern-day North Dakota and South Dakota, proudly reported: "Three years ago the 'tom-tom' (drum) was in constant use, and the sun dance, scalp dance, buffalo dance, kiss dance, and grass dance, together with a number of feast and spirit dances, were practiced with all their barbaric grandeur; but all these are now 'things of the past.'"[74]

The most catastrophic conflict arose over a newly created ritual called the Ghost Dance. It was promoted in the 1890s by a Northern Paiute prophet named Wovoka, who in 1889 reported that he had died and traveled to heaven, where God taught him a new dance and gave him a set of messages. If the Indians led good, honest, peaceful lives, he said, the dead would come back to life and the land would once again be full of buffalo and game. Illness and death would be banished. And then there was the part that drew special attention from the non-Indian population: if the dances were performed properly, a great cataclysm, perhaps a flood or an earthquake, would wipe out the whites. His message was similar to the millennial promise of Mormons, evangelical Christians, and many other faiths that look forward to the End of Days and the advent of a new Kingdom of God—with two differences: a dance would trigger the arrival of paradise, and white Christians would have no place in it. By one account, Wovoka believed that God's vision would not spare the Indians' tormentors. "When Old Man [God] comes this way, then all the Indians go to mountains, high up away from whites. Whites can't hurt Indians then. Then while Indians way up high, big flood comes like water and all white people die, get drowned. After that, water go away and then nobody but Indians everywhere and game all kinds thick."[75]

He told his followers to dance for four consecutive nights and then repeat this six weeks later.[76] The ritual was preceded by a purification fast or sweat lodge ceremony.[77] The dancers wore special shirts—the yoke was sky-blue, and the rest was decorated with images of the moon, stars, eagles, crows, and buffalo. These "ghost shirts" were said to repel bullets.[78] They danced in a circle, hand in hand, gradually increasing the pace. As they glided around, dancers called out the names of their dead relatives, throwing dirt in their hair to signify grief. Excitement grew, and those who left the circle, said historian Rani-Henri Andersson, "fell to the ground with trembling limbs and lay motionless, seemingly dead."[79]

Leaders from the Sioux, Shoshone, Arapaho, Cheyenne, and other tribes across the country traveled by train to present-day Nevada to size up Wovoka. Each recounted the meetings differently. Sometimes Wovoka was described as a prophet. At other times, he was Christ returned. In another account, Jesus was an Indian who had been driven from Earth by immoral whites. "God blamed the whites for his crucifixion," the story went, "and sent his son Wovoka back to the Indians, since the whites were bad."[80]

Word of Wovoka and the dance spread from tribe to tribe, aided by the telegram and the railroad. By 1890, at least thirty tribes participated, and it had become a most unusual phenomenon: a pan-Indian ceremony.

Remarkably, most accounts of Wovoka contained strong Christian elements. Several witnesses reported seeing wounds in Wovoka's palms. Fast Thunder, a Christian who performed the Ghost Dance, recounted:

> As I looked upon his fair countenance, I wept, for there were nail prints in his hands and feet, where the cruel white men had fastened him to a large cross. There was a small wound in his side also, but as he kept his side covered with a beautiful blanket of feathers, this wound could only be seen when he shifted his blanket.[81]

Rather than viewing the Christian elements as a sign that their theology was penetrating Indian consciousness and declaring victory, the missionaries saw the telltale signs of Satan. The devil, explained one missionary, had cleverly made a beguiling "combination of the old heathen dance and the idea of a Messiah brought in by a gleam of Christianity."[82]

After visiting one of the dance camps at White River, Father Florentine Digman reported that there was no uprising afoot but that the Indians were enraged that the agents had threatened to cut off their rations if they kept dancing.

"Obey [the] order then and quit dancing," the priest advised. "Why after all are you bent on dancing?"

"This is our way of worshipping the Great Spirit," responded one of the Indian leaders.

"I fear it is another spirit that leads you astray."

The Indian pointed out that the Christian missionaries couldn't even agree with each other over the right way to pray. "Let us alone then, and let us worship the Great Spirit in our own way."[83]

Government agents were less sanguine; they feared that the Ghost Dances would lead to violence. It's important to understand the context. The Indians, especially the Sioux Indians in the Plains states, were in dire straits. The government had recently taken a big chunk of land to give to white settlers and the railroads, cutting their reservation in half. The Indians had so little land that they could no longer base their economy on hunting. The property they had left was difficult to farm, and 1890 saw a horrible drought. "The Indians were brought face to face with starvation," wrote James Mooney, a government official who surveyed the area.[84] The government's response: to increase the Indians' incentives to farm, they cut their rations.

In August 1890, two thousand Sioux gathered at White Clay Creek (near Pine Ridge in modern-day South Dakota) to perform the Ghost Dance. The government agent, H. D. Gallagher, sent twenty police officers to break them up, but the effort was unsuccessful.[85] Partisan politics inflamed the situation. A South Dakota newspaper said that Gallagher, a Democratic appointee, had been too soft, allowing the Indians to "leave their children and stock to care for themselves and spend their time in dancing and wild religious orgies."[86] Gallagher was soon replaced by a Republican, Daniel F. Royer, who tried to convince the Indians to stop. The leaders laughed at him and told him they would "keep it up as long as they pleased."[87] A few weeks later, a panicked Royer reported that almost thirteen hundred Indians were joining in the dances.[88] He telegrammed Washington, DC, repeatedly, pleading for troops. A massive Indian uprising was brewing, he wrote. "Indians are dancing in the snow and are wild and crazy. We need protection and we need it now."[89] In October there were almost daily Ghost Dances on the four Lakota reservations.[90]

Press coverage mostly made matters worse, suggesting or asserting, with no evidence, that the Ghost Dances were a part of Indian war preparations. By mid-December there were seventeen correspondents in the area. The *Washington Post* and *Chicago Tribune* quoted a military source who said that the "incantations and religious orgies" would soon lead to trouble.[91] The *New York Times* ran an article with the headline "How the Indians Work Themselves Up to a Fighting Pitch," which explained, "The spectacle was as ghastly as it could be: it showed the Sioux to be insanely religious."[92] A *Washington Post* piece blamed the whole thing on the Mormons.[93] Relying on military sources, the press accounts tended to exaggerate the number of potential warriors, printing estimates of fifteen thousand to twenty-seven thousand when the number was probably more like five thousand. More to the point, extensive historical research has found that the dancers were not planning an uprising.[94] Settlers became alarmed and started leaving the area.

The news accounts also reflected the view that the real driver of the dancing was Sitting Bull, the renowned leader then living at Pine Ridge. That wasn't true. Sitting Bull had heard of the dancing late in the game and was reportedly ambivalent about it. But as the man who had defeated Custer, Sitting Bull—still an ardent opponent of the whites—was the most frightening Native American alive, and he was an easy villain for reporters intent on hyping a dramatic showdown. Royer pushed that line too and demanded that Sitting Bull be arrested.

In Washington, President Benjamin Harrison was weighing political as well as military factors. Harrison and the Republicans, argues historian Heather Cox Richardson, figured that taking military action would convince the white settlers that the government had their back. The president told the secretary of war to intervene.

On December 15, a group of Indian policemen at Standing Rock Indian Reservation moved to arrest Sitting Bull, but the operation went horribly wrong. A scuffle ensued, and an Indian policeman shot Sitting Bull in the head. As word spread, Indians exited the area.

Some of the fleeing Indians—a wagon train of about three hundred men, women, and children from the Miniconjou tribe—were stopped by US Army troops and ordered to return with them to their camp near Wounded Knee Creek.

The next day, on December 29, the Indians were told to turn in their guns. Some were surrendered, but the soldiers believed there were more, so they went from tent to tent, pulling out knives and other weapons. The soldiers, now about five hundred strong, were tense, having read newspaper articles about how the Ghost-Dancing Indians were preparing for war.[95] One Indian—some say he was deaf, others that he was crazy—raised his gun in the air, declaring in Lakota that he had paid good money for the new Winchester and was not about to give it up. The soldiers grabbed him, and a shot was fired into the air.

Hundreds of soldiers opened fire on the Indians. Two-pound shells from the Hotchkiss cannons poured down. In just a few minutes, two hundred Indian men, women, and children were dead, along with twenty-five soldiers, most of whom were killed by friendly fire.[96] Women and children who tried to flee the scene were shot as they ran. Bodies were found almost two miles away from the scene. One witness reported seeing a newborn infant nursing from its dead mother's breast.[97] Another recalled: "I saw a boy and a girl, probably 8 or 10 years old, running from the field in a southeast direction toward the creek, and I saw two soldiers drop down each on one knee, and taking a knee and elbow rest of their pieces, kill these little children who, when hit, carried by the momentum of running, went rolling over."[98]

After the massacre, snow buried the dead. A cleanup party was sent on January 1, 1891, but the bodies were frozen under the bloodstained white covering. Yet several babies were found alive, lying beside their dead mothers. Other victims were frozen in grotesque positions where they had fallen. Some children were wearing their school uniforms.[99] The soldiers stripped many of the bodies naked—in part to get the "ghost shirts" as souvenirs—and 146[100] frozen bodies were dumped into a mass grave.[101]

Most of the public reaction was positive. Twenty of the soldiers were awarded the Congressional Medal of Honor.

It would be an exaggeration to say that the massacre at Wounded Knee was primarily an act of religious violence. Economic, social, and political factors helped fuel Indian passions and white paranoia. But the whites' inability to see the Ghost Dance as a religious phenomenon—thanks to their deep ignorance of, and arrogance about, Native American spirituality—led them to wildly misinterpret its significance. They also underestimated the rage that suppressing it would cause. Whites didn't view their war on the Ghost Dance as an assault on religious freedom, but the Indians surely did.

The Land

No history of the assault on American Indian religion is complete without a consideration of the spiritual impact of the loss of land. Of course, settlers took land from the Indians mostly for reasons unrelated to religion. But Native American religion is intimately connected to the land in ways that Abrahamic religions are not. Indians have occupied North America for thousands of years. When Moses was leading the Hebrews out of Egypt, Indians were already deeply ensconced in North America. Native American spirituality is grounded in a belief that all nature is imbued with life spirit. But tribes also bonded to specific areas. Some were the birthplaces of gods; others were places where people could commune with spirits. The Navajo point to specific mountains from which their people arose from the underworld.[102] The Hopi believe that the emissaries of the gods reside in the San Francisco peaks. The Tsistsista and Lakota believe that humans were created within the Bear Butte area of the Black Hills of South Dakota.[103] When a government agent tried to convince the Shahaptian to switch from hunting and fishing to farming, Smohalla, their chief, explained: "You ask me to plow the ground. Shall I take a knife and tear my mother's bosom? Then when I die she will not take me to her bosom to rest. You ask me to dig for stone. Shall I dig under her skin for her bones? Then when I die I cannot enter her body to be born again. You ask me to cut grass and make hay and sell it, and be rich like white men. But how dare I cut off my mother's hair?"[104] Every forced removal from an ancestral homeland left a profound spiritual wound.

While the religious harm was often an unintentional side effect of other agendas, sometimes it was the point. John Wesley Powell, the noted explorer who became the head of the Smithsonian Institution's Bureau of American Ethnology, argued that the government should try to shatter the Indians' "attachment to his sacred homeland." He advised the secretary of the interior as follows:

> When an Indian clan or tribe gives up its land it not only surrenders its home as understood by civilized people but its Gods are abandoned and all its religion connected therewith, and connected with the worship of ancestors buried in the soil: that is, everything most sacred to Indian society is yielded up.[105]

Although the attacks on the religious freedom of Native Americans and slaves are the most extreme in American history, even here lessons can be learned about the broader trajectory of religious liberty.

When Americans are inclined to deprive a group of its religious freedom, they often deny that they are suppressing an actual religion. The literature of the period is full of comments such as that of Wilkinson Call, a US senator from Florida, who declared that to promote morality, the Indian children should be "put under the guardianship of religion."[106] Religion in this case meant Christianity, written on the blank slate of a Native American soul.

While those attempting to deprive the Mormons and Catholics of their religious rights (and, later, Jews and Muslims) had to go through contortions to racialize their differences, Native Americans were already viewed as savages. As with slaves, the public commitment to religious liberty was not sufficiently strong to overpower other forms of bigotry. Rights were very much alienable.

Whites did not embrace religious freedom as a universal right, nor did they feel that their own rights were defined by how they treated Indians. The majority figured that one benefit of religious liberty was having the latitude to convert others, sometimes forcibly. In some cases, they believed the Indians were not only mistaken in their beliefs but also guided by Satan. These cases pose a particular challenge to the Madisonian model for religious competition. It's hard to maintain free market sensibility— may the best religion win!—when one group sees the other as animals or humans led by the forces of darkness.

Few religious leaders defended the Indians. Those advocating religious liberty meant something quite limited: the freedom to choose between Protestantism and Catholicism. The agent at the Siletz Indian Agency in Oregon in 1889, Beal Gaither, said with sweet pride that he had "endeavored to secure the Indians the privilege of religious liberty." His proof: "During the short time I have been in charge there have been about forty members taken into the Methodist Church and about the same number have been baptized to the Catholic Church."[107]

The Native American experience again illustrates the interconnectedness of our rights. Indians did not have the right to vote and therefore could not bring political pressure to bear on their situation, as Mormons, Catholics, and Jews eventually did.

The treatment of the Indians also reveals the importance of the press— this time in undermining religious freedom. By failing to understand or explain the genuine spirituality of Native Americans, the media enabled Americans to default to their fears.

Interestingly, the Native Americans began to make more progress in protecting their spiritual lives when they cast their appeals in the language of religious freedom. When the commissioner of Indian affairs limited dancing during the Fourth of July celebrations of the Blackfeet in Montana in 1917, an Indian representative named Wolf Tail used analogies that the whites would understand. "These gatherings are to us as Easter is to white people. We pray, and baptize our babies only instead of water we paint them."[108] Protesting limits placed on their ceremonies in 1916, leaders of the Ojibwa of the Red Lake Indian Reservation in Minnesota explained, "The beating of the Drum is simply an accompaniment to the songs of praise uttered by the congregation," just as "in every Church of the White man a Piano or Organ is found for the same purpose."[109] Thus they demanded the freedom to practice "the Chippewa religion." As scholar Tisa Wenger put it, "The demand for religious freedom relied on re-interpreting indigenous practices in Christian terms."[110]

Though Native Americans still must fight for their religious rights, there was a seismic shift for the better in the 1930s. President Franklin Roosevelt appointed as his commissioner of Indian affairs a man named John Collier, who had a dramatically different attitude. Collier declared point-blank that the Bureau of Indian Affairs had been "making it a crime to worship God."[111] In 1934, he issued Circular No. 2970, which ended most of the government's repressive policies.[112]

Congress did eventually codify the religious freedom rights of the Native Americans. The American Indian Religious Freedom Act decreed that the government could not interfere with Indian worship ceremonies or despoil sacred sites. "It shall be the policy of the United States to protect and preserve for American Indians their inherent right of freedom to believe, express, and exercise the traditional religions." The law declared clearly, for the first time, that Native Americans now merited the protections of the First Amendment.

The law passed in 1978, a mere 199 years after the First Amendment was ratified.

A march in Washington, DC, 1925

Chapter Nine

THE KKK, AL SMITH, AND THE FIGHT FOR THE PUBLIC SCHOOLS

The surge in Catholic immigration prompts an ugly Protestant backlash.

In the 1920s, the Ku Klux Klan was best known for burning crosses, wearing white hoods, and sowing terror among minorities. Less well known was that they also loved to sing. To cultivate a family-friendly Main Street image, the Klan sponsored glee clubs around the country, such as the Detroit Klan Quartette and the 100% Americans. Klan fans created more than one hundred songbooks, which often included reworks of Christian hymns, such as "Onward, Christian Klansmen" and "Let the Fiery Cross Be Burning."[1] They'd belt out these songs at chapter meetings and picnics.

Tellingly, most of the songs focused not on blacks but on Catholics. For instance, nine of the ten songs in the *Ku Klux Klan Song Book* were anti-

Catholic, including "Yes, the Klan Has No Catholics," sung to the tune of "Yes, We Have No Bananas," which included the following couplet:

> Oh the Klansmen are Protestant people, they want nothing only
>   their own.
> Their [sic] not a going to be ruled by the Catholics, nor by that
>   Dago Pope in Rome.[2]

That the Klan would attack the pope may not be surprising. What does seem strange is what its members focused on when it was time to get practical: defending public schools. They proclaimed support for a single public school system, not one set of common schools alongside a parallel system of Catholic schools. A checklist for would-be Klan members titled "Am I a Real American?" asked candidates whether they "believe that our free public school is the cornerstone of good government and that those who are seeking to destroy it are enemies of our republic and are unworthy of citizenship."[3] A Klansman's manual suggested this pledge for new members:

> I swear that I will most zealously and valiantly shield and pre-
> serve, by any and all justifiable means and methods, the sacred
> Constitutional rights and privileges of . . .
>
> – 1 Free public schools.
>
> – 2 Free speech and free press.
>
> – 3 Separation of church and state.[4]

If the image of a hooded Klansman expressing reverence for the "separation of church and state" seems bizarre, that's because the fight over religious freedom took some dramatic turns in the first decades of the twentieth century. Many Protestants were taking another shot at asserting their legal dominance. The concept of separation now became a cudgel used against Catholics. The anti-Catholic sentiment, exemplified by but not limited to the Klan, was astonishing. Again, mass media played a role in fanning the flames of fear, especially in Thomas Nast's horrifically offensive anti-Catholic cartoons. As in the 1830s, Protestants and Catholics fought over whose Bible should be used in the schools, with the result that no Bible was used. But unlike the situation in the Know-Nothing era of the 1840s and 1850s, this time the Catholics were strong enough to effectively fight back. The climax of the Catholic counterpunch was the presidential campaign of Alfred Emanuel Smith, a half-Irish Catholic immigrant, which triggered a wave of anti-Catholic activity but also permanently transformed urban politics. In the end, it was politics, not the courts, that brought Catholics some success, thereby strengthening religious freedom for everyone.

The Second Catholic Surge

Sometime toward the end of the nineteenth century, Roman Catholicism became the largest Christian denomination in America.

From 1870 to 1920, 9 million Catholics landed in the United States, many from Ireland, Italy, Germany, Austria-Hungary, and Poland, to work in the factories of the Industrial Revolution.[5] The share of the US population that was Catholic rose from 5 percent in the 1850s to 20 percent by 1910,[6] and among the religiously active the percentage jumped to 32 percent.[7]

The Catholic Church created an impressive infrastructure to sustain and assimilate these immigrants, providing social service agencies, schools, and thousands of new churches that offered Mass in a breathtaking range of languages. The number of priests in the United States rose from five hundred in 1840 to nine thousand in 1890.[8] The Church created an extraordinary social safety net that helped bring strength to millions of families and prevent society from rupturing. By 1916, there were 543 Catholic hospitals and 645 orphanages serving 130,000 children, mostly staffed by women in religious orders. Nuns—so often the objects of sexually obsessed ridicule—were integral, their numbers growing from 270 in 1820 to 49,620 in 1900.[9]

Although the mobilization of social services proved the founders' belief that religion would enrich the Republic, many Protestants didn't see it that way. Rather, they feared a massive power shift, and they weren't wrong. Around the country, Catholics were winning political office. In 1880, William R. Grace became the first Catholic mayor of New York City, prompting the *New York Times* to fret that the public schools would soon be "Romanized."[10] Four years later, Boston—where the Ursuline Convent had been torched—elected its first Catholic mayor. Soon, Catholics led the political machines or occupied mayoralties in Chicago, St. Louis, Kansas City, Omaha, St. Paul, Minneapolis, Indianapolis, and Detroit.[11]

As in the 1830s, the fight between Protestants and Catholics after the Civil War often focused on the schools. In the second part of the nineteenth century, the common schools grew, along with the assumption that they were vehicles for teaching Protestant Christianity. Many young women became teachers as a quasi-missionary calling. "Of all important requisites in a teacher, Christianity is certainly the foremost," one educator explained.[12] The National Teachers Association—the forerunner of the National Education Association—strongly supported teaching the Bible in public schools. Of 946 schools that responded to a survey in 1896, 454 said the Bible was read in all schools in the district, 295 said the readings were irregular, and just 197 (20 percent) said there was no Bible reading.[13]

How did the prevalence of Bible reading in schools square with the ideals of religious freedom? Common school advocates believed schools would stay within the bounds of the Constitution as long as they were both religious *and* "nonsectarian."[14] Protestants defined sectarianism as the promotion of a particular denominational doctrine—such as the Calvinist emphasis on predestination or the Baptists' belief in adult baptism. Education reformer Horace Mann argued that the Bible by itself—when presented without commentary—was pure and universal, making "the perfect example of Jesus Christ" lovely in their eyes.[15]

Catholics thought that the Protestant definition of "nonsectarian" was absurd. Requiring Catholic school children to read the Protestant version of the Bible at taxpayer-funded schools was, to them, a rather obvious violation of religious freedom. Beyond that, anti-Catholicism pervaded the public school curriculum. In a comprehensive study of public school textbooks, Professor Ruth Miller Elson concluded, "No theme in these school books before the 1870s is more universal than anti-Catholicism."[16] Among the common messages: the Roman Church opposed democracy, intentionally kept the masses ignorant, and forbade parishioners from reading the Bible. History books taught that English conquerors yearned to bring God to the Indians, while the Spanish and French were in it only for the money.[17] A reader created by Alexander McGuffey included passages describing Franciscan friars "who eat the bread of other people's [labor], and have no plan in life, but to get through it in sloth and ignorance, *for the love of God*."[18] A popular geography textbook explained that southern Europeans were "generally indolent . . . [and] less virtuous" compared with those in central and northeastern countries, "where the Bible is best known and Christianity most pure."[19] The introduction to another textbook promised "to contrast particularly the religion of Christ and his apostles, with the religion of the Popes and Mahomet."[20]

Emboldened by their new numerical clout, some Catholic leaders took an aggressive stance, arguing that taxpayers should subsidize parochial schools. By creating these religious schools, they maintained, the Church had removed a financial burden from towns, so Catholic schools should get a pro rata share of public funds.[21] This rarely happened, but the few notable exceptions gave mountains of grist to fearful Protestants. In 1860, New York City's Tammany Hall political machine got the state legislature to quietly slip $412,000 to Catholic schools.[22] The law was repealed the next year but provided a warning that Catholics would try to get money for their religious schools.[23]

While the Catholics didn't oppose public education—in fact, the majority of Catholic children attended public schools—their leaders tended to deprecate it. Besides disliking their anti-Catholic educational materials, they felt the schools were insufficiently moral. The Vatican's Sacred Congregation de Propaganda Fide (yes, its real name) worried that Catholics in public schools would be exposed to "evils of the gravest kind."[24] Whether it was because they felt shut out of the Protestant-flavored public schools or disapproved of their methods, the American Catholics spent heavily to build a parallel Catholic school system. By 1895, a staggering four thousand Catholic schools had been built, serving 755,038 children, a rise of 50 percent over the previous decade.[25]

During the post–Civil War period, the popes complicated matters by issuing statements that seemed to justify Protestants' claims that Catholicism and democracy were incompatible. In 1864, Pope Pius IX issued the Syllabus of Errors, which listed as a grave mistake the notion that "the Church ought to be separated from the State, and the State from the Church."[26] In 1870, the pope declared the pontiff's decisions to be infallible. In 1895, Pope Leo XIII warned against the pluralistic model of American religious freedom.[27] In 1906, in *Vehementer Nos*, Pius X said the idea of separation of church and state was "eminently disastrous and reprehensible."[28]

American Catholics found themselves in an awkward position. To a surprising extent, they often courageously stated their support *for* separation despite the pope's admonitions. Archbishop John Ireland of St. Paul, Minnesota, suggested that the American approach provided an "estimable advantage" to the Catholic Church: "Here she is as free as the eagle upon Alpine heights, free to unfold her pinions in unobstructed flight."[29] A prominent Catholic theology professor, John Ryan, declared that "practically all American Catholics" believed "that separation of church and state is the best arrangement for the United States."[30] As for the pope, Ryan straight-up said that "Catholics in the United States owe him no allegiance as a temporal sovereign; their obedience to him is entirely in the spiritual order."[31]

The clearest sign of how acceptable a certain type of noxious anti-Catholicism had become can be seen in the illustrations of Thomas Nast, the nation's most famous political cartoonist. Starting in 1870, he launched a series in *Harper's Weekly* that depicted Irish Catholics as apelike trolls. Nast may have developed his anti-Catholic feelings in Europe; his family had left Bavaria in the 1840s amid the spate of European revolutions in which the Vatican mostly opposed the forces of liberalism. *Harper's* was also a virtual organ of the Republican Party, while Catholics were part of the Democratic Party coalition.

In "The American River Ganges," Catholic clergy take the form of crocodiles, paddling ashore to devour American schoolchildren. Since

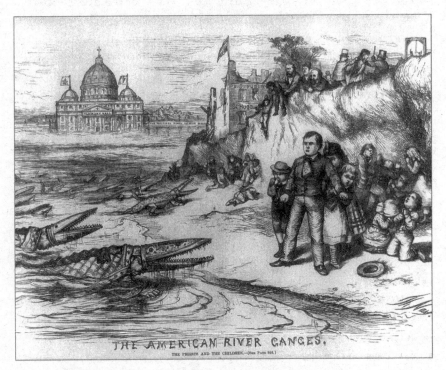

"The American River Ganges"

"DON'T BELIEVE IN THAT."

WHAT THE IRISH ROMAN CATHOLIC CHILDREN WILL BE TOLD TO DO NEXT.
"Kick it out *Peaceably!*"

"Don't Believe in That"

the defenders of public schools were also fighting to keep the (Protestant) Bible in class, one child clutches a Bible while bravely confronting the croco-clergy. In the background, a bombed-out building labeled "US Public Schools" is under attack.[32]

The cartoon titled "Don't Believe That" refers to a Bible-in-the-schools controversy that erupted in Long Island City, Queens, in 1875. The school

"Church & State"

board had required readings from the King James Version; Catholic students could either sit in the room during the exercise or leave for the day. In a gutsy form of civil disobedience, the Catholic children responded by blocking their ears as the principal read from the Bible. As the weeks went on, some students also shouted, "I don't believe in that!" In this cartoon, the Roman Catholic children are drawn with baboonlike features. They kick the Holy Bible in the air as a bishop looks on with a sinister grin.

In another cartoon, Lady Liberty is shackled to a box labeled "Fraudulent Votes." Simian Irishmen and diabolical bishops, one of them holding a bag labeled "Public School Money," look on as the banner of church and state—which had been previously separated—is tragically sewn back together. Get it?[33]

And then there's one that spells out what Nast believed was the pope's sinister intentions for the United States. In it, the pope stands atop the dome of St. Peter's Basilica, pointing across the Atlantic Ocean toward America. The caption reads "The Promised Land."

As these cartoons indicate, issues of religious freedom increasingly became entangled with partisan politics, with Democrats aligned with

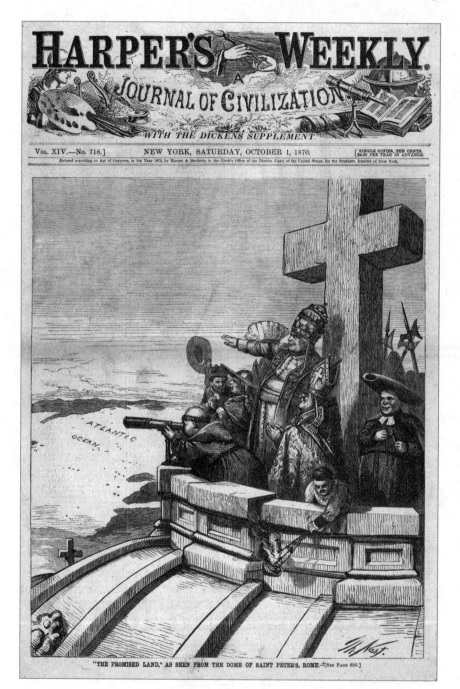

HARPER'S WEEKLY.
A JOURNAL OF CIVILIZATION
WITH THE DICKENS SUPPLEMENT.

VOL. XIV.—No. 718.]   NEW YORK, SATURDAY, OCTOBER 1, 1870.   [SINGLE COPIES, TEN CENTS. $4.00 PER YEAR IN ADVANCE.

Entered according to Act of Congress, in the Year 1870, by Harper & Brothers, in the Clerk's Office of the District Court of the United States, for the Southern District of New York.

"THE PROMISED LAND," AS SEEN FROM THE DOME OF SAINT PETER'S, ROME.—[See Page 626.]

" 'The Promised Land' "

urban Catholics and Republicans representing their Protestant opponents. In 1875, Republican president Ulysses S. Grant declared, "Encourage free schools, and resolve that not one dollar appropriated for their support shall be appropriated to the support of any sectarian schools." He did not address the pervasively Protestant nature of the public schools at the time but rather declared, "Keep the church and the state for ever separate."[34] Ominously, the man who led one of the armies in the Civil War predicted that if another such grand conflict were to arise, it would be "between patriotism and intelligence on the one side, and superstition, ambition and ignorance on the other." "Superstition" was a code word for Catholicism. Despite the anti-Catholic tinge of Grant's rhetoric, he was at least consistent, proposing to ban the teaching of any religion.[35] The Speaker of the House of Representatives, James G. Blaine, who was challenging Grant for the Republican nomination, attempted to one-up the general by proposing a constitutional amendment ensuring that no taxpayer money "shall ever be under the control of any religious sect."[36]

Evangelical Protestants had conflicted feelings about this ideologically consistent position. They liked the attacks on Catholics but didn't want to make the public schools fully secular. They mostly handled this contradiction by insisting that it didn't exist. Government support for Catholic schools was a heinous violation of the First Amendment, but allowing public schools to teach the King James Version was obviously sensible. While the House of Representatives approved the Blaine Amendment banning government spending for sectarian schools by a vote of 180 to 7, the Senate added a new clause clarifying that "the reading of the Bible in any school or institution" would still be allowed. Senator Frederick Frelinghuysen of New Jersey, an evangelical, explained that the Bible "is a religious and not a sectarian book."[37]

Although the Blaine Amendment ultimately failed, its politics lived on. Some thirty-eight states banned government funding for Catholic schools.[38] Many included an asterisked clarification that the ban shouldn't be construed to apply to (Protestant) Bible reading in public schools.[39] Rutherford B. Hayes, the Republican nominee in 1876 and an evangelical, supported Bible reading, he said, because education must promote "religion, morality and knowledge."[40] In case there was any doubt about what he meant, he confided in his diary that continuing the King James Version readings marked a "defeat for subserviency to Roman Catholic demands."[41]

While politicians could sometimes muscle through a plan that embodied contradictory principles—for example, support for Protestantism in the schools is grand; support for Catholicism is terrible (and religious freedom is the best thing ever)—judges were more sensitive to the logical contradictions. The conflict came to a head in Edgerton, Wisconsin, where public school teachers had been leading their classes in readings of the King James Version. Catholic parents complained. "Wisconsin Catholics: Are You Willing That the King James Bible Be Read in the Schools You Are Taxed to Support?" read the headline in a local Catholic publication. School administrators insisted that it was nondiscriminatory because Catholic students were free to leave the room. Their explanation of why the Bible was not sectarian was particularly creative: it "was responsible for freedom (including freedom of conscience)" and therefore "could not possibly be sectarian or an infringement on anyone's religion."[42] Besides, the Catholics' real purpose was to destroy public education, they charged, citing the pope's statements in the Syllabus of Errors that the church was responsible for education.

The Wisconsin Supreme Court was not convinced. All five of its justices (all of them Protestants) supported the Catholic plaintiff. The King James Version was, in fact, sectarian (!), their opinion stated, and reading Bible passages was a form of worship (!), which therefore violated the state constitution. The jurisprudence was catching up to demographics. Catholics made up almost half of Wisconsin's churchgoers by the 1890s.[43] This was one of the first major cases in which the courts declared that the use of religion in public schools needed strong limits.[44]

Protestants eventually retreated to what they viewed as a more defensible position, albeit one with serious moral drawbacks. If they taught the Bible as *literature* instead of religion, then it wouldn't violate religious freedom. Stanley Matthews, an attorney who was involved in similar Bible litigation in Cincinnati, suggested that the Bible passages be taught "not as the words that fell from the second person in the Godhead . . . but as a beautiful specimen of English composition."[45] As the scholar Steven K. Green wrote in *The Bible, the School, and the Constitution*, "the practices were generally constitutional, but at a cost to their integrity."[46] Protestants would use the same sleight of hand in the coming decades. For instance, in order to preserve blue laws that banned work on the Sabbath, Christians argued that the statutes were intended to encourage public order and social cohesion, not to enforce a religiously ordained day of rest. To justify the inclusion of the words "under God" in the Pledge of Allegiance, it was argued that they buttressed patriotism, not faith. In Indiana, courts decreed that Good Friday could be an official holiday because it wasn't religious (it was just an opportunity to enjoy a long weekend).[47] In Oklahoma, the legislature allowed local governments to display the Ten Commandments as an important historical document, not a religious one.[48]

Toward the end of the nineteenth century, the public schools gradually did become more secular. A survey by the Woman's Christian Temperance Union in 1887 found that only one-third of schools were reading the Bible.[49] The share of readings in the McGuffey series that were religious dropped from 30 percent in 1844 to just 3 percent in 1901.[50] Schools that wanted to instill religion tended to shift toward prayer—which was easier to personalize than the Bible. Meanwhile, Catholics softened their position as well, in part as a response to a practical problem. They couldn't build Catholic schools fast enough—or raise enough money to sustain them—so in several areas they agreed to merge the parochial schools with the public schools and accept that some of their parishioners would get a secular education during the week.

Neither Protestants nor Catholics really got what they wanted during this period. Both preferred that schools actively teach religion, including the Bible. But Protestants could not abide the idea that Catholic texts would be taught alongside Protestant ones and thereby be granted a moral equivalence. Horace Mann once commented that such a system encouraged children to think "there is no such thing as truth"—as if Ptolemy were taught in one classroom and Copernicus in another—leading to "an extinction of the central idea of all moral and religious obligations."[51] Catholics figured that since they were not likely to get a public school system to their liking, they should focus on building parochial schools. As a result, the Bible was removed from public schools.

In our own day, when conservative Protestants and Catholics unite to demand more religion in schools, one can only wonder what might have happened if Protestants had been open to the radically pluralistic approach offered by the Catholics in the nineteenth century, allowing for the use of both Catholic and Protestant Bibles. Of course, that would have required them to cede the idea that Protestantism was the true religion of America—to give up on *winning*.

Protestant resistance stiffened in the first decades of the twentieth century, in large part because of the rise of Protestant fundamentalism. In the 1910s, a group of conservative theologians released a set of essays called *The Fundamentals: A Testimony to the Truth.* A reaction against the liberalizing trends in Protestantism, these essays embraced an ardent biblical literalism. "The Bible, the whole Bible, nothing but the Bible is the standard and the rule of Christianity," wrote T. W. Medhurst in one of the essays. They abhorred the Catholic view that the Bible should be studied with the guidance of the Church. The Bible was meant to be read individually, Medhurst insisted, "but Romanism denies all this; and therefore, Romanism is not Christianity."[52]

The Politics of Catholicism

Anti-Catholic fervor intensified in the 1920s. The reborn Ku Klux Klan had enrolled as many as 4 million members at its peak in the middle of that decade, when the US population was less than one-third of what it is today. Its largest chapters were not in the South but in Indiana and Ohio. While less violent than the original Klan of the Reconstruction era, it achieved tremendous power through more traditional means. Klan members wielded effective political control in Indiana and Ohio; Klan-backed candidates won the governorships of Oregon, Colorado, Indiana, and Kansas. US senators from Texas and Colorado were Klansmen.[53] In 1925, thirty thousand robed Klansmen paraded past the US Capitol.[54]

The KKK's most stunning victory was in Oregon. The state's Catholic population was only 8 percent, but a sensational story of a convent kidnapping ("The Escaped Nun from Mount Angel Convent, or the Last Stand of Desperate Despotism") had rocked the state in 1913.[55] In 1922, the Klan and the Masons backed a successful state referendum that required all children to attend public schools, effectively banning Catholic schools. "We are not against the way the Catholics worship but we are against the Catholic machine which controls our nation," a local kleagle explained. "We believe in the separation of church and state."[56] Their triumph was short-lived. In 1925, in *Pierce v. Society of Sisters*, the Supreme Court overturned the law.[57]

Some four hundred thousand Ohioans joined the Klan. Unlike the situation in Oregon, Catholics were a large and growing presence, making up about 35 percent of Ohio's churchgoers.[58] One Catholic resident remembered "crosses burning almost every night" near her home, while another recalled massive Klan parades several times a year.[59] Almost thirty-two thousand Dayton Protestants gathered at the fairground down the road from the University of Dayton, a Catholic school, for a festival that featured an airplane with a cross illuminated in red lights and a massive hundred-foot flaming cross.[60]

In Maine, the Klan targeted Catholic immigrants from French Canada. A Klan organizer said their purpose was "to keep Protestant Americans in the lead, not only in numbers but in fact,"[61] while a Protestant minister from Portland declared, "It's the rising of a Protestant people to take back what is their own."[62]

The Klan even showed strength in New York City. In 1923, the First Presbyterian Church in Queens hosted a KKK official who liked to be called "the Human Dynamo." Mr. Dynamo, along with thirteen other robed Klansmen, marched down the aisle as the congregation sang "Stand Up for Jesus."[63] He told the crowd of five thousand that they stood ready to block Alfred E. Smith, the Catholic governor of New York, from winning the presidency: "There are 6 million people in the United States who have pledged their lives that no son of the Pope of Rome will ever sit in the Presidential chair."[64] In 1927, one thousand white-robed Klansmen joined the regular Memorial Day parade in Queens. The Knights of Columbus, a Catholic group, pulled out of the parade to protest the Klan's inclusion.[65] Police and Klan members fought, with the police claiming that the Klan had violated a pledge to go hoodless. Klan members subsequently claimed that "Native-born Protestant Americans" were being "assaulted by Roman Catholic police of New York City." Their propaganda included the "one school" message that proved so popular in other parts of the country. "Liberty and Democracy have been trampled upon when native-born Protestant Americans dare to organize to protect one flag, the American flag; one school, the public school; and one language, the English language."[66]

One of seven people arrested during the rally was Fred Trump, Donald Trump's father, according to 1927 news accounts. Some newspaper articles said all of those arrested were Klansmen, but another account said Trump was detained "on a charge of refusing to disperse from a parade when ordered to do so" and that he was "discharged" at the arraignment.[67] A separate article in the *Brooklyn Daily Eagle* described five of the seven—but not including Trump—as Klan members. Donald Trump denied that any of this even happened.[68]

Nationally, the Klan sharply divided the Democratic Party. At the 1924 Democratic National Convention in New York City, Klan opponents offered an amendment to the party's platform denouncing the organization. But a staggering 343 delegates were members of the Klan, and many others were sympathizers.[69] The anti-Klan resolution lost by two votes.

Four years later, the Democrats conducted a laboratory experiment in American tolerance by nominating Al Smith, who embodied every negative stereotype peddled by fearful Protestants—a Catholic, Tammany Hall–connected, anti-Prohibition Irish Italian American. To have one of their own nominated by one of the two major parties was an extraordinary milestone for American Catholics. The four-term governor of New York was a beloved progressive, whose policies laid much of the groundwork for the New Deal.

But his candidacy brought a level of religious vitriol not seen since the Jefferson-Adams election of 1800. At the Democratic convention in Houston, where Smith was nominated, several Klansmen dragged a life-size effigy of Smith into the convention hall, slit its throat, and threw fake blood on its chest.[70] Throughout the campaign, Smith was depicted as the pope's puppet. Klansmen claimed that a photo of the recently completed Holland Tunnel in New York City actually showed a newly built secret pathway from Rome to the United States, through which the pope would arrive and take over the country.[71] One widely distributed cartoon, titled "Cabinet Meeting—If Al Were President," showed a big boardroom filled with priests and bishops. The pope is sitting at the head of the table and Al Smith is off in the corner, dressed as a bellboy, carrying a jug of whiskey on a serving platter.[72] Klan members and their supporters speculated about where the pope would camp after his arrival. Some figured Georgetown University was being outfitted with guns aimed at the White House.

Around the country, signs appeared making it clear what the main issue was: "For Hoover and America, or For Smith and Rome. Which?"[73] One KKK flier showed an image of a priest throwing a baby into a fire, with the title "Will It Come to This?"[74] In Muncie, Indiana, a twofer conspiracy theory spread: the Catholics had invented a powder that would bleach the skins of black men so they could seduce and marry unsuspecting white women.[75] Other fliers claimed that if Smith were elected, Protestant marriages would be annulled.[76] As Smith arrived in Oklahoma City, he could see the burning crosses of the KKK across the countryside.[77]

The attacks did not come just from the hooded. "Protestants of America are determined to keep Popery out of the White House," declared Senator J. Thomas Heflin of Alabama.[78] The school board of Daytona Beach, Florida, had each student carry home a note reading "We must prevent the election of Alfred E. Smith to the Presidency. If he is elected President, you will not be allowed to have or read a Bible."[79] The *Fellowship Forum*, a publication owned by a member of the Republican National Committee, distributed two hundred thousand copies of a campaign piece that declared, "It has been the everlasting unwritten law of this nation since its creation . . . that only a Protestant shall be President of the United States."[80]

Smith opponents resented the suggestion that their attacks on Catholicism amounted to bigotry. Lou Hoover, wife of the Republican nominee, Herbert Hoover, explained, "there are many people of intense Protestant faith to whom Catholicism is a grievous sin. And they have as much right to vote against a man for public office because of that belief" as anyone else.[81]

Perhaps most disappointingly (and yet not surprisingly), Protestant religious leaders—including some of the leading voices—joined in the attack. The *Christian Century*, the most respectable Protestant publication in the country, opposed Smith as "a representative of an alien culture, of a medieval Latin mentality, of an undemocratic hierarchy and of a foreign potentate in the great office of President of the United States."[82] Out of 8,500 Southern Methodist preachers, 4 admitted to supporting Smith.[83] In Atlanta, a group of ministers declared, "You cannot nail us to a Roman cross and submerge us in a sea of rum."[84]

For religious Protestants, it was hard to disentangle Smith's Catholicism from his opposition to prohibition. The temperance movement had always had anti-Catholic elements, viewing drinking, immigration, and urban squalor as branches of the same vine. In 1916, the Prohibition Party even included in its platform a call for "absolute separation of church and state."[85] Smith's opponents called him Alcohol Smith and spread false rumors that he was a drunk.[86] The popular evangelical preacher Billy Sunday referred to Smith's supporters as "the damnable whiskey politicians, the bootleggers, crooks, [and] pimps."[87] Most creatively, John Roach Straton, the minister of New York's Calvary Baptist Church, preached that Smith represented "card playing, cocktail drinking, poodle dogs, divorces, novels, stuffy rooms, dancing, evolution, Clarence Darrow, overeating, nude art, prize fighting, actors, greyhound racing and modernism." Historians offer no explanation for how stuffy rooms and poodles got on the list.[88]

Though Smith had certainly experienced anti-Catholicism before, including during the 1924 race, he was overwhelmed by its volume and breadth. He sometimes responded with humor. Told that Lutheran voters might not get past the schism that had occurred a few hundred years before, Smith reportedly said, "Well, holy smokes. They are going back pretty far to get an issue against me."[89] When challenged with the content of a papal encyclical that was supposedly incompatible with American democracy, he quipped, "Will somebody please tell me what in the hell an encyclical is?"[90]

His most thorough explication of his views on religious freedom, though, came in 1927, in response to a lengthy article in the *Atlantic* magazine by a Protestant named Charles C. Marshall, who cited various Vatican rulings to prove that Smith would have to defer to the pope. Marshall's article anticipated many of the warnings against the dangers of Muslim Sharia law that are circulating in our own day.

> Here arises the irrepressible conflict. Shall the State or the Roman Catholic Church determine [legal issues]? The Constitution of the United States clearly ordains that the State shall determine the question. The Roman Catholic Church demands for itself the sole right to determine it, and holds that [it is] superior to and supreme over the State.[91]

Smith responded with an extraordinary essay of his own, mostly written by a Jewish advisor, Judge Joseph Proskauer, and the exchange garnered press coverage throughout the country.[92] Smith argued that the behavior of actual American Catholics bore no resemblance to the scare version conjured from bits of papal encyclicals or the dark chapters of European history. For starters, Smith said he'd never had any trouble putting the interests of New Yorkers foremost in his four terms as governor. In response to Marshall's suggestion that parochial schools teach hostility to America and democracy, Smith countered:

> I and all my children went to a parochial school. I never heard of any such stuff being taught or of anybody who claimed that it was. That any group of Catholics would teach it is unthinkable.

Marshall complained about a case in which American courts refused to give a woman a divorce but a papal court provided an annulment. Smith responded by saying this was no different from when Protestant religious bodies pass judgment on family matters. These rulings may be important within the religion, but they cannot trump civil laws.

> Your Church has its tribunals to administer its laws for the
> government of its members as communicants of your Church.
> But their decrees have no bearing upon the status of your
> members as citizens of the United States.

Smith made the point that was missing from so much of the anti-Catholic literature—and from modern-day discussions about Islam and other religions. There's a difference between how a religion might be interpreted through a particular sacred text or encyclical and how it is lived by Americans. When Marshall challenged Smith to respond to comments from different popes, the governor responded:

> You seem to think that Catholics must be all alike in mind and
> in heart, as though they had been poured into and taken out of
> the same mould. You have no more right to ask me to defend
> as part of my faith every statement coming from a prelate
> than I should have to ask you to accept as an article of your
> religious faith every statement of an Episcopal bishop, or of
> your political faith every statement of a President of the United
> States. So little are these matters of the essence of my faith that
> I, a devout Catholic since childhood, never heard of them until
> I read your letter.

For Al Smith, winning in politics meant not only appealing to his base but also bringing new people into his coalition. To do that, he had to depart from the Vatican's position and instead support separation of church and state. He concluded:

> I summarize my creed as an American Catholic. I believe in the
> worship of God according to the faith and practice of the Roman

Catholic Church. I recognize no power in the institutions of my
Church to interfere with the operations of the Constitution of the
United States or the enforcement of the law of the land. I believe
in absolute freedom of conscience for all men and in equality of
all churches, all sects, and all beliefs before the law as a matter
of right and not as a matter of favor. I believe in the absolute
separation of Church and State and in the strict enforcement of
the provisions of the Constitution that Congress shall make no
law respecting an establishment of religion or prohibiting the free
exercise thereof. I believe that no tribunal of any church has any
power to make any decree of any force in the law of the land, other
than to establish the status of its own communicants within its
own church. I believe in the support of the public school as one
of the cornerstones of American liberty. I believe in the right of
every parent to choose whether his child shall be educated in the
public school or in a religious school supported by those of his
own faith. . . .

In this spirit I join with fellow Americans of all creeds in a
fervent prayer that never again in this land will any public servant
be challenged because of the faith in which he has tried to walk
humbly with his God.[93]

Smith lost in a landslide. Hoover's seventeen-point margin was the
fourth biggest in American history up to that point. Political scientists believe Smith's religion was the decisive factor.[94] But in some ways that election also marked a positive turning point for Catholics. Statistical analysis
revealed that 1928 saw both a massive increase in urban populations and
a shift in urban voting to the Democrats, the birth of a new coalition that
would sweep Hoover out of office in 1932. "The Republican hold on the
cities was broken not by Roosevelt but by Alfred E. Smith," declared political scientist Samuel Lubell.[95] While Hoover took 200 previously Democratic counties in the south, Smith won 122 Republican counties in the
north, about half of which remained Democratic thereafter.[96] In Chicago,
the Polish and Czech wards voted 40 percent for Democrats in 1924 but
70 percent in 1928. Jews flocked to Smith too. He won the twelve largest
cities, and overall he got 64 percent more votes than any previous Democratic nominee.[97]

Catholics made progress in other ways during this period. Positive Catholic characters began to emerge in popular culture. Babe Ruth was raised in a Catholic orphanage, and both Gentleman Jim Corbett and John Sullivan, the man he defeated to win the heavyweight boxing championship, were Catholics. The heroic priest began to be a staple in movies, a character type that reached its apotheosis with Spencer Tracy's Father Flanagan in *Boys Town* in 1938. With the election of Franklin Roosevelt, Catholics for the first time were full players in a winning presidential coalition, and they were rewarded accordingly. Approximately 25 percent of Roosevelt's judicial appointees were Catholic.[98] Catholics became major leaders in the labor movement too.[99]

This period illustrated several patterns that would reappear in later years. First, the impulse for majoritarianism was persistent and strong. When a group risks losing its perch atop the heap, it fights back hard, even if it means jeopardizing universal rights. The mainstreaming of the Ku Klux Klan showed that the language of religious freedom can be easily perverted, turned into a weapon *against* religious minorities. As some conservatives are doing today with their attacks on American Muslims, anti-Catholics cast their adversary as disloyal, un-American, and primitive. Being a good Catholic meant being a bad American. American Catholics were tarred with the worst attributes, real or imagined, of Catholics in history and in other nations. The partisan media again played an important role, sometimes working to dehumanize an unpopular religious minority. We also saw that attacks on religious freedom can end up advancing secularism. The result of the Protestant-Catholic fight over the Bible in schools was the removal of religion from classrooms.

But religious freedom marched forward. As Catholics grew in number, they gained the strength to defend themselves. In the Madisonian arena of religious competition, it was ultimately Catholic voting power that denied Protestants the ability to impose their religious views. Catholics also learned that they would have to compromise. Hobbled by a Vatican whose ideology was out of step with American sensibilities, American Catholics carefully charted a course that was both respectful to Rome and loyal to the Constitution. When they attempted to use their newfound political clout to get taxpayer funds for parochial schools, they were throttled and redoubled their efforts to prove their love of the First Amendment. In his quest for the White House, Al Smith declared his own unwavering support for separation of church and state. Catholics moved deeper into the twentieth century with a new playbook for advancing their faith and their religious liberty at the same time.

While millions of Catholics exerted great influence through the electoral process, it left open the question of would happen when a persecuted minority was both unpopular and tiny.

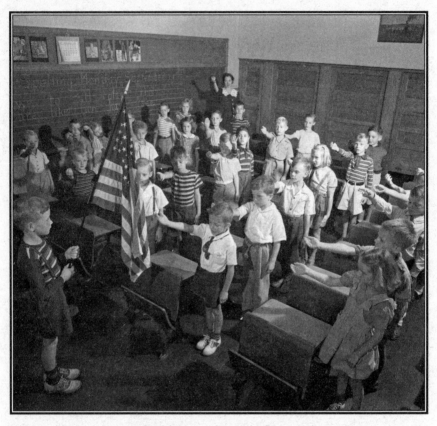

Schoolchildren saluting the flag, 1943

Chapter Ten

THE WITNESSES

*A tiny, reviled, and obnoxious American
religion forces the nation to define what
religious liberty really means.*

Robert Fischer was trying to escape from Litchfield, Illinois, when the mob caught up with him. The crowd pulled him out of his car and started destroying his Jehovah's Witnesses literature. It was June 16, 1940, war hysteria was mounting, and the residents were livid that Fischer and the other Witnesses refused, as a matter of conscience, to salute the American flag.

To demonstrate their love of flag, the crowd draped one over the front of the car—and slammed Fischer's head against it, demanding that he kiss Old Glory. Fischer wouldn't. Again, they smashed his head against the flag-covered hood. Again. Again. And again, for thirty minutes. The town's chief of police sat nearby watching.[1]

The attack was part of a wave of violence against Jehovah's Witnesses that began in the 1930s. The Witnesses were a small group, just forty thousand people, quirky and original—exactly the sort of religious startup that the Madisonian free market allows. But their unusual theology and aggressive proselytizing prompted what Brigham Young would have called "mobocracy." Witnesses were beaten, jailed, tarred and feathered, and, in one case, castrated. The response: an equally aggressive effort by the Jehovah's Witnesses to use the American courts to protect their rights. At least thirty-seven religious freedom cases involving Jehovah's Witnesses were argued in front of the United States Supreme Court.[2] The decisions that were handed down changed the understandings of, and rules for, religious freedom. Because of their efforts, religious freedom was finally guaranteed at the state and local levels, as James Madison and John Bingham had hoped. "Seldom, if ever, in the past has one individual or group been able to shape . . . our vast body of constitutional law," legal scholars John Mulder and Marvin Comisky wrote in 1942. "But it *can* happen, and it *has* happened, here. The group is Jehovah's Witnesses."[3]

The Jehovah's Witnesses' emphasis on constitutional law turned out to be crucial because when a religious minority is small and unpopular, it will not be able to gain protection through political clout. It must gain strength from the *idea* of religious freedom—which can be actualized only through an independent judiciary. The Witnesses worked the courts, prompting federal judge Edward Waite to ask: "If 'the blood of the martyrs is the seed of the Church,' what is the debt of Constitutional Law to the militant persistency—or perhaps I should say devotion—of this strange group?"[4]

"Worse than Traitors"

In 1869, seventeen-year-old Charles Taze Russell was working in his father's clothing store in Allegheny, Pennsylvania. One Sunday, he heard an Adventist minister preach about the imminent return of Christ. Intrigued, he started a Bible study group. He published a pamphlet, *The Object and Manner of Our Lord's Return*, and then other pamphlets and books. Russell initially described his project as more of a faith-based publishing operation than a new religion (to this day, Witnesses who work full-time call themselves "peak publishers").[5]

Over time, Russell developed his own theology of biblical literalism, which maintained that Christ would return to restore paradise on Earth, not destroy it. He laid out in great detail a schedule for Christ's return and the specific steps his followers would need to take to gain salvation. By the time of his death in 1916, Russell's books and tracts had sold 20 million copies.

Soon after Russell's death, the controversial views of the International Bible Students Association (as the Witnesses were called back then) began to enrage the authorities. The government believed that the writings of Joseph Rutherford, who had taken over as head of the movement, would stir resistance to the World War I draft. They pointed to this passage in Russell's *Finished Mystery*:

> Nowhere in the New Testament is patriotism (a narrowly minded hatred of other peoples) encouraged. Everywhere and always murder in its every form is forbidden. And yet under the guise of patriotism civil governments of the earth demand of peace-loving men the sacrifice of themselves and their loved ones and the butchery of their fellows, and hail it as a duty demanded by the laws of heaven.[6]

They were not traditional pacifists. The Bible passages that drove them were not so much Jesus's teachings about nonviolence as apocalyptic writings about the ultimate battle between Jehovah and Satan. All governments, including that of the United States, were controlled by the devil, they believed. (The theological roots: Satan had taunted Jehovah by saying that no one would remain faithful if subject to the devil's influences. Jehovah took the bet and allowed Satan to run the governments, and all religious institutions too, as a test.)[7]

Though *The Finished Mystery* is a turgid, difficult-to-follow collection of Bible verses, exegeses, and excerpts from other writings, the US Department of Justice thought it could go viral. "The only effect of it is to lead soldiers to discredit our cause and to inspire a feeling at home of resistance to the draft," stated a memorandum from the US attorney general.[8] He was not convinced that the Bible Students were actually driven by religious views. "The International Bible Students Association pretends to the most religious motives, yet we have found that its headquarters have long been reported as the resort of German agents."[9]

The US government indicted eight leaders under the Espionage Act of 1917 for "unlawfully and willfully conspiring to cause insubordination, disloyalty, and refusal of duty of the military."[10] Judge Harland B. Howe wrote that the Bible Students' "religious propaganda" was "a greater danger than a division of the German Army." The sincerity of their religious convictions made them potentially more persuasive. "They are worse than traitors," he declared. "You can catch a traitor and know what he is about. But you cannot catch a man who does what they did under the guise of religion."[11] The leaders were convicted and sentenced to an astonishing twenty years in prison. Though the charges were later thrown out, Rutherford served nine months in a federal penitentiary.

For Rutherford, the experience was searing. It not only cemented his attitude toward government but also stoked his antagonism toward other religious groups, as many religious leaders had cheered the war, and some had even applauded the arrest of the Bible Students. The organization, renamed Jehovah's Witnesses in 1931, poured out writings about the coming Armageddon and the sinister behavior of the Catholic Church. The Church was "the chief visible enemy of God, and therefore the greatest and worst public enemy," declared Rutherford.[12]

As World War II approached, the Witnesses' beliefs about patriotism got them into trouble again—at first, with the Nazis. Jehovah's Witnesses in Germany refused to say "Heil Hitler," offer the salute of loyalty, or join the army. Hitler shut down the Witnesses' printing presses and banned them outright.[13] After the draft was instituted, thousands more were arrested for refusing to serve in the army. Some ten thousand Witnesses were sent to prisons and concentration camps, where they were identified with purple triangles.[14] They were frequently tortured—and yet also offered their freedom if they signed an affidavit renouncing their faith. In one case, the Witnesses in a concentration camp were gathered together outside and forced to watch as one of their leaders was shot to death. The Nazis then handed out pieces of paper granting the other Witnesses their freedom if they denounced their religion. None did, and most likely they all died.[15] In all, approximately two thousand Witnesses were killed by the Nazis. "The Jehovah's Witnesses were literally the only martyrs of the Holocaust," said Michael Berenbaum of the United States Holocaust Memorial Museum. "The Jews were victims because their experience was not a matter of choice. But the Witnesses did have a choice. They are people to be respected for not giving in."[16]

The Witnesses rankled American authorities too. States pushed to inculcate patriotism in schools, often by having children salute the flag. The Witnesses had two problems with the practice. Since governments were controlled by Satan, the law "that compels the child of God to salute the national flag compels that person to salute the Devil."[17] Satan was fond of the flag salute rules because it turned the flag into an object of worship, violating the first of the Ten Commandments ("Thou shalt have no other gods before me. Thou shalt not make unto thee any graven image . . . thou shalt not bow down thyself to them, nor serve them").

The flag had become a new god, more important than Jehovah, they believed. Saluting it was no minor infraction. Witnesses were thought to have entered into a covenant with God, predicated on following the laws precisely. A Witness who broke faith would lose the possibility of everlasting life. Rutherford generously allowed that, of all the Satanic governments of the world, the United States was definitely the best—but he insisted that resistance to the flag salute was nonnegotiable. In a book called *Children*, Rutherford explained:

> Satan influences public officials and others to compel little children to indulge in idolatrous practices by bowing down to some image or thing, such as saluting flags and hailing men, and which is in direct violation of God's commandment (Exodus 20:1–5).[18]

In 1935, Carleton Nichols, a brave third grader in Lynn, Massachusetts, stood quietly, hands at his side, during a flag ceremony. He explained that as a Jehovah's Witness, he couldn't honor "the Devil's emblem." After the school punished Nichols and his parents, Rutherford went on the radio to praise Carleton for "declaring himself for Jehovah God and his kingdom. . . . All who act wisely will do the same thing."[19] Rutherford noted that the American flag salute was awfully similar to the salute that Germans were giving Hitler. (At the time, the custom was to extend one stiff arm upward while reciting the pledge. In 1942, after the United States entered World War II, Congress amended the US Flag Code, stipulating that the right hand should be placed over the heart instead.)[20]

Among those who heard Rutherford's remarks was the family of Walter Gobitas of Minersville, Pennsylvania, a working-class coal-mining town.[21] Lillian, a seventh grader, and Billy, a fifth grader, both decided to stop saluting the flag. Billy explained in a note, "I love my country and I love God more and I must obey his commandments."[22]

They were expelled. School superintendent Charles Roudabush believed that the patriotic rituals were crucial and the religious objections bogus. Those who abstained were "aliens."[23] The family, with the help of the American Civil Liberties Union (ACLU) and the Witnesses' main office, appealed the ruling. During the trial, Roudabush had this exchange with the district court:

> ROUDABUSH: We feel it is not a religious exercise in any way and has nothing to do with anybody's religion.
>
> THE COURT: Do you feel that these views to the contrary here held by these two pupils are not sincerely held?
>
> ROUDABUSH: I feel that they were indoctrinated.

THE COURT: Do you feel their parents' views were not sincerely held?

ROUDABUSH: I believe they are probably sincerely held, but misled; they are perverted views.[24]

In 1940, in *Minersville School District v. Gobitis*, the US Supreme Court ruled 8–1 against the Witnesses.[25] As it had sixty-one years before, in its ruling against the Mormons, the Court concluded that the First Amendment did not license behaviors that the local community finds destructive.

The next three years saw a massive increase in persecution of Jehovah's Witnesses. Whether it was caused primarily by the *Gobitis* decision or by the Witnesses' decision to start proselytizing on street corners (in addition to going house to house), the attacks on Witnesses became horrific.

In Lookout, West Virginia, Witnesses were brought to the mayor's office, where they were roped together like cattle, at two-foot intervals, and forced to drink castor oil. In the midst of the attack, liquored-up American Legion members, with no sense of irony, declared that their purpose was to "promote peace and good will on earth."[26]

In Nebraska, two men appeared at the home of Witness Albert Walkenhorst. They claimed to be coreligionists and asked him outside to discuss the Bible. Then they grabbed him, brought him to a grove of trees, and castrated him. "There, that will hold you for a while," one of them joked.[27]

In Little Rock, Arkansas, a group "armed with guns, pipes and screwdrivers . . . mercilessly beat all the Witnesses they could find," according to a report by the ACLU.[28]

In Connersville, Indiana, several middle-aged female Witnesses were charged with flag desecration because they had given out literature opposing the flag salute requirement. Two pleaded not guilty and were sentenced to two to ten years in prison. Their attorney was beaten and run out of town.[29]

In Flagstaff, Arizona, a Witness reported that residents asked him if he would salute the flag.

> When I replied that I respected the flag but was consecrated to do God's will and did not salute or attribute salvation to the flag they cried, "Nazi spy!" knocked me down, beat me badly, and finally knocked me out—then dragged and pushed me across the street to a service station and again tried to make me salute the flag. I was

dizzy, befuddled and don't clearly remember anything further except that a considerable crowd had gathered yelling "Nazi spy!—Heil Hitler!—String him up!—Chop his head off!"[30]

Witnesses' businesses were boycotted. In Belleville, Illinois, they were kicked off relief rolls. In Clarksburg, West Virginia, local unions forced the firing of seven Jehovah's Witness glass cutters.[31] Often, the attacks were led by members of the American Legion, with the active support or at least acquiescence of local law enforcement.[32] The Witnesses got little help from the press ("44,000 Americans Join Freak Cult That Hates Everything!" blared the *Chicago Daily Tribune*).[33]

The scale of the harassment and persecution grew and grew. From 1933 to 1951, there were 18,866 arrests of Witnesses.[34] From 1940 to 1943, 843 instances of persecution were reported to the US Department of Justice's Civil Rights Division, according to an analysis by historian David Manwaring.[35] The ACLU estimated that more than two thousand students had been ejected from school by 1943. In many cases, families put the kids in Kingdom Schools after they were expelled—and were then prosecuted for truancy.[36] In Monessen, Pennsylvania, Witnesses set up a Kingdom School to accommodate those who had been kicked out of local schools, but the mayor viewed it as communistic, padlocked the school, and seized literature. When 146 Witnesses went to Monessen to protest, the mayor put them all in jail overnight.[37]

Just as the Mormon claims were mocked as being not genuinely religiously grounded, many found it hard to believe that the Witnesses' refusal to salute the flag was truly a matter of conscience. "To symbolize the Flag as a graven image and to ascribe to the act of saluting it a species of idolatry," the Florida Supreme Court declared, "is too vague and far-fetched to be even tinctured with the flavor of reason."[38]

But the Witnesses continued to resist the flag salute law and proselytize on the streets. The reason is important. While Russell had believed that only 144,000 people would be saved, making it pointless to exert much energy converting people, Rutherford had amended the theology. There was a second class of people, the Jonadabs, who would live in the new Edenic paradise that Jesus would be leading. But only those who had become Witnesses by the time of Jesus's arrival—which was any day now—would be saved, so time was of the essence.[39]

They also passionately believed that the courts could help. By 1933, the organization's leadership had pledged to appeal all unfavorable rulings and provide lawyers to carry forward the cases.[40] That may have been partly because their leader, "Judge Rutherford," was an attorney.[41] At Witness conventions, the organization offered special training in legal procedures. They distributed a pamphlet, the *Order of the Trial*, to help Witnesses defend themselves in court. The ACLU, which helped bring many of the cases, also offered rewards in communities for information leading to the prosecution of anti-Witness assailants.[42] Rutherford's faith in the legal system was not groundless; Witnesses won more than one hundred decisions from state supreme courts.[43]

Breakthrough

Newton Cantwell and his son Jesse went to spread the gospel in a Catholic neighborhood in New Haven, Connecticut. They brought a portable hand-cranked phonograph and played bits of Rutherford's book *Enemies*, which includes passages such as "The Roman Catholic hierarchy is a selfish and devilish organization, operating under the misleading title of 'Christian religion,' and desperately attempting to gain control over all the people of the earth." This enraged local residents, and the sheriff arrested the Cantwells and charged them with violating a Connecticut law forbidding the soliciting of funds without a license. Under the law, the secretary of the local public welfare council got to determine whether an organization was a bona fide religion. Like the Baptists in the 1700s, the Witnesses did not believe in government certification and thus refused to seek such permits.

The Witnesses wanted to challenge the law, but there was an obvious problem with the case: the violation of their religious liberties in this case was being perpetrated by a *local* government. The compromise forged by James Madison around the First Amendment meant it would apply (much to his disappointment) only to actions by the federal government. Although John Bingham had intended the Fourteenth Amendment to repair that flaw, for eighty years the courts had refused to do so. But the Witnesses' lead attorney, Hayden Covington, knew that the Supreme Court had already taken a big step toward what would become known as "incorporation"—the idea that the Fourteenth Amendment had applied the Bill of Rights to the states and not just the federal government. In *Gitlow v. New York* in 1925, the Court had ruled that the First Amendment protected freedom of speech on the state and local levels because of the

Fourteenth Amendment. The Court then incorporated freedom of assembly in 1937. Covington wondered: could freedom of religion be next?

In 1940, in *Cantwell v. State of Connecticut*, the Supreme Court unanimously ruled for the Jehovah's Witnesses, declaring that, thanks to the Fourteenth Amendment, the "free exercise of religion" was indeed guaranteed to all. No longer could local governments trample religious freedom rights without the Bill of Rights having something to say about it.

There it was. Madison had failed to apply the principle of religious freedom to the states, but thanks to the Civil War, the Radical Republicans, John Bingham, the United States Supreme Court, and finally the Jehovah's Witnesses, religious liberty was now an inextricable part of the national creed, enforceable in every jurisdiction.

In taking this historic step, the Court said that while religious freedom was not an unlimited right, the state must not "unduly" infringe on it. States could regulate only when there was a "clear and present danger of riot, disorder, interferences with traffic upon the public streets, or other immediate threat to public safety, peace, or order." The Court would spend the next seventy-five years assessing when religious liberty went too far. But from that day forward, all religious freedom questions—even local matters—were potentially matters for the federal courts to decide, governed by the First Amendment of the United States Constitution.

Madison would have been particularly tickled by the Court's grappling with the diversity of viewpoints in America. In *Cantwell*, the Court acknowledged how messy religious competition could be. "In the realm of religious faith, and in that of political belief, sharp differences arise," Justice Owen Roberts noted. "In both fields, the tenets of one man may seem the rankest error to his neighbor." Yet even when religious views are deemed strange or even harmful, they must be given wide berth. Under the "shield" of religious freedom, Roberts wrote, "belief can develop unmolested and unobstructed." Acknowledging the centrality of this concept in a pluralistic society, he concluded, "Nowhere is this shield more necessary than in our own country, for a people composed of many races and of many creeds."[44]

A year later, the United States entered World War II. As the American Legion unleashed a national campaign "to foster and perpetuate a one hundred percent Americanism," cities, states, and school boards around the country stepped up their efforts to encourage patriotism in part by having schoolchildren pledge allegiance to the flag.[45] Emboldened by *Cantwell*, the Witnesses decided to again challenge the flag salute laws.

In a way, the Witnesses' efforts to strike down flag salute laws were more audacious than their efforts to protect their proselytizing work in the streets. Decreeing that a religion can't hand out its tracts is a clear restriction of its "free exercise." But flag salute laws were a bit different. They did not target Jehovah's Witnesses or stop them from expressing themselves. The statutes had a secular goal, encouraging patriotism.

But a few things had changed since the last flag salute case, *Gobitis*, was decided against the Jehovah's Witnesses. One was the *Cantwell* ruling, which had opened up local school boards to the scrutiny of federal courts when it came to religious questions. Just as important, the reaction to *Gobitis* had been negative. The *New Republic* had mocked the Court for "heroically saving America from a couple of schoolchildren whose devotion to Jehovah would have been compromised by a salute to the flag." Legal experts were also aware of the wave of persecution that had followed it and the courageous sincerity of the victims.

The Witnesses' lead attorney, Hayden Covington, found his test case near Charleston, West Virginia. In 1942, the state board of education had issued a rule requiring kids to salute the American flag—"in the spirit of Americanism"—and declared that refusal "would be regarded as an Act of insubordination." Ten-year-old Marie and eight-year-old Gathie Barnett, the children of a pipe fitting helper at a local DuPont factory, refused to salute during a ceremony at Slip Hill Grade School.[46] They were expelled. The Witnesses appealed all the way to the highest court.

In his brief to the US Supreme Court, Covington compared the *Gobitis* decision to *Dred Scott v. Sandford* as a case that would live in infamy. He argued that freedom of speech—which had been gaining greater protection from the Court—must include the freedom not to speak.[47]

In *West Virginia State Board of Education v. Barnette*, the Court in 1943 sided with the Witnesses, overturning the *Gobitis* decision of just three years earlier. Three of the justices who had voted against the Witnesses switched sides.[48] Justice Robert H. Jackson noted that, because of the Fourteenth Amendment, the Supreme Court had not only a right but an obligation to intervene on a local level because the "small and local authority may feel less sense of responsibility to the Constitution."

Surprisingly, Jackson objected to the flag salute requirement not so much because it forced religious beliefs on Jehovah's Witnesses, but because it forced beliefs in general on anyone. "Those who begin coercive elimination of dissent soon find themselves exterminating dissenters," wrote Jackson, the specter of European Fascism evident between the lines.

"Compulsory unification of opinion achieves only the unanimity of the graveyard." In one of the most famous sentences from a Supreme Court decision, he declared, "If there is any fixed star in our constitutional constellation, it is that no official, high or petty, can prescribe what shall be orthodox in politics, nationalism, religion, or other matters of opinion."[49]

This was an important moment for religious liberty—and it would create scores of new dilemmas for the United States in the years that followed. With *Barnette* and other cases of that era, the Court gave more power and deference to religious believers. From then on, even if a law wasn't intended to hurt a religion, it might still be viewed as unconstitutional if the harm it inflicted was significant or if the law's secular purpose wasn't important enough. The devil, as it were, was in defining "enough": what secular purpose could be so important that it justified inflicting collateral damage on a religion? What if religious groups felt that taxation infringed upon their rights? Or what if they believed that teaching evolution in schools violated their religious beliefs? How far should we go to accommodate religious Americans?

In his dissent, Justice Felix Frankfurter prophesied that this new world would be fraught with constitutional danger. The justice, a Jew, began with an unusually personal bit of credibility building: "One who belongs to the most vilified and persecuted minority in history is not likely to be insensible to the freedoms guaranteed by our Constitution." Nonetheless, he said, religious minorities could end up with *too many* "new privileges."

> [The First Amendment] gave religious equality, not civil immunity. Otherwise, each individual could set up his own censor against obedience to laws conscientiously deemed for the public good.

Noting that there were 250 distinctive religious denominations in the United States, he wondered whether the Court would now have to assess the sincerity or significance of each of their beliefs. After all, if a belief is a minor part of a theology, perhaps the government should be less worried about infringing upon it. Frankfurter's dissent unearthed a great irony: the Court's desire to protect religion from the state could force it to become *more* involved in sensitive judgments about religious claims. Frankfurter's *Barnette* predictions proved prescient. The Court was entering a new era in which society would be increasingly sensitive to the rights of religious groups and, as a result, drawn into difficult balancing acts. The Court took the right path, but that didn't mean it would be smooth.

From 1940 to 1944, the US Supreme Court heard a variety of religious freedom cases, many involving the Jehovah's Witnesses. Case by case, the Court sketched out new principles, sometimes ruling against the Witnesses but more often in their favor. Yes, the Witnesses (and other people of faith) could proselytize without having to get a permit. Yes, they could do so even if it was in a company town. No, they couldn't have eight-year-olds do it in violation of child labor laws. Yes, they could do it without paying a tax. No, they could not hold a parade in which marchers carried signs reading "Religion Is a Snare and a Racket" without obtaining a license.[50] No, they could not tell the local marshal that he was "a damn fascist and a racketeer." No, they could not avoid both military and civilian service (and some 4,300 Witnesses were jailed for their refusal).[51] And yes, they could hold worship services in the park. Gradually, this despised religion won expanded rights for all believers.

Why was it that the Jehovah's Witnesses ended up playing such a critical role in the expansion of religious liberty? As with the Mormons, the Witnesses' obnoxiousness made all the difference. Because their own salvation depended on their success at saving others, they were famously pushy. Because their theology required them to tell "the truth" about not only their own faith but others' (i.e., the harlots, dupes, and pawns of Satan), they excelled at provoking overreactions. Because they were biblical literalists and millennialists, they adopted extraordinarily unpopular positions, such as being avowedly unpatriotic in the midst of both world wars. Because they were religiously intolerant, they alienated potential allies among other religions. Alone and unpopular, they could not influence legislatures. But because they were litigious, they forced the courts to probe the real meaning of the First Amendment. Because they published their controversial views—and then spread them on street corners—they were able to gain additional protection from the First Amendment's guarantees of freedom of press, speech, and assembly.

In a way, the rise and role of this ornery faith fit the Madisonian model perfectly. It was a religious startup—invented by a seventeen-year-old possessed with the belief that he'd found a better way. This grew into a movement of ordinary Americans who challenged those in power, won, and brought expanded rights for everyone. But their path to success was different from that of the Catholics and Mormons, who gained acceptance in part through their numerical clout. The Witnesses did not have that option. They needed to rely on the law, for, in the words of Justice Jackson, "the very purpose of a Bill of Rights was to withdraw certain subjects from the vicissitudes of political controversy, to place them beyond the reach of majorities." It turned out that the Madisonian model could not rely only on a multiplicity of sects; it also had to make that "parchment barrier"—the declaration of rights—become a powerful force. For that to happen, the nation needed an assertive, independent judiciary.

As a legal matter, the Jehovah's Witnesses cases triggered two seismic shifts. First, the Constitution now protected Americans from the tyranny of state and local governments (as Madison and Bingham had wanted). Second, America would from then on have to seek ways to accommodate the sensitivities of religious believers in those gray areas where secular laws inadvertently infringe upon religious convictions. It was no longer enough to not persecute a group—America would have to bend over backward to give religions room to breathe. This new era of accommodation has drawn the courts and legislatures into many more religious controversies but in the service of a more expansive notion of liberty.

Over time, the Jehovah's Witnesses became less aggressive and insulting, which is part of the reason that there are more than 8 million of them around the world today. Undoubtedly, they've benefited from sanding off their rough edges. But fortunately the Witnesses in the 1940s were still plenty abrasive.

Issued in 1948 by the US Postal Service

Chapter Eleven

WORLD WAR II AND THE JUDEO-CHRISTIANS

*To defeat Hitler and the Communists,
America elevates and redefines religious
freedom—and invites Jews to the table.*

On February 3, 1943, a German torpedo struck the SS *Dorchester*, a 368-foot transport ship that was carrying 902 American soldiers and sailors to Greenland. It blew a hole right below the waterline, killing many of them instantly. Some were asphyxiated by ammonia gas; some drowned. Others were crushed under bunk beds that collapsed.

But hundreds survived the initial blast and scrambled up to the deck. There they encountered the ship's four chaplains: John Washington, a Catholic priest; George Fox and Clark Poling, both Protestants; and a thirty-two-year-old rabbi named Alexander Goode. Born in Brooklyn, Goode represented the fourth generation of Goodekowitzes (the family's original name) to join the rabbinate. It was not an easy time to be Jewish in America. According to polls, the peak year for American anti-

Semitism was 1944.[1] Goode volunteered right after Pearl Harbor and was disappointed when he was assigned to Greenland, as he wanted to be in the thick of the action, where he would be more needed.

Now, on the *Dorchester*, Rabbi Goode proved himself invaluable. Panic was on the verge of killing as many soldiers as the torpedo had. Some jumped overboard and were torn apart by the ship's propeller. One became so distressed that he tried to choke one of the chaplains. Others refused to leave the ship. The chaplains calmly ushered them one by one into the lifeboats.[2] "So long, boys, good luck," one of the chaplains shouted from the deck as the last of the lifeboats drifted away, according to eyewitnesses.

One man couldn't get a life jacket on because of an injured shoulder. Rabbi Goode pulled the laces from his boots and tied the life preserver to the man's arm. The chaplains helped him over the side of the ship and into the water. When the life jackets ran out, the chaplains offered theirs.

As the *Dorchester* began to sink, the four chaplains could be heard praying separately—together—in English, Latin, and Hebrew—a babel of languages that offered hope instead of confusion. Rabbi Goode chanted the Sh'ma: "Hear, Israel, the Lord is our God, the Lord is One."[3]

One survivor, John Ladd, said the chaplains were still standing arm in arm as the ship disappeared beneath the waves, just twenty-seven minutes after the torpedo hit. "It was the finest thing I have seen or hope to see this side of heaven," he said.

Some of the other ninety-six chaplains who died during the war no doubt performed comparable acts of bravery. But there was something about this story that resonated widely. In 1944, the four clergymen were posthumously awarded the Distinguished Service Cross. On May 28, 1947, the US government issued a postage stamp in their honor (usually stamps did not feature individuals until at least ten years after their death). The main title was "These Immortal Chaplains"; in finer print were the words "Interfaith in action." In a White House ceremony celebrating the stamp, President Harry Truman declared, "The greatest sermon that ever was preached is right here on this stamp."[4]

America's conception of religious liberty dramatically changed during World War II and its aftermath. First, for a combination of reasons—including the Holocaust and the birth of Israel—it was the moment when American Jews got their place at the civic table.

Second, the presence of two major existential threats, Fascism and Communism, forced the nation to emphasize the central role that religious liberty played in the American identity. The concept started to permeate the American consciousness, not just of constitutional scholars but of ordinary Americans. Three presidents—Franklin Roosevelt, Harry Truman, and Dwight Eisenhower—for their own reasons and in their own ways, each took significant steps to elevate the principle to near sacred status. As a defining characteristic of American success, religious freedom became as important as religious passion.

Tolerance Trios

The Founding Fathers had a soft spot for the Jews. In his famous letter to the Touro Synagogue in Rhode Island, George Washington wrote:

> May the children of the stock of Abraham who dwell in
> this land continue to merit and enjoy the good will of the
> other inhabitants—while every one shall sit in safety under
> his own vine and fig tree and there shall be none to make
> him afraid.[5]

That's not to say that Jews enjoyed equal rights in the colonial era. Far from it. Peter Stuyvesant tried turning away the "very repugnant" Jews from New Amsterdam (now called New York) in 1654 and prohibited them from building a synagogue. After the English took over and renamed the city New York, twenty Jewish families asked to create a house of worship, but the city's common council said no, explaining, "Publique worship is Tolerated . . . but to those that professe faith in Christ."[6] In 1737, the New York Assembly affirmed that court testimony from Jews was inadmissible.[7] Jews were often viewed as greedy scoundrels. A popular Mother Goose rhyme cheerfully warned:

> Jack sold his egg
> To a rogue of a Jew
> Who cheated him out
> Of half of his due.[8]

During the Revolutionary War period, ten of the thirteen colonies banned Jews from holding office,[9] and some barred Jews from practicing law.[10] State laws discriminated against Jews, long after state churches were disestablished. Connecticut refused to recognize a Jewish congregation until 1843.[11] "The Jews," complained the *New Haven Register,* "have outflanked us here, and effected a footing in the very centre of our own fortress."[12] Jews were not allowed to hold office in New Hampshire until 1876.[13]

But hostility toward Jews in the eighteenth century was relatively muted compared with, say, that directed toward Catholics, because there were so few of them. At the conclusion of the Revolutionary War, there were about one thousand to two thousand Jews in the United States, less than 0.05 percent of the population[14] (just slightly more than the portion Baha'is now make up in America).[15] As late as 1840, there were only fifteen thousand, an even smaller percentage of the population.[16]

This all changed with the massive European immigration in the late nineteenth and early twentieth centuries. Between 1880 and 1924, some 2 million Jews[17] arrived from Eastern Europe, and the welcome they received was not exactly warm. A historian of Brownsville, Brooklyn, recalled that "it was enough that a Jewish boy appeared on the street for gangs to set upon him."[18] Ironically, few were more hostile to the Jews than Irish Catholics, the group that had been the most discriminated against in America. On July 30, 1902, Irish workers from a printing press factory on New York's Lower East Side threw metal objects and dumped buckets of water on a Jewish funeral procession. When the police arrived, they also attacked the mourners, shouting, "Kill those Sheenies!"[19] On July 23, 1911, a group of Irish in Malden, Massachusetts, yelling "Beat the Jews" and "Kill the Jews," attacked local Jews and smashed store windows. On another occasion, an Irish mob, including three policemen, ransacked a synagogue after a rumor spread that Jews had murdered a Gentile girl and used her blood for a religious ritual.[20]

When Congress cracked down on immigration in 1924, one consequence was a slowing of Jewish immigration. The head of the US Consular Service explained that such limits made sense because Polish Jews had been so frequently the victims of religious persecution that they could not possibly function in a democratic society. They were, he wrote, "abnormally twisted because of [a] reaction from war strain" and suffered from "the dullness and stultification resulting from past years of oppression and abuse."[21] A State Department report claimed, "Eighty-five to ninety percent [of Jewish immigrants] lack any conception of patriotic or national spirit."[22] University of Wisconsin sociologist E. A. Ross wrote that Eastern European immigrants "reach here moral cripples, their souls warped and dwarfed by iron circumstance."[23]

Obstacles to immigration persisted into the 1930s, so hundreds of thousands of Jews who attempted to flee the Nazis were unable to reach the United States.[24] In 1938, after German attacks on Jews during Kristallnacht, American pollsters asked, "Should we allow a larger number of Jewish exiles from Germany to come to the United States to live?" With unemployment still sky-high, 72 percent of Americans responded no.[25] Congress rejected a proposal in the late 1930s to allow just twenty thousand Jewish children in from Germany.[26] And in 1939, the United States turned away the MS *St. Louis*, carrying nine hundred Jewish refugees, a quarter of whom ultimately died in death camps.

Recent evidence indicates that the family of Anne Frank was among those likely thwarted in part by America's immigration limits and bureaucracy. Since the United States did not have a refugee policy, her father, Otto Frank, applied for a regular American visa in 1938. Nothing happened for two years, at which point the consulate in Rotterdam was bombed and the paperwork destroyed.[27] After the United States entered into the war, the government tightened up further to keep out German spies. The Franks continued to try. "I am forced to look out for emigration and as far as I can see USA is the only country we could go to," Otto Frank wrote to an American friend. Amazingly, in 1941, despite a growing waiting list of Jews seeking to emigrate, the United States admitted only 62 percent of its quota for Germany. Having no success, the Franks went into hiding in 1942.[28]

Housing covenants proliferated to explicitly exclude Jews, blacks, and other unwanted groups. A 1934 study reported that "the invasion of any particular area by Jews is often accompanied by the withdrawal or flight of the Gentiles, unless—and often, even when—the Jewish newcomers are persons of recognized social worth."[29] In Washington, DC, at least fourteen neighborhoods restricted Jews. Most social clubs banned Jews, and elite universities instituted quotas. Harvard University's president, A. Lawrence Lowell, explained that admitting too many Jews would "ruin the college" by driving away good Protestant students.[30] At the same time, anti-Semites often criticized Jewish separatism, a supposed unwillingness to blend into the rest of society. Thus the *Christian Century* in May 1936 urged the Jew to convert or at least assimilate faster, since he "will never command the respect of the non-Jewish culture in which he lives so long as he huddles by himself, nursing his own 'uniqueness.'"[31]

The beloved automobile pioneer Henry Ford campaigned obsessively to convince Americans that Jews controlled global finance, and he republished the bogus conspiracy screed, *The Protocols of the Elders of Zion*. His anti-Semitic newspaper, the *Dearborn Independent*, had a circulation of seven hundred thousand.[32] It became increasingly permissible to express anti-Semitic views in public settings, as when a minister in Illinois called a mass meeting to discuss "The Problem of the Jew, or How Shall We Get Rid of Him?"[33] In a 1939 survey, 41 percent said that "measures should be taken to prevent Jews from getting too much power in the business world," while 10 percent said they should be deported.[34]

Too many mainstream Christian religious leaders contributed to the tone. In July 1936, the *Christian Century* stated that Jews "must be brought to repentance—with all the tenderness, in view of their age-long affliction, but with austere realism, in view of their sinful share in their own tragedy."[35] That was tolerant compared with what regularly came from Catholic leaders. The *Catholic Transcript* of Hartford, Connecticut, declared that the Jews "are hated because they are too prosperous, too successfully grasping." Father Charles Coughlin, a popular radio personality, blamed Jews for the Russian Revolution and said, "When we get through with the Jews in America, they'll think the treatment they received in Germany was nothing."[36] Most of his anti-Semitic radio addresses were approved by the Catholic hierarchy.[37]

Fortunately, the rise in anti-Semitism prompted a powerful, history-changing response. In 1924, the National Conference of Christians and Jews was formed, bringing together Protestants, Catholics, and Jews for common projects—for instance, defending Al Smith from anti-Catholic attacks in 1928. In 1933, three of the leaders—Everett Clinchy, Rabbi Morris S. Lazaron, and Father John Elliot Ross—did something novel: they launched a thirty-eight-city tour to promote interfaith understanding. *TIME* magazine dubbed them the Tolerance Trio.[38] They won over audiences by soliciting charged questions—such as whether Catholics coveted political power or Jews were inherently greedy—and then tackling them with good humor.

The idea caught on. A trio dubbed the Corn Belt Crusaders traveled eleven thousand miles through Iowa, Kansas, and Illinois. In just 1939, various trios attended ten thousand meetings in two thousand communities in forty-eight states. An essay in the *Saturday Evening Post* titled "Satan, Be Warned" predicted that this "united moral front" may "prove to be one of the most remarkable forces that ever ganged up on the devil." It's hard to prove that this was the exact moment when the universe was given the tri-faith bar joke—"A rabbi, a priest, and a minister walk into a bar . . ."—but there can be no doubt that these newfangled trinities were in vogue. "Priests, rabbis and ministers speaking from single platforms on social affairs is becoming 'the usual thing,'" stated the 1932 annual report of the National Conference of Christians and Jews. By 1941, the organization estimated that these "trialogues" had happened more than 250,000 times.[39]

When the United States entered into World War II, this multifaith approach was broadly embraced—by Presidents Franklin Roosevelt, Harry Truman, and, a few years later, Dwight Eisenhower. Indeed, each leader played a significant role in bringing more religion to the public sphere while simultaneously encouraging the idea of "tri-faith" America, or, as it came to be known, our "Judeo-Christian" heritage.

Franklin Roosevelt took a historic step by declaring religious freedom to be a defining characteristic of American patriotism. Eleven months before the Japanese attacked Pearl Harbor, Roosevelt became convinced that Europe would be overrun if we didn't help Britain right away. Many Americans opposed getting involved in the European war, so to mobilize support for aiding Britain, Roosevelt explained that the efforts were needed to preserve four essential freedoms. Rather than reciting the Bill of Rights, Roosevelt came up with his own list: freedom of speech and expression; freedom from want; freedom from fear—and the "freedom of every person to worship God in his own way—everywhere in the world."

Roosevelt expertly offered language that was vague enough to be unifying and meaningful enough to be inspiring. He believed that freedom of religion was a prerequisite for democracy.

> Religion, by teaching man his relationship to God, gives the individual a sense of his own dignity and teaches him to respect himself by respecting his neighbors.

Democracy, the practice of self-government, is a covenant among free men to respect the rights and liberties of their fellows.

International good faith, a sister of democracy, springs from the will of civilized nations of men to respect the rights and liberties of other nations of men.

In a modern civilization, all three—religion, democracy and international good faith—complement and support each other.[40]

In truth, Roosevelt thought that freedom of religion mostly meant the beneficent rule of liberal Protestantism. He said privately in 1942 that the United States was "a Protestant country and the Catholics and Jews are here under sufferance."[41]

Publicly, however, he pushed a universal vision of religious liberty. The "Declaration by United Nations," a statement of values embraced by the allied nations in 1942, drew from the Four Freedoms, declaring that "complete victory over their enemies is essential to defend life, liberty, independence and religious freedom." To help sell war bonds, the beloved illustrator Norman Rockwell created four posters about the freedoms for the *Saturday Evening Post*. The freedom of worship illustration that ran on February 27, 1943, was not a generic image of worshippers at church or Pilgrims settling a new land. Rather, it was a group of easily identifiable contemporary believers—a Catholic woman clutching a rosary, a white-haired woman with hands clasped in prayer, and, right in the foreground, a man with a yarmulke clutching a Jewish prayer book.

More Tolerance Trios fanned out to military bases around the world. Speakers stressed that religious freedom was central to the democratic system they were defending. After one such event, a member of the National Conference of Christians and Jews (NCCJ) reported, "The three speakers . . . had those 36,000 men on their feet cheering, applauding, whistling, yelling—one of the most tremendous ovations I have ever seen given to men in my life."[42] After an intramural football game at Fort Benning, Georgia, the marching band formed a giant Star of David and played "Ein Keloheinu"—and then re-formed into a giant cross and played "Onward, Christian Soldiers."[43] By the end of the war, trios had spoken to more than 9 million Americans at 778 bases.[44] In the words of historian Kevin Schultz, author of *Tri-Faith America*, "the trios became new symbols of American moral righteousness, focused on confronting problems directly, being honest, and promoting the Golden Rule."[45]

The wartime pop-culture propaganda effort incorporated the interfaith message too. Frank Sinatra talked about tolerance at the end of his CBS *Old Gold* radio show. In one episode he explained, "Religion doesn't make any real difference, except to a Nazi or a dope." RKO Pictures followed up with an eleven-minute short about a group of kids poised to beat up a Jewish boy. Sinatra sets them straight and then serenades them with a celebration of American diversity: "The children in the playground, the faces that I see; all races, all religions, that's America to me."[46] The NCCJ distributed a comic book called *Three Pals*, which told the true story of Gershon Ross (a Jew), Blaine Kehoe (a Catholic), and George Foster (a Protestant), who went to high school together before they were killed in the war. "Their spirits mingle as in days of old, Catholic, Protestant, Jew," the comic book declared. "They died, as they lived, in true brotherhood . . . Americans All!"[47]

Significantly, some important Christian leaders enthusiastically embraced the approach. Bishop Fulton J. Sheen, probably the most influential Catholic in America, even sketched areas of theological common ground, noting that Jews historically "are the roots of the Christian tradition [and] religiously are one with the Christian in the adoration of God." James Cannon Jr., a well-known Methodist bishop, said that America needed to save the Jews, who "wrote the Scriptures we read every Sunday, but whom we allowed to be murdered by the diabolical wretches of Nazism."[48]

To be clear, no one pitched the war as an effort to save the Jews. In fact, Jewish leaders were quite sensitive to the implication that Jews had gotten America into the war. Rather, religious discrimination became that thing that the enemy did. "Anti-Semitism was no longer merely one of many American prejudices," explained historian Edward Shapiro in *A Time for Healing.* "Since anti-Semitism was the key element in the ideology of Nazi Germany, the American anti-Semite was in effect allying himself with America's mortal foe."[49]

During this period, one of the leaders of the NCCJ, Everett Clinchy, began using the term "Judeo-Christian." The phrase had popped up in intellectual circles for more than a century but now was being used to convey a spirit of inclusive religiosity. "Political party machines, led by Nazi Hitler, Communist Stalin and Fascist Mussolini alike, deny the sovereignty of God above all else, pour contempt on the spiritual values of the

Judeo-Christian tradition, and refuse to recognize those natural rights of freedom of conscience," Clinchy said. "Never before in history have Protestants, Catholics and Jews been as aware of each other's suffering and as willing to mobilize spiritual forces as American citizens." The phrase conveyed both religiosity and tolerance at the same time. One of the NCCJ's pamphlets declared the global conflict to be a "war of ideas between Totalitarian dictatorship and the essentials in our Judeo-Christian tradition."[50]

Was there actually a Judeo-Christian theology behind all this? Scholars have debated this question for years, and this period featured an increase in such discussions. Obviously, one can look at the Jewishness of Jesus, the common teachings of the Old Testament, and much more. But in truth, the impulse behind the trios—and the term "Judeo-Christian"—was not to synthesize a collective theology; it was to forge political and cultural unity.

One other factor affected the way Americans perceived each other. Because the military draft was universal, men and women of different religions really did serve side by side—as evidenced by the Four Chaplains. Aboard the *Dorchester*, soldiers noticed the collaboration between the clergymen. "I was raised Catholic in an Irish neighborhood, and there the Catholics didn't talk to any Protestants, and none of us Protestants and Catholics spoke to the few Jews who were there," recalled one soldier, Michael Warish. "To see these men in the same uniform but of different faiths getting together and actually talking and laughing and smiling and joking with each other was unheard of."[51]

Hollywood loved interfaith plot lines. In the 1949 John Wayne film *Sands of Iwo Jima*, a Jewish character dies while chanting the Sh'ma. Overtly and self-consciously Jewish characters appeared in *Action in the North Atlantic, Air Force, Bataan, Guadalcanal Diary, The Purple Heart, Winged Victory, Objective, Burma!*, and *A Walk in the Sun*. In *Pride of the Marines*, a Jewish soldier declares, "Maybe some guys won't hire me because my name is Diamond and not Jones. 'Cause I celebrate Passover instead of Easter. . . . We need a country to live in where no one gets booted around for any reason."[52]

Godless Communism

After World War II ended, American leaders worked to convince a war-weary nation that they remained in a cosmic battle—now against Communism. As the Soviet Union consolidated power in Eastern Europe, it suppressed local religions and promoted an aggressive atheism. President Truman explained the Cold War as follows:

> There has never been a greater cause. There has never been a cause which had a stronger moral claim on all of us.
> We are defending the religious principles upon which our Nation and our whole way of life are founded. We are defending the right to worship God—each as he sees fit according to his own conscience. We are defending the right to follow the precepts and the example which God has set for us. We are defending the right of people to gather together, all across the land, in churches such as this one.
> For the danger that threatens us in the world today is utterly and totally opposed to all these things. The International Communist movement is based on a fierce and terrible fanaticism. It denies the existence of God and, wherever it can, it stamps out the worship of God.[53]

Truman took a symbolic step to illustrate the American approach to religion. On January 20, 1949, he had a Jew offer a benediction for the first time at a presidential inauguration. Rabbi Samuel Thurman of the United Hebrew Congregation of St. Louis was an immigrant who had come over from Russia as a child around the turn of the century, exactly the kind of Jew that had provoked such a fierce reaction.[54] The next six presidential inaugurations featured a rabbi as well as a Protestant, a Catholic, and, for several years, a Greek Orthodox priest.

Truman's background prepared him well to be an evangelist of pluralism. His business partner in Independence, Missouri, had been Jewish, and his political patron, the St. Louis boss Tom Pendergast, was Roman Catholic. Remarkably, when the Ku Klux Klan was in its most reputable phase, Truman briefly joined, thinking it would help him with his campaign for the county judgeship, but he quit when he was told it would mean he'd have to fire Catholic city employees. Truman himself was raised as a Baptist. Although he made no reference to the history of persecution of Baptists, he did explain that the nature of the denomination—"whose church authority starts from the bottom up—

not the top"—contributed to his small-*d* democratic impulses.[55] All of his ecumenical tendencies were magnified a hundredfold by the war. "Minor, and even major, differences in how we choose to worship God strike me as being of relatively little importance in the face of an aggressive foe threatening to destroy all freedom of worship and other individual liberties," Truman said.[56]

Many of the interfaith efforts that began during the war continued after the fighting ended. The Ad Council ran a public service campaign from 1946 to 1952 called "United America." A typical print ad featured an illustration of a bird hanging up a sign reading "No Catholics, Jews, Protestants," prompting another bird to scold, "Only silly humans do that!" The United America campaign made more than 293 million listener impressions on the radio.[57] Even the etiquette mavens got in on it. In 1952, socialite Amy Vanderbilt's *Complete Book of Etiquette* included a chapter on interfaith courtesy and understanding.[58] As part of a massive public service campaign sponsored by the American Heritage Foundation, crowds recited en masse "The Freedom Pledge."

> I am an American. A free American.
> Free to speak—without fear
> Free to worship God in my own way
> Free to stand for what I think right
> Free to oppose what I believe wrong. . . .[59]

Hollywood's posture continued to evolve. Although several studios had Jewish leaders, they had shied away from depicting anti-Semitism, fearing it would cause a backlash. After the war, they started to address it directly. In 1947, 20th Century Fox, run by a non-Jew, produced *Gentleman's Agreement*, about a Gentile journalist (played by Gregory Peck) who passes as Jewish to see how he's treated in the elite country club circles. This sophisticated depiction of genteel anti-Semitism won an Oscar for Best Picture and, more surprisingly, was one of Fox's highest-grossing films of the year.

Celebrities can affect both the majority culture's acceptance of religious minorities and the self-image of the members of those faiths. On September 2, 1945, the twenty-one-year-old Bess Myerson—who hailed from the Shalom Aleichem Houses in the North Bronx—was crowned

Miss America. No hyperassimilated Jew, she came fully loaded with risky characteristics: Jewish surname, immigrant roots. She rejected pageant managers' requests that she change her name, and she wore her Judaism, and her borrowed swimsuit, with pride. "It was remarkable for a Jew—especially the child of poor, radical, New York immigrants—to become the exemplar of American womanhood at a time of anti-Semitism and opposition to large-scale immigration of Jewish refugees," wrote Edward Shapiro.[60]

That same month, a man who had grown up just five miles away from Meyerson, in the South Bronx, also smashed cultural stereotypes when he hit a ninth inning grand slam, allowing the Detroit Tigers to win the pennant. Hank Greenberg was tough, big, athletic, and one of the best hitters of the day. Best of all, Greenberg had served in the military for more than four years, busting another anti-Semitic stereotype, that Jews shirked military service. He too was showered with anti-Semitic epithets—"Jew bastard," "pants presser," and "kike son of a bitch"—but shrugged them off and even refused to work on Yom Kippur.

Of course, the place of Jews after the war was profoundly affected by two seismic events: the Holocaust and the birth of Israel.

The newsreels began showing evidence of genocide in May 1945, but it would be decades before it was fully processed. It did fairly quickly make Jews realize that lying low was no longer an option; anti-Semitism could metastasize into something more dangerous than a block on upward mobility. "To accept quietly any form of anti-Semitism, many believed, would be a cowardly betrayal of the six million European Jewish victims of Hitler," wrote Shapiro.[61] For instance, national Jewish groups had previously been quite cautious about challenging the Christian imprint on public schools lest it cause an anti-Jewish backlash, especially while they were trying to build interfaith bridges. After the Holocaust, while some Jewish leaders maintained that reticence, others aggressively pursued legal advocacy for separation of church and state. The American Jewish Congress, guided by its associate counsel Leo Pfeffer, became a leading player in US Supreme Court challenges to prayer in school and other First Amendment cases.[62] "It represented an epochal transformation in their self image," wrote Gregg Ivers in *To Build a Wall*.[63] What's more, American Jews had been handed the mantle of leadership, as the United States was now the home of the most important Jewish community in the world.[64]

In 1948, the state of Israel was created, giving Jews great pride and also providing another reason for Gentiles to support Jews. Other Americans viewed it as an important element in the Cold War scramble to win the Middle East. Truman recognized Israel over the strong objections of his own Department of State, explaining later that, despite resistance from Arab allies, he could protect American interests "while at the same time helping these unfortunate victims of persecution to find a home."[65]

The growing Jewish assertiveness and self-confidence took place during a period when religion in general played a greater role in public life. Some of this was driven by demographics and economics. As the suburbs mushroomed, communities built more and more churches and synagogues. Rabbis, priests, and ministers had a lot of work to do.

Ike, Under God

To a degree rarely acknowledged, a key figure in defining the role of faith and religious freedom was Dwight Eisenhower, who didn't even belong to a church when he arrived at the White House. It was during the Eisenhower administrations that Congress added the phrase "Under God" to the Pledge of Allegiance and "In God We Trust" to our paper currency. In 1956, In God We Trust replaced E Pluribus Unum as the national motto. Eisenhower began his cabinet meetings with a moment of prayer. He initiated the presidential "Prayer Breakfast," a tradition that persists to this day. And he delivered probably the most religion-soaked inaugural address in American history. Jefferson would have been appalled, as Eisenhower began with a prayer that he composed himself, asking God to bring about a spirit of cooperation between people of different politics.[66] He then called for "a conscious renewal of faith in our country," contrasting the American approach with that of the Communists, who "know no god but force, no devotion but its use." Privately explaining his hope for his inaugural address to his advisors, Eisenhower said he wanted to mobilize the nation into a "spiritual crusade"[67] and "to point out that we were getting too secular."[68] In the speech, he used the word "faith" fourteen times.

And to make sure questions weren't raised about his own piety, ten days after being sworn in as president, Eisenhower was baptized as a Presbyterian.[69]

Significantly, Eisenhower did not cast this as a Christian crusade. He spoke broadly of God and faith, not Christ. When he signed the legislation in 1954 that inserted "under God" into the Pledge, Eisenhower declared: "In this way we are reaffirming the transcendence of religious faith in America's heritage and future; in this way we shall constantly strengthen those spiritual weapons which forever will be our country's most powerful resource, in peace or in war."[70]

In fact, he was the first president to use the term "Judeo-Christian." It happened a month before he was sworn in, when he was explaining that our rights came from the Creator.

> In other words, our form of government has no sense unless it is founded in a deeply felt religious faith, and I don't care what it is. With us of course it is the Judeo-Christian concept, but it must be a religion that all men are created equal.[71]

Some mocked his "I don't care what it is" line. As one critic put it, Eisenhower seemed to be "a very fervent believer in a very vague religion."[72] But in his own way, he captured well the way most Americans were increasingly approaching faith—with a combination of passion and tolerance. Eisenhower understood that a surge in "God talk" *required* a parallel emphasis on pluralism. Overtly describing America as a Christian nation was uncomfortable, even during the war. The scholar Mark Silk wrote, "After the revelations of the Nazi death camps, a phrase like 'our Christian civilization' seemed ominously exclusive; greater comprehensiveness was needed for proclaiming the spirituality of the American Way."[73] The society that boasted to the world about its tolerance could not then rhetorically exclude religious minorities. On the other hand, Eisenhower could not promote secularism, which was both out of sync with America and a poor contrast to godless Communism. So, he fashioned a modern synthesis: assertive but pluralistic religiosity.

Two other factors must be considered when contemplating Eisenhower's role. While most US presidents have become deeply familiar with the facts about the Holocaust, only one witnessed it with his own eyes. As supreme commander of the Allied Expeditionary Force, Eisenhower toured multiple concentration camps and—in a historically important step—insisted that both lawmakers and the news media come in to document the atrocities. After visiting the Ohrdruf concentration camp near Gotha, Germany, he cabled to his superior, George C. Marshall:

> The things I saw beggar description. . . . The visual evidence
> and the verbal testimony of starvation, cruelty and bestiality
> were so overpowering as to leave me a bit sick. In one room,
> where there were piled up twenty or thirty naked men, killed
> by starvation, George Patton would not even enter. He said
> that he would get sick if he did so. I made the visit deliberately,
> in order to be in a position to give first-hand evidence of these
> things if ever, in the future, there develops a tendency to
> charge these allegations merely to "propaganda."[74]

He didn't say much about how the Holocaust affected his posture as president, but surely it must have contributed to his inclusive approach.

Finally, there's the mysterious matter of Eisenhower's own religious upbringing. He was raised a Jehovah's Witness. Yes, the religion that earned such obloquy by its opposition to the draft, militarism, and patriotism, was the childhood faith of the man who led the Allied forces in World War II. For years, Eisenhower and his brothers downplayed their Jehovah's Witnesses upbringing (one brother even deleted references to the Witnesses from a biography),[75] but subsequent historians have said that the case is pretty clear. Not only were his parents believers; they were leaders in the Jehovah's Witnesses community in Abilene, Kansas. Their house served as the venue for Witness meetings, and the children often participated, offering their interpretations of scriptural readings. His mother, Ida Eisenhower, was a pacifist; she was deeply disappointed with Eisenhower's decision to attend West Point.

Eisenhower left the Jehovah's Witnesses when he joined the military, but he always praised his mother's faith—and he was sworn in on the Bible that she gave him, which used the word "Jehovah" instead of "God" throughout. He could not have been oblivious to the intense persecution of the Witnesses during World Wars I and II.

Good for the Jews

While the rise of the Judeo-Christian terminology was, on one level, a triumph for tolerance—and beneficial for all three religions—it was especially good for the Jews. As a small, historically despised minority, they had the most to gain by being treated as an equal part of an American faith triumvirate. The more deeply the notion of Judeo-Christian heritage became entrenched, the less likely it was that anti-Semitism could receive official sanction. The change made it more difficult for Christians to argue that the United States was in any legalistic way a Christian nation. Solutions to church-state controversies now had to accommodate the views of Jews. The rise of the Judeo-Christian heritage model meant the death of Christian America as the dominant archetype.

To be sure, anti-Semitism has persisted up until the present day, and even increased significantly in 2016 and 2017. The worst attack on Jews in American history took place not in 1918 but in 2018, at the Tree of Life synagogue in Pittsburgh. At a certain point, if one fears being murdered when attending shul—or if full religious liberty now requires having an armed guard perpetually stationed outside the doors of your house of worship—then it may feel like an emptier freedom.

But it does matter that structural and official anti-Semitism mostly has fallen away. In 1948, the US Supreme Court invalidated restricted covenants on housing, whether applied against blacks, Asians, or Jews. In 1960, Pope John XXIII removed the word "perfidious," as in "perfidious Jews," from the Good Friday liturgy. Evangelicals gradually became enamored of Israel—in part because they viewed it as a sign of the coming of Christ's millennial reign (indeed, support for Israel has become a central plank in the evangelical platform). Universities eased their anti-Jewish quotas. Public opinion polls showed a dramatic drop in anti-Semitism. In 1940, more than 25 percent said they wouldn't want to work alongside Jews; by the 1960s, almost no one would admit to that.[76] Remarking on the dramatic turnaround, the sociologist Seymour Martin Lipset declared, "Their energy and achievements are viewed with admiration. . . . Jews have arrived."[77] Noting the strong support offered the Jewish community following the Pittsburgh attacks, John Podhoretz, editor of *Commentary*, wrote, "The philo-Semitic response to this unspeakable act of anti-Semitism reveals how American Jews are anchored in America in a way that Jews who live anywhere else outside of Israel are not. . . . On this day of all days it needs to be said: America has been a blessing for the Jewish people unlike any other blessing given any other people in the history of the world."

The World War II period offers important lessons about religious freedom more broadly. The three wartime leaders used religious freedom, as much as religion, as a rallying cry. The concept had gained such strength that it could serve as a source of national cohesion. It had already been clear that having a variety of faiths would keep one of them from dominating. Now, it became clear that the very *idea* of religious freedom could also unify.

In the twentieth century, we also see the rise to power of leaders from groups that had been persecuted in the nineteenth century. Harry Truman was the first president raised as a Baptist, the same faith that was persecuted in Madison's backyard. Eisenhower was raised as a Jehovah's Witness. His vice president, Richard Nixon, was a Quaker. None of them invoked the persecution of their forebears to explain their contemporary actions, but it's not hard to imagine that the historical scars affected the way they approached religious freedom.

Again, the immigration that had initially stirred religious conflict—in this case the arrival of Eastern European Jews—eventually strengthened religious pluralism.

The rise of tri-faith Judeo-Christian America fully cemented the idea that religious freedom was a matter of rights not toleration. The importance of the concept to Jews in particular had been evident even to George Washington. It was to the Touro Synagogue in Rhode Island that he wrote:

> It is now no more that toleration is spoken of as if it were the
> indulgence of one class of people that another enjoyed the exercise
> of their inherent natural rights, for, happily, the Government of the
> United States, which gives to bigotry no sanction, to persecution
> no assistance, requires only that they who live under its protection
> should demean themselves as good citizens.[78]

After World War II, few would challenge that idea.

America had to adjust to a new way of resolving religious disputes. If the majority no longer got to decide by itself what counted as fair-minded, who would? Take the issue of nondenominational prayer in public schools. Before World War II, Protestants generally adjudicated whether a given prayer was sufficiently broad-minded. Fairness was in the eye of the majority. But if religious minorities had greater voice, they might read that same prayer differently, and say so.

It turned out that the mechanism for resolving these disputes would change too. Moving from toleration to rights meant moving from the political system to the judicial system. Going forward, the primary locus of conflict would no longer be Congress, the state legislature, or the local school board.

It would be the United States Supreme Court.

Amish men attending Supreme Court case, 1971

Chapter Twelve

ENTER THE SUPREME COURT

The full power of the First Amendment is finally felt as the Court becomes a major player.

Ellery Schempp's historic act of civil disobedience began with a charmingly nerdy bit of propaganda. On little strips of paper, the sixteen-year-old typed a quote from Thomas Jefferson—"I have sworn eternal hostility against every form of tyranny over the mind of man." He then scattered them in classrooms throughout his Philadelphia-area public high school.

Ellery was protesting what had become a daily ritual at his school. Every morning, the students listened as Bible verses were read over the school's public-address system. The students then stood to recite the Lord's Prayer. Mind you, Ellery was not anti-religion. He and his family attended services at a Unitarian church in the Germantown section of Philadelphia every Sunday. But the Bible readings gnawed at him. Perhaps reading Thoreau's *Civil Disobedience* in English class had stirred a rebellious strain. Or maybe he'd absorbed the tolerance-loving theology of the Unitarians. How could the United States Constitution permit a public school to have group Bible readings? Was this some sort of mistake? What he did that fall of 1956 triggered a series of events that, according to many people, undermined religious freedom in American—or, in the view of many others, including myself, powerfully safeguarded and cemented those liberties.

On November 16, Ellery's homeroom teacher asked students to clear their desks so they could focus as a student volunteer read ten Bible verses over the public-address system. Ellery instead took out a copy of the Quran and perused a random page. This, he later explained, was his "particular way of showing that there is another religious tradition and another holy book that is respected by zillions of people around the world, and it has equal status in the global perspective with the Christian Bible."

Then the taxpayer-funded teacher asked the students to stand for the Lord's Prayer. Ellery remained seated.

> *And lead us not into temptation, but deliver us from evil: For thine is the kingdom, and the power, and the glory, for ever. Amen.*

He then stood for the Pledge of Allegiance, but that did not assuage his teacher, who sent him to the principal's office. There, the assistant principal asked him, "All those other students, three thousand students, they're all doing it, and why can't you?"

It was, Ellery responded, "a matter of religious freedom."[1]

The school was not impressed by his idealism. After Tufts University accepted Ellery, the principal urged the university to retract its acceptance, given his misbehavior. But Ellery had the last laugh, twice. Tufts did not revoke his acceptance, and in 1963, the United States Supreme Court issued a landmark ruling declaring that he had been right. In *School District of Abington Township v. Schempp*, the Court ruled 8–1 that the Pennsylvania law mandating Bible readings was unconstitutional because the state— through the law and the behavior of the government-paid teachers— showed a clear preference for Christianity. When the government favors a particular religious approach, the Court concluded, it undermines the freedoms of others.

Modern religious conservatives view this case, along with *Engel v. Vitale*, a prayer case decided in 1962, as among the worst decisions of the century. Senator Strom Thurmond spoke for many, then and since, when he described it as a "conspiracy to throw God completely out of national life."[2] How can Americans have real religious freedom when God is excluded from such an important institution? They also suspected, with some justification, that this was the first step toward removing religion from public spaces more generally. The *Washington Evening Star* stated: "God and religion have been all but driven from the public schools. What remains? Will the baccalaureate service and Christmas carols be the next to go? Don't bet against it."[3] In later years, many Christians concluded that the prayer decisions led to an unraveling of America's social fabric. Influential Christian historian David Barton penned a book arguing that the prayer decisions helped cause everything from rising crime to lower SAT scores.[4]

These decisions also awakened Americans to a new reality: that the United States Supreme Court was now a central player in the fight over religious freedom. To modern ears, that may seem odd. Wasn't the Supreme Court always the main adjudicator of religious freedom? Actually, no. Its deep involvement—a central facet of modern religious freedom debates—arose only after World War II. For most of American history, the First and then the Fourteenth Amendments had limited reach. That changed with the Court's ascendance.

If the Madisonian model required a competitive religious marketplace, it would also need to make sure the competition was fair, especially to those who had little political clout. It would need a powerful umpire actively interpreting the religious freedom clauses of the First Amendment. This chapter attempts to describe how the Court has handled this new responsibility. Though politicians have debated whether this Supreme Court justice or that supported or opposed religious liberty, that's a silly framing. They have all supported religious freedom. There are more interesting questions: Through whose eyes did they view the issue? Did they err on the side of protecting freedom of action for the majority religion or the minority religion? The government or the individual?

At any given moment, the Court might seem inconsistent and confused. The longer arc is clearer: on balance, the Court over the past fifty years has dramatically expanded and strengthened religious freedom, but not in the ways one might expect. The general philosophy that has emerged is that government involvement in overt religion should be limited, but also that, as a society, we should bend over backward to make sure that secular laws don't inadvertently do any damage to religious freedom.

The States of Religious Freedom

From 1620 until around 1947, the religious liberties of Americans were mostly in the hands of local governments. By World War II, most state constitutions had language both defending the rights of "conscience" and thanking God. Though it's hard to generalize, most states protected the right to private worship, wrote the scholar John Witte Jr., who did an exhaustive survey of state regulations of religion.

Most religious individuals were granted rights to assemble, speak, publish, parent, educate, travel, and the like on the basis of their religious beliefs. Most religious groups were generally afforded the rights to incorporate, to hold property, to receive private donations, to enforce religious laws, and to maintain buildings, schools, and charities for their voluntary members.

But at the same time, many states allowed, or even required, "patronage of one common public religion." They did not accept Madison's view that the mingling of church and state—or attempts to have a "public religion"—would ultimately undermine religious freedom. The majoritarian bias, Witte explained, sometimes meant that religious minorities received shoddy treatment.

The New England states, for example, continued to resist the missionizing efforts of Quakers, Baptists, and Methodists, routinely delaying delivery of their corporate charters, tax exemptions, and educational licenses.

New York, New Jersey, and Pennsylvania were similarly churlish with Unitarians, Adventists, and Christian Scientists, often turning a blind eye to private abuses against them. Virginia and the Carolinas tended to be hard on conservative Episcopalians and upstate Evangelicals alike.

Many Southern states were notorious in their resistance to Catholic churches, schools, missions, and literature. Few legislatures and courts, outside of the main cities on the Eastern seaboard, showed much respect for the religious rights of the few Jews or Muslims about, let alone the religious rights of Native Americans or enslaved African Americans.[5]

Government routinely abandoned neutrality and expressed public support for religion and, often, for Protestantism or Christianity.

Crucifixes were erected in state parks and on statehouse grounds. Flags flew at half mast on Good Friday. . . . Subsidies were given to Christian missionaries on the frontier. . . . Property grants and tax subsidies were furnished to Christian schools and charities. . . . Employees in state prisons, reformatories, orphanages, and asylums were required to know and to teach basic Christian beliefs and values. . . . Blasphemy and sacrilege were still prosecuted.[6]

And the Bible was read in many public schools. After World War II, two dozen states permitted Bible reading, and twelve required it.

All this was possible because the US Supreme Court had not interpreted the Fourteenth Amendment the way John Bingham had wanted. For almost eighty years, conservative judges continued to defer to the states, as they had before the Civil War. That began to change in 1940, through one of the Jehovah's Witnesses cases, *Cantwell v. State of Connecticut*, in which the Court ruled that the Free Exercise Clause protected people from discriminatory acts of state and local governments.

In 1947, in *Everson v. Board of Education*, the Court then also "incorporated" the establishment clause of the First Amendment, which declares that "Congress shall make no law respecting an establishment of religion."[7] This tends to be the part of the First Amendment that is in play when judges consider questions touching on the separation of church and state.

Once the United States Supreme Court had declared its intention to judge local laws, it then merely had to define religious freedom.

Separation of Church and State

In *Everson*, the Court focused on the meaning of the Establishment Clause. Did that cryptic phrase intend merely to block the establishment of a state religion? Or did it prohibit taxpayer support for religion more generally? The Court disagreed with a New Jersey taxpayer who objected that his tax dollars were being used to subsidize the transportation of students to parochial schools. But it offered a set of guidelines and then these controversial words: "In the words of Jefferson, the clause against establishment of religion by law was intended to erect 'a wall of separation between Church and State.'"

As we saw in chapter 2, some modern conservatives maintain that the idea of a separation of church and state was concocted by the Supreme Court in that 1947 *Everson* ruling. As one writer put it, "Where then did the doctrine of 'separation of church and state' originate? The answer is in the U.S. Supreme Court's 1947 decision of *Everson v. Board of Education*."[8] Many sermons note (accurately) that the phrase "separation of church and state" does not appear in the Constitution. But Madison as well as Jefferson explicitly pressed the idea of separation repeatedly. Madison in particular thought separation would help religion flourish. "Every new & successful example therefore of a perfect separation between ecclesiastical and civil matters, is of importance," he wrote. "And I have no doubt that every new example, will succeed, as every past one has done, in shewing that religion & Govt. will both exist in greater purity, the less they are mixed together."[9] The term was used by the Court itself in 1878 and came up routinely during political debates, including the fight over the Blaine Amendment and the treatment of American Indians. The motives for using the phrase varied. The Klan was concerned less with advancing religious freedom than with crushing Catholics.[10] There's room for debate about what the phrase means, who embraced it, or whether it's even a useful metaphor. But the idea that it was invented, or even rescued from obscurity, by the Court in 1947 is nonsense.

In *Everson*, the Court laid out what it thought the Establishment Clause meant:

> Neither a state nor the Federal Government can set up a church.
> Neither can pass laws which aid one religion, aid all religions, or
> prefer one religion over another. Neither can force nor influence a
> person to go to or to remain away from church against his will or
> force him to profess a belief or disbelief in any religion. No person
> can be punished for entertaining or professing religious beliefs
> or disbeliefs, for church attendance or non-attendance. No tax in
> any amount, large or small, can be levied to support any religious
> activities or institutions, whatever they may be called, or whatever
> form they may adopt to teach or practice religion.[11]

The full implications of this approach became apparent when the Court limited prayer and Bible reading in public schools. The year before deciding Ellery Schempp's case, the Court struck down a prayer that the State of New York crafted for voluntary use by local school districts. The prayer in question:

> Almighty God, we acknowledge our dependence upon Thee, and
> we beg Thy blessings upon us, our parents, our teachers and our
> country. Amen.

The plaintiffs in *Engel v. Vitale*—three Jews and two "spiritual" people who did not belong to an organized religion—objected to their children having to recite prayers. The Court agreed 6 to 1, with three Republican-appointed justices joining three appointed by Democrats. In hindsight, it seemed constitutionally fairly clear-cut: the prayer had actually been written by the state and offered for distribution through state employees (teachers) to impressionable youngsters. The prohibition of an "establishment," they explained, did not merely block government from setting up an official church; it means the state cannot use its "power, prestige and financial support" to support "a particular religious belief."[12]

Many believers were outraged. The prayer seemed to them quite generic—Jesus is not mentioned—and exactly the sort that the founders regularly sprinkled into their own proclamations. But religious language is rarely truly neutral. The phrase "we beg Thy blessings upon us" assumes the existence of a God that hears and responds to prayers. The phrase "we acknowledge our dependence upon Thee" assumes a personal God that is intimately involved in the affairs of the living, at odds with the beliefs of Unitarians, Buddhists, some Quakers, and many Reform Jews.

In both *Schempp* and *Engel*, the court ruled that students need to be protected not only from coercion but also from pressure. Allowing students to leave the room during the prayer was not sufficient. Those students were being placed on a lower plane, treated unequally.[13]

Many religious groups opposed the rulings. The most surprising was the Catholic Church. In the 1830s and 1920s, the Church had been brutally persecuted for opposing state-sponsored prayer in school. But this time the Church switched sides. "No one who believes in God can approve such a decision," said Cardinal Francis Spellman of New York.[14] With Protestant-Catholic antagonism declining, Catholics now focused more on how separatism could undermine their own public expressions of faith and their continued desire to win tax support for parochial schools.

Implicit in these rulings, and in many others, is a core idea that some Protestants have long resisted. When it comes to religion, the majority cannot get special privileges. In recent decades, a cottage industry has sprung up making the case that America is a Christian nation and that both the Constitution and the founders intended to codify that preference. These advocates largely make their case by offering various quotations from Founding Fathers about the importance of Christianity in their lives and to the health of the nation. Then they put forth a great non sequitur—that because many founders loved Christianity as individuals, they therefore wanted the state to promote Christianity. But the idea that America is a Christian nation in a legal or constitutional sense is not embraced today by even the most conservative Supreme Court justices and scholars.

When it came to constitutional law, the tri-faith alliance began to erode. The American Jewish Congress and its lead attorney, Leo Pfeffer, played important behind-the-scenes roles in driving forward the *Engel*, *Everson*, and *Schempp* cases. They pressed strict separation despite the resistance or queasiness of the other major Jewish organizations, the American Jewish Committee and the Anti-Defamation League, which feared that such a strategy would disrupt efforts to improve relations with the Catholic and Protestant groups, potentially inviting an anti-Semitic reaction.[15] But Jewish leaders came to see separation as a proxy for equality. "For [Jews]—but not for others—the separation of church and state constitutes and defines their individual and group status in American society, because to breach separation is to Christianize America, relegating Jews to second class citizenship," wrote Peter Medding.[16] Sure enough, the Catholic magazine *America* zeroed in on the Jewish role in these cases: "What will have been accomplished if our Jewish friends win all the legal immunities they seek, but thereby paint themselves into a corner of social and cultural alienation?"[17]

The Supreme Court has struggled to devise rules governing these church-state Establishment Clause questions. Its most significant early attempt occurred in *Lemon v. Kurtzman* in 1971, when the Court ruled 8–1 that a Pennsylvania education law was unconstitutional because the state reimbursed religious private schools. This was not a leftist putsch: five of the eight justices in the majority were appointed by Republican presidents, and the opinion was written by Chief Justice Warren Burger, who was appointed by Richard Nixon. Burger suggested three tests:

– First, the law must have a secular legislative purpose.

– Second, its principal or primary effect must be one that neither advances nor inhibits religion.

– Third, the statute must not foster "an excessive government entanglement with religion."[18]

The Court emphasized that the legislative brain must be focused on secular goals. This is in sync with Madison's suggestion that religion should not be in the "cognizance" of government. But it also conflicted with various noncontroversial uses of religion in public life. The Court sessions begin with an exhortation from the marshal: "God save the United States and this Honorable Court!" What is the secular purpose of that? And what about all the presidents who invoke God, or the "under God" phrase of the Pledge of Allegiance? Or the countless other steps government takes to encourage religion? Don't those violate the *Lemon* test by advancing religion?

Over time, the Court concluded that the *Lemon* test was too rigid and sometimes led to religion being penalized. For instance, a state could give college scholarships to all students except those getting divinity degrees. There was a narrow logic: taxpayer money should not go to a religious institution. But it also went against the spirit of the First Amendment by discriminating *against* religion.

The Supreme Court has continued to tinker, with mixed success. In *Marsh v. Chambers*, the Court said that the Nebraska legislature could have a clergyman open the sessions with a prayer because of the "unique history" of chaplains playing this role. If it was okay with the founders, it's okay with us. That's not really an argument that stands up if you think about it too hard. The founders disagreed with each other about taxpayer-funded chaplains. Still, the Court was at least trying to find a practical way of avoiding the perils of state involvement while allowing for some religious expression in public situations. The conservative, or anti-separationist, view hardened around the idea that as long as government didn't promote a particular religion, it could encourage religion in general and give room for people to express themselves.

As with the Bible fights of the nineteenth century, the twentieth-century efforts to bring more religion into the public sphere came with a cost: a weakening of the integrity of the very prayers and symbols being put forward. To pass Court muster, lawmakers and activists concocted secular purposes for religious acts. In *Marsh v. Chambers*, the Court said that a prayer before the legislature was fine because it wasn't so much a religious expression as it was an acknowledgment of the religiosity of the community.

That's right: a prayer wasn't a religious expression.

In *Lynch v. Donnelly* (1984), the Court said that the crèche that the city fathers of Pawtucket, Rhode Island, had displayed downtown since 1943 (along with a Santa Claus house, a Christmas tree, and a "Seasons Greetings" banner) had only "remote" and "indirect" religious content because it "merely happens to coincide or harmonize with the tenets of some . . . religions." It was really, they said, a *history* presentation. "The crèche in the display depicts the historical origins of this traditional event long recognized as a National Holiday."[19]

The Court later separately concluded that a menorah was not a religious symbol because it was juxtaposed with Christmas trees, and everyone knows that Christmas trees long ago lost their spiritual pizzazz.

Just by being near the Christmas trees, the menorahs got secularized too. Another judge suggested that a menorah could be transformed from a religious symbol to a secular symbol if Christmas lights were strung on a nearby tree.[20] You may recall that in order to require readings of the King James Version of the Bible in the 1920s, Protestants argued that it was a work of literature. The State of Pennsylvania tried the same thing in defending the Bible reading and Lord's Prayer recitation during Ellery Schempp's case. "We're teaching morality without religion," the attorney for the school district said.[21]

There are two problems with this approach. First, it invites religious leaders to deceive themselves and the public. To claim that a crèche—a depiction of the birth of the savior from his virgin mother—is not a religious scene is just flat-out disingenuous. In order to get the courts to agree to having the Ten Commandments posted in two counties in Kentucky, the state argued that the tablets weren't religious; they were symbols of "the foundations of American Law and Government."[22]

More important, this approach of cutely sneaking religion in through the secular backdoor has the effect of stripping symbols of their spiritual meaning. One has to ask: What's the point of getting people to read the Bible if you have to declare, in effect, that it's *not* a revelation from God? Don't believers lose more than they gain from this gambit?[23]

Liberals, meanwhile, have also become ensnared in a legal trap of their own making. Legal philosopher Martha Nussbaum argues that the Court, and progressive scholars, have come to mistakenly think of separation of church and state as an end in itself. Separation for separation's sake can lead to strange outcomes or bizarre hostility to religion, which was not Madison's intention. For instance, no one would want a city to forbid its firefighters from putting out a fire in a church. Strict separation might also require that someone laid off from a job at a religious organization not collect unemployment benefits. But that too would be a perverse result: penalizing religion in order to protect it.

Over time, different justices offered new formulas to capture the spirit of the First Amendment better than just "separation of church and state." They coalesced around the idea of "neutrality," as one interpretation of what Madison and the other founders were really after when they advocated for separation. But the justices disagreed about what neutrality means. Separationists usually argue that government neutrality means not favoring religion over nonreligion. The traditionalists argued that government *could* show preference for religion in general so long as it did not favor one religion over another.

Justice Sandra Day O'Connor suggested that the Court focus on equality rather than separation. Government should not be allowed to take steps that could be seen by an objective party as endorsing a particular religion. Under this logic, a crèche by itself would violate the Constitution, but a crèche alongside a menorah wouldn't. The former looks like the government backing Christianity; the latter looks like the government, as a public service, making space to honor the religious traditions of various citizens. Diversity becomes the solution rather than the problem. "The Madisonian conception of equality is richer and more substantive [than the idea of separation of church and state]: it means that the public realm respects and treats citizens as people of equal worth and entitlement," Nussbaum wrote.[24]

Consensus has eluded the Court. It continues to experiment with ever more fine-grain distinctions. For instance, it has frowned upon legislative appropriations for religious organizations but allowed charitable tax deductions for donations to religious organizations because in the latter case it is the individual, not the government, making the choice. Some vouchers for students going to private schools may be tolerable, since the choice of a religion is made by a parent, not a legislator.[25] Schools cannot have religious instruction on school grounds,[26] but they can allow students to go off-site for religious instruction[27] (a movement known now as Weekday Religious Instruction).[28] In *Wallace v. Jaffree*, the State of Alabama had set aside a moment of silence for "meditation or voluntary prayer." The majority concluded that moment-of-silence periods were fine, but this particular one was not. The reason: the legislative history showed that Alabama intended this to have a religious purpose (one of the sponsors boasted that the point of the law was to "return voluntary prayer" to the schools). The words were constitutional, but the intent was not. "Few areas of law today are so riven with wild generalizations and hair-splitting distinctions, so given to grand statements of principle and petty applications of precept, so rife with selective readings of history and inventive renderings of precedent," grumbled Witte.[29]

In fairness to the Court, this muddiness reflects the founders' own disagreements and ambivalence about the interplay of church and state. They wanted strict limits on the involvement of government in religion and vice versa—yet simultaneously hired chaplains and issued prayer proclamations.

Modern jurists are no different—they have a general desire for religious freedom but are inconsistent about what on earth that means.

Free Exercise

The cases discussed so far in this chapter have related to church-state conflicts governed by the Establishment Clause. We now turn to the second clause—the right to freely "exercise" your religion. Here, the same Court that "kicked out God" then expanded religious freedom and, indeed, has given religion a privileged position in American society.

Legislatures cannot make laws designed to harm a particular religion. That's easy. But the Court repeatedly wrestled with the tougher question of what happens when a secular law hurts a religion as an unintended side effect. Government has long carved out exceptions to help religious groups in such situations. For instance, since the beginning of the country, states and the national government have recognized the idea of conscientious objection—allowing Americans to avoid military service if their religion forbids participation in war. As president, James Madison personally pardoned a group of Quakers who had refused to fight in the War of 1812.[30] Congress also exempted Quakers from the requirement that they swear an oath in courts, allowing them to pledge truthfulness in their own way. In 1798, the Rhode Island state legislature exempted Jews from anti-incest laws because Jewish law at the time allowed marriages between an uncle and a niece.[31] A particularly important case arose in 1812 in New York when a Catholic priest named Anthony Kohlmann became entangled in a local burglary case. Kohlmann had come into the possession of some stolen property and returned it to the victim. When the police demanded information about the thief, the priest refused to cooperate because he had learned the incriminating information during a confession. Mayor DeWitt Clinton, a Protestant, ruled in favor of the priest, declaring that preservation of priest-parishioner confidentiality was "essential to the free exercise of a religion." Once again, the normal rule—in this case the law against covering up a crime—was put aside in order to protect religious freedom.[32] (Clinton would go only so far, though, commenting that if Hindus burned widows or pagans pushed "bacchanalian orgies or human sacrifices," the state would have to insist on enforcing the law.)[33]

But deciding when government should offer such exceptions can be difficult. In 1879, for instance, the Court had refused to accommodate the Mormon's religiously motivated practice of polygamy.

The Court's first major twentieth-century attempt involved Adele Sherbert, a textile worker in Beaumont Mills, South Carolina.[34] The factory that employed her instituted a six-day workweek—Monday through Saturday. But Sherbert was a Seventh-day Adventist, which teaches that the Sabbath is Saturday (Exod. 31:15: "Six days may work be done; but in the seventh is the Sabbath of rest, holy to the LORD: whosoever doeth any work in the Sabbath day, he shall surely be put to death"). Sherbert quit and applied for unemployment benefits but was rejected on the grounds that she had left her original job voluntarily and turned down opportunities to work at other factories (which also required work on Saturdays). The State of South Carolina had a reasonable position. The law didn't target Seventh-day Adventists; the state was blind—or noncognizant, as Madison might have said—as to whether it hurt or helped a particular religion. The law was the law.

The Court issued its ruling in *Sherbert v. Verner* on June 17, 1963—the same day it invalidated prayer in school. The Court that had, in the view of religious believers, ejected religion from schools, in the very next breath gave religion a stunningly privileged status. The Court ruled 7–2 in favor of Sherbert, saying that the state should have *accommodated* her religious practices. Justice William Brennan, appointed by President Eisenhower, offered a two-part test to guide decisions. First, determine whether the law in question burdens or pressures someone to forgo a religious practice. That can be in the form of coercion or the denial of a benefit.

Second, the government *can* infringe upon someone's religious practice but only if there is a "compelling state interest" and no other regulation could be conjured to achieve that same goal.

If the law doesn't meet either of those tests, then the state must "accommodate" the person's religious practice. In lay terms, the state had to bend over backward to avoid making a religious person choose between the law and his or her faith.

This fundamentally transformed the nature of religious liberty. No longer would it be defined only by the absence of intentional persecution. The ideal would now be something more expansive, more nuanced—a system that grants people tremendous space in which to live their faith, even when that conflicts with laws that other people have to abide by. For instance, in 1972, in *Wisconsin v. Yoder*, the court held that Amish children could be exempted from laws requiring school attendance after the eighth grade. In a sense, the Court had adopted the view of Roger Williams that conscience was fragile, and the freedom to pursue one's own spiritual path was "the most precious and valuable Jewel."[35]

The problem was, having expressed the idea that the government had a duty to "accommodate" religion, the Court then had to sort through a variety of claims for special treatment. Some state laws are so important, it ruled, that individuals cannot claim religious exemptions. In 1989, for instance, it allowed California to prosecute a Christian Scientist who had refused to give medical care to her four-year-old daughter on religious grounds. The girl died of meningitis.[36] In another case, the Court rejected the claim of an Amish employer who said his religion precluded him from providing Social Security benefits because support of the elderly was the moral obligation of the Amish themselves.[37] The Court figured that allowing individuals exemptions from taxation would destroy the tax system, so while the Amish were certainly burdened, the state interest was plenty compelling.

But at other times, the Court has sided with the religious groups. It chastised the City of Hialeah, Florida, for blocking the animal sacrifice rituals practiced by adherents of Santeria, an African American religion with roots in the slave culture of the Caribbean. The Court saw through the city's claim that the law was for public health (it allowed many other animals to be killed in other situations). Although neutral on its surface, the law actually was targeted against a particular religion.[38] The lawmakers' intent mattered.

These cases exposed something curious about the First Amendment—its two religious clauses occasionally conflict with each other. In order to have a lush, expansive approach to guaranteeing "free exercise" of religion, the government must make accommodations, which is to say, give certain religions legal exemptions. Isn't allowing a particular religion to skip out on a particular law exactly the sort of preferential treatment that the Establishment Clause is supposed to prevent?

The Court has also made a point of protecting disbelievers. In 1961, in *Torcaso v. Watkins*, the Court unanimously struck down a Maryland law requiring that all public office holders offer "a declaration of belief in the existence of God." The Court said government couldn't "aid all religions as against non-believers." But in truth, the efforts to exempt religious behavior from some secular laws do usually privilege religion over non-religion. We can refuse to work on Saturdays if it violates our religion but not because, say, we have to take care of a sick parent. So, when modern conservatives claim that the liberal courts are anti-religion, they're ignoring how progressive judges have approached religious expression. On this, the Court is dramatically pro-religion, to the point that would have likely worried Madison, who wanted government to be religion-blind.

As the Court turned the pieces of the Rubik's Cube in the second half of the twentieth century, a paradox became apparent. Well-intentioned efforts to provide accommodations to religious practice get the government more involved in the inner workings of religious organizations and the thinking of religious people. For instance, the Court has said it's fine for government to provide aid to religious schools or other organizations if they use the money for secular purposes—like remedial education in the case of a Catholic school, or provision of meals through a church-based homeless shelter. But that means the government has to police whether the institutions are keeping the pots of money separate. Congress wants religions to have certain benefits in the tax code—but that means the Internal Revenue Service has to decide what actually counts as a religion. It was, for instance, the IRS that had to pass judgment on the murky question of whether the Church of Scientology is a legitimate religion. (It said yes.)

The problem came to a head in the case of a man named Al Smith, who was definitely no relation to the Catholic New York governor but had other remarkable connections to earlier themes in religious history. Smith was a Native American who had been sent to Christian boarding schools as a boy. He ran away numerous times and ultimately became an alcoholic. Eventually, he found Alcoholics Anonymous, sobered up, and joined the Native American Church, an entrepreneurial new religion that sprang up late in the nineteenth century in the wake of the decimation of Native American tribes. It combined Christianity, a pan-Indian message, and the ingestion of peyote, a hallucinogen that had been used by Native American tribes in North America for at least five hundred years. Smith maintained that peyote use was an essential part of the religion and helped him to stay sober. But he was fired from his job on the staff of an addiction center and then was denied unemployment benefits by the state because he'd used an illegal drug. He argued that this was a violation of his religious freedom, on the basis of the *Sherbert* case.[39]

In 1990, in *Employment Division v. Smith*, the US Supreme Court ruled against Smith—and ditched the *Sherbert* standard. In his opinion for the majority, Justice Antonin Scalia wrote that because the law was neutral in intent, there could be no exemption for religiously motivated behavior. Scalia, a hero with conservatives, restricted religious freedom. To use the flexible standard of the *Sherbert* case would, Scalia wrote, "lead towards anarchy." We'd end up with "religious exemptions from civic obligations of almost every conceivable kind." Scalia's argument about the practical problems of allowing religious groups to easily claim religious liberty violations echoed what Felix Frankfurter had written in his *Barnette* dissent and what the Supreme Court had decided in the nineteenth century when it upheld banning polygamy.

While this may seem incompatible with one strain of conservative ideology (that governments should show deference to religions), it was consistent with another thread of conservatism, favoring "majority rule" over "minority rights." In religious liberty cases, what often defined the conservative position was a reluctance to allow the religious freedom rights of minorities to constrain either the government or Americans who practiced the majority religion. The liberal bloc tended to view the questions more through the eyes of religious minorities.

In this case, though, public reaction to the *Smith* decision was harshly negative among liberals and conservatives alike. In 1993, Congress proposed the Religious Freedom Restoration Act, which reestablished the *Sherbert* test. Testimony during the congressional debate brought home some of the repercussions of the *Smith* decision. William Nouyi Yang, a Laotian immigrant, described the tragedy of his teenage son's death—and his shock when Rhode Island authorities autopsied his body against the family's wishes. Yang's belief system, animism, teaches that mutilation of the body will interfere with reincarnation. A district court at first ruled that the autopsy had violated the family's religious rights, but after the *Smith* ruling, the lower court felt compelled to reverse itself. "Why did he take away our rights and our hope?" Yang asked later. "Why are we excluded from the First Amendment, deprived from constitutional rights?"[40]

The bill's main sponsors in the House of Representatives, where it passed unanimously, were two Jews, Charles Schumer and Stephen Solarz. Its sponsors in the Senate, where it passed 97–3, were Ted Kennedy, a Catholic whose grandparents had told him about the "No Irish Need Apply" signs that used to be posted outside businesses in Boston, and Orrin Hatch, a conservative Mormon from Utah. "As a member of the Church of Jesus Christ of Latter-day Saints," Hatch wrote, "I know of the failures of the state to protect the faithful. I am a member of a faith that, in this Republic's short history, was brutally, murderously persecuted."[41]

In two other instances, Congress stepped in to give religious groups more rights than the Supreme Court had been inclined to offer. In 1984, Congress passed the Equal Access Act, which established the right of religious groups to use public school facilities, even for Bible study.[42] In 1994, the American Indian Religious Freedom Act Amendments restored Native Americans' rights to perform ceremonies at sacred sites on public land. The right to use peyote in religious rituals was established as well.

Given its inconsistency, is it possible to generalize about the role of the Supreme Court in the story of religious freedom since World War II? The thrust has been to expand, refine, and enshrine religious freedom. In the free exercise cases, the Court, despite some zigzags (and sometimes with a push from Congress), has moved in the direction of providing greater rights to individuals. The government can inadvertently infringe but now has to have a damn good reason. Few other countries have such a robust, bend-over-backward approach. As a nation, we moved from defining religious liberty as an absence of persecution to a collective commitment to special sensitivity. This gives America's religious freedom model a higher-order level of refinement, but it has also, just as Frankfurter and Scalia predicted, led to a thicket of difficult questions (as we'll see in chapter 15). The price of this pro-religion approach is more controversial gray-area cases and more judicial involvement in religious freedom disputes. So, when we get frustrated over this or that Supreme Court inconsistency, we should remind ourselves that the alternative—a clear, easy-to-understand rule that secular laws always triumph over religious sensitivities—would greatly restrict our religious freedoms.

At the same time, in the Establishment Clause cases—the church-state fights—the Court has leaned toward restricting the government's role in religion. That too has been beneficial to religious minorities, but it has also diminished the presence of religion in the public sphere and thus feels hostile to some religious people. Conservatives and advocates for traditional religious groups have forced a helpful course correction, demanding that the separation of church and state at least not disadvantage religion.

This conversation continues, often with so much passion that it seems like nothing has been resolved. On the contrary. When we step back from the headlines and take a longer view, it's clear that the Supreme Court has been a powerfully positive force for religious freedom. Of course, this debate is dynamic. New issues continue to force recalibrations. For instance, by the twenty-first century it had become clear that one of the new challenges would be how religious freedom would change if, somehow, there were tens of millions of Americans outside the "Judeo-Christian tradition."

A naturalization ceremony, 2017

Chapter Thirteen

"ALIEN BLOOD"

*Millions of Muslims, Hindus, and
Buddhists enter America—transforming
the dynamics of religious freedom—thanks
to the immigration act of 1965.*

Venkatachalapathi Samuldrala's big moment came on September 14, 2000. The priest of the Shiva Vishnu Temple of Parma, Ohio—a full-service temple celebrating Hindu holidays and performing puja services for a variety of different deities—had been invited to open a session of the US House of Representatives. Samuldrala did not mention Krishna or Vishnu but rather prayed that all Americans would be free from disease and misery.

> O God, You are Omnipresent, Omnipotent, and Omniscient. You are in everything and nothing is beyond You. You are our Mother and Father and we are all Your children. Whatever You do is for our good. You are the ocean of mercy and You forgive our errors. You are our teacher and You guide us into righteousness.

The Family Research Council, one of the leading Christian conservative groups, denounced the House's decision to allow a prayer from a Hindu priest. Its statement no doubt spoke for millions of Christians.

It is one more indication that our nation is drifting from its
Judeo-Christian roots. . . . Alas, in our day, when "tolerance"
and "diversity" have replaced the 10 Commandments as the only
remaining absolute dictums, it has become necessary to "celebrate"
non-Christian religions—even in the halls of Congress.[1]

Robert Regier and Timothy Dailey, the authors of the statement, asserted
that the founders envisioned this as a Christian nation and never intended
to give legitimacy to non-Christian faiths.

Our founders expected that Christianity—and no other religion—
would receive support from the government as long as that support
did not violate people's consciences and their right to worship.
They would have found utterly incredible the idea that all religions,
including paganism, be treated with equal deference. . . .

As for our Hindu priest friend, the United States is a nation that
has historically honored the One True God. Woe be to us on that
day when we relegate Him to being merely one among countless
other deities in the pantheon of theologies.

But then something curious happened. The Family Research Council
partly retracted the statement. The council no doubt still believed that
Christianity was, is, and always should be the driving force in America,
but its executive vice president, Chuck Donovan, issued a clarification.

It is the position of the Family Research Council that governments
must respect freedom of conscience for all people in religious
matters. . . . We affirm the truth of Christianity, but it is not our
position that America's Constitution forbids representatives of
religions other than Christianity from praying before Congress.

The conservative Christian world was really struggling with how to process the march of pluralism—and this time the religious minorities that
were challenging their worldview were not even Christian.

In fact, more than 19 million Americans practice a religion that is not
Christianity—a statistical average of about 44,000 people per congressional district. As of 2017, the United States counted approximately 3,727
synagogues;[2] 2,100 mosques; 810 Hindu temples; 290 Sikh gurdwaras;

2,340 Buddhist centers; 150 Baha'i temples; 60 Afro-Caribbean churches; and 90 Jain worship centers.[3]

The influx of non-Christians once again forces the majority to adjust how it thinks about religious liberty. It challenges the idea that, even as a statistical matter, the United States is a "Christian nation." And it has made it increasingly difficult for Protestants to act like a monopoly power, capable of dictating the terms of religious freedom. In Madisonian terms, it has brought the fullest manifestation of the "multiplicity of sects."

How did this happen? The short answer: the Immigration and Nationality Act of 1965. When signing this legislation, Lyndon Johnson dramatically understated the impact it would have: "This bill that we will sign today is not a revolutionary bill. It does not affect the lives of millions." He was wrong. That law turned US immigration patterns upside down, leading to a flood of newcomers from around the world—including millions of people from Asian and Middle Eastern countries where Christianity was not the majority religion.

Consider: in the 1820s, the top ten countries sending immigrants to the United States were all majority Christian nations. That was still true in the 1960s, before Johnson signed the bill. But after the effects of the 1965 act had fully kicked in, the melting pot became filled with very different ingredients. From 1986 to 2012, three of the top five countries sending immigrants—China, India, and Vietnam—were majority non-Christian. The Pew Research Center estimates that from 1992 to 2012, 25 percent of immigrants followed non-Christian religions, with the largest groups being Muslims (10 percent), Hindus (7 percent), and Buddhists (6 percent). Roughly 14 percent were religiously unaffiliated. In any given year, about 260,000 non-Christians settle in America.[4]

America is still, to be sure, a majority Christian nation. But it is no longer a Protestant majority nation. What's more, almost 23 percent of Americans are unaffiliated and 6 percent are non-Christian. In the context of religious freedom, 6 percent is a huge number. That's a bigger share of the population than Catholics were in the 1830s or Mormons were in the 1870s.[5]

As we've seen, immigration has powerfully affected the fights over religious freedom throughout American history. There have been severe backlashes, followed by adjustments. But in terms of the dynamics of religious freedom, this most recent wave is distinctive: millions have arrived who cannot be considered part of the "Judeo-Christian" tradition.

The Barred Zones

Most Founding Fathers were pro-immigration. George Washington declared that "the bosom of America is open to receive not only the opulent
and respectable stranger but the oppressed and persecuted of all nations
and religions."[6] In the Declaration of Independence, the colonists complained that King George II prevented "population of these states." There
was lots of land and not enough people, so Americans mostly supported
immigration until the nativist period in the 1830s.

Although early efforts to curb immigration focused on Catholics, policies evolved that excluded a broad range of different religions. These
efforts generally emphasized matters besides religion, such as race or economics. But the effect was that for much of American history, people practicing non-Christian religions were barred.

The Chinese Exclusion Act of 1882 was driven by racist theories of ethnic superiority and some concerns about Chinese competing for American
jobs. Eugenics was on the rise and taken quite seriously. A report from a
congressional committee explained that there was "not sufficient brain capacity in the Chinese race to furnish motive power for self-government"
and that "there is no Aryan or European race which is not far superior to
the Chinese."[7] The law banned immigration from China and decreed that
those currently legally in the country could never become citizens. "We
have this day to choose whether we will have for the Pacific coast the
civilization of Christ or the civilization of Confucius," said Senator James
Blaine of Maine in 1879.

Congress didn't view "Hindoos," or people from India, as any better.
Though they arrived in smaller numbers than the Chinese, they faced
similar types of opposition. In 1907, a mob of five hundred men in Bell-
ingham, Washington, broke into lumber mills where several hundred
Indian immigrants were working. They robbed them, set fire to their
bunkhouses, and forced them onto trains to Canada.[8] In 1911, the United
States Immigration Commission declared that the "East Indians" on the
West Coast were the "least desirable race of immigrants thus far admitted to the United States."[9] A representative from California predicted that
because they came from tropical countries, they "cannot stand the rigors
of Northern climate" and would "become burdens upon the communities
to which they go."[10]

In 1917, Congress created the "Asiatic Barred Zone," targeting India (including the parts that are now Pakistan and Bangladesh), Southeast Asia

(Vietnam, Cambodia, Laos, and Thailand), Indonesia, and Malaysia. Representative John Raker, the main advocate for Indian exclusion, explained to colleagues that he had wanted to exclude "Hindus . . . by name" but that international sensitivities encouraged him to be more oblique, "glossing it over, making it smooth so that it may be swallowed without naming anyone."[11] The Asiatic Barred Zone also included the four largest Muslim countries in the world—the lands now known as Pakistan, India, Indonesia, and Bangladesh. Under this new law, each of those countries was granted just one hundred slots per year.

Between 1880 and 1920, a tidal wave of immigration, much of it from Eastern and Southern Europe, transformed America, especially in urban areas. The population of cities tripled between 1880 and 1910,[12] and almost two-thirds of city residents in the Northeast were foreign-born.[13] By 1920, a strong backlash had grown, as witnessed by the rise of the Ku Klux Klan and a movement in Congress to ensure that the country's European "stock" was not diluted. "Biological laws tell us that certain divergent people will not mix or blend," Calvin Coolidge explained to readers of Good Housekeeping magazine. Although "the Nordics propagate themselves successfully," others don't, and immigration policy should pay close attention to "ethnic law."[14] A congressman from Arkansas drew applause from the chamber when he called for the preservation of white Christian America: "We have admitted the dregs of Europe until America has been Orientalized, Europeanized, Africanized, and mongrelized to that insidious degree that our genius, stability, greatness, and promise of advancement and achievement are actually menaced."[15]

In 1924, Congress imposed a numerical quota system for each country. At first glance, the formula appeared neutral. Rather than picking and choosing favorite countries, each would get a fixed percentage based on its contribution to the American population. But there was a catch: instead of pegging it to the population reality of 1924, the law required that the immigrant makeup mirror the population of 1890—before the surge of immigrants from Eastern Europe.[16] Some 70 percent of the slots were reserved for three countries: Great Britain, Germany, and Ireland. The law's chief author, Representative Albert Johnson of Washington, explained his racial purity goals.

> Today, instead of a nation descended from generations of
> freemen bred to a knowledge of the principles and practice of
> self-government, of liberty under law, we have a heterogeneous

population no small proportion of which is sprung from races that, throughout the centuries, have known no liberty at all. . . . In other words, our capacity to maintain our cherished institutions stands diluted by a stream of alien blood, with all its inherited misconceptions respecting the relationships of the governing power to the governed. . . .

The United States is our land. . . . We intend to maintain it so. The day of indiscriminate acceptance of all races has definitely ended.[17]

The restrictions loosened slightly during World War II. President Franklin Roosevelt feared that the Chinese exclusion provisions undermined the war effort because, in radio broadcasts throughout the Pacific, the Japanese were accusing the United States of hypocrisy for rejecting Asian immigrants.[18] Roosevelt believed that China, an ally in the war against Japan, needed to be rewarded and encouraged. In 1943, some Chinese immigrants were allowed in. Then, in 1945, the War Brides Act allowed for immigration of Asian spouses and children of veterans.[19]

Over Harry Truman's veto, Congress in 1952 approved the Immigration and Nationality Act of 1952 (the McCarran-Walter Act),[20] which maintained restrictions for southern and Eastern Europe, in part because of fears that the nation had already taken in too many Jews[21] (in 1939 and 1940, about half of immigrants to the United States had been Jewish).[22] But it added a significant new provision: citizens' spouses were exempted from immigration quotas.

As the American economy heated up later in the 1950s, public opinion began to shift. In 1956, both the Republican and Democratic party platforms endorsed eliminating the national origins quotas. President Dwight Eisenhower declared that McCarran-Walter "does in fact discriminate."[23] Congressman John F. Kennedy took an interest in the issue as well. Just as important as his own family's experience with anti-Irish discrimination, Italians in his district complained that the current laws prevented them from bringing over their families.[24] As president, JFK proposed that we focus less on ethnicity and more on the "reuniting of families" and the attracting of immigrants with useful skills. The legislation had made little progress, though, when Kennedy was assassinated.

In 1965, Lyndon Johnson made it a priority. The Democrats had a massive congressional majority, and immigration reform seemed a sibling of the Voting Rights Act of 1965, the Civil Rights Act of 1964, and the abolition of the poll tax. Johnson pushed hard, perhaps influenced by his experience during World War II, when he helped smuggle forty-two Jews out of Europe by having them emigrate first to Latin America and then to the United States through Texas.[25] Though there wasn't a popular groundswell for the law, crucially, organized labor came out in support. The unions had previously feared the impact of immigration on American workers, but they supported the focus on family reunification because they thought it would bring in less-skilled workers who would be less likely to compete with their members.[26] A liberalized immigration system was also seen as a key tool in the Cold War.[27] As Senator Kenneth Keating of New York explained it, if we are "discriminating against individuals because of race or national origin, what trust can we in turn expect from the emerging nations of Asia and Africa?" Jewish[28] and Catholic[29] groups supported the bill,[30] as did members of Congress who represented Italians, Greeks, Portuguese, and Poles.

A key moment came when Michael Feighan, a conservative Democrat who defended the existing restrictive system, became convinced that an emphasis on family reunification would helpfully freeze the current system in place. He altered the legislation to put *more* emphasis on family reunification, a change that brought support from even some anti-immigrant groups, such as the American Legion.[31] The reasoning was as follows: there weren't that many Asians and Africans here to begin with, so there weren't many families to unify. Johnson and his allies rolled with this argument. "There will not be, comparatively, many Asians or Africans entering this country," explained Representative Emanuel Celler.[32]

Their prognostications turned out to be a tad off. Attorney General Robert Kennedy predicted about 5,000 people coming in from the Asia-Pacific Triangle. In 2015, 405,000 Asians got permanent resident status.[33] Secretary of State Dean Rusk estimated that India would send about 8,000 immigrants over five years. From 2011 to 2015, 329,000 people came from India. In the 1950s, Europeans made up 56 percent of new immigrants; by the 1990s, they made up just 13 percent.

Why were the legislators so wrong? They underestimated the effects of family reunification. Before the act, half of the exemptions from quotas were awarded to "highly skilled immigrants whose services are urgently needed in the US." After the act, only 20 percent went to those categories, with 74 percent of the slots going to family reunification.[34]

Although policy makers at the time understood the potential chain effect, they assumed it would bring in more Europeans. But as Europe's economy improved, fewer Europeans emigrated. Meanwhile, as many Third World countries achieved independence in the 1950s, 1960s, and 1970s, their residents had more freedom to make their own migration choices. The growth of the airline industry made it easier for people to travel, and improvements in phone service made it less expensive for immigrants to communicate with relatives back home.

And then there were the wars. When the United States sends its troops to foreign lands, we often end up taking back a lot of their people. America's involvement in Korea, Vietnam, and Iraq significantly affected the religious makeup of American immigrants. The first immigrants from Korea were women who married American soldiers; then Americans adopted thousands of Korean babies.[35] Korea is religiously diverse, with millions of Christians, but the majority of Koreans practice some form of Confucianism, sometimes combined with Buddhism, Taoism, or Shamanism.

The Vietnam War produced another wave of non-Christian immigrants. In the 1980s, a stunning 581,000 refugees came from the countries most affected by the Vietnam War: 324,000 from Vietnam, 143,000 from Laos, and 114,000 from Cambodia. The majority religion in all of those countries is Buddhism. As they became citizens, they began to bring over family members.[36] Another 565,000 immigrants came from Vietnam after 1990.[37]

The Iraq War prompted an increase in the number of Muslim immigrants from the Middle East. In 2015, 21,107 Iraqis came to the United States, 90 percent of them as refugees.[38] Earlier, the overthrow of America's ally, the shah of Iran, led to a mass exodus of Western-friendly Iranians. Immigration from Iran rose from 9,059 in the 1960s to 98,000 in the 1980s.

With India, the effects of the 1965 act were compounded by a 1990 law that provided more work-based visas for skilled workers.[39] In 2014, 70 percent went to Indians. Between 1980 and 2013, the Indian population of the United States skyrocketed from 206,000 to 2.04 million.[40]

The number of student visas jumped as well—from 110,000 in 2001 to 524,000 in 2012. Incredibly, all of the top twenty cities of origin for student visas were in majority non-Christian areas.[41] About 55 percent came from just four countries: China, India, South Korea, and Saudi Arabia, where the dominant religions are Buddhism, Hinduism, Confucianism, and Islam.[42] America has benefited in particular from an influx of immigrant doctors, with the top countries of origin being India, China, the Philippines, Korea, and Pakistan.[43]

Ironically, the shift to non-Christian religions would be even greater if not for the presence of more than 11 million undocumented immigrants. Most of them come from Latin America, so 83 percent are Christian. The "illegals" make America more Christian. If they were all expelled, the United States would have 9 million fewer Christians.[44]

The changes in immigration law, combined with the impact of military interventions, altered the complexions—ethnically and religiously—of the immigrants. From 1930 to the 1960s, Asians constituted 5 percent of legal immigrants. That grew to 12 percent in the 1960s, 34 percent in the 1970s, and 37 percent in the 1980s. Those opposed to Asian immigration had warned that they were unlikely to assimilate, but it turns out that Asian immigrants become citizens at a high rate—which means that they can bring over family members more quickly.[45] The faster the assimilation rate, the more dramatic the chain-immigration factor.

The increase in numbers of non-Christians came at a time when the globalization of pop culture and communications made it possible for Eastern religions to gain rapid acceptance in American society. The Beatles' George Harrison engineered the importation of Indian musical styles and, later, Hindu concepts, popularizing meditation and even easing the arrival of yoga. "It would not have happened" without Harrison, says Deepak Chopra, the Indian doctor who himself popularized so many Eastern concepts. "Overnight [the Beatles] made the world aware of Indian spirituality."[46] As Buddhists immigrated to the United States, elements of their faith became popular with Westerners seeking a rich spirituality not connected to revelation-based Western religion. Buddhism's sudden cultural acceptance—before you knew it, there seemed to be as many movie stars who were Buddhist as there were Christian—was helped along by the broad popularity of the Dalai Lama, who put an inspiring and nonthreatening face on a previously alien faith. He was routinely listed as one of the most respected world leaders,[47] with his poll numbers in the United States usually hovering in the same range as those of the most respected Christian leader, Billy Graham.[48]

In the long run, the challenge posed by Hindus and Buddhists might be even more complex than that presented by Muslims. Not only are they not Christian; Hindus are not fully monotheistic, and Buddhists are not fully theistic. The nature of their theism is a topic of some debate in both religious traditions. Some Hindus argue that while they worship multiple gods, they are not polytheistic because all of them are manifestations of a single spiritual presence called Brahman. But most scholars view Hinduism as non-monotheistic. Buddhists believe they do not need an all-powerful deity, at least not one that centrally guides the faith. So ultimately even phrases like "In God We Trust" may rankle a small but growing part of the population.

Hindoos and Mahometans

The founders were surprisingly cognizant of these non-Christian religions. In some cases, they expressed admiration for them and speculated about how they would fit into the American landscape. Late in life, Thomas Jefferson recalled that an amendment had been offered to the Virginia Statute for Religious Freedom specifically citing Jesus Christ as its inspiration. But this idea "was rejected by a great majority," proving, he said, that the law was also intended to protect "the Jew and the Gentile, the Christian and Mahometan, the Hindoo, and Infidel of every denomination." John Adams carefully read the Upanishads, a central work of Hinduism, though he proclaimed Christianity and "the Hebrews" to be superior. Ben Franklin hoped his great meeting hall in Philadelphia would be used by a wide range of thinkers, including Mohammedans.

This point can be overstated. When the founders imagined a world of religious liberty, they were not mostly thinking of Muslims and Hindus (or, for that matter, of Jews, Catholics, or Russian Orthodox practitioners). But whether they specifically focused on non-Christian religions or not, the crafters of both the First Amendment and the Fourteenth Amendment advocated for principles that would endure in scenarios they couldn't imagine. In today's technology world, this is called "future-proofing" a product. One of those unimaginable scenarios happened in 1965, when Lyndon Johnson signed that bill that he said would have only a minor impact on the country. The resulting chain of events changed how we think about religious liberty—and, in the end, strengthened our system by fragmenting religious power.

We now must accept that non-Christian faiths will be players in the debate. That has specific policy implications. If you want government support for religious schools, you have to be willing to subsidize Muslim madrassas. If you want prayers opening the sessions of the House of Representatives, you now have to welcome the likes of Venkatachalapathi Samuldrala.

Pope John Paul II and President Ronald Reagan, 1984

Chapter Fourteen

POLITICAL BEDFELLOWS

*The poison gets drained from the
Protestant-Catholic relationship, in part
because of the rise of the religious right.*

During the 1960 presidential campaign, a group of Protestant ministers in Georgia put their names to an advertisement declaring that
they could not vote for John F. Kennedy because he was Catholic.
One of the signatories was Dr. Martin Luther King Sr.

"Daddy King," the father of the civil rights leader, was like a lot of traditional Protestants, white and black. He viewed Catholics with suspicion
or hostility. He changed his attitude in October 1960 after his son was
imprisoned for eating at a segregated lunch counter in Atlanta, Georgia.
Martin Jr.'s wife, Coretta, was terrified that he would be killed in jail.
John F. Kennedy, the Democratic Party candidate, had been cautious on
civil rights, but his advisor, Harris Wofford, convinced him that a simple
phone call would make a huge difference. Kennedy told Coretta that he
was thinking of them and wished them well.

Daddy King was impressed. On the night his son was released from
jail, he explained, with jarring candor: "I had expected to vote against
Senator Kennedy because of his religion. But now he can be my president,

Catholic or whatever he is. It took courage to call my daughter-in-law at a time like this. He has the moral courage to stand up for what he knows is right. I've got all my votes and I've got a suitcase and I'm going to take them up there and dump them in his lap." The campaign quietly distributed a pamphlet, known as "the Blue Bomb" because of the color of its paper, in African American communities to publicize the call.[1] Kennedy won 68 percent of the black vote, a seven-point improvement over the previous Democratic nominee.[2]

Shortly before Election Day, Wofford was alone with Kennedy. The future president said, "Did you see what Martin's father said? He was going to vote against me because I was a Catholic, but since I called his daughter-in-law, he will vote for me. That was a hell of a bigoted statement, wasn't it? Imagine Martin Luther King having a bigot for a father!"[3]

Many American Protestants held Catholics in disdain for 350 years of America's history. And then, suddenly, at least in terms of the long arc of history, this changed. Between roughly 1960 and 1990, the pace at which Catholics were accepted accelerated. This chapter attempts to explain why. We're accustomed to thinking that religion shapes politics, but during this period, it worked in reverse. The exigencies of electoral coalition building helped pull down walls between religions. It happened first on the left, as the nomination of a Catholic Democrat, combined with the dynamics of the civil rights and anti-war movements, forged new Protestant-Catholic alliances. Then an even more dramatic (and less understood) reshuffling occurred among conservatives and religious traditionalists. The rise of the religious right led to more religious pluralism. Conservative Protestants and Catholics united around opposition to abortion, Communism, and secular liberalism, casting aside their traditional theological differences and long-standing cultural animosities.

This period also saw perhaps the greatest example yet of how American values can sometimes alter the complexion of even ancient religions. A dramatic effort by Catholic leaders in the United States, led by an academic named John Courtney Murray, prodded the Vatican to embrace the American approach to religious liberty. This further eased the integration of Catholics into American society by removing any inconsistency between their position and that of Rome. Religious freedom, it turned out, could become an American export.

Anti-Catholicism in the mid-twentieth century was not limited to fundamentalists. Many liberals viewed the Catholic Church as a powerfully

regressive force. A bestselling anti-Catholic book in 1949 by the civil lib-
ertarian Paul B. Blanshard, *American Freedom and Catholic Power*, criticized
state support of Catholic schools, the Church's censorship of movies and
books, and the ban on birth control in Catholic hospitals. He called for a
"resistance movement" against the "Catholic plan for America" and its
"undemocratic system of alien control."[4] Some liberals also associated the
Church, strongly anti-Communist, with the excesses of McCarthyism and
anti-Semitism.[5]

Kennedy's campaign, just thirty-two years after Al Smith's drubbing,
eroded anti-Catholicism on the left. Like Daddy King, many Democrats
who had been suspicious of Catholics found reason to open their minds.
Kennedy's tactical decisions helped. On September 12, 1960, before the
Greater Houston Ministerial Association, he laid out a vision that was
quintessentially Madisonian but at odds with the traditional approach of
the Catholic Church.

> I believe in an America where the separation of church and state is
> absolute, where no Catholic prelate would tell the president (should
> he be Catholic) how to act, and no Protestant minister would tell
> his parishioners for whom to vote; where no church or church
> school is granted any public funds or political preference; and
> where no man is denied public office merely because his religion
> differs from the president who might appoint him or the people
> who might elect him.[6]

The speech reflected a shift for Kennedy, who earlier in his career had
backed government support for Catholic schools. Now, to win on the national instead of the local stage, he opposed such measures as "clearly
unconstitutional."[7] The speech's message was similar to that of Al Smith,
but times had changed. The rise of the tri-faith ethos elevated Catholics as
well as Jews. The Catholic vote had become significant, possibly helping
Kennedy as much as it hurt him in the 1960 election. In a sign of just how
much Catholic fortunes had changed, when Kennedy became president
in 1961, both the majority leader of the House of Representatives, John W.
McCormack, and the senate majority leader, Mike Mansfield, were also
Catholic.

Meanwhile, the civil rights and anti-war movements further strengthened relations between liberal Catholics, Protestants, and Jews. Martin

Luther King Jr. reached out to religious leaders around the country to join the march in Selma, Alabama, in 1965 and was thrilled to see that more than nine hundred Catholics, including scores of priests and nuns, answered the call.[8]

The other Catholic breakthrough in the 1960s involved the Vatican itself. Recall that earlier papal encyclicals and pronouncements had criticized the American approach to religious pluralism. Like modern Muslims, Catholics were held accountable for doctrines over which they had minimal control. If anything, American Catholics were in more of a bind: while Islam has no central religious body, Catholics were supposed to follow guidance from Rome.

Remarkably, in the 1960s the American Catholic leadership pushed back, helping to reshape Vatican theology. A prominent Jesuit scholar, John Courtney Murray, had been writing for more than a decade that the Vatican's approach to religious freedom had become antiquated and that American pluralism offered new possibilities. Since the Church can't just change its mind willy-nilly, Murray argued that previous papal proclamations had been appropriate, context-specific reactions to a type of modernism exemplified by the French Revolution, which had perverted the idea of religious freedom to attack the church. But in the United States, Murray argued, "the Church is completely free to be whatever she is."[9] The Church should still, of course, insist that its spiritual vision was correct, but it should no longer seek government enforcement of those views.

Murray was initially resisted by other Catholic theologians, who argued that "no other form of religion has any right by divine law to exist or to propagate. . . . Ours is the only religion that has a right to exist."[10] Encouraging religious freedom would promote "indifferentism," the idea that one faith is as good as another.[11] As one hostile bishop complained, Murray's approach conferred the same rights to both "truth and error."[12] For a time, these conservatives successfully silenced Murray. One friend in the Vatican advised him to stay out of trouble by focusing on his poetry.[13]

But in 1962, Pope John XXIII announced the Second Vatican Council, an international conclave of bishops and cardinals to review Catholic teaching. The American Catholic hierarchy mobilized to change the Church's position on religious freedom. With Murray as their intellectual guide, the American bishops pushed to get American notions of church-and-state separation adopted by the rest of the church. The council debated the topic over several years. A key outside endorsement came from Archbishop Karol Wojtyla of Krakow, Poland, who would later become Pope John Paul II.[14] Cardinal Josef Beran of Czechoslovakia, who had been imprisoned by the Nazis in the Dachau and Theresienstadt concentration camps and then by the Communists a decade later, movingly told his fellow cardinals that "the principle of religious freedom and freedom of conscience must be set forth clearly and without any restriction flowing from opportunistic considerations."[15] In the end, the conclave voted 1,997–224 to issue new guidance on religious freedom. The resulting document, *Dignitatis Humanae*, stated, "This Vatican Council declares that the human person has a right to religious freedom." Remarkably, according to the Roman Catholic Church, the primary role of government now was promoting not religion but religious liberty: "government is to assume the safeguard of the religious freedom of all its citizens, in an effective manner."[16]

The Vatican position was now fully aligned with the United States Constitution.

Indeed, *Dignitatis Humanae* was used later by reformers within the Catholic Church who were fighting Communism and other tyrannies. Pope John Paul II's biographer, George Weigel, argues that he owed his effectiveness, as both archbishop of Krakow and pope, to this Madisonian document. "Absent *Dignitatis Humanae*," he wrote, "Pope John Paul II would have been lacking one of the most powerful weapons in his moral armamentarium: the standing of the Catholic Church, post-*Dignitatis Humanae*, as defender of the religious freedom of all."[17]

Pluralism on the Right

Abortion would eventually help raze barriers between conservative Protestants and Catholics—though not at first. The politics of abortion in the 1960s little resembled today's lineups. Consider the drama that played out in California in 1966. Illegal abortions were happening routinely, killing hundreds of women. The legislature moved to liberalize the laws—allowing abortions if the pregnancy endangered the life or health of the woman or if she was the victim of rape or incest. The Catholic Church fought hard against the bill. Cardinal James McIntyre compared it to Herod ordering the slaughter of "Holy Innocents" in Bethlehem.[18] But the legislature passed the landmark abortion liberalization, which was then signed into law by the new governor—Ronald Reagan.

Back then, many abortion opponents were Catholic Democrats, while many conservative Republican Protestants wanted nothing to do with the issue, viewing it as the province of Catholics, their theological adversaries. Francis Schaeffer, an evangelical professor who later became a major anti-abortion activist, at first refused to get involved. After his son, Frank, pushed him to join the anti-abortion movement, Schaeffer exasperatedly blurted out, "They're Catholics!"

"How can you say you believe in the uniqueness of every human being if you won't stand up on this?" the son yelled.

"I don't want to be identified with some Catholic issue. I'm not putting my reputation on the line for them!" Francis shouted back.[19]

The evangelicals' ambivalence on abortion, an issue they now consider to be at the sacred heart of their morality, is striking. The year after California's abortion liberalization law passed, Billy Graham declared that he supported loosening the laws so rape and incest victims could get abortions, and the Baptist State Convention of North Carolina took no position. Other Bible Belt states behaved similarly. "I have always felt that it was only after a child was born and had a life separate from its mother that it became an individual person," said the fundamentalist minister W. A. Criswell, the former president of the Southern Baptist Convention.[20]

Some Protestants doubted there was biblical justification for the Catholic view that human life began at conception. Twenty-five evangelical scholars in 1968 concluded that the "human fetus" was either "an actual human life or at the least, a potential and developing human life," so physicians should "exercise great caution" when prescribing an abortion.[21] "Hardly any evangelical Protestants joined Catholics in lobbying against the abortion law reform efforts of the late 1960s," wrote Daniel K. Williams in *Defenders of the Unborn*.[22] Evangelicals certainly did not view the "right to life" as an important issue. "The Evangelicals' attitude was that 'it's not our problem,'" recalled Paul Weyrich, the conservative activist, who was Catholic. "They had a ghetto mentality and didn't foresee the impact of the [*Roe v. Wade*] decision."[23]

But over the next decade, their views changed dramatically. For one thing, the 1973 *Roe v. Wade* decision led to a dramatic increase in legal abortions, from 750,000 in 1973 to 1 million in 1975 to 1.5 million in 1980.[24]

Many conservative Protestant groups that had supported the modest lib-eralization of abortion laws had second thoughts. *Christianity Today*, the leading evangelical intellectual magazine, stated afterward: "Christians should accustom themselves to the thought that the American state no longer supports, in any meaningful sense, the laws of God."[25] Protes-tants became energized in part by an influential movie created by Francis Schaeffer and C. Everett Koop, *Whatever Happened to the Human Race?*

The process of turning the evangelical-Catholic détente into a polit-ical alliance began in the late 1960s with Richard Nixon. His aides Pat Buchanan and Kevin Phillips made the case that abortion was poten-tially a wedge issue that could separate Catholics from the Democratic Party. Abortion, Buchanan wrote in a private memo, was "a rising issue and gut issue with Catholics."[26] Nixon's position had been virtually the same as George McGovern's, but as he got closer to the 1972 election, he began making pro-life gestures, such as directing the Pentagon to rescind the abortion regulations it had issued the year before.[27] In May 1972, he rejected a report on population growth that he had commissioned two years earlier, arguing that "unrestricted abortion policies would demean human life"—a thoroughly Catholic phrasing.[28] Mostly, Nixon associated abortion with a general moral degeneracy, captured by the three A's that McGovern would supposedly bring to America in abundance—amnesty, acid, and abortion. The canniest leaders understood that abortion politics could help conservatism, and vice versa. Weyrich explained to his fellow conservatives that abortion should be "made the keystone of their orga-nizing strategy, since this was the issue that could divide the Democratic Party."[29]

During the Jimmy Carter administration, what came to be known as the religious right began to take shape. A key impetus was the Internal Revenue Service's attempt to remove Bob Jones University's tax-exempt status because it banned interracial dating. In 1979, Paul Weyrich joined together with a Baptist minister named Jerry Falwell to form a new multi-faith religious group to advocate conservative cultural issues. They called it the Moral Majority.

The prevalence of Catholics in the leadership of the religious right, lit-tle noticed by the press at the time, helped elevate abortion as an issue and bridge the Catholic-Protestant divide. At a rally in Dallas, James Robison, an evangelical preacher, introduced Weyrich by saying, "Weyrich is a brother Cath-o-lic, and if any of you want to leave, do it now, because

I don't want you in the room."[30] By 1980, abortion politics had reached a tipping point. The Republican presidential nominee, Ronald Reagan, endorsed a constitutional amendment to *ban* abortion, cementing together a new political coalition of conservative Protestants, Catholics, and Mormons.

Over the next four decades, the religious right grew in strength, as did the conservative Protestant-Catholic alliance. On January 31, 2006, Samuel Alito was sworn in as a justice to the United States Supreme Court— becoming the fifth Catholic then serving on the nine-person court. All five of the Catholic justices were appointed by Protestant Republican presidents who owed their elections to this coalition. A surprising number of conservative activists even converted to Catholicism. Among the Protestant conservatives who joined the Holy Roman Church were columnist Robert Novak;[31] Supreme Court Justice Clarence Thomas;[32] former Speaker of the House of Representatives Newt Gingrich; former Florida governor Jeb Bush; Judge Robert Bork; Kansas governor Sam Brownback; and pundit Laura Ingraham.[33]

Anti-Communism also helped reshuffle the Protestant-Catholic relationship. The Catholic Church had always taken a strong anti-Communist stance, and many of America's most prominent anti-Communist leaders had been Catholics, including Senator Joseph McCarthy. William F. Buckley, the founder and editor of the *National Review*, united different strands of conservatism against Communism and in the process raised the status of Catholic intellectuals. Later, Protestant conservatives who put anti-Communism at the center of their worldview would develop a crush on Pope John Paul II. Deal Hudson, a conservative Catholic leader, explained:

> He spoke with the zeal of an evangelist, in the language of a
> biblical scholar, and with the depth of a Catholic intellectual. He
> appealed to everybody, except the secular left. His leadership
> energized the pro-life movement, the religious conservatives who
> supported Reagan and the Bushes, and the growing cooperation
> between Evangelicals and Catholics. Where theologians had
> limited success building consensus, John Paul II broke down the
> barriers with the rallying cry to build a "culture of life."[34]

His alliance with Ronald Reagan, beloved among American evangelicals, helped too, and in June 1981, 91 percent of Americans approved of his papacy.[35] No longer the diabolical leader of a threatening foreign power, the pope was now a beloved ally in America's war against evil. Consider the changing rhetoric of America's favorite evangelical preacher, Billy Graham. In 1960, Graham wrote an article for *Life* magazine in which he argued that America should not have a Catholic president. Three and one-half decades later, Graham told columnist Cal Thomas that the pope was "the strong conscience of the whole Christian world."[36]

Although modern conservatives often complain that the Second Vatican Council ushered in an era of liberalism and disrespect for Church authority, it also helped bring together traditionalist Protestants and Catholics. As we've seen, one of their biggest points of contention in the past had been the Bible. Catholics viewed the emphasis on reading of the Bible—especially the King James Version—as a Protestant thing. In November 1965, the Second Vatican Council urged a stunning new approach in a statement called *Dei Verbum*, or "The Word of God." Catholics, it stated, should "learn by frequent reading of the divine Scriptures the 'excellent knowledge of Jesus Christ.'" After centuries of ambivalence about Bible reading, the conclave declared that "ignorance of the Scriptures is ignorance of Christ."[37] Vatican II also allowed for Mass to be conducted in the local language, which meant the in-service Bible readings would be understandable to those who didn't know Latin. Over time, as Bible study became more common among Catholics, an entirely new lingua franca developed between them and Protestants, especially evangelicals. Richard Mouw, the former president of the Fuller Theological Seminary, an evangelical school, recalled coteaching with Father Raymond Brown, a Catholic Bible scholar who had described how Catholics were discouraged from reading the Bible. Afterward, a mother and daughter came up to the two men. The mother, a Catholic, told them that the two had fallen out when the daughter became an evangelical. "Hearing the two of you talk about the Bible—well, now we see that we are both OK!"[38]

Evangelical and conservative Catholic intellectuals found common ground on an ever-expanding set of issues. In 1994, the group Evangelicals and Catholics Together was formed by Father Richard John Neuhaus, an influential conservative Catholic, and Chuck Colson, the Watergate figure who became the evangelical founder of the Prison Fellowship ministry. In its first statement, the group declared its solidarity against a new enemy: secularism. "Influential sectors of the culture are laid waste by relativism, anti-intellectualism, and nihilism that deny the very idea of truth," it declared. The group came to embrace a similar approach on the issue of religious freedom too. While the two denominations had for decades used the term as a club against each other, they now believed that government's hostility to religion threatened liberty.

> We strongly affirm the separation of church and state, and just as strongly protest the distortion of that principle to mean the separation of religion from public life. . . . As a consequence of such distortions, it is increasingly the case that wherever government goes religion must retreat, and government increasingly goes almost everywhere. Religion, which was privileged and foundational in our legal order, has in recent years been penalized and made marginal.[39]

Policy compromises developed. For instance, while Protestants earlier had opposed government funding for Catholic schools, in the late twentieth century evangelicals came to support vouchers for religiously run private schools.

Just as World War II had prompted an interfaith moment, the culture wars had turned old enemies into allies. Conservatives would (mostly) accept religious pluralism—the lions lying down with the lambs, the Protestants with the Catholics. Protestants gave up their conviction that Catholicism was a fraudulent religion, while Catholics dropped some demands for government support. Even Mormons were eventually welcomed in, the breakthrough being the nomination of Mitt Romney as the Republican presidential candidate in 2012. The multiplicity of sects once again helped strengthen religious freedom as faith factions and political factions danced, swapped partners, and danced again.

Traditionalist Protestants no longer sought dominance but rather embraced a pan-Christian ideology that put aside ancient denominational differences in favor of common conservative views on abortion, the sexual revolution, and Communism. Indeed, throughout American history, whenever the majority has been on the verge of losing control it has shape-shifted, reassembling in order to maintain its dominant size. Whereas Protestant denominations warred with each other in the eighteenth century, they coalesced as a Protestant majority when combating Catholics in the nineteenth century. In the twentieth century, they invited in Catholics and even Jews to become the Judeo-Christian majority. As the twentieth century came to a close, the internecine fighting between right-of-center Christians mostly ended. The new conservative ecumenical alliance focused instead on what they considered a growing hostility to their traditional worldview.

Rallying against the Affordable Care Act's contraception provision

Chapter Fifteen

THE "WAR" ON "CHRISTIANITY"

Evangelical Christians go from "moral majority" to persecuted minority.

C hristianity is under tremendous siege," said Donald Trump during the 2016 presidential campaign. "The Christians are being treated horribly because we have nobody to represent the Christians." Trump pledged that with his election, "the Christians" would at long last have a champion. "As long as I am your president no one is ever going to stop you from practicing your faith or from preaching what's in your heart."[1]

Trump even claimed that *he* had been persecuted for his deeply held faith. When asked why his businesses had been audited by the Internal Revenue Service, he didn't mention the voluminous evidence of shady practices and instead suggested it was "Maybe because of the fact that I'm a strong Christian."[2] After all, he reminded us, he has "a great relationship with God."[3]

Trump's Joan of Arc positioning resonated because conservative evangelicals believe they are victims of a rampant persecution. "Christians have been singled out for discrimination," explained David Limbaugh in his book *Persecution*. FOX News personality John Gibson argued that there was a "liberal plot to ban" Christmas. The "war on Christianity is alive and well," warned Glenn Beck.[4] Religious leader Tony Perkins warned that your own family could be at risk: "Christians you know are targets . . . maybe Christians in your own home."[5] Mike Huckabee said the United States was moving toward a "criminalization of Christianity."[6] One report declared that in public schools, town squares, and pop culture, "hostility to religion in America is rising like floodwaters."[7] Never to be outdone, Pat Robertson explained: "Just like what Nazi Germany did to the Jews, so liberal America is now doing to the evangelical Christians. It's no different. It's the same thing."[8]

Are conservative Christians being reasonable or paranoid? This chapter sorts through what has become a confusing and politicized debate and makes these related arguments:

- There is a germ of truth in the idea that there is growing hostility toward religion.

- But the notion that we are in the midst of a horrible wave of hostility against American Christians is untrue. Indeed, the profligate use of the term "religious freedom" by some Christian leaders and conservative media outlets, often for partisan or commercial purposes, threatens to bleach the phrase of its meaning.

- From a legal perspective, religion has never been more privileged.

- The loss of demographic dominance for white Protestants, though a cause of much angst, will ultimately prove to be a great blessing for evangelicals. We have finally arrived at the purest form of Madison's "multiplicity of sects"—a religious landscape so fragmented that no denomination is big enough to dominate. That will safeguard religious liberty for Christians and for everyone else.

Fear of Religion

We were sitting in the audience at my son's elementary school concert in Brooklyn, New York, beaming at the sight of him up there in his white button-down shirt and khaki pants amid a lineup of singing cutie-pies. The class was belting out Don McLean's "American Pie."

> *Did you write the book of love*
> *And do you have faith in God above*
> *Everybody tells you so. . . .*

Wait. "Everybody tells you so"? I could have sworn the lyrics were "if the Bible tells you so." Did they really just cut a reference to the Bible out of "American Pie"? Yes, they did.

The incident, which somehow never made it to FOX News, nicely captures a genuine shift in the place of religion in American culture. No, this was not a case of separation of church and state run amok. It's a private school; they can do whatever they want. Nor was it a case of non-Christian animus against Christians. The school leaders were mostly Christian. They just figured it would be safer to gently excise a phrase that might offend. But it didn't occur to them that deleting the "the Bible" might bother those who take scripture seriously. They assumed that the sensitivities needing protection belonged to secular people or religious minorities, not devout Christians.

Throughout the country, efforts to separate church and state have sometimes given religion a second-class status.

- The federal government ruled that student loan forgiveness could be provided to graduates taking a wide variety of public service jobs but not to those who become clergy.[9]

- The Federal Emergency Management Agency refused to provide financial support to assist churches after devastating hurricanes in Texas.[10]

- A group of atheists sued, unsuccessfully, to get the National September 11 Memorial & Museum to pull down a seventeen-foot cross that had been formed by steel beams left from the World Trade Center.[11]

- A group of residents in Acton, Massachusetts, sued to block the state from using historic preservation funds to preserve old churches along with secular buildings.[12]

These kinds of examples can make religious people feel under attack—especially given the broader demographic context. Sometime around 2013, according to Gallup surveys, the country passed a milestone that would have stunned its founders: less than half the population was Protestant. In 1964, Protestants made up 70 percent of the US population; by 2016, the number was 47 percent.[13] The share describing itself as white evangelical Protestants is declining too, in one study falling from 23 percent in 2006 to 17 percent in 2017.[14] And the future looks worse for evangelicals. Only

11 percent of young millennials (born 1990–1996) say they're evangelical, compared with 35 percent of baby boomers.[15]

At the same time, "nones" are on the rise. The percentage of people describing themselves as atheists, agnostics, and people "not affiliated" with any religion jumped from 5 percent of Americans in 1972 to 23 percent in 2016.[16] They're not all secular: 48 percent of the "not affiliateds" pray regularly. Still, the percentage of Americans who believe religion does more harm than good is now significant, around 13 percent. That's more than double the number of Jews, Muslims, Hindus, and Buddhists combined.[17] And secularism is projected to grow, especially if immigration is curtailed. A stunning 39 percent of young adults between the ages of eighteen and twenty-nine say they are not affiliated with a religion. While the growth of non-Christians—Muslims, Buddhists, and Hindus—poses challenges, those groups might at least be counted on to support some religion in the public square. Not so for the "nones," who may be irritated by believers strutting their stuff in public places.

So, while Protestants aren't nearly as victimized as they think, they do face a new world in which they will be merely the largest religion rather than the utterly dominant one. Remember, for many evangelical Christians, as for other believers, religion is not merely about private worship. It is about living one's life according to biblical values, including professing their faith to others. As the public realms in which that is permissible shrink, it can feel as if freedom is contracting too.

Many conservative Christian leaders, politicians, and media celebrities have exploited those fears of victimization, regularly engaging in what might be called persecution inflation. Among the examples of "persecution" listed in Limbaugh's book by that name was the time that a high school in Reno, Nevada, told members of its Bible club that they couldn't hand out "Jesus Loves You" candy canes to other students. Had Limbaugh maintained a proper sense of perspective, he might have noted that (a) the *public* high school has a happily functioning Bible club and (b) the administrators ultimately overruled the decision.[18]

FOX News pushed a story with the blood-boiling headline "VA Hospital Refuses to Accept 'Merry Christmas' Cards."[19] Actually, the hospital had decided that cards from strangers could not go straight to families without first passing through a committee of chaplains, who would make sure the appropriate messages got to the right soldiers.[20] In *No Higher Power*, Phyllis Schlafly reported that "[President Barack] Obama's Department of Veterans Affairs had banned any mention of Jesus Christ during burials at Houston National Cemetery."[21] Banned mentions of Jesus! That is quite the assault. In reality, the veterans' agency had told staff that its employees could not read religious texts unless asked to do so by the family of the deceased. "Invoking the name of God or Jesus is not only allowed, it is common at VA National Cemeteries across the country," said a spokesman for the US Department of Veterans Affairs.[22]

Let's put these "attacks" on Christians into some in perspective. Of the 1,679 religiously based hate crimes catalogued in 2017 by the Federal Bureau of Investigation, 58 percent were against Jews, 19 percent were against Muslims, and less than 2 percent were against Protestants (with 10 percent against all Christians). There were 40 attacks on Protestants, compared with 1,266 against gays and lesbians.[23] Yet because of the drumbeat from the conservative media and some Christian leaders, rank-and-file evangelicals view themselves as the most persecuted group. In 2017, 57 percent of white evangelicals said they face "a lot of discrimination," compared with 44 percent who said Muslims do.[24]

The effort to find, fight, and win a "war on Christmas" illustrates how a charge can have a grain of truth while also being mischievously exaggerated to stir rage, mobilize votes, or boost ratings. There have indeed been absurd instances of cities or individuals who, in their hyperattentiveness to the sensitivities of nonbelievers, have purged innocuous Christmas symbols. For instance, a member of the Parent-Teacher Association at an elementary school in Frisco, Texas, advised parents not to have Christmas trees or use the colors green and white. (The suggestion was quickly overruled.)[25]

But these slights have been cast as part of a "war" to prevent Christians from practicing their faith. In outlining the "Liberal Plot to Ban the Sacred Christian Holiday," John Gibson of FOX News claimed that "it's no longer permissible to wish anyone Merry Christmas."[26] Mysteriously, despite the demise of Christmas, 90 percent of Americans celebrate the holiday[27] and 25 million Christmas trees manage to insinuate themselves into homes and town squares every year[28]—including the ninety-four-foot-tall Christmas tree at Rockefeller Center, a few hundred yards from Gibson's office. In addition to massively overhyping the threat, the war on Christmas folks misstate the motives of those who say "Happy Holidays" instead of "Merry Christmas." Some retail stores have shifted greetings to avoid alienating potential customers, a pragmatic market-driven decision. December also includes Hanukkah, Kwanzaa, and, occasionally, Ramadan.[29] For all that conservative Christians talk about the Judeo-Christian heritage, the insistence on "Merry Christmas" mostly serves to exclude Jews from the sentiment. Conservatives sometimes confuse pluralism (or plain courtesy) with secularism.

In fact, the rage expressed on FOX News is not shared by most people on either side of the debate. Polls show that of those who prefer "Merry Christmas," only 19 percent are "offended" by those who say "Happy Holidays." Of those who like "Happy Holidays," only 11 percent are offended by "Merry Christmas." Most view it for what it actually is: an attempt to be slightly more inclusive, a moderate solution to a minor problem. Merry Christmas? Sure, say most Jews and Muslims. Happy Holidays? That's nice too, think most Christians. Most Americans are secret Madisonians. Of course, the small number of people who are offended get the airtime.

When religious rights are infringed, the cause is often ignorance, not maliciousness. The courts and the legislatures actually allow quite a bit of church-state mingling, but those charged with administering the rules sometimes mistakenly think that more is forbidden.[30] A study of 115 teachers in a southwestern school district found that when presented with church-state dilemmas that had been settled by courts, the teachers got it right only 55 percent of the time.[31] They often erred on the side of restricting religious expression too much, but sometimes they erred the other way, indicating that the problem may not be a bigoted urge to harm Christianity but confusion about the law.[32]

Nonetheless, leading conservatives have claimed that there is an assault on Christians' freedom—led by liberal Democrats. They argued that the greatest opponent of religious freedom in history was Barack Obama, who instigated a "sweeping abuse of the American people's religious liberty" (Phyllis Schlafly);[33] was "waging war on religion" (Mitt Romney);[34] and was attempting to "abrogate America's priceless religious freedom in the name of leftist social engineering" (Congressman Trent Franks).[35]

The most commonly cited example of Obama's hostility to religious liberty—the Obamacare contraceptive mandate—was a misdemeanor described as a felony. The Obama administration issued a rule in 2012 stating that contraception needed to be covered by health insurance plans under the Affordable Care Act. They exempted houses of worship from the requirement but did not extend that exemption to religiously oriented nonprofits such as schools and hospitals. That was a thumb in the eye of religious groups, which would have been forced to pay for health coverage for their employees that might conflict with their religious teachings. Religious believers were right to jump on this, and progressives proved clueless, ethically and politically, when they dismissed these concerns as frivolous or bigoted.

But then something happened that neither side likes to fully acknowledge: the administration capitulated and issued a sensible new rule.[36] Under the new proposal, religiously *oriented* organizations could also opt out of the contraceptive requirement, and the insurer would pay for the service instead. While some religious groups declared victory, most pronounced this to be a mere accounting gimmick and escalated their attack. They found the perfect plaintiffs, a kindly group of nuns called the Little Sisters of the Poor, who sued to block the rule.[37] When he became president, Donald Trump issued an executive order reversing the Obama policy. He gave the Sisters the good news that he was thereby "ending the attacks on your religious liberty" and "your long ordeal."[38]

To understand how the term "religious liberty" was being misused, let's consider the nature of the "attacks" on the Little Sisters of the Poor. The revised rule maintained that religious organizations did *not* have to pay for or provide coverage for contraception in the health insurance plans of their employees. They were excused from having to abide by that law. They merely had to inform the insurance company that they wanted out. They did not have to pay a penny toward providing contraception. The Little Sisters' attorneys argued that it was nonetheless unconstitutional because they were still involved in the system as a whole; nonreligious employees at the organization could choose to get contraception (at their own expense); and the government could have found even less burdensome ways of exempting them. That's it. The government imposed a tiny burden but maybe could have found a *teeny* tiny burden instead. Rather than an example of religious oppression—"the attacks against the Little Sisters of the Poor"[39]—the case was an arcane argument about the right ways to balance different interests. And to state the obvious, none of those ways bore any resemblance to the heinous violations of religious freedom that Catholics had themselves suffered in this country in the past—or that Muslims are experiencing in this country today.

Another case in which a small theoretical problem was exaggerated into a partisan war cry involved the so-called Johnson Amendment. As a senator, Lyndon Johnson added a rule to the tax code that tax-exempt nonprofits could not endorse political candidates. In the 1990s, the IRS revoked the tax benefit of the Church of Pierce Creek in Binghamton, New York, after it placed a newspaper advertisement saying it would be sinful to vote for Bill Clinton—and then told readers that donations to help defray the cost of that ad would be tax-deductible.[40] The courts upheld the IRS position, but the rule proved so controversial that the IRS has rarely enforced it. Still, it's theoretically possible that the government could remove a tax benefit on the basis of words spoken from a pulpit, so it became a cause among religious conservatives around 2016. In attempting to scale back the rule, President Trump falsely declared, "For too long, the federal government has used the power of the state as a weapon against people of faith, bullying and even punishing Americans for following their religious beliefs."[41]

The issue became significantly distorted, with activists and the press reporting that the rule prohibited churches from engaging in "political activity" or "political speech." The law never prohibited houses of worship from expressing political views; it put a limit on their ability to *endorse candidates*. Even then, they could do it, but only if they sacrificed their tax benefit. What's more, the rule applied to all nonprofits, including liberal groups such as the American Civil Liberties Union, not just churches. The Trump administration's proposed solution would have made James Madison cringe. Someone who gives a campaign donation to a church that has endorsed a candidate would get a tax deduction, while those who give to a political party would not. That would strongly incentivize the creation of bogus religious institutions to act as financing vehicles for political campaigns, or entice existing religious organizations to become more partisan. The overhyping of a minor problem led to a solution that would do far more harm to the integrity of both our politics and our religious institutions than the ailment it was supposed to cure.

Donald Trump promised not only to protect Christians from persecution but also to restore their faith to dominance. "Other religions, frankly, they're banding together and they're using it. And here we have, if you look at this country, it's gotta be 70 percent, 75 percent, some people say even more, the power we have, somehow we have to unify. We have to band together. . . . Our country has to do that around Christianity." A Trump administration, he promised during the 2016 campaign, would be a Christian administration. "We're going to bring [Christianity] back because it's a good thing. It's a good thing. They treated you like it was a bad thing, but it's a great thing."[42] A 2018 study by scholars Andrew Whitehead, Samuel Perry, and Joseph Baker found that the single most important determinant of Trump support was whether voters expressed what the authors called "Christian nationalism"—the hope that Christians not only would be protected from persecution but also that they would re-claim their rightful role as the primary crafters of American values. The voters who supported him the most strongly responded affirmatively to all of these statements:

> "The federal government should declare the United States a Christian nation."

> "The federal government should advocate Christian values."

> "The federal government should allow the display of religious symbols in public spaces."

> "The success of the United States is part of God's plan."

> "The federal government should allow prayer in public schools."[43]

As they have felt less secure, many evangelicals have turned toward more pugnacious assertions of identity. Like other minorities, they some-times seem to be looking for opportunities to declare their defiant pride. This can be seen, oddly enough, in the prayers given at presidential in-augurations. From 1937 until 1993, presidents invited a multifaith cast of clergy to open the festivities.

In 1993, President Bill Clinton decided instead to have one minister, Billy Graham, who he thought could speak to the whole nation. Graham gave a broadly ecumenical prayer, closing "in the name of the one that's called Wonderful Counselor, Mighty God, the Everlasting Father and the Prince of Peace." At the next inauguration, Graham went softly Chris-tian, invoking "the Father, the Son and the Holy Spirit." But at George W. Bush's inauguration in 2001, the honors went to Graham's son Franklin, who called on the diverse crowd to "acknowledge You alone as our Lord, our Savior and our Redeemer. We pray this in the name of the Father, and of the Son, the Lord Jesus Christ, and of the Holy Spirit." He intentionally offered a prayer to which many in the audience could not respond with "Amen."

LGBT Rights and Religious Freedom

Many examples of the so-called war on religion involve clashes over les-bian, gay, bisexual, and transgender (LGBT) rights, in which Christians are supposedly discriminated against because of their biblically inspired opposition to homosexuality. "For this, we are despised," evangelical leader James Dobson declared. "Jesus Himself told us we would be hated for what has been the 'offense of the cross.'"[44] Again, the recipe is one cup exaggeration, one cup disingenuousness, and a pinch of valid grievance.

The core argument: orthodox Christians believe, as a matter of faith, that homosexuality is wrong. Therefore, those who support LGBT rights are opposing the Christians' religious beliefs. And if you're opposing "Christian beliefs," you're hostile to Christianity, Christians, and religious freedom.

Many examples of supposed religious persecution are actually instances of policies advanced to promote tolerance of LGBT people. For instance, as evidence that Obama was warring against religion, Phyllis Schlafly cited his decision to extend federal benefits to same-sex partners of federal employees and the US Department of State's "bizarre new mission . . . the promotion of gay rights abroad."[45] David Limbaugh argued that efforts to make gays and lesbians feel less stigmatized in public schools had the effect of persecuting Christians. He rejected the rationale for these steps, that bullying causes high rates of suicide among gay teens, suggesting instead that the deaths "might be linked to the lifestyle behaviors themselves." Beyond that, "the real civil rights issue here is the discrimination against students who uphold traditional religious beliefs about homosexuality."[46] When the Eastman Kodak Company had a "Coming Out Day," an employee, Rolf Szabo, sent a broadly distributed group email saying he found this disgusting. He was fired for refusing to apologize, which Limbaugh cited as proof that Kodak had "encroach[ed] on Szabo's right to religious freedom."[47]

Indeed, the term "religious freedom" has often become interchangeable with the right to oppose LGBT-friendly policies. A 2016 article on Christian Post, an evangelical website, listed "7 Signs That America Declared War on Christianity." Six of the seven related to fights between conservative Christians and local governments over LGBT rights.[48] Being in favor of gay rights, or legal abortion, for that matter, apparently now means you're anti-Christian. Former FOX News host Bill O'Reilly explained, "Some far-left people aided by a sympathetic media are now smearing Americans who oppose things like abortion and gay marriage. No question it is open season on Christians."[49]

The sloppy logic: to oppose a particular position held by some Christians is now considered to be against Christianity. Modern Christians have the right to oppose same-sex marriage but can't at the same time persuasively claim immunity from criticism on the grounds that their beliefs have religious roots.

But in 2015, a real problem emerged for Christians opposed to same-sex marriage. The Supreme Court ruled, in *Obergefell v. Hodges*, that gay men and lesbians had a federal constitutional right to get married. Suddenly Christians who opposed gay marriage were fighting not merely a policy but rather a judicially protected *right*. There was now a logic to the idea that Christians could have less freedom to express their religiously held opposition to homosexuality as a result. For instance, the IRS in the 1970s had attempted to revoke the tax-exempt status of Bob Jones University because it violated anti-discrimination rules by banning interracial dating. Couldn't the government now take a similar posture against Christian schools that opposed same-sex marriage? When Justice Samuel Alito asked that question of the solicitor general of the United States, Donald Verrilli, his answer did not exactly reassure religious conservatives.

> JUSTICE SAMUEL ALITO: Well, in the Bob Jones case, the Court held that a college was not entitled to tax-exempt status if it opposed interracial marriage or interracial dating. So would the same apply to a university or a college if it opposed same-sex marriage?

> SOLICITOR GENERAL VERRILLI: You know, I—I don't think I can answer that question without knowing more specifics, but it's certainly going to be an issue. I—I don't deny that. I don't deny that, Justice Alito. It is—it is going to be an issue.[50]

Part of the difficulty with the issue of same-sex marriage is the speed with which public opinion shifted. Same-sex marriage was considered a fringe idea even in the LGBT communities up through the 1990s. Barack Obama publicly opposed it until 2012. Religious beliefs usually take centuries to evolve. With *Obergefell*, same-sex marriage passed from marginal to acceptable to required within two decades. For conservative Christians, the ground fell out underneath them. Ideas that had been taught to them their whole lives—and to their ancestors before them—suddenly became proof not of piety but of bigotry.

When gay men and lesbians got rights, it did diminish the clout of those who opposed them. For instance, once Congress overturned the ban on openly gay, lesbian, and bisexual Americans serving in the military, the top brass told chaplains to stop railing against the immorality of gays. In one sense, that was a straightforward enforcement of an anti-discrimination provision, but it did restrict the conservative chaplains' speech.[51] Some were so upset that they joined a group called the Chaplain Alliance for Religious Liberty, which pledged to combat the "rising tide of threats to religious liberty," one of which was the "destructive effects of providing official approval of and protection for deviant lifestyles and behaviors which Scripture and orthodox Christian tradition and teaching condemn."[52] Many American Christians watched with alarm as the professional societies for lawyers in Canada ruled that they would no longer license graduates of Trinity Western University's law school, which required students to avoid sex outside of heterosexual marriage.[53] Some conservative organizations have been labeled "hate groups" because of their anti-LGBT position. Merits aside, doesn't that mean that efforts to curtail "hate speech" could, by that logic, target conservative churches that believe the same things?

Even when they're not in legal jeopardy, conservative Christians have felt increasingly culturally ostracized. The owners of Memories Pizza in Walkerton, Indiana, told a local television station that on the off chance that someone asked them to cater a wedding, they would not provide a pizza for a same-sex celebration because it violated their religious beliefs. They were deluged with attacks, made easier by social media. The restaurant's Yelp ratings increased from 2 to 1,200, and it had to close down temporarily because the staff could not tell which phone orders were pranks.[54] (On the other hand, a GoFundMe campaign netted the restaurant more than $846,000.)[55] Newt Gingrich, with his characteristic knack for unapt historical analogies, declared that there was "a lynch mob underway."[56]

While conservatives' pre-*Obergefell* arguments mostly seemed ridiculous, after the decision they developed a more plausible case. Just as a Catholic nurse gets a "conscience exemption" so she doesn't have to participate in abortion counseling, evangelical bakers suggested that they should not be forced to provide cakes for same-sex weddings. Forcing them to provide creative services at such an event violated their religious rights, they said, because their opposition to such marriages was grounded in biblical teaching.

But there are huge risks to this strategy—not so much in terms of the law but rather in terms of the aspirations of Christianity. Remember, like other freedoms in the Bill of Rights, religious liberty doesn't trump *everything*. The United States Constitution allows some burdening of religious liberties—*if* there is a compelling enough reason to justify it. For instance, states can no longer ban interracial dating on the grounds that the Bible disapproves of such relationships. Advocates for gay equality argued—and most Americans would agree—that the right for people to marry whom they love most certainly is one of those compelling purposes.[57]

To override something as profound as the right to marry, conservatives find themselves casting their opposition to same-sex marriage as a deeply significant part of their faith. This is no B-list plank of Christianity. In pulpits and on talk shows, preachers and politicians repeatedly deploy the shield of religious liberty to justify anti-LGBT positions—and, in so doing, send a strong message about the centrality of the anti-LGBT teachings to the religion. That message is being received: some 39 percent of young people who have left Christianity to become a "none" said it was because of "negative religious teachings about treatment of gay and lesbian people."[58]

Conservative evangelicals are having what we might think of as a "Mormon moment." During the second half of the nineteenth century, Mormon leaders argued that Congress violated their religious freedom when it banned polygamy. That practice, they said, was a genuinely important part of their creed. It wasn't just a belief; it was one of *the* beliefs that defined their faith. In the public mind, Mormonism became the religion that promoted polygamy. Mormons were scorned. They were accused of using bogus "religious freedom" claims to defend the indefensible, just as evangelicals are today. For decades, Mormon leaders said they would rather be ostracized than give up the practice. Eventually the leadership made a fateful decision—that polygamy was not actually a *core* belief for the Church of Jesus Christ of Latter-day Saints. In subsequent years they grew rapidly in membership and clout. It was a moment of self-definition for them, as this era is for conservative evangelical Christians.

Golden Age of Religious Liberty

Despite the passion of the culture wars, when it comes to the classic church-state fights, there is now actually much agreement. The Supreme Court has better balanced the religious rights of minorities with the desire to have religion expressed in public places. Congress has made adjustments too, passing several important laws that established broader religious rights, including the Equal Access Act (1984), the Religious

Freedom Restoration Act (1993), and the Religious Land Use and Institutionalized Persons Act (2000). And a directive from the George W. Bush administration, *maintained by the Obama administration,*[59] concluded as follows:

- During school hours, students are allowed to pray, read their Bibles or other religious books, and discuss their faith.

- Students have a right to hold prayer meetings or organize religious clubs and to publicize their meetings.

- Students may express their faith through classwork and homework.

- Teachers may help students organize Bible studies or other religious meetings so long as they do not do so in their official capacities.

- Students are allowed to leave campus to attend Bible studies during school hours.

- Students can express their faith during school events.

- Students can reference or express their faith during graduation ceremonies.

Indeed, society now privileges religion in all sorts of ways we don't think about. For instance, some 42 percent of all noncommercial radio station licenses were held by religious broadcasters in 2012.[60] Efforts to restrict the dominance of religious broadcasting have been resisted on the grounds that doing so would violate the First Amendment. The tax code provides billions of dollars in subsidies to religion. Scholars estimate that local governments lose about $7.8–$12.6 billion[61] from not collecting property taxes on houses of worship.[62] Unlike other nonprofit organizations, religious institutions do not have to file disclosure reports to the IRS, meaning they have virtually no oversight. While three thousand to four thousand audits are done each year of nonprofit tax-exempt organizations, only about twenty of them are for churches or other houses of worship.[63] Efforts to better police tax abuse have been resisted on religious freedom grounds. Court rulings on religious accommodations routinely provide exemptions for religious but not secular purposes. People can avoid working on Saturdays to visit the church but not to visit the nursing home. And while believers may sometimes feel ostracized, one group is even more mistrusted: nonbelievers. Americans repeatedly tell pollsters that they could not vote for, or allow their kids to marry, atheists.[64]

Christians have gained legal clout through a fascinating new strategy. They have started to think of themselves, and litigate, as a minority. In 2014, in *Burwell v. Hobby Lobby Stores, Inc.*, the Supreme Court ruled that not only can religious organizations and individuals avoid the contraception mandate, but so should corporations, as long as they are mostly owned by religiously motivated people. Tellingly, the Court based its ruling on the Religious Freedom Restoration Act (RFRA) of 1993, which was sponsored by Senator Chuck Schumer and other progressives in part to safeguard religious minorities. Protections won by the Jehovah's Witnesses or members of the Native American Church are now shielding evangelical Christians. These cases helped establish the idea that the government must be hypersensitive when secular laws clash with religious beliefs—a principle at the heart of the claims made by the Little Sisters of the Poor about contraception policy and by Hobby Lobby when it came to same-sex marriage. "Two decades later, it's clear that the main beneficiaries of RFRA are the Christian right and other religious conservatives," complained liberal writer Katha Pollitt in the *Nation*.[65]

In fact, it's fair to ask whether religious freedom is now invoked too often, just as Antonin Scalia and Felix Frankfurter warned. The Catholic Archdiocese of Milwaukee claimed that the RFRA and the First Amendment protected it from liability claims by the victims of pedophile priests.[66] In Lancaster County, Pennsylvania, a group of nuns sued a federal agency attempting to put a natural gas pipeline through their property, arguing that the move violated their religious freedom because "God calls humans to treasure land as a gift of beauty and sustenance."[67] (That argument didn't work so well for the Native Americans back in the day, but perhaps the nuns will have more luck.) Timothy Anderson in 2015 claimed that his arrest for selling heroin violated his religious freedom because he had distributed the drug to "the sick, lost, blind, lame, deaf and dead members of God's Kingdom."[68] The court rejected the claim on the grounds that the heroin recipients didn't realize they were partaking because of their religion.

The most vivid example comes from Brooklyn, the same borough that brought us the deletion of "if the Bible tells you so" from "American Pie." Brooklyn has a large community of ultra-Orthodox Jews. Some conduct a practice called *metzitzah b'peh*—in which, after an infant is circumcised, the religious leader who performs the procedure uses his mouth to suck blood from the baby's penis. The practice is performed on about 3,600 infants each year. This tradition is said to come from Talmudic instruction that circumcision must be accompanied by "suction."

City officials believed that this was unhealthy. The public health department reported that at least eleven infants who were on the receiving end of that suction contracted herpes between 2000 and 2015, with two dying and two suffering brain damage. Though it didn't ban the practice, the city required families to sign a consent form. The Orthodox rabbis responded that the herpes claims were a "blood libel." One of the mohels who performed metzitzah b'peh, Rabbi Avrohom Cohn, was a Holocaust survivor and viewed the city's actions as a grotesque infringement on his religious freedom. "Now I am here in America all these years, and I am terribly disappointed religion is being interfered with," he said. "If they want me to go to jail, I will go to jail."[69]

"You may ask, 'what's the big deal?'" Rabbi Gedaliah Weinberger declared, echoing the Little Sisters of the Poor. "'All they are asking for is a consent form.' The problem is that it not only intrudes on our religious practice, but it intrudes on our religious decision making. Already it has had a damaging impact."[70]

The rabbis sued the city, charging that the policy was a violation of their religious freedom. "By essentially starting a public intimidation campaign that forces private citizens to spread the government's beliefs, they are shaking the core of our democracy," their spokesman said.[71] A lower court agreed with the city, an upper court agreed with the rabbis, and the fight continued. Apparently, religious freedom is sometimes under attack and at other times running amok.

To some extent, such conflicts have increased in number because we have collectively moved to a new definition of religious freedom— one that requires more sensitivity to religious people than ever before. Many of the instances in which modern Christians claim victimhood are "accommodation" cases, which is to say that they're being harmed only incidentally, as a by-product of some secular law that wasn't targeting them. We have come to think of this new kind of religious freedom as the moral equivalent of earlier claims against overt oppression. Requiring someone to fill out paperwork in order to be excused from a secular law is now in the same category—religious freedom!—as hanging a Quaker from a tree.

This is not an argument against the nuanced attempts to accommodate religious beliefs in those circumstances. This broad definition of liberty helps make the American approach to religious freedom rise above others. But there is a significant risk to invoking religious freedom too often. If we always play the music at the same volume—whether for egregious violations or gray-area cases—we will lose any sense of perspective. We could misunderstand the phrase "religious freedom" and might even become blinded to real persecution when it's right under our noses.

Wallace Deen Mohammed

Chapter Sixteen

ALL-AMERICAN
ISLAM

*Muslims are on their way to becoming
the latest fully mainstreamed American
religion. Until 9/11.*

In 1955, the sociologist Will Herberg wrote that although America embraced religious freedom, certain faiths were more equal than others. "Americanness today entails religious identification as Protestant, Catholic, or Jew," he wrote. On the other hand, being a Buddhist or Muslim would "imply being foreign."[1]

In 1999, Sulayman Nyang, one of the foremost Muslim American scholars, proposed an amendment to Herberg's work. "If the present and the recent past are any sort of guide to the future, then we can here conclude that Islam as a minority religion has a promising future. . . . Their religion will join Christianity and Judaism as the third branch of the Abrahamic tradition."[2] In a Beliefnet article titled "Islam: The Next American Religion," Muslim author Michael Wolfe wrote that because of its pluralism, its Abrahamic roots, and its interest in mysticism, his faith was poised to break out. "There's a new religion on the block now, one that fits the current zeitgeist nicely. It's Islam." That article was published a few months before the terrorist attacks of September 11, 2001.

In the next chapter, we will see how American Muslims have become targets of a historic wave of persecution. But it's important to understand that before the backlash began, Muslims had been well on their way to becoming mainstream, in part because the American model of religious freedom was working so well. Immigration created tremendous diversity within the American Muslim community. Muslim women began to assert an Americanized approach to their roles, forcing liberal American values even on conservative Muslims who had come from other nations. Among African Americans, Wallace Deen Mohammed—one of the most significant unheralded figures in American religious history—led a mass migration out of the Nation of Islam toward mainstream Sunni Islam. Cultural figures such as Muhammad Ali and Kareem Abdul-Jabbar helped normalize Islam. Notably, even the 9/11 attacks did not immediately stem the progress, in large part because of the leadership of President George W. Bush. American Muslims were demonstrating the effectiveness of the Madisonian model—a distinctive religion had evolved, fitfully but persistently, in a way that allowed for both deep spirituality and assimilation, full, free, and thoroughly American.

African American Islam

In the early twentieth century, religious entrepreneurs attempted to appeal to African Americans by recalling the substantial Islamic presence among slaves. Timothy Drew, who took the name Noble Drew Ali, founded the Moorish Holy Temple of Science in Newark, New Jersey, in 1913, arguing that all African Americans were Moors, and Muslim. Claiming to be a Muslim prophet, he recruited adherents in Philadelphia, Pittsburgh, Detroit, and Chicago. The FBI tracked and harassed Ali in part because he was what they considered "a fanatic on the subject of equality for all races." In Anderson, Indiana, agents seized the temple's possessions and closed its offices.[3]

The group faded away after Noble Drew Ali died in 1929, but it likely influenced Wallace D. Fard, a silk peddler in Detroit, who created the Nation of Islam. Fard taught that American blacks descended from a tribe called Shabazz that whites had enslaved. He disappeared in 1934 and was replaced by an autoworker named Elijah Poole, who changed his name to Elijah Muhammad and would lead the Nation of Islam from 1934 until 1975. The Nation of Islam offered a powerful message of self-reliance and empowerment that attracted thousands of "black Muslims," including

Malcolm X, Muhammad Ali, and Louis Farrakhan. It also advanced an extreme, separatist mythology: that white people are devils created by an evil scientist named Yakub; that Wallace Fard had been God incarnate; and that blacks in America should establish their own separate nation.

The trajectory of the organization—and of Islam in America—took a sharp turn in 1975. On February 25 of that year, Elijah Muhammad died and was replaced by one of his sons, Wallace Deen Mohammed. That same day, W. D. went to the Nation of Islam's temple on the South Side of Chicago to present himself to the world. He mourned his father, praised his greatness, and then revealed that he was going to make a few changes. He held up a copy of the Quran and said, "We have to take this down from the shelf." Laying the groundwork for a historic shift, he declared, "What my father taught that is in this book, we will keep. What is not in this book, we have to give up."[4]

Having read the Quran carefully while serving in prison for refusing military conscription, W. D. Mohammed moved to correct what he deemed the Nation of Islam's mistaken or blasphemous theology. Wallace Fard was not God. The last prophet was Muḥammad, not W. D's father, Elijah.

Within two years, the temples were renamed "mosques." The pews were removed and replaced by prayer carpets. Quotations from the Quran, often in classical Arabic writing, began to adorn the walls. The ministers became imams and were asked to learn Arabic and brush up on their Quran. Adherents were encouraged to pray five times a day, fast during Ramadan, try to make the pilgrimage to Mecca, and read the holy book.[5] Mohammed encouraged them to take Muslim surnames instead of using "X," as most Nation of Islam members had.

Mohammed also required all of the mosques to add one more sacred object to the décor—an American flag. His New World Patriotism Day on July 4 in Chicago attracted baby-kissing pols of all colors and encouraged African American Muslims to "come into the American spirit and identify with the land and flag."[6] He endorsed the racial self-empowerment of the earlier Nation of Islam but recrafted the message: Islam was a way to reclaim their African roots.

His most notable convert was Muhammad Ali. Many Americans were exposed to the Nation of Islam after the boxer Cassius Clay became Muhammad Ali and regularly thanked "the Honorable Elijah Muhammad." He refused induction into the military because of his Nation of Islam faith and was banned from boxing for three years. Ali's religion was held in contempt by many Americans, including some in the media. The *New York Times* insisted on calling him Cassius Clay in more than one thousand articles after Ali announced the name change.[7] But Wallace Deen taught the boxer that the Nation of Islam ideology—including its racial separatism—was un-Islamic. "Wallace taught us the true meaning of the Quran," Ali said later. "He showed that color don't matter. He taught that we're responsible for our own lives and it's no good to blame our problems on other people. And that sounded right to me so I followed Wallace."[8] By the time he lit the torch at the 1996 Summer Olympics, Ali was viewed as a world treasure, his religion no longer disqualifying him from iconic status.

It's not an exaggeration to say that Wallace Deen Mohammed risked his life in breaking away from the Nation of Islam. (Malcolm X was assassinated in part for following the same path.) As of mid-2018, about one-quarter[9] of the roughly 3.4 million[10] Muslims in the United States were African American, most of them practicing Sunni Islam rather than the theology of Elijah Muhammad. When W. D. Mohammed died, in 2008, he was the spiritual leader of about 185 mosques.[11]

The mainstreaming of African American Islam can also be seen in the spiritual evolution of another sports legend, basketball star Kareem Abdul-Jabbar. Like Cassius Clay, Lew Alcindor rejected his "slave name." Both were influenced by Malcolm X, in Ali's case through personal conversations and in Abdul-Jabbar's from reading *The Autobiography of Malcolm X* in 1966 as a freshman at the University of California, Los Angeles. But Abdul-Jabbar soon came under the tutelage of another Sunni Muslim teacher named Hamaas Abdul Khaalis, who also rejected racial separatism. "Don't ever say that this isn't your country," he told him. "Your ancestors lived and died in this country. And this *is* your country."[12] Abdul-Jabbar said his mentor went on to "cure me of racism" by emphasizing the Quran and Islam's universal, nonracial themes.[13] The Nation of Islam, he said, "took the name of Allah and soiled it."[14] His switch from Lew Alcindor to Kareem Abdul-Jabbar when playing for the Milwaukee Bucks was not uncontroversial. "Some fans took it very personally," he recalled, "as if I had firebombed their church while tearing up an American flag. Actually, I was rejecting the religion that was foreign to my American culture and embracing one that was part of my black African heritage."

Compared with Ali's, Abdul-Jabbar's conversion was tellingly smooth. The press almost immediately obliged his wish to be called by his new name.[15] Most tried hard to adjust. When his coach, Larry Costello, slipped up—sputtering "Lew . . . Kareem . . . Lew . . . Kareem"—Abdul-Jabbar was touched that he "was very self-conscious about not saying the wrong thing."[16] To some degree, Abdul-Jabbar benefited from Ali's having paved the way. But Abdul-Jabbar's adherence to a more traditional Islam made his approach seem less political—less a rejection of the United States—and more of a spiritual commitment. It also helped that he is considered one of the greatest basketball players ever. By the time Abdul-Jabbar retired, his religion was a nonstory. Sports fans had long since become accustomed to hearing Muslim names in team lineups.

Muslim Immigrants

In the early twentieth century, African American Muslims were joined by a smattering of Muslim immigrants. Syrians and Lebanese, fleeing the Turks, settled in Ross, North Dakota, in 1902.[17] In 1916, the Ford Motor Company in Detroit counted 555 Arabic-speaking employees, many from Lebanon, Syria, and Albania.[18] But overall, the US population of Muslims was small. During World War II, the dog tags for soldiers included three options: *P* for Protestant, *C* for Catholic, and *J* for Jewish.[19] (In 1953, at the request of a Muslim World War II veteran, President Dwight Eisenhower, ever the pluralist, added an *I* for Islam.)[20]

Passage of the Immigration and Nationality Act of 1965 led to a surge in the number of Muslims—from 500,000 in 1960 to at least 3.45 million in 2018 (some estimates put it closer to 9 million).[21] Islamic institutions proliferated. The number of mosques increased from 1,209 in 2000 to 2,106 in 2015.[22]

Some were escaping from America's enemies. By 1980, about 27 percent of American Muslims (some 880,000 people) were from Eastern Europe, many of them leaving Communist countries where Islam was suppressed along with other faiths.[23] Others immigrated from Afghanistan after the Soviet invasion in 1979. Kurds fled Saddam Hussein, and then more Muslim refugees escaped danger during and after the US wars in Afghanistan and Iraq.

As a result, the Muslim population in the United States became quite diverse. In 2011, 33 percent of American mosque attendees came from South Asia (Pakistan, India, Bangladesh); 27 percent from Arab countries; 9 percent from sub-Saharan Africa; and 2 percent from Europe. Some 24 percent were native African Americans.[24]

Most Muslim immigrants assimilated well, in part because many were well educated. Between 1966 and 1988, 76 percent were professional or technical workers or their dependents.[25] For the most part, Muslims were happy with their lot in America, with about 42 percent describing their economic situation as excellent or good.[26] They became American citizens at a healthy clip.[27] To be sure, as with previous immigrant groups, pockets of Muslims have remained in separatist, orthodox subgroups, resistant to American values.[28] Immigrants from Islamically conservative countries have often brought their more fundamentalist beliefs to the United States. And prisons have sometimes incubated a militant form of Islam among inmates. But compared with Muslim communities in the rest of the world, according to a 2007 survey by the Pew Research Center, American Muslims were "middle class and moderates, largely assimilated, satisfied with their lives."[29]

Starting in the 1970s, global politics began to shape Americans' perceptions of Muslims. The Iran hostage crisis in 1979 shined a spotlight on hatred of the West among many Shia Muslims in the Middle East. When Iranian clerics called for the death of novelist Salman Rushdie in 1989 for his book *The Satanic Verses*, the Union of Islamic Students Association in Europe actually supported the fatwa.[30] Most American Muslims took a different stance, but the incident highlighted the darker side of global Islam.[31]

Arguably the biggest obstacle to successful Muslim integration in the United States has been the role of money from Saudi Arabia. The boom in mosque construction in the past few decades was financed in part by money from Saudi Arabia, which advances an ultra-conservative form of Islam.[32] At one point, more than half the budget of the Islamic Assembly of North America, which sends Qurans to prisons, came from Saudi Arabia.[33] Many American mosques received books that peddled fundamentalist doctrine, including hatred of non-Muslims.[34] For instance, the Muslim Student Association distributed at a local mosque copies of a booklet, *Women in the Shade of Islam*, published by Saudi Arabia's Islamic Propagation Office. The pamphlet encourages Muslims to hit their wives in some cases, albeit "without hurting, breaking a bone [or] leaving blue or black marks." A pamphlet available at the King Fahad Mosque in suburban Los Angeles, built with Saudi money, instructed Muslims to oppose non-believers.[35] For some time, W. D. Mohammed provided the approvals for Americans wishing to make hajj to Mecca and was paid by Saudi Arabia.[36] Sometime in the 1990s, he decided that the money came with too many strings. "They wanted him to be their boy," his biographer, Muhammad

Frazier-Rahim, said. "So he stopped taking their money."[37] The head of one Muslim American group, the Muslim Public Affairs Council, rejected overseas Saudi money on grounds that sound strikingly similar to the warnings given by James Madison and the eighteenth-century Baptists. "We believe that a community that cannot sustain itself does not probably deserve to be," said Maher Hathout. "And if people believe in you and in your line, they will support you."[38]

In some ways, Muslims have had an easier time crafting an Americanized version of their faith than Catholics did. Islam has no pope and no unity around Quranic interpretation. The relative independence of American Muslims can be seen through the role of women. Certain Muslim-controlled countries are among the most regressive, sexist countries in the world. Some immigrants carried these conservative traditions with them to the United States. For instance, the Muslim Students Association of the U.S., which was funded in part by Saudi Arabia, initially excluded women.[39] But Muslim American women objected and were soon admitted.

Muslim women have made persistent progress in opening up Islamic institutions and taking leadership positions generally. In 2001, the Islamic Center of Greater Toledo selected Cherrefe Kadri to be the first woman to serve as president of a mosque in the United States. About half of Muslim congregations in the US allow women on governing boards, and most African American mosques do.[40] (Still, about two-thirds of Muslim American women pray in a separate space.)[41] In America, according to one study, it is often Muslim women who initiate the creation of a new mosque.[42] In 2006, the Islamic Society of North America, the largest Muslim group in America, named Ingrid Mattson—a white woman—as its head. When a new translation of the Quran by Laleh Bakhtiar, an American, indicated that the holy book had not in fact given Muslims the green light to beat their wives, Mattson defended the new version. "We have long been concerned with the misuse of Islam to justify injustice toward women," she declared.[43] In 2015, a group of women in Los Angeles opened the Women's Mosque of America, the first female-run Islamic worship center in the country.[44] In November 2018, voters in Detroit elected the first Muslim woman to Congress. Her comments sounded both patriotically traditional and modernly feminist. "Today I was being thankful, embracing how incredibly blessed I am to grow up here, to have this tremendous opportunity," said Rashida Tlaib. When attending mosque, she prays in the women's area, and yet "sometimes I say, 'Thank her,' because my Allah is She."[45]

Muslim American women have been able to change their standing because of two factors we sometimes take for granted. First, the United States government, in defending freedom of worship for Muslims, does not favor a particular Muslim doctrine.[46] Second, America hosts the most diverse Muslim community in the world, with adherents coming from at least sixty-eight different countries.[47] This makes it impossible for a particular strain of Islam to dominate and more likely that American values of pluralism will triumph. Madison's "multiplicity of sects" theory works within Islam too. Shiite and Sunni Muslims, often in bitter conflict in other parts of the world, sometimes worship in the same mosques in the United States.[48] (Some American Muslims jocularly blur the lines between Sunni and Shia by describing themselves as "Sushi Muslims.") The Islamic Center of Greater Toledo, which had the first female president, has members from twenty-one different countries, including both Sunni and Shia.

Muslims sometimes have more freedom to practice Islam in the United States than they did in their Muslim-run countries of origin. Ahmadiyya Muslims, who are harshly persecuted in Pakistan, have flourished in the United States. Shahina Bashir, an Ahmadiyya Muslim living in Silver Spring, Maryland, described the nonjudgmental reaction of most residents. "I kept standing there and thanking God for allowing me to have this opportunity," she told the local paper as she dispensed food in a soup kitchen.[49] American Muslims also have had more freedom than in France, England, and other Western countries. In the United States, Muslim women are free to wear, or not wear, head scarves.[50] As assimilation proceeded, the American Muslim population remained mostly moderate; radicalism rarely took root.

This progress occurred while court rulings were strengthening the rights of religious minorities, including Muslims. In 1988, a US court of appeals ruled that the town of Starkville, Mississippi, had violated the constitutional rights of Muslims by denying a permit for construction of a mosque. The town had granted approval for nine churches and had never before turned down a request.[51] Jurists increasingly treated Islam as a mainstream religion worthy of the same rights as Christianity and Judaism.[52]

Some Christians even began to acknowledge the obvious theological similarities between Islam and the other Abrahamic faiths. "I think Islam is misunderstood too," said Billy Graham in 1997. "Muhammad had a great respect for Jesus. He called Jesus the greatest of the prophets except for himself. I think that we're closer to Islam than we really think we are."⁵³ He was right about that. The Quran accepts, reveres, and builds on the stories and teachings of both the Old and New Testaments. There are more references to Mary in the Quran—seventy—than in the Bible. (An example can be found in chapter 3, verse 42: "O Mary, God has chosen you, and purified you; He has chosen you above all the women of creation.") The Quran, like the Book of Genesis, begins with Adam and Eve and tells the stories of Noah, David, Job, Jonah, Solomon, and Moses. Muslims view themselves as descendants of Abraham.⁵⁴ In the greatest example of interfaith cooperation relayed in Muslim tradition, it was Moses who suggested to Muhammad that he ask God to reduce the number of times that the pious should pray from fifty to five times a day. (Insert here your own tasteful and politically sensitive joke about the Jewish prophet haggling with God to get a better deal on prayer requirements.)⁵⁵

By the 1990s, the Muslims-have-arrived milestones were coming faster and faster. In 1991, Charles Bilal became the first Muslim mayor of an American municipality, the mostly white town of Kountze, Texas.⁵⁶ In 1992, W. D. Mohammed became the first Muslim to give a benediction before the United States Senate. In 1996, First Lady Hillary Clinton hosted an iftar dinner at the White House to celebrate Ramadan. That same year, President Bill Clinton invited W. D. Mohammed to give a prayer at his second inauguration. In 2001, the US Postal Service released an "Eid Greetings" postage stamp.⁵⁷ Perhaps most important, in New York City, halal chicken and rice gradually supplanted the hot dog with mustard and sauerkraut as the iconic street food.⁵⁸

Gradually, Muslims became influential and appreciated for accomplishments having nothing to do with being Muslim. Fazlur Khan, a structural engineer, designed the Sears Tower. Ayub Ommaya, a neurosurgeon, developed a better way to treat brain tumors. Ibtihaj Muhammad won a bronze medal for the US Olympic fencing team, while wearing a hijab. Just as important, as their numbers grew, Muslims became ordinary parts of the lives of ordinary Americans. About 3 percent of American physicians are Muslim, more than three times their percentage of the general population.⁵⁹ (The first time my hijab-wearing dentist, Dr. Muhammad, walked into the room, I was grateful for America's system of religious liberty. Now I'm just relieved that she's a talented dentist and can save my tooth without making me cry.) Not surprisingly, the role of religion in the lives of American Muslims bears little resemblance to the picture painted by anti-Muslim activists. In a 2017 study by the Pew Research Center,

American Muslims reported that "believing in God," "working for justice," and "protecting the environment" were more essential to being a Muslim than eating halal foods or dressing modestly. Two-thirds said that the most important thing in their life was "being a good parent," the same percentage as the non-Muslim population in America.[60]

One surprising reason Muslims integrated so well in the United States was their politics. While Jewish immigrants had been cast as socialists, Muslim Americans were often conservative. In some ways, the group they resembled most before 9/11 was evangelical Christians. In one poll, 61 percent of Muslims said society should discourage homosexuality.[61] Listen to W. D. Mohammed talk about family values: "Respect for life is lost when people do not keep healthy family values. Great nations have not toppled because society failed, but because the family institution failed."[62] Mohammed endorsed President George H. W. Bush in 1992.[63] Another major Muslim group endorsed George W. Bush in 2000,[64] and that year's Republican National Convention was the first to feature a Muslim prayer.[65] Approximately 72 percent of Muslims voted Republican in 2000,[66] including a large number in Florida, which helped provide George W. Bush with his razor-thin margin of victory there.[67]

In his inaugural address, President George W. Bush added Muslims to the standard praise patter about religious groups. "Church and charity, synagogue and mosque lend our communities their humanity, and they will have an honored place in our plans and in our laws."[68] When Bush announced an initiative to give government grants to faith-based programs that helped with social problems, he made it clear that Muslims should participate. Despite his strong support from evangelical Christians, in an interview with Beliefnet in 2000, Bush advocated pluralism.

> BELIEFNET: How would you feel if government money instead was, say, subsidizing the Muslim group that taught prisoners the Qur'an?
>
> BUSH: The question I'd be asking is what are the recidivism rates? Is it working? And secondly, is there a secular alternative available? So the answer to your question is I wouldn't object at all if the program worked.
>
> BELIEFNET: Even though, effectively, it would mean that taxpayer money would be going to help a group teach the Qur'an or the Bible?

BUSH: Right, that's right. . . . A results-oriented world says "Let's achieve some common objectives and some common goals," and if teaching Bible study or the Qur'an is a method that works, we should welcome it.[69]

About a year after that interview, on September 11, 2001, nineteen terrorists—all of them Muslim—killed 2,996 people. Bush's attitudes about Islam would prove to be far more important than anyone could have imagined during the campaign.

The Post-9/11 Wave of Tolerance

When false rumors spread in the 1830s that Catholic priests had imprisoned a young woman in a Boston convent, a mob came and burned down the building. When false rumors spread during World War II that Jehovah's Witnesses were plotting with the Nazis, Witnesses were beaten and castrated. When false rumors spread in 1838 that Mormons were plotting to take Missourians' land, they were massacred.

So when the accurate news was reported in the days and weeks after September 11, 2001, that the terrorists were militant Muslims; that their leader, Osama bin Laden, had said, "We are the children of an Islamic Nation, with Prophet Muhammad as its leader, our Lord is one"; and that he had been given safe harbor in Afghanistan by a radical Islamic organization called the Taliban—it would not have been surprising if the people of the United States had blamed Islam. But when public opinion surveys were released in November 2001, they revealed a remarkable development: Americans had become *more* sympathetic to Islam. While in March 2001, 45 percent had a favorable opinion of Muslim Americans, after the attacks, 59 percent did. Favorable views about Muslims among conservative Republicans skyrocketed from 35 percent to 64 percent.[70]

In some ways, it was a vivid demonstration of how completely Americans had absorbed once-alien notions about religious tolerance. But much of the credit should go to President George W. Bush. His administration has been harshly criticized on many grounds, but Bush's posture toward Islam in the months after the attack should rank among the greatest examples of leadership in the realm of religious freedom. When he heard reports of attacks on American Muslims, he recalled the internment of Japanese Americans during World War II, in part because his secretary of transportation, Norman Mineta, had been detained as a child.[71]

A few days after the attacks, Bush decided to visit a local mosque. On September 17, he entered the Islamic Center of Washington, took off his shoes, and walked into the prayer room. His statement began with the most elemental point: American Muslims, our neighbors, are grieving too. Therefore, Americans who harassed American Muslims were unpatriotic, he said. "Those who feel like they can intimidate our fellow citizens to take out their anger don't represent the best of America, they represent the worst of humankind, and they should be ashamed of that kind of behavior." Part of what made America great was, he said, its approach to religious freedom—its equal treatment of all its citizens.[72]

Controversially, Bush described Islam as a great religion worthy of respect.

> Islam is peace. These terrorists don't represent peace. They
> represent evil and war. When we think of Islam we think of a faith
> that brings comfort to a billion people around the world. Billions
> of people find comfort and solace and peace. And that's made
> brothers and sisters out of every race.

He would later be harshly criticized for the "Islam is peace" line, which anti-Muslim activists cited as an example of the US government's blindness to Islam's threat. But in that moment, Bush successfully set a tolerant tone. His strategic goal was to undermine the ability of the terrorists to cast the conflict as the West versus Islam. He wanted to assemble a coalition for the war in Afghanistan that would include Muslim countries. "Bush immediately understood [that] we could not get into a war with the Islamic world," recalled Peter Wehner, one of Bush's speechwriters. "You want to keep it from becoming a clash of civilizations."

In Bush's dramatic speech a few days later to a joint session of Congress, he spoke directly to Muslims around the world.

> We respect your faith. It's practiced freely by many millions of
> Americans, and by millions more in countries that America counts
> as friends.
> Its teachings are good and peaceful, and those who commit evil
> in the name of Allah blaspheme the name of Allah. The terrorists
> are traitors to their own faith, trying, in effect, to hijack Islam
> itself.[73]

Just as critics in earlier eras had suggested that Mormonism and Catholicism were inherently hostile to democracy, some argued that majority

Muslim nations could not become civilized. Bush rejected that view: "It should be clear to all that Islam—the faith of one-fifth of humanity—is consistent with democratic rule." Noting that more than half of Muslims live in democratic nations, he said, "A religion that demands individual moral accountability, and encourages the encounter of the individual with God, is fully compatible with the rights and responsibilities of self-government."

Bush's approach flowed not so much from a deep reading of Islamic history or theology as from an optimistic view of faith in general. Muslims, he said, "succeed in democratic societies, not in spite of their faith, but because of it."

For a time, Bush's strategy worked. The vast majority of Americans drew the distinction between Muslim terrorists and rank-and-file Muslim Americans. But this moment would soon pass.

Protesters opposing construction of Islamic community center
near former site of World Trade Center, 2010

Chapter Seventeen

"AN ENEMY INSIDE OUR PERIMETER"

A major attack on religious freedom is launched against American Muslims, accelerated by a new kind of media and a new kind of leader.

E arlier in American history, those who wanted to suppress a particular religion had to confront a challenging question: Doesn't doing that violate the First Amendment?

They often gave a brazen response: no, it doesn't, because the despised minority faith in question wasn't really a religion, at least not in an appropriate way. This claim was made about Mormons, Catholics, and Native Americans. Whenever this argument has surfaced, egregious assaults on religious liberty were sure to follow.

So it was ominous when, in 2007, the popular Christian televangelist Pat Robertson said, "Ladies and gentlemen, we have to recognize that Islam is not a religion. It is a worldwide political movement bent on domination of the world. And it is meant to subjugate all people under Islamic law."[1] Over the next decade, the claim that Islam was not a legitimate religion gained popularity. Echoing Samuel Morse's comments about Catholics, Michael Flynn, Donald Trump's main campaign advisor on national security, declared that "Islam is a political ideology. It definitely hides behind being a religion."[2] Ben Carson, the former surgeon and presidential candidate who became secretary of housing and urban development, said that Islam is "a life organization system," not a religion. Steve Bannon, the former head of Breitbart News Network and an important early advisor to President Trump, told *Mother Jones* that Islam is "a political ideology." In case there was any doubt about *why* they pushed this argument, the veil was lifted by retired Lieutenant General William G. "Jerry" Boykin, the deputy undersecretary for intelligence under President George W. Bush. Because Islam is "a totalitarian way of life," he said, it "should not be protected under the First Amendment."[3]

To be clear, a noxious, fundamentalist strain of Islam *is* spreading and feeding the rise of global terrorism. The problem is not endemic to the entire religion, but it involves more than just a few extremists. At its worst, a bastardized version of Islam has energized or provided a pretext for ISIS, Al-Qaeda, the Taliban, and other militant groups. In some parts of the world, Muslim hatred of the West is pervasive. A few years after 9/11, Osama bin Laden still had a favorability rating of 65 percent in Pakistan.[4] The populations in Jordan and Morocco felt similarly. Some Muslim majority countries have picked the most barbaric elements of Islamic law to undergird their systems of justice. One of those nations, Saudi Arabia, has used its tremendous oil wealth to spread a radical form of the faith. Meanwhile, persecution of Christians is growing around the world, often (though not exclusively) driven by Muslim governments.[5]

Moreover, some Muslims in the United States have embraced the idea that God wants them to kill innocent Americans. Radicalized American Muslims committed massacres at the Pulse nightclub in Orlando, at a Christmas party in San Bernardino, at Fort Hood, and at the 2013 Boston Marathon. American law enforcement officials have no choice but to increase surveillance of Muslims, including, in some cases, at mosques. When politicians and journalists insist that terrorists are simply isolated actors, disconnected from any religious motives, they are as wrong as those saying that all Muslims are terrorists.

That said, the treatment of Muslims in America in recent years has constituted a historic, grotesque attack on religious freedom. Regressive ideas and actions that were once common, and then banished as beyond the pale, are back. Anti-Muslim activists have blocked the construction of mosques and cemeteries. They have wiped away distinctions between Muslim terrorists and Muslim Americans. They have asserted that Islam itself is so inherently depraved that most Muslims are, by definition, terrorists or terrorist sympathizers. Attacks on American Muslims have been disseminated and normalized via digital media, faster and more effectively than were attacks on other groups in earlier eras. And we have witnessed the election of a president who made hostility to one American religion a centerpiece of his campaign. All in all, we've seen a revival of patterns we thought had been expunged, to such a degree that religious freedom itself now seems more precarious than it has in decades.

The Growth of Anti-Muslim Activism

President Bush delayed anti-Muslim sentiment from taking root,[6] but within a year or two, conservative Christian leaders started taking a different tack. A stark example of the shift in approach among evangelical leaders can be found within the family of the beloved Christian evangelist Billy Graham. While he had complimented Islam in 1997, his son Franklin Graham in 2002 called Islam a "wicked, violent religion." Later, he mocked Bush's "Islam is peace" line. "There was this hoo-rah around Islam being a peaceful religion," he said. "But then you start having suicide bombers, and people start saying, 'Wait a minute, something doesn't add up here.'" The dam broke, and other Christian leaders rushed in to criticize not only the terrorists but the Islamic religion and its founder. Jerry Falwell called Muhammad "a terrorist." Jerry Vines, the former head of the Southern Baptist Convention, the nation's largest Protestant denomination—the sect that had led the charge for religious freedom in the eighteenth century—called Muhammad a "demon-possessed pedophile." The Christian book industry quickly capitalized with titles such as *The Everlasting Hatred: The Roots of Jihad*; *Religion of Peace or Refuge for Terror?*; and *War on Terror: Unfolding Bible Prophecy*.[7]

Public opinion shifted dramatically. Immediately after 9/11, only 25 percent of Americans said "Islam is more likely to encourage violence," but by July 2004, 46 percent did.[8] Verbal attacks then morphed into concrete assaults on Muslims' religious freedom—including one of the most basic, the freedom to establish houses of worship. In Tennessee, the Islamic Center of Murfreesboro had been established in 1982 for Muslim families in the community, about thirty miles outside Nashville. The Muslim population grew with the arrival of refugees fleeing Saddam Hussein and of Somalis displaced by civil war. Many other international students came to attend nearby Vanderbilt University and Tennessee State University. As of 2010, about one thousand Muslim families were sharing a 1,200-square-foot space to worship; the women watched on closed-circuit television in a converted garage. Members raised $600,000 for a new 12,000-square-foot building located on the outskirts of town. With the support of the Republican mayor, the city planning commission approved the mosque. But after word of the project spread, protests began.[9]

The campaign against the Murfreesboro mosque featured many elements found in past assaults on religious minorities. First, fearful of genuine Islamist terrorism, local residents lost the distinction between radicals in Afghanistan and restaurant owners in Murfreesboro. After someone set fire to construction equipment at the mosque site, one resident said, "I think it was a piece of their own medicine. They bombed our country."[10] Another agreed that the "they" over there were the same as the "they" next door. "Everybody knows they are trying to kill us," she declared. "Somebody has to stand up and take this country back."[11] Another said, "Something's going on, and I don't like it. We're at war with these people."[12] A billboard appeared declaring "Defeat Universal Jihad Now."[13]

Second, they too maintained that Islam was not a real religion and therefore not worthy of First Amendment protection. Ron Ramsey, a candidate for lieutenant governor, suggested, "You could even argue whether being a Muslim is actually a religion, or is it a nationality, way of life, cult or whatever you want to call it?"[14] A local Republican candidate for the US House of Representatives, Lou Ann Zelenik, explained that Islam was a political organization "designed to fracture the moral and political foundation of Middle Tennessee."[15]

Third, they flipped the script and claimed that it was the Muslims who were endangering the religious freedoms of non-Muslims. In one of the lawsuits filed against the mosque, opponents argued that mosque members were "compelled by their religion to subdue non-Muslims."[16] Therefore, "why would we give any religion the right to cancel our rights under the United States Constitution?"[17]

Encouragingly, despite local opposition, the courts upheld the basic principles of religious freedom. A local judge at first ruled for the protesters, finding that the planning commission had not given adequate notice of the meeting at which the permit was approved.[18] But a US district court ruled that the mosque could open, and other courts agreed.[19] The US Department of Justice helped by filing a brief explaining that Islam is, indeed, a religion.[20]

Efforts to block Muslim houses of worship were not limited to Tennessee. In 2012, the Pew Research Center's Forum on Religion & Public Life counted at least fifty-three instances when proposals for mosque construction or expansion were contested by local residents.[21] When the Islamic Society of Milwaukee applied for permission to build a mosque, a rally was held to protest "the growing threat of Islam." One resident explained that "a mosque is a Trojan Horse in a community. Muslims have not come to integrate but to dominate."[22] During a zoning board meeting in Bayonne, New Jersey, residents railed against the "so-called religion."[23] Protests against a mosque in Temecula, California, drew signs such as "Mosques are monuments to terrorism." A local pastor said: "I see people blowing up, being killed, beheaded, murdered, every day in the news. And I see that they are very often—virtually all the time—they have a Muslim connection. I don't see every day in the paper Baptists beheading, killing, burning, looting, suicide bombing."[24]

The protests became so prevalent that the United States Department of Justice stepped up its efforts to intervene. From 2010 to 2016, the Justice Department joined or initiated seventeen cases in which, it believed, opposition to mosque construction violated the religious freedom of American Muslims.[25] For instance, the Justice Department argued in a case in Culpeper County, Virginia—the same county where Baptists had been persecuted in the time of James Madison—that on twenty-six other occasions the town had approved the type of permits that it denied the mosque.[26]

Even deceased Muslims scared the increasingly agitated populace. Residents in at least four communities attempted to block Muslims from creating cemeteries. West Pennsboro Township, Pennsylvania, objected on the (false) theory that Muslims' burial practices would contaminate the groundwater, since they don't place caskets in metal-lined vaults. In Farmersville, Texas, residents officially complained about the location of the cemetery, but some were up front about the real roots of their opposition: "People don't trust Muslims. Their goal is to populate the United States and take it over," one resident said. Town leaders tried to reassure residents by distributing material stating that there would be "no terrorist activity associated with" the cemetery.[27]

The Sharia Scare

In 2010, Newt Gingrich, the former Republican Speaker of the House of Representatives, urged a mainstream conservative audience at the prestigious American Enterprise Institute to wake up to a new enemy. It was not ISIS, nuclear proliferation, immigration, or social polarization. No, it was something called "Shariah" that was "a mortal threat to the survival of freedom in the United States and in the world as we know it."[28] To casual observers this may have seemed like a quixotic obsession, but Gingrich was tapping into a growing fear that Islamic law, with associated barbaric punishments, was infiltrating America. From 2010 to 2016, lawmakers introduced 120 anti-Sharia laws in forty-two states. In Tennessee, a bill provided for a fifteen-year prison sentence for anyone who helped a "Sharia organization," which was defined as two or more people acting to "support" Sharia. Six states—Louisiana, Oklahoma, Tennessee, Arizona, Kansas, and South Dakota—approved laws aimed at blocking Sharia. Conservative funders bankrolled the placement of 28 million copies of *Obsession*, a video about Islamic terrorists, in seventy newspapers.[29] Sharia was "the pre-eminent totalitarian threat of our time," declared an urgent report from the Center for Security Policy, a leading anti-Islamic activist group run by a former official of the Ronald Reagan administration named Frank Gaffney.[30]

To be clear, the Sharia threat in America is made up. Yet it gained prominence and legitimacy with stunning speed—exemplifying how the modern techno-media system can turbocharge attacks on religious freedom.

Sharia law refers to a broad set of religious rules assembled over hundreds of years to guide Muslim behavior. It covers religious and ethical practices—such as how many times a day to pray, what kinds of food Muslims should eat, how to treat animals, what kind of loans are permissible—and a wide variety of other topics. It addresses family law, including rules for marriage, divorce, and inheritance. It can, in some countries, include legal punishments for crimes; in a handful of Muslim countries, authorities even cite the Quran in occasionally cutting off the hands of thieves. Mostly, Sharia is similar in nature to the Halacha rules that govern some Orthodox Jews and to Catholic Canon Law, which affects all practicing Catholics.

Anti-Muslim activists have thoroughly distorted both the content of these rules and how they're used by Muslims around the world. They describe Sharia as a take-it-or-leave-it, all-inclusive package of rules that all Muslims around the world must, and do, follow. Sharia, they say, *requires* violent jihad against nonbelievers, so Muslims within the United States will inevitably follow those orders. Violence, barbarism, sexism, and hatred of democracy will grow as American courts and communities are forced to accept Sharia.

Let's start with the most basic point. For any particular Sharia rules to become law in the United States, they would have to be approved by state legislatures and city councils. The same is true for Halacha and Catholic Canon Law. Orthodox Jews may opt to eat only kosher food, but to block other Americans from eating shellfish, the United States Congress would need to ban lobster rolls. Same with Sharia. Muslims can use parts of Sharia as a private personal code, but to force it on other Americans, those rules must be approved by state legislatures or Congress. It is true that civil courts are sometimes asked to adjudicate cases in which individuals have made contracts or decisions based on their personal religious views. For instance, a couple who divorced following the procedures of a rabbinical or Sharia court might then present that agreement to an American court for enforcement. The courts pretty much treat these the way they treat other contracts, assessing factors such as whether they were created under duress or violate American laws. To do that, judges sometimes need to understand the nature of those religious rulings.[31] But American courts do not accept the contracts if the terms violate American law.

The second fallacy is that if a Muslim abides by any of Sharia's rules, he or she must abide by all of them, following the most extreme possible interpretations. In other words, if you eat halal chicken and rice, you pretty much have to kill infidels too. In fact, on this score, Islam is like, well, every other religion in the history of the world: its practitioners have interpreted religious law in a wide variety of ways. There are certainly fundamentalist countries that interpret the Quran to justify inhumane rulings. For instance, 85 percent of those in Afghanistan believe in stoning as a punishment for adultery, and even in the more moderate Turkey, 29 percent agree.[32] But the idea that Sharia requires opposition to democracy is widely rejected by Muslims around the world. Some 93 percent of Muslims in Indonesia say it is "good that others are very free to practice their faith."[33] Even among Muslims who do want Sharia applied pervasively, many believe it should apply only to Muslims.[34]

Of course, the real worry for the American political system should be whether *American* Muslims want Sharia imposed. They don't. Not a single major American Muslim group has asked for Sharia to be enshrined in the American legal system. While 79 percent of Muslims in the world said

Sharia should be "a source" for legislation, just 37 percent of American Muslims did.[35] And many Muslims say they support Sharia in the same way that 55 percent of Americans say the Bible should be a source for legislation.[36] They mostly mean biblical values should inform the law, not that judges should, say, adopt the suggestion in Deuteronomy that rapists be required to marry their victims. Most American Muslims say there are multiple valid interpretations of Islam, and only one-third even say Islam is the "one true faith," about the same percentage as American Christians who make that claim for their own religion. American Muslims benefit more from religious freedom than any Muslims in the world; they're not eager to trade American law for the rules of Pakistan. In fact, 66 percent of American Muslims believe life here is better than in most Muslim countries, compared with 8 percent who say it's worse.[37]

Catholics in the 1830s, in the 1920s, and in 1960 had to answer a similar charge that they owed allegiance to a foreign authority and set of laws. In his attack on Al Smith in 1929, Charles C. Marshall argued in the *Atlantic* that if a Catholic were elected to the US presidency, decision making on marriage, education, and other topics would be "wrested from the jurisdiction of the State." Catholics would have no choice but to obey the "foreign and extraterritorial" rules.[38] American Muslims are freer to ignore fundamentalist interpretations of Sharia than Catholics of the 1920s were in disregarding the Vatican.

In short, American Muslims have not tried to impose Sharia and don't want to—and even if they did want to, they couldn't.

In truth, most of those warning about Sharia were not taken seriously for much of the 2000s. Anti-Islam activist Frank Gaffney was excluded from some conservative political gatherings because of his fringe views.[39] Then, starting around 2010, the anti-Sharia movement began to take off. When controversy erupted in New York over plans—approved by local authorities and churches—to construct an Islamic community center a few blocks from the site of the World Trade Center, Sharia became part of the opposition campaign. Robert Spencer of Jihad Watch explained how the center would invariably spawn terrorism. "They say it will be different but they will be reading the same Quran and teaching the same Islamic law that led those 19 hijackers to destroy the World Trade Center and murder 3,000 Americans."[40]

The battles over anti-Sharia laws in the state legislatures intensified. In November 2010, the voters of Oklahoma approved the Save Our State amendment to the state's constitution, which decreed that their courts "shall not consider international law or Sharia law." State senator Rex Duncan, the sponsor of one anti-Sharia bill, admitted that there were no examples of Sharia being imposed but claimed that the bill was a "preventive strike" to help ensure "the survival of America." The bill's other sponsor, Representative Mike Reynolds, explained, "America was founded on Judeo-Christian values, it's the basis of our laws and some people are trying to deny that."[41] After a federal judge, Vicki Miles-LaGrange, struck down the amendment, Robert Spencer reposted an article titled "Taliban Chops Off Man's Hand for Theft" and asked, "Isn't it great that Judge Vicki Miles-LaGrange has made Oklahoma safe for Sharia?"[42]

Being against Sharia became a way for lawmakers to signal their conservative toughness. A stunning 630 different Republican legislators sponsored or cosponsored anti-Sharia laws from 2010 to 2016.[43] Since Sharia was thought of as an indivisible package, they figured even minor accommodations to Muslim traditions would lead inexorably to adoption of full Sharia. When schools in Dearborn, Michigan, began providing halal meals for their large Muslim population, Pamela Geller's organization tweeted, "Halal meals increasing in Dearborn schools. What's next???"[44] When some cities set aside female-only swim times in public pools, in part to accommodate Muslim women, Geller pleaded, "Stop the Islamization of America."[45] She reported that "in a little-known strike against freedom," Butterball turkeys were slaughtered in a halal-compliant way and should be boycotted.[46] Bryan Fischer of the American Family Association seriously warned, "Every single Butterball turkey sold in the United States of America has been sacrificed to Allah."[47]

Like the argument that Islam was not a religion, the anti-Sharia drive could be used to break apart First Amendment protections. "Far from being entitled to the protections of our Constitution under the principle of freedom of religion," Frank Gaffney wrote, Sharia "is actually a seditious assault on our Constitution which we are obliged to prosecute, not protect."[48] Claiming that "over eighty percent" of American mosques are "shariah-adherent," he concluded that they are not houses of worship but rather "incubators of, at best, subversion and, at worst, violence and should be treated accordingly."[49] A report issued by his Center for Security Policy, signed by numerous notable anti-Muslim activists, recommended a stunning array of legal restrictions for those who "espouse or support shariah," that is, *most American mosques*:

- Muslims who back Sharia should be prohibited from holding elective office or serving in the military.

- "Shariah-compliant" finance (i.e., Islam-friendly financial products) should be banned.

- Mosques that "advocate shariah in America" must be "subject to investigation and prosecution."[50]

Imagine the above sentences with "Catholic Canon Law" or "Jewish rules of Halacha" substituted for the word "Sharia": *Jews who espouse or support Hebrew law should not be allowed to hold public office. Catholic churches that advocate the use of Catholic Canon Law must be subject to investigation and prosecution.*

The practical damage of these laws has so far been limited. In 2012, a US court of appeals ruled that the Tennessee law violated the First Amendment's religious freedom protections. Later state efforts more narrowly tailored the attacks toward blocking the influence of "foreign laws" in general rather than just Islamic law.

Just as important, other religious groups joined the fight against these laws, seeing that such a flagrant attack on religious freedom would inevitably hurt them too. An organization representing Orthodox Jews concluded that the laws undermined Jewish religious courts, the *beit din*, and "would be a terrible infringement on our religious freedom." Weighing in on a proposed law in Arizona, an alliance of Jewish groups said, "It would apparently prohibit the courts from looking to key documents of church, synagogue or mosque governance—religious law—to resolve disputes about the ownership of a house of worship, selection and discipline of ministers, and church governance." Abraham Foxman, the longtime head of the Anti-Defamation League, had a nonlegal explanation for the anti-Sharia movement. "People don't know what Sharia means, it's a foreign word," Foxman told the Jewish Telegraphic Agency. The proposed anti-Sharia laws, he said, are "camouflaged bigotry."[51]

Rotten to the Core

The anti-Sharia attack was part of a larger drive by anti-Muslim activists to destroy George W. Bush's initial framing. Islam had not been hijacked but rather was rotten to its core. Terrorists commit terror, they argued, because they're good Muslims, not because they're bad Muslims.

Their most important contention: Islam is *inherently* violent. It's quite easy to make a misleading but plausible-sounding argument to that effect. Terrorists shout "Allahu Akbar!" as they murder innocents. Some Muslim clergy declare that the Quran supports suicide bombers. And passages in the Quran promote violence. In these arguments, conservatives have been joined by some liberals and libertarians such as Bill Maher and Sam Harris.

The first flaw in the arguments is that many of the Quranic quotes are torn out of their contexts and sometimes amputated as well. Muhammad was a military leader defending Muslims from attacks; in that historical context, the Quran was partly a battle guide. Muhammad urges his troops to attack, but once victory is at hand, to relent. Critics often quote the passage "Kill them wherever you find them." They often leave off the rest of the quote: "But if they desist, then lo! Allah is forgiving and merciful."

Second, while there's plenty of violence in the Quran, it's really no worse than the Bible. In addition to oft-quoted messages of peace, both the Old and New Testaments include scenes that make the Quran seem like Teletubbies. For instance, Yahweh decrees that because the people of Samaria rebelled, they will have "their pregnant women ripped open."[52] The psalmist offers this message for the Babylonians: "How blessed will be the one who seizes and dashes your little ones against the rock."[53] While hard-line orthodox Muslims target "nonbelievers," the New Testament makes clear the fate awaiting those who do not accept Jesus: "In flaming fire taking vengeance on them that know not God."[54]

Some modern Christians acknowledge that the Olde Time believers— the Crusaders or the leaders of the Spanish Inquisition—deployed their faith in the service of violence too. But, they say, Christians have matured, while Muslims have not. There's an element of truth to that; in the twenty-first century, religiously motivated violence more commonly arises in predominantly Islamic countries than in Christian countries. But Christians shouldn't get cocky. Biblically ordained sadism is found in recent history. To take just one example, in 1992, Christian Serbs put Bosnian men and boys in concentration camps for the crime of being Muslim. Serbian sharpshooters on the heights above Sarajevo shot down pedestrians in the streets as if they were hunting fowl. Bosnian Serb leader Radovan Karadzic justified his 1992–95 campaign of ethnic cleansing as "just and holy."[55] Here in the United States, it was just a few generations ago that American Christians used the Bible to justify slavery.[56] Leviticus 25:44–46 was cited often: "Your male and female slaves are to come from the nations around you; from them you may buy slaves." The *Richmond Enquirer* concluded, "Whoever believes that the written word of God is *verity itself*, must consequently believe in the absolute rectitude of slave-holding."[57] Bans on interracial marriage, which survived until 1967, sometimes rested on biblical justifications.[58] More recently, Christian opposition to the morality and even the legality of homosexuality has relied heavily on passages from the Bible.

The point is not that the holy books, or the faiths, are equal (or unequal) but that the reality of religious practice has always been determined by how believers interpret doctrine at that moment in time. Some Muslims—far too many—are choosing to deploy the Quran in the service of violence, sexism, bigotry, and even terrorism. But most are not—including, crucially, almost all the Muslims in the United States. Perhaps the best proof that Islam isn't inherently regressive is how American Muslims practice it.

Anti-Muslim activists ignore the ways in which American Muslims have attempted to chart a new course for Islam. "We should not look to the Muslim world any more for leadership," declared W. D. Mohammed, probably the most significant Muslim leader in America, after 9/11. "The hope is not there. Don't expect anything from these governments but more disappointment, until they repent."[59] He argued that the Quran and the Hadiths could guide American Muslims toward a truer form of the faith. "We see the world of Islam in the condition that it is in and that alone should make us more spirited, more courageous, more determined to establish a beautiful society of Muslims in America which is the highest mountain on earth in terms of government."[60]

In *Taking Back Islam*, published in 2002 by Beliefnet, American Muslims asserted the right to define their religion, just as American Catholics and Jews had before them. "September 11 forced a reckoning of sorts," wrote Michael Wolfe, who edited the anthology.

> And it has led us to be more self-reliant. When any religion
> is new to a place, as Islam is new to America, the tendency to
> take one's cues from the Motherland is strong, wherever that
> Motherland is perceived to be. *And then there comes a moment
> to grow up.* For many American Muslims, that moment arrived
> in the weeks following September 11, when a substantial
> number grew disenchanted with the habit of looking abroad
> for leadership. The near extinction of Afghanistan at the hands

of the Taliban, the abysmal state of education in Pakistan, the murderous mullahs of al-Qaeda misquoting the Qur'an on video, along with a host of other glaring moral failures, have led many American Muslims to suspect that Islam's "traditional lands" have less to teach us than they claim.[61]

Not surprisingly, American Muslims have been in the vanguard of liberalization. Some 64 percent of them say there's more than one way to interpret Islam.[62] And 92 percent say they're proud to be Americans, which is why it's not so surprising that as of 2015 there were 5,896 Muslims serving in the US military.[63] Those who find it difficult to believe that American Muslims may be patriots might write on the back of their hand these names: Daniel Isshak, Omead H. Razani, Humayun Saqib Muazzam Khan, Kendall Damon Waters-Bey, Mohsin A. Naqvi, James M. Ahearn, Kareem R. Khan, Rasheed Sahib, Azhar Ali, and Ayman A. Taha.[64] They are Muslim American soldiers who died defending their country, the United States, after 9/11.

Ironically, the only two groups that truly believe that Islam *requires* violent jihad are the "murderous mullahs" and American anti-Muslim activists. Both groups would contend that truly devout Muslims should wage war against infidels. American Muslims such as Wolfe who do not share that interpretation are, well, just not reading their Quran carefully enough. Brigitte Gabriel, leader of ACT for America, claimed: "Behind the terrorist attacks is the purest form of what the Prophet Mohammed created. It's not radical Islam. It's what Islam is at its core." If you're a devout Muslim, you by definition cannot be a loyal American, she has argued. "A practicing Muslim who believes the word of the Koran to be the word of Allah, who abides by Islam, who goes to mosque and prays every Friday, who prays five times a day—this practicing Muslim, who believes in the teachings of the Koran, cannot be a loyal citizen to the United States of America."[65] Christian conservative leader Bryan Fischer put it clearly: "The greatest long-term threat to our security is not radical Islam but Islam itself."[66]

The casual assertion that American Muslims have no agency—or that if they dislike terrorism, it's only because they're sloppy Muslims—recalls the arguments of anti-Catholic activists in earlier eras. Even if well-meaning, Catholics had no choice but to follow Rome. There was little recognition of the myriad ways that American Catholics had been Americanizing Catholicism.

Destroying the Moderates

The George W. Bush and Barack Obama administrations did not argue that Islam was flawless. Rather, they maintained that there was, in effect, a civil war within Islam—and therefore the most effective response was not only fighting radicals but also bolstering reformers and moderates. But American anti-Muslim activists had a different assessment: the moderates were terrorists in waiting. They began attacking mainstream American Muslims and Muslim institutions. Huma Abedin, Hillary Clinton's top aide, was accused of connections to terrorists, a charge so baseless that several Republican senators came to her defense.[67] Khizr Khan, the Muslim father who spoke at the 2016 Democratic National Convention about his son who was killed fighting in the US Army in Iraq, was subsequently attacked as a terrorist sympathizer because he criticized the Republican presidential nominee. InfoWars.com, a popular conspiracy website that became mainstreamed during the 2016 election, ran an article with the subhead "Khan Defends Sharia Law Responsible for the Executions of Gays and Women in 11 Countries."[68] A reality TV show, *All-American Muslim*, depicting the lives of regular Muslims, was boycotted by the Florida Family Association, a conservative evangelical group, on the grounds that it was "propaganda clearly designed to counter legitimate and present-day concerns about many Muslims who are advancing Islamic fundamentalism and Sharia law."[69]

And then there was the demonization of Imam Feisal Abdul Rauf, the would-be builder of the Islamic center in lower Manhattan (to have been called Cordoba House, in homage to the area of Spain where Muslims, Jews, and Christians ostensibly lived together harmoniously in the tenth century). Rauf had been one of the nation's leading advocates for interfaith cooperation and a regular denouncer of Islamic terrorism. The Bush administration hired him after 9/11 to speak in other countries about the status of Muslims in America, with one official explaining in 2007, "His work on tolerance and religious diversity is well-known and he brings a moderate perspective to foreign audiences."[70] But after he advocated creating the Islamic community center—including a swimming pool, basketball court, and library—in lower Manhattan, he was recast as a bin Laden clone who wanted to build a "victory mosque" to celebrate 9/11.[71] On *FOX & Friends*, Newt Gingrich argued, "Nazis don't have the right to put up a sign next to the Holocaust Museum in Washington."[72] Sean Hannity declared, "I'm not talking about shredding our Constitution and putting Sharia law as the law of the land in America, as [Rauf] is,"[73] and at another point asked, "Should he even be in the U.S.?"[74] Hannity's evidence that Rauf wanted to shred the Constitution? Rauf's assertion that America already is "Sharia compliant" because it "upholds, protects, and furthers" the "God-given rights" of "life, mind (that is, mental well-being or sanity), religion, property (or wealth), and family (or lineage and progeny)."[75] Rauf was making the argument that *real* Islam is fully compatible with democratic values—and he was attacked for it. The physical threats against Rauf became so severe that police instructed him to live in a secret safe house for months during the controversy. His wife, the Muslim feminist activist Daisy Khan, received hate letters such as one that included an image of herself labeled "Daisy (the new face of terror) Khan=another whore of Muhammed."[76]

As with other religious groups in American history, not all Muslim groups have spotless records. One of the most controversial has been the Council on American-Islamic Relations, which has operated as a mainstream group defending Muslims against attack yet was founded by men affiliated with the radical Middle East group Hamas.[77] But anti-Muslim activists paint with the broadest possible brush. The Islamic Society of North America—the same group that chose a feminist white woman as its president—was cast as a front for fundamentalist terrorist organizations.[78] The anti-Sharia report by Frank Gaffney's group, the Center for Security Policy, included in a list of "institutions supporting shariah law" bastions of American education, including the Section on Islamic Law of the Association of American Law Schools and the Islamic Legal Studies Program at Harvard Law School. The Center for Security Policy made it clear that mainstream Muslim leaders were among those to be feared: "We have an enemy inside our perimeter."[79]

Even those Muslims who happen to be doctors, basketball players, or congressmen should be scrutinized, they suggested, because most Muslims are at least terrorism sympathizers. Robert Spencer, one of the most quoted anti-Muslim activists, made the preposterous claim that 300 million Muslims around the world were poised to murder Westerners—and that those who weren't willing to pull the cord on the suicide bomb vest were warmly supportive of those who were. "The Muslims who are not fighting still understand that that is something good and proper to be done and they applaud those who do it," Spencer argued on FOX News.[80] Former Wisconsin governor Scott Walker said during the 2016 Republican presidential campaign that there were a "handful of reasonable, moderate followers of Islam."[81] A *handful*.

One alleged "proof" that American Muslims are complicit in terror is that they supposedly never denounce terrorism. "There's been a lot of silence in the Islamic community when America and Americans have been attacked by acts of terror from the Muslim community," said Tony Perkins, head of the conservative Christian group the Family Research Council.[82] Given the magnitude of the problem, Muslim leaders could no doubt do more—but they do a lot. In the years after 9/11, Muslim leaders issued hundreds of condemnations.[83] Indeed, many not only denounced Islamic extremism but also took the far gutsier step of criticizing fundamentalist Muslim culture. Ingrid Mattson, who has served as the head of the Islamic Society of North America, was quite candid about the clout of Muslim extremists.

> Let me state it clearly: I, as an American Muslim leader, denounce
> not only suicide bombers and the Taliban, but those leaders of
> other Muslim states who thwart democracy, repress women, use
> the Qur'an to justify un-Islamic behavior, and encourage violence.
> Alas, these views are not only the province of a small group of
> terrorist or dictators. Too many rank-and-file Muslims, in their
> isolation and pessimism, have come to hold these self-destructive
> views as well.

Because American Muslims have both freedom and affluence, they have an obligation, she argued, to champion a more enlightened Islam. "Muslims who live in America are being tested by God to see if we will be satisfied with a self-contained, self-serving Muslim community that resembles an Islamic town in the Epcot global village, or if we will use the many opportunities available to us to change the world for the better—beginning with an honest critical evaluation of our own flaws."[84]

Despite this, people like Mattson have been attacked. Anti-Muslim activists have insisted that American Muslims are part of the problem—and that they refuse to help weed out terrorists. "When they see trouble they have to report it," said Donald Trump. "They are not reporting it. They are absolutely not reporting it and that is a big problem."[85] In fact, the evidence is overwhelming that law enforcement has been able to thwart a huge number of attacks because of the cooperation of rank-and-file Muslim Americans. Out of the 120 violent terrorist plots that were thwarted between 2001 and 2015, the tips came from American Muslims in 48 of them.[86]

The anti-Muslim crusaders cast American Muslims as the enemy within in order to build support for limiting their freedom. If American Muslims are anti-American and Islam isn't really a religion, then taking steps to close mosques, ban Muslims from office, or refuse to accommodate legitimate religious practice don't violate the United States Constitution. As Frank Gaffney's Center for Security Policy put it, "Today, we are facing a threat that has masked itself as a religion and that uses the tolerance for religious practice guaranteed by the Constitution's First Amendment to parry efforts to restrict or prevent what amount to seditious activities."[87] Even though antipathy to different religious groups has persisted throughout American history, opponents have rarely overtly argued that the unpopular groups should not be covered by the First Amendment. Yet that argument has been made repeatedly by anti-Muslim activists. In 2010, Harvard professor Martin Peretz, then editor in chief of the *New Republic*, an influential progressive, pro-Israel magazine, put it most baldly. "Muslim life is cheap, most notably to Muslims. . . . So, yes, I wonder whether I need honor these people and pretend that they are worthy of the privileges of the First Amendment which I have in my gut the sense that they will abuse."[88]

The Media's Role

Why, when we'd come so far, have we suddenly experienced such a powerful threat to religious freedom? An entirely new media system has changed how such attacks congeal and metastasize. Granted, bigots in the past have gained national platforms. For instance, Father Charles Coughlin was given radio time to utter anti-Jewish tirades on national radio and Henry Ford published his anti-Semitic views in his newspaper. But their power tended to be limited in duration and breadth. For a while, that was true for anti-Muslim activists too.[89] Over time, though, the activists-formerly-known-as-extremists gained massive clout and credibility thanks in part to the revolution in social media and the rise of a new conservative media establishment. One characteristic of social media, of course, is that voices on the margins can far more easily find audiences. That was certainly true for the anti-Muslim groups. According to author Nathan Lean, tweets sent by Pamela Geller had massive viral appeal, generating 150 million impressions for every 1,000 tweets (about three months' work for her). Robert Spencer's comments were retweeted 300,000 times, generating

81 million impressions during the 93 days he analyzed. In the month of July 2015 alone, 215,246 anti-Muslim tweets were sent.[90] With reach came influence and ultimately respectability.

As if the social media engine weren't powerful enough, they got some help from the Russians too. In order to destabilize American democracy, Russian hackers and operatives pushed inflammatory anti-Muslim content. One Instagram post showed an image of a woman, eyes peering out of a black burka, and this message: "SHARIA LAW SHOULD NOT EVEN BE DEBATABLE. STOP ALL INVADERS. YOU CANNOT ENTER A FOREIGN COUNTRY AND SET UP YOUR OWN SET OF LAWS AND REGULATIONS THAT CONTRADICT MOST OF THE WORLDS MORAL STANDS." It was shared 235,000 times.[91] The Russians clearly decided that attacking Sharia would serve their goal of dividing Americans. They created a fake anti-Muslim group to organize a rally in Houston, Texas, in May 2016 and a fake pro-Muslim group to counterprotest. Innocent Texans, thinking the calls to action were real, attended the event, unaware that they'd been sent there by Russian hackers.[92]

Leading conservative media outlets gave platforms to fringe figures. Robert Spencer, the one who said that 300 million Muslims were poised to strap on suicide vests, was regularly published by the Breitbart News Network, one of the most influential conservative news outlets, and appeared on the radio show hosted by Breitbart chief Steve Bannon, who called him "one of the top two or three experts in the world on this great war we are fighting against fundamental Islam."[93] Frank Gaffney, whose group called for the shutting down of most mosques, had appeared on Steve Bannon's radio show twenty-nine times as of early 2017.[94]

Most important, extreme anti-Muslim activists regularly appeared on the FOX News Network. FOX commentator Jonathan Hoenig said we needed to "stop having Ramadan and Iftar celebrations in the White House" and learn from our history: "The last war this country won, we put Japanese-Americans in internment camps, we dropped nuclear bombs on residential city centers. So, yes, profiling would be at least a good start. It's not on skin color, however, it's on ideology: Muslim, Islamist, jihadist."[95] FOX radio show host Mike Gallagher proposed a special line at airports where all Muslims would be forced to assemble.[96] Bill O'Reilly declared in one of his FOX commentaries: "Is Islam a destructive force? There are exceptions, but they are few."[97] Brian Kilmeade of *FOX & Friends* suggested, "There was a certain group of people that attacked us on 9/11. It wasn't just one person, it was one religion. Not all Muslims are terrorists, but all terrorists are Muslims."[98]

After FOX host Jeanine Pirro assailed Islamic terrorists, she targeted respected Muslims who had participated in interfaith religious ceremonies. "Muslims were even invited to worship at the national cathedral in Washington, DC. . . . They have conquered us through immigration. They have conquered us through interfaith dialogue."[99] On Sean Hannity's show, Brigitte Gabriel declared, "We're talking about 300 million people who are ready to strap bombs on their bodies and blow us all up to smithereens."[100] While criticizing President Obama for offering praise for Islam's achievements, FOX commentator Andrea Tantaros shifted seamlessly between terrorists and Islam in general.

> They've been doing this for hundreds and hundreds of years. If you study the history of Islam, our ship captains were getting murdered. . . . You can't solve it with a dialogue. You can't solve it with a summit. You solve it with a bullet to the head. It's the only thing these people understand. And all we've heard from this president is a case to heap praise on this religion, as if to appease them.[101]

And the patriarch of FOX, Rupert Murdoch himself, tweeted that even peaceful Muslims needed to be accountable for the actions of the violent radicals: "Maybe most Moslems peaceful, but until they recognize and destroy their growing jihadist cancer they must be held responsible."[102] Remember, Kareem Abdul-Jabbar: *you* are responsible for ISIS.

The anti-Muslim rhetoric goes well beyond FOX, of course. Conservative talk radio, websites, and social media stars hit these same themes with, if anything, even less nuance. It's easy to find extreme statements on the fringes of any ideology, so in fairness let's focus on the voices with the greatest influence. According to audience size, the top conservative talk radio personalities in 2017 were Rush Limbaugh, Sean Hannity, Michael Savage, Glenn Beck, and Mark Levin.[103] All of these pundits regularly blurred the lines between radical Islam, terrorists, and the Islam practiced by most American Muslims.

Rush Limbaugh, who has an audience of at least 14 million, asserted that Islam was "not even a religion"[104] and that Americans *should* conflate radical Islam and Islam. "[We distinguish] Muslim terrorists from other Muslims. In a more sensible time, we did not say 'German Nazis'—we said 'Germans' or 'Nazis' and put the burden on non-Nazi Germans, rather than on ourselves, to separate themselves from the aggressors."[105]

Michael Savage, who reaches more than 10 million listeners through Cumulus Media Networks, once opined, "They say, 'Oh, there's a billion of them [Muslims]. I said, 'So, kill 100 million of them, then there'd be 900 million of them.' I mean . . . would you rather us die than them?"[106]

Mark Levin, also on Cumulus, declared that "the Muslim Brotherhood has infiltrated our government."[107]

Glenn Beck has simultaneously made distinctions between Muslims and Islamic extremists in one sentence and then blurred those lines in the next. When Beck hosted Keith Ellison, the first Muslim congressman, he said, "What I feel like saying is, 'Sir, prove to me that you are not working with our enemies.'" Beck added: "I'm not accusing you of being an enemy, but that's the way I feel, and I think a lot of Americans will feel that way."[108] His book, *It Is About Islam*, explains, "In America we like to believe that all religions are equal. But that's not the truth. A religion that believes in stoning and killing people who don't share their views and values is not equal to the rest."[109]

Some of the most influential voices are on neither radio nor television. The most popular conservative website in 2017 was Breitbart.com. Here are some of its recent headlines:

"The West Vs. Islam Is the New Cold War—Here's How We Win"[110]

"Political Correctness Protects Muslim Rape Culture"[111]

"6 Reasons Pamela Geller's Muhammad Cartoon Contest Is No Different from Selma"[112]

"Roger Stone: [Clinton Aide] Huma Abedin 'Most Likely a Saudi Spy' . . ."[113]

More important, other social media platforms—including Twitter, Facebook, and Reddit—enable fringe voices to gain mainstream followings. Social media has minimized or wiped out the two primary obstacles to the spread of attacks on religious minorities—cost and social stigma. Those wanting to assail, say, Mormons or Catholics or Jews in the nineteenth and twentieth centuries could do so, but few would hear their voices unless they owned a publication and had the money to disseminate it widely, as Henry Ford did with his *Dearborn Independent*. Now it's fast, free, and fun. As for social stigma, Facebook in many ways *rewards* people with extreme views, including hostility to Islam. Posts that evoke strong reactions, either agreement or rage, are deemed by its algorithms to be more valuable and are more widely distributed. Social media doesn't create hate, but it certainly psychologically incentivizes it. It's not surprising, then, that people who you'd think would be embarrassed to make bigoted comments come to believe they have important ideas to share. The following examples all involve local *public officials* who got in trouble for posting on Facebook:

- A member of the conservation commission of Easton, Massachusetts, posted a photo of a nuclear mushroom cloud with the headline "Dealing with Muslims . . . Rules of Engagement."[114]

- A member of the Board of Education in Elmwood Park, New Jersey, wrote: "Go back to your own country; America needs to get rid of people like you."[115]

- The Minnesota Republican Party posted a photo of Minnesota congressman Keith Ellison, a Muslim, on its page, under the headline "Minnesota's Head Muslim Goat Humper."[116]

- A county commissioner in Mifflin County, Pennsylvania, posted an image of a mosque with a red "No" symbol slashed through it and the headline "No Islam Allowed."[117]

- A Republican committeewoman in California posted: "I DO NOT WANT ANY TYPE OF MUSLIMS IN OUR COUNTRY, PERIOD! I DON'T WANT TO HEAR THERE ARE GOOD MUSLIMS. LOOK AT MY STATE OF MICHIGAN. . . . STOP THE MUSLIM INFLUX!!!"[118]

Spend time reading regular-folk posts against Muslims and you'll spot something right away: the messages are quite similar to those espoused on talk radio, on FOX News, and by anti-Islam activists. It's hard to prove causation, but 58 percent of Republicans who listed FOX News as their most trusted news source believed that American Muslims wanted to establish Sharia, compared with just 33 percent of Republicans who didn't watch FOX News.[119] Elites influence regular listeners, users, and viewers, and vice versa. It's far easier than it used to be for public officials to have impact by attacking a minority religion. Their public statements, in turn, provide safe cover for people to voice toxic opinions that are already on the tips of their fingers.

Clearly, fear drives as much of this as prejudice. Psychologically, it's easy to drift into thinking that because many terrorists are Muslims, many Muslims are terrorists. Countering this tendency would require leaders who pour water on the fire rather than gasoline.

The President

Religious freedom has been sustained not just by laws and court rulings but also by an informal consensus that past attacks on minority religions have been so explosive, un-American, corrosive, and liable to spiral out of control that we just won't do that anymore. When the president of the United States doesn't demonstrate respect for that idea, the consensus can unravel quickly.

Donald Trump began airing his anti-Muslim message during his drive to prove that Barack Obama wasn't really a US citizen. In March 2011, he said to radio host Laura Ingraham, "Now, somebody told me—and I have no idea if this is bad for him or not, but perhaps it would be—that [on his birth certificate] where it says 'religion,' it might have 'Muslim.'"[120] Later, on FOX News, he criticized Obama's visit to a mosque: "I think that we can go to lots of places. . . . I don't know if he's—maybe he feels comfortable there."[121] As Trump understood, partisan antipathy to Obama could be juiced if tied to anti-Muslim sentiment, and vice versa. After criticizing Obama for not attending Justice Antonin Scalia's funeral, Trump tweeted, "I wonder if President Obama would have attended the funeral of Justice Scalia if it were held in a Mosque?"[122]

At first, Trump's attacks on American Muslims were indirect. On September 18, 2015, at a town hall meeting in Rochester, New Hampshire, a supporter asked: "We have a problem in this country. It's called Muslims. Our current president is one. We know he's not even an American. We have training camps growing where they want to kill us. That's my question: When can we get rid of them?" When John McCain was asked a similar question in 2008, he defended Obama. Trump, by contrast, responded, "A lot of people are saying that and a lot of people are saying that bad things are happening out there. We're going to be looking at that and a lot of different things."[123] His rhetoric escalated in the two months before the first primaries, a period that coincided with two terrorist attacks—the mass killing orchestrated by ISIS on November 13, 2015, in Paris and the tragedy in San Bernardino, California, on December 2, when two Muslims killed their coworkers at a Christmas party.

Trump deployed many of the same lines of attack used by the anti-Muslim activists. While insisting that he was going after extremists, he also routinely equated radical Islam with Islam per se. "I think Islam hates us," he said.[124] Asked if he meant all Muslims, he said, "I mean a lot of them. I mean a lot of them."[125] Just as some in earlier eras had claimed that Jews, Mormons, and Catholics would not assimilate, Trump maintained, "They come—they don't—for some reason, there's no real assimilation."[126]

Chillingly, he promoted the idea that American Muslims generally support the terrorists. While Jehovah's Witnesses were cast as Nazi supporters during World War II, Muslims were deemed insufficiently patriotic and maybe even dangerous. Trump claimed, falsely and repeatedly, that he saw "thousands and thousands" of Muslims in New Jersey cheering the destruction of the Twin Towers on 9/11.[127] He claimed, falsely, that American Muslims avoid reporting suspicious activity. "They're not turning them in," he said.[128] He renewed the suggestion, after the San Bernardino attack, stating, falsely, "If you look at San Bernardino as an example, San Bernardino, they had bombs all over the floor of their apartment. And everybody knew it, many people knew it. They didn't turn the people over. They didn't do it."[129] (Police never found any evidence that Muslim neighbors or friends knew. The closest thing: a local news station interviewed an out-of-town visitor who claimed that a friend of his who lived near the attackers had noticed the couple working a lot in their garage and receiving large packages but didn't report it because she didn't want to racially profile.)[130]

Most important, in December 2015, Trump called for a "total and complete shutdown of Muslims entering the United States until our country's representatives can figure out what is going on." Gone was the idea that we should focus on Islamic fundamentalists or terrorists. No Muslims of any kind could be trusted. "It's obvious to anybody the hatred is beyond comprehension," said Trump.[131]

Justifying the policy, Trump explained that Muslim refugees were "trying to take over our children and convince them how wonderful ISIS is and how wonderful Islam is."[132] As proof that the Muslim ban was not beyond the pale, he pointed to Franklin Roosevelt's internment of Japanese Americans during World War II as justification. "So, you're for internment camps?" ABC News correspondent George Stephanopoulos asked. No, he said, but "what I'm doing is no different than FDR," who was "a president highly respected by all."[133]

Trump had taken the rhetorical conflation of Muslim terrorists and Muslims in general and turned it into policy. Restriction of immigration on the basis of religion was unprecedented. Although the Immigration Act of 1924 had been designed in part to reduce the number of Jews entering the country, its advocates rarely said so publicly, and that position was not championed by the president. Even in the 1830s, when anti-Catholic nativism was rampant, or in the 1920s, when the Ku Klux Klan was winning elections, successful presidential candidates did not come out and call for the banning of a particular religious group from America's shores.

Just as stunning, Trump said he would "absolutely" require American Muslims to register in a special database to make it easier for the government to track them. "They have to be," he said. "They have to be." Reporters probed for specifics, asking, for instance, whether the government would use mosques as the places to register all the Muslims. "Different places. You sign up at different places. But it's all about management. Our country has no management."[134] And finally, he said that "there's absolutely no choice"[135] but to close down some American mosques as a way of combating extremism. "We have to be very strong in terms of looking at the mosques, you know, which a lot of people say, 'Oh, we don't want to do that. We don't want to do that.' We're beyond that."[136] Asked if he would consider warrantless searches on mosques and Muslims, he said, "We're going to have to do certain things that were frankly unthinkable a year ago."[137]

Nothing like this had ever been proposed by a successful presidential candidate.

Notably, to back up his proposals, Trump campaign officials cited surveys allegedly proving that a high percentage of American Muslims were radical. The surveys came from none other than Frank Gaffney, who had gone from outcast to legitimated media pundit to information source for a presidential candidate.

Public opinion about Muslims, which had been worsening for a decade, darkened as the election approached. The percentage of Republicans who said at least half of Muslims living in the United States were anti-American jumped from 47 percent in 2002 to 63 percent in 2016. (In the same poll, 92 percent of Muslims said they were "proud to be an American.")[138] From 2001 to 2010, 29 percent of Republicans expressed negative views of Muslims; by 2016, 58 percent did.[139]

Trump no doubt found the political appeal irresistible. Islam-bashing drew together several distinct strains of the Republican electorate. Religious conservatives had led the charge against Islam, in part because they viewed themselves as being in a global competition with the religion. Conservative Zionists liked the toughness on Muslim majority countries that had harassed Israel. National security hawks who had criticized Obama's alleged softness on Islamic terrorism loved Trump's willingness to single out Islam. Opposition to Islam had filled in the gap left by the fall of Soviet Communism—providing an overarching ideological foe that could explain evil in the world and mobilize advocates of American military vigilance. That study by Whitehead, Perry, and Baker that found Trump doing especially well among those who wanted a Christian nation also reported that those same voters had high levels of animosity toward Muslims. They tended to approve of these statements: "Muslims hold values that are morally inferior to the values of people like me," "Muslims want to limit the personal freedoms of people like me," and "Muslims endanger the physical safety of people like me." Trump's antagonism toward Muslims increased his appeal to a large group of conservative Christians.[140]

After his election, Trump appointed men allied to the most extreme anti-Muslim activists. Michael Flynn, his first national security advisor,[141] was on the advisory board of Act for America, the group run by Brigitte Gabriel, whom he called "a national treasure."[142] (She's the one who said that practicing Muslims cannot be loyal Americans.) Flynn dismissed Muslims' claims that they should be protected by the First Amendment as a treacherous tactic. "It will mask itself as a religion globally because, especially in the west, especially in the United States, because it can hide behind and protect itself behind what we call freedom of religion." And he warned that groups friendly to the terrorists had infiltrated the American government.[143]

Steve Bannon, chief strategist during the campaign and senior advisor in the early part of the Trump administration, played a major role in promoting the anti-Muslim activists. Bannon called Frank Gaffney "one of the senior thought leaders and men of action in this whole war against Islamic radical jihad" and Pamela Geller "one of the top world experts in radical Islam and Shariah law and Islamic supremacism."[144]

Mike Pompeo, who would become director of the Central Intelligence Agency and later secretary of state in the Trump administration, suggested that mainstream American Muslims were soft on terrorism, un-American, or both. After two Muslim Americans exploded bombs at the Boston Marathon, every major Muslim group quickly denounced the attack, but Pompeo subsequently claimed that the "silence of Muslim leaders has been deafening"[145] and that therefore "these Islamic leaders across America [are] potentially complicit in these acts."[146] He was also a frequent guest on Gaffney's radio show between 2013 and 2016.[147]

John Bolton, Trump's third national security advisor, was a fan of Pamela Geller, Frank Gaffney, Robert Spencer, and other anti-Muslim activists. He endorsed Geller's book *Fatwa* and Spencer's book *Stealth Jihad*.[148] As his chief of staff, Bolton appointed Fred Fleitz, the senior vice president of Gaffney's Center for Security Policy, the same group that said Sharia-supporting American Muslims should not be allowed to hold public office.[149]

Ben Carson, the brain surgeon appointed to be secretary of housing and urban development, said during his own presidential campaign that he could not support a Muslim ever being president: "I would not advocate that we put a Muslim in charge of this nation. I absolutely would not agree with that. . . . I do not believe Sharia is consistent with the Constitution of this country."[150] Those statements did not disqualify him from being in Trump's cabinet.

After the election, Trump altered the Muslim ban to be a restriction on immigration from certain Muslim majority countries.[151] The first version of the ban also included another unprecedented idea—an explicit preference for Christian refugees over Muslims, even if the lives of both groups were equally in danger.[152] This policy would, he said, right a horrible wrong. "Do you know if you were a Christian in Syria it was impossible, at least very tough, to get into the United States? If you were a Muslim you could come in, but if you were a Christian, it was almost impossible," Trump maintained.[153] (Actually, from 2002 to 2015, 46 percent of refugees from Syria were Christian, while 32 percent were Muslim.)[154]

Trump continued to use his bully pulpit to blur the lines between Muslim thugs and Muslims in general. As president, he retweeted to his 43 million followers, "VIDEO: Muslim migrant beats up Dutch boy on crutches!" The man, as it turned out, was not a migrant and most likely not a Muslim.[155] The source of the video was Britain First, an avowedly fascist organization.[156] Trump's aides continued to treat Islam as if it were a curse word. In 2018, Trump's lawyer, Rudy Giuliani, decided that an effective way to tarnish the character of former Central Intelligence Agency director John Brennan was to say that he "claims to be a great lover of Islam."[157]

In some ways, the attacks on American Muslims have actually revealed the strength of our modern religious freedom model. After Trump announced his "travel ban," thousands of protestors flooded airports.[158] The courts forced him to recast it as a prohibition on travel from a handful of Muslim countries. The courts then threw out that narrower version because it still prioritized Christian refugees over Muslims. The administration revised it again to drop the preference for Christians, add non-Muslim countries, and drop some Muslim ones. That version was approved 5–4 by the US Supreme Court. In one sense it was sad day: a policy that originated with blatant religious animus had been implemented. But there's another way to look at it. The courts and public opinion forced the administration to play by a modern set of religious liberty rules.

There were other signs that the religious liberty apparatus was holding up. Local courts and planning boards brushed aside many efforts to block construction of mosques and Islamic cemeteries. We've also seen some non-Muslim religious leaders expressing farsighted solidarity. Republican senator Orrin Hatch, a conservative Mormon, defended the rights of Muslims to build the so-called ground zero mosque.[159] After Trump floated the idea of creating a national registry of Muslims, the head of the Anti-Defamation League responded that he too would register as a Muslim. As assaults on Jews from far-right groups have increased, Muslim leaders have, in turn, shown their own solidarity. After the massacre at the Tree of Life synagogue in Pittsburgh in October 2018, two Muslim groups organized a fundraiser to pay all the funeral costs of the Jewish victims.[160]

But the attacks on Muslims still need to be taken seriously because they reflect a return to dark tendencies we thought we'd vanquished forever, and this bodes ill not just for Muslims but for religious freedom in general. We can see all the elements from prior bouts of persecution. A minority religion is cast as alien, foreign, undemocratic, and not a valid faith. Ethnic and religious fears blend and reinforce each other. Irresponsible press coverage spreads ignorance and fear. A previously persecuted denomination forgets its own history and turns on a new unpopular religious minority. Political leaders are rewarded rather than punished for stoking religious antagonism. The majority perceives itself as losing status and lashes out.

Popular support for religious freedom is more fragile than we thought. In December 2015, the month in which Trump was calling for a ban on Muslim immigrants and a registry, pollsters asked Republicans whether Islam should be made illegal in the United States. The results: 26 percent said Islam should be banned, and 21 percent weren't sure.[161] Only half of Republicans were willing to say that Islam should be legal in America.

During this same period, violent attacks on American Muslims grew.

It's impossible to say what role the normalization of anti-Muslim rhetoric played—ISIS was increasing its horrific activity in those years too—but something shifted. Hate crimes against American Muslims in 2016 were twice as high as they were in 2014.[162] The 2015 tally included 12 murders, 8 anti-Muslim arsons, 9 shootings or bombings (mostly of mosques), and 29 assaults.[163] Almost one-third of the attacks in 2015 came in December as Trump's anti-Muslim campaign hit full gear.[164] Here's a small sample from the final quarter of 2015:[165]

- October 17, Bloomington, Indiana. An Indiana University student yells "Kill them all!" at a Muslim woman prior to slamming her head into a table and attempting to pull off her hijab.[166]

- November 1, Burlington, Massachusetts. The Islamic Center is spray-painted with the letters USA.[167]

- November 6, Coon Rapids, Minnesota. A Muslim woman dining with her family at Applebee's has a beer mug smashed across her face.[168]

- November 14, Meriden, Connecticut. An area mosque is shot up with bullets.[169]

- November 16, Pflugerville, Texas. Feces are smeared on the door of the local Islamic center.[170]

- November 19, New York City, New York. Three students assault a sixth-grade Muslim student during recess. They call her "ISIS," punch her, and try to pull off her hijab.[171]

- November 26, Pittsburgh, Pennsylvania. A Muslim taxi driver is shot by a passenger asking about ISIS.[172]

- December 1, Anaheim, California. A bullet-riddled copy of the Quran is left for the owner of Al-Farah Islamic Clothing.[173]

- December 6, Castro Valley, California. A woman throws hot coffee at Muslims in Alameda County Park.[174]

- December 7, Philadelphia, Pennsylvania. A bloody pig's head is placed outside the door of the Al-Aqsa Islamic Society.[175]

- December 7, Vandalia, Ohio. While riding on a school bus, a seventh grader threatens to shoot a Muslim schoolmate, calling him "towelhead," "terrorist," and "son of ISIS."[176]

- December 10, Coachella Valley, California. A mosque is fire-bombed.[177]

- December 13, Hawthorne, California. Vandals deface two mosques, writing "Jesus is the way" on one of them.[178]

- December 13, Grand Rapids, Michigan. A robber calls a convenience store clerk "terrorist" and then shoots him in the face.[179]

- December 24, Richardson, Texas. A shooter yells "Muslim!" as he murders one man and injures another.[180]

Nazar Naqvi was one American Muslim who could not understand why his people have become the objects of such rage in the past fifteen years. "Why are we Muslims being blamed for something done by 19 people? Why? Why is that? We are patriotic Americans." His plaintive questions were posed during his visit to Evergreen Memorial Park in Colonie, New York. His son, Mohsin, is buried there. Mohsin was killed in Afghanistan in 2008, having signed up for the US Army four days after 9/11.[181]

Chapter Eighteen

PRESERVING RELIGIOUS FREEDOM

*Why it took so long, how we might lose
it, and how we can save it.*

T hrough push and pull, blood and ballot, prayer and protest, the nation has over time crafted a new, distinctly American model of religious freedom.

What *is* this American approach? "Separation of church and state" is
a component but does not fully capture the essential elements. We have
developed certain rules—most of which seem self-evident now, but which
were won through the courageous efforts of religious freedom fighters.

Religious freedom is a right.

The "state" must not favor one religion over another.

The majority religion does not get to regulate or push around minority
religions.

People define for themselves what a religion is.

Religions are largely left to govern themselves.

Religious expressions by public officials in public places should be
inclusive.

Our society must often make special accommodations for the religious. We avoid, if possible, forcing people to choose between their faith and the law. That's why Seventh-day Adventists don't have to work on Saturdays, Quakers don't have to serve in the military, and Catholic hospitals don't have to perform abortions. Religious excuses get special respect. Jews can skip school for Yom Kippur, but Italians cannot take off for Columbus Day.[1]

But the American model of religious freedom does not rely only on constitutions, laws, and regulations. It's a dynamic system that ensures its own perpetual self-improvement. It's like a free market for religion, operating best when it has both good rules (what James Madison called "parchment barriers") and many competitors ("a multiplicity of sects"). Over the decades, a virtuous circle developed. Religious liberty allowed for more sects, and those minority faiths in turn demanded more freedom. Thanks to that forward motion, government's role changed from promoting religion to promoting religious freedom.

Finally, the American approach has an important unstated premise: Religious freedom should not only prevent persecution; it should also lead to religious vibrancy.

Taken together, this is the American model of religious freedom.

We've seen how modern reality compares with America's past. It also contrasts well with the global present. Consider other countries still struggling with issues we have resolved.

In 2017, Russia banned Jehovah's Witnesses. This happened after years of the Russian Orthodox Church and the Russian state growing closer under Vladimir Putin. Orthodox leaders attacked the Witnesses on the grounds that they insulted the Russian Orthodox Church and, in the words of one court ruling, advocated "the exclusivity of one religion over another, thus indicating the presence of signs of incitement of interreligious hostility."[2] Dozens of Witnesses were indicted, and, according to the United States Commission on International Religious Freedom, there have been frequent incidents of "law enforcement officers interrupting religious services suddenly bursting into Kingdom Halls, wearing masks and brandishing their automatic weapons, when children, women and elderly people were present."[3] The Russian government has also harassed Muslims, Pentecostals, evangelicals, Mormons, atheists, and Hare Krishnas.

In India, the world's largest democracy—and one of the most religious nations—the government favors one religion over all others. Since the rise of a Hindu nationalist party in the first two decades of the twenty-first century, persecution of Muslims and Christians has risen dramatically. In 2002, anti-Muslim riots left more than two thousand dead.[4] In December 2017, police arrested thirty priests and seminarians for singing Christmas carols. When other priests attempted to come to their rescue, the crowd attacked them as the police watched.[5] In 2016, Hindu extremists kidnapped a Pentecostal minister and a friend, dragged them into the forest, and beat them. "The police found them eight hours later tied to a tree," the US Commission on International Religious Freedom reported. "Instead of arresting the attackers, authorities detained the Christians under the state's anti-conversion law."[6] As Joseph Smith learned, religious freedom depends on the state being willing to intervene to protect unpopular religious minorities from mobs.

Pakistan has used anti-blasphemy laws—of the sort employed by the Puritans in the seventeenth century—to brutally persecute those not following a fundamentalist form of Islam. As of June 2016, the government had given death or life imprisonment sentences to at least forty people for insulting Muhammad, the Quran, or Islam.[7] Most victims were Muslim, but authorities have also targeted Christians.[8] Two human rights activists were assassinated after defending a Christian woman, Aasia Bibi, who had been imprisoned for violating anti-blasphemy laws.[9] In January 2013, another Christian was accused of blasphemy, prompting about three thousand rioters to destroy 150 Christian homes, businesses, and churches.[10]

In Saudi Arabia, a court sentenced a twenty-eight-year-old man to ten years in prison and two thousand lashes because he had tweeted in favor of atheism. Saudi regulations make it a crime to "call . . . for atheist thought in any form," demonstrating that nonbelievers and believers have a common interest in a robust system of religious freedom.[11]

France has long offered an instructive contrast. With its doctrine of laïcité, or secularism, the state embraces separation of church and state but without the additional American commitment to making special accommodations for religious practice. In 2004, it passed a law banning the wearing of religious clothing, including hijabs and other religious symbols, in schools. In 2010, they banned full-face veils. Many experts believe that ardent secularism contributed to the tendency for French Muslims to feel more ghettoized and militant than in the United States. More recently, in the face of Muslim immigration and rising Islamic terrorism, French secularism became even less even-handed. The right wing political leader Marie LePen declared, "If French Muslims wish to practice their faith, they need to accept the fact that they are doing so on soil that is culturally Christian. This means that they cannot have the same rank as the Christian religion."[12]

In general, while the rise of Islamic fundamentalism fueled restrictions on religious freedom in the earlier part of this decade, the more recent growth of right-wing nationalist movements has led to harassment of religious minorities—usually Muslims and Jews—in Europe, Latin America, and even America.[13]

While we celebrate the fact that we are doing better than India, Russia, Saudi Arabia, or Pakistan, we should nonetheless tremble at the thought that core tenets of our time-tested approach have lost popular support. To preserve our religious freedom, we need to understand why it developed so slowly, why it ultimately did take root, and how it is truly threatened. Then we can have a clear sense of how to ensure its preservation.

What Took So Long?

Though we now think of James Madison's ideas as obvious, they were actually audaciously counterintuitive. Take the principle that religious liberty requires each of us to accept the legitimacy of other faiths. While the founders (and this book) used the appealing "marketplace of faith" metaphor, it's quite difficult to cheerfully accept the existence of a religion that you believe consigns millions of souls to eternal torment. You've found the *truth*. You have an obligation to spread it and to make sure it permeates the culture. Tolerating another faith can feel like an abdication of responsibility.[14] The Madisonian sensibility in some ways runs against the very nature of religious belief.

Madison's approach to the role of government was also counterintuitive. If you want to aid faith, *stop* supporting it? This, too, conflicted with a consensus established over several thousand years, including a few hundred in the colonies. In Madison's mind, putting the weight of the state behind a particular faith would harm both minority religions (by oppressing them) and the majority religion (by making it lazy and corrupt). But for many people, government neutrality seemed like an insult to God.

These approaches were so alien—in world history as well as on our continent—that we probably had to learn them through painful experience. For quite a while, many Americans mistakenly believed that religious liberty meant having the ability not only to practice their faith but also to impose it on others. That misunderstanding led them to undermine the liberty of others, including Baptists, Quakers, Catholics, Native Americans, African slaves, Mormons, Jehovah's Witnesses, and Jews. They did offer toleration to minorities as long as they remained relatively unthreatening. (It's easy to support a free market of religion when you have 90 percent market share.) But they vehemently resisted when challenged by rapidly growing sects, such as Catholics and Mormons.

Instead of seeing diversity as strengthening the religious freedom model, many Americans became fearful that it would erode the culture or enable dangerous theological errors to spread. In particular, the depth of the Protestant mistrust of Catholics, built up over centuries, made a live-and-let-live attitude difficult to embrace. Pluralism was especially challenging for those who believed not only in the living God but also in the living devil. If we're in an ongoing battle between the forces of good and evil, it's irresponsible to let the chips fall where they may.

We have struggled as a nation with the concept of "public religion"—the use of religious language in official or ceremonial settings or in public spaces. Many held the idea that America was being watched over by God and that we must therefore publicly acknowledge that fact, thank Him, and ask for continued protection. That was relatively noncontroversial for a long time, but there was always an inherent tension between religious liberty and the widespread desire to express a collective spiritual worldview. Despite our aspirations to religious freedom, many Americans deep down believed that their form of Protestantism was the semi-official American religion. Dissenting Protestants and then Catholics challenged that assumption. We still figured that, despite diversity, we could surely find widely shared concepts and aspirations. That has proven difficult. Ostensibly non-controversial religious passages—such as the Ten Commandments—turn out to be far from neutral.

At several moments, American Protestants' confidence that they had already found the true religion combined nastily with their deep ignorance about other faiths. Most people snorted with disgust and amusement at the idea that Native American dances had a religious meaning. Many simply did not believe Jehovah's Witnesses when they insisted that their refusal to salute the flag was driven by a genuine religious conviction. In our worst moments, Americans denied the legitimacy of entire religions, thereby letting everyone off the hook for violating religious freedom rights. Residents of Charlestown, Massachusetts, believed the stories about nuns suffocating infants, so burning down the convent seemed just. The men who massacred LDS families at Haun's Mill viewed them as subhuman, so they wouldn't lose sleep over blowing out the brains of a Mormon child. After all, "nits make lice."

Thanks to our short memories, victims of persecution in one generation have not sufficiently rallied to defend victims in the next. Puritans fled religious harassment in Europe and then hanged Quakers in Massachusetts. Catholics were abused in the nineteenth century, but some joined attacks against Jews in the twentieth century. Evangelical Christians led the way for religious freedom early in our history, but many of their leaders have turned against it in our own time.

Some of these problems persisted because the nation did not adopt Madison's proposal that religious liberty apply on the state and local levels. In theory, the passage of the Fourteenth Amendment solved this problem, but two generations of states' rights–oriented judges meant that it was not until the middle of the twentieth century that the federal Bill of Rights could finally provide full protection.

Taking Root

Americans ultimately demanded that their realities live up to the promises of the US Constitution. For this, we must thank Mary Dyer, Robert Fischer, the Catholic children who refused to say Protestant prayers, John Leland, hundreds of imprisoned Mormons, the Native American Ghost Dancers, Lillian Gobitas, Ellery Schempp, Rabbi Alexander Goode, Ingrid Mattson, "slaves who gathered in hush harbors," John Murray, W. D. Mohammed, and countless others who risked their reputations or lives.

A number of factors ultimately led to religious freedom moving forward.

Religious fragmentation proved to be a positive force, reducing the ability of the majority to squelch other faiths. The collapse of the religious establishments, combined with the natural tendency for religions to splinter, led to great diversity within Protestantism. There could be no uniform "Protestant way"; intra-Protestant warfare was too intense. Homegrown religious innovators—Mormons, Jehovah's Witnesses, Seventh-day Adventists—further contributed to the joyful noisiness of America's religious landscape.

Immigration has strengthened religious freedom. The continuous arrival of new people with new religions increased diversity and forced the majority repeatedly to recalibrate. Catholics from Ireland, Mormons from England and Canada, Jews from Eastern Europe, Buddhists from Asia, and Muslims from Pakistan, Iraq, and other nations—their presence eliminated the possibility that one faith could dominate, brought new forms of religious practice and increased demands for religious liberty protections.

At this point, it's accurate to say we are not only a nation of immigrants; we are a nation of religious minorities. The original American majority was composed of Anglicans and Congregationalists. Those denominations now make up 1.7 percent of the American population.[15] Most everyone else descends from a group that was once considered a religious minority. Our system reflects that.

As fragmentation grew, another significant trend altered the way Americans perceived each other. In the second half of the twentieth century, Americans grew more and more likely to have friends or spouses from other faiths. While only 19 percent of Americans in 1960 had a spouse from a different religious group, 39 percent did by 2015.[16] Studies have shown that greater exposure to other faiths increases tolerance. "It is difficult to demonize the religion, or lack of religion, of people you know and, especially, those you love," write sociologists Robert D. Putnam and David E. Campbell. As a result of this "religious churn," America is "graced with the peaceful coexistence of both religious diversity and devotion."[17]

Politics has played a complex role. Sometimes electoral campaigns have been a theater for demagoguery, as certainly was the case in 2016. But at other times, religious minorities have gained acceptance because of their rising political clout. Mormons entered the Union in part because Republicans wanted to win over western states. Catholics asserted power through their sheer numbers in the cities. The need to create coalitions sometimes eroded historical divisions. In their quests for the White House, both Alfred E. Smith and John F. Kennedy broke with Vatican policy by stressing the separation of church and state. With the rise of the religious right in the 1980s and 1990s, conservative alliance building melted decades of deep antagonism between Protestants and Catholics.

However, when religious groups are small, or powerless, electoral politics offers little help. The Constitution then has to assert itself—championed by an independent judiciary. In the twentieth century, the courts have strengthened religious freedom. Liberals and conservatives both deserve credit. Liberal justices in the United States Supreme Court pushed to limit the role of government in religion and to have the rights of religious minorities accommodated in ways that deepened the freedom of all Americans. Conservatives demanded a course correction when separation of church and state began to create legal hostility to religion. Although the rulings of the Supreme Court have often seemed inconsistent or muddled, in the big sweep the judicial system—because it was insulated from electoral pressure—has brought the First Amendment fully into play. The actions of governments large and small must now be judged against the principles in the Bill of Rights.

When other civil liberties gained strength, religious freedom benefited. The Jehovah's Witnesses won their cases in part because they tied religious rights to freedom of expression. Having seen how efforts to punish slaves also ended up harming freedom of press and religion, advocates of the Fourteenth Amendment believed that strengthening one right would safeguard others.

America also has had an advantage unavailable to many other countries: land. When the Puritans grew tired of Roger Williams, they didn't kill him. They hounded him out of town. When Deborah Moody was banished, she moved to New Amsterdam (now known as New York). When Mormons faced persecution in Missouri and Illinois, they moved to Utah, where they flourished. Much of the Protestant-Catholic conflict played out through competition over who would cultivate new western territories. Though fierce, it would have been worse if entirely focused within eastern cities.

We tend to think of religious fights as being about absolutes, but throughout American history, the minority faiths have adjusted and even sacrificed some of their principles. Mormons had to give up a key tenet of their faith, polygamy, to gain acceptance into the Union. Catholics in the United States diverged from Church doctrine on separation of church and state and eventually even helped prompt change within the Vatican. Religious minorities must always defend their integrity, but the nation is well within its rights to demand that they abide by certain core American principles.

Electing farsighted leaders in the right places at the right times surely helped. Arguably the most significant were James Madison, George Washington, John Bingham, Dwight Eisenhower, Franklin Roosevelt, Harry Truman, and George W. Bush. Each could have appealed to his base (and their baseness) but instead advocated for the loftier principles that made America great.

War has, ironically, often promoted religious harmony. The American Revolution and World War II forced us to manage our diversity in a way that helped ensure military victory. Washington, Roosevelt, Truman, and Eisenhower each viewed religious liberty as a weapon, not a vulnerability. These grand conflicts invited us to identify those few principles that truly distinguish the United States. Religious freedom emerged as a unifying value.

Gradually, many Americans came to see an attack on one American faith as an attack on us all. The ideas of religious tolerance and pluralism ascended to a higher level of civic status. Our ancestors sacrificed so we could have the freedom to worship, or not, as we saw fit. Blood had been spilled. Religious freedom therefore needed to be revered and protected. It became a sacred liberty.

The Threats

Though religious freedom in America is highly developed—especially relative to the rest of the world and our earlier history—it nonetheless faces four threats. Three are small, and one is significant.

First, there is a small but genuine possibility that secularism will become so prevalent that religious people will be meaningfully disadvantaged. If this happens, it will sap America's spiritual robustness, which stems not only from the freedom to worship privately but also from the ability to live one's full life out in the public world, according to the dictates of one's conscience or the light of the divine. This threat is exaggerated, but it is not fabricated. A misinterpretation of the separation of church and state has occasionally led to the subordination of religion. A live-and-let-live secularism has increasingly been replaced by a pissed-off secularism. Angered by religion's intolerance, more voices promote intolerance of religion. It's important that we remain aware of this threat so we don't end up with a French-style effort to protect ourselves from religious excess by entombing faith, ripping off our collective hijabs in the name of repelling religious ugliness. Still, the threat of pervasive secularism is merely incipient. Religion is still quite privileged in the United States.

The second small threat stems from exaggerating the first. Religious conservatives are crying "religious freedom" so often that they're bleaching all meaning from the phrase. If you support gay rights, you're against religious freedom! If you think churches shouldn't be endorsing political candidates while benefiting from a tax exemption, you're against religious freedom! If you oppose a mohel sucking blood off the penises of babies, you hate religious freedom! Just as the overuse of charges of racism, sexism, and anti-Semitism can dilute their meaning, the misuse of the term "religious freedom" risks undermining the strength of our model. During World War II, religious freedom became a defining American ideal, cross-partisan, multifaith, and profound. That sense of exaltedness gave it power. If "religious liberty" becomes viewed primarily as another tactic to win votes, weaken political rivals, sell books, raise money, boost ratings, or secure benefits, it will lose potency. Religious freedom will become viewed as a profane partisan weapon.

One subtle but unsettling misuse of religious freedom came after the 2018 massacre of eleven Jews in a Pittsburgh synagogue. Although all American leaders condemned anti-Semitism, some attempted to cast the attacks as part of the same war on religion that has led to prayer being purged from schools or "Merry Christmas" being "banned" from department stores. Kellyanne Conway, a senior advisor to President Trump, said the attacks derived from "anti-religiosity in this country—that it's somehow in vogue and funny to make fun of anybody of faith." Religious Christians, she implied, were victims, too. The assailant was secularism; the solution was less separation of church and state. "This is no time," she concluded, "to be driving God out of the public square."

Third, religious freedom could become so muscle-bound that it undermines democracy. Conservatives have increasingly taken up the principle—previously championed by liberals—that secular laws should not be allowed to force believers to take actions contrary to their religious code. Right now, the model has a decent balance between Madison's desire that government not be cognizant of religion—sometimes manifest as separation of church and state—and a more modern desire to accommodate religious practice even when it conflicts with secular law. But Justices Antonin Scalia and Felix Frankfurter were not wrong when they warned that such an approach would undermine the rule of law if followed without limits. If we go too far in the direction of accommodation—with government vigilantly thinking about how to exempt religious people from the law—we could lose that equilibrium. We could end up with a system of constant cognizance, with government continually weighing how to create conscience exceptions for an ever-growing array of religious groups. Over time, our system will seem absurd instead of inspiring. If, for instance, the Supreme Court were to rule in favor of the mohels over the New York City public health department, it would signal that religious freedom now hinders the creation of a just democracy rather than strengthening it.

The greatest threat to religious liberty, though, is the powerful effort to demonize, marginalize, and persecute Muslims in the United States. Every other threat is minor compared with this one—not only because it harms Muslims but also because it represents a disintegration of the basic compact that sustains religious freedom for everyone. Many of the lines of attack are strikingly similar to historical efforts to stigmatize or disenfranchise Catholics, Mormons, Jews, Baptists, and Jehovah's Witnesses. Like those earlier groups, Muslims are cast as unassimilable, undemocratic, alien, and disloyal. We've seen rising violence against the members of this faith, along with attacks on their houses of worship. Many voters aren't sure whether the religion should even be legal.

Donald Trump's legacy on this issue can seem confusing. He talks about defending religious freedom more than almost any other president. His administration has taken a few positive steps, such as deciding that the Federal Emergency Management Agency could give disaster relief to houses of worship and raising concerns about persecution of Christians overseas. "Nobody's done more for Christians or evangelicals or frankly religion than I have," Trump said in November 2018.[18] But much of his religious liberty agenda involves efforts, focused largely on helping conservative Christians, that are minor, symbolic, or actually damaging.[19] Most important, in his attacks on Muslims, he has violated most of the principles that have sustained religious freedom by favoring one religion over another; ignoring First Amendment protections; blurring the distinctions between Americans practicing their faith and extremists overseas; and proposing that practitioners of one faith should have second-class citizenship. He has made the concept of religious freedom partisan instead of universal, a way to divide rather than unite.

Meanwhile, the increased aggressiveness of far-right hate groups in the United States—which Trump did nothing to stop and arguably helped to fuel—led to an increase in attacks on both Muslims and Jews.

How does he compare with other presidents? James Buchanan sent the army to Utah to remove Brigham Young from power, but the conflict never materialized. Millard Fillmore received the presidential nomination from the overtly anti-Catholic nativist party the Know-Nothings, but he lost. Ulysses S. Grant dog-whistled against Catholics by pledging that "not one dollar" would be appropriated for "any sectarian schools," but he also wanted the government to avoid funding Protestant groups.[20] Rutherford B. Hayes may be Trump's closest competitor, having argued that the United States Congress should attempt to "destroy the temporal power of the Mormon Church." But he did not hit that note persistently, did not make it a major theme of his election campaign, and was not a decisive player in the anti-Mormon efforts. Richard Nixon was a raving anti-Semite, but only in private. Notably, most of the presidents with comparably poor records were in the nineteenth century.

This moment is also especially perilous because we have never before had such a powerful array of media voices attacking a particular American religion, nor have we had an informal information-sharing system that allows bigots to gain credibility and followers so easily. We have little idea how to combat these anti-democratic strains without violating another part of the First Amendment, freedom of speech.

Finally, this is happening in the context of a political system that now deemphasizes coalition building. At several points in the past, politicians' desire to expand their support beyond their core constituencies led them to reach across religious boundaries or even embrace religious freedom directly. But political parties now focus on mobilizing their bases. Rousing the passions of religious groups that already support them has become more important than trying to win over those who do not.

The most significant test of how far this anti-Muslim rot has spread will come if Muslim extremists conduct a terrorist attack on American soil. Some will no doubt use that moment to take stronger steps against American Muslims. How will the rest of America react?

Strengthening Religious Freedom

Like that sword in the window described by the eighteenth-century Baptist author, religious freedom got sharper as a result of the fires that touched it. Unlike the sword, it has changed over time, adapting to new circumstances. For religious freedom to remain strong—and for us to rise to the occasion during future crises—we will have to stand by some immutable principles while also changing some of our thinking. On the basis of what we've seen in the past, religious freedom will have a greater likelihood of surviving if the following occur:

Religious groups must cultivate a heartier all-for-one, one-for-all solidarity around religious freedom. Efforts to help minority religions help all religions—

for example, when the Supreme Court protected Jehovah's Witnesses, it carved out more room for other faiths to express themselves and live out their beliefs. When a Muslim prisoner earns the right to grow a beard, it enables an Orthodox Jew to wear a yarmulke. And we've seen the opposite too, as when efforts to suppress Mormonism in the nineteenth century led to a narrowing of rights for others. Religious freedom that isn't universal isn't religious freedom; it's special pleading for a particular denomination. And as Madison noted, a government that has the authority to favor one religion today can favor a different one tomorrow.

No religious leader who stands silently by as Muslims are attacked should be taken seriously when he or she talks about religious freedom. Political leaders who participate in such efforts should be held in low esteem, and media outlets that mimic the worst bigots of the nineteenth century will earn their place in history alongside Father Coughlin, Henry Ford, and other infamous anti-American demagogues. To attack our "sacred liberty" is a form of civic blasphemy, an assault on a hard-won communal achievement.

Americans should come to appreciate each person's right to seek God, even when they detest the person's theology. The conservative writer who opposed a Hindu priest opening a session of Congress claimed: "Many people today confuse traditional Western religious tolerance with religious pluralism. The former embraces biblical truth while allowing for freedom of conscience, while the latter assumes all religions are equally valid, resulting in moral relativism and ethical chaos."[21] That's wrong. Pluralism does not imply the validity of any religion's claims. Rather, it accepts the legitimacy of its quest for spiritual truth. A Christian who sees a Hindu priest offering a benediction can believe that Hinduism is wrong while also relishing how exceptional America is for allowing a Hindu priest to open a session of Congress.

Those who cannot bring themselves to respect the faith journeys of heretics can at least understand that religious freedom is in their own self-interest. Throughout history, diversity has strengthened freedom through a process akin to the "mutually assured destruction" doctrine that governed international relations during the Cold War. Neither the United States nor the Soviet Union had an incentive to attack the other because such a move—even if brilliantly executed—would end up destroying the whole world. With religion, it has become clear that attempts to achieve religious dominance tend to backfire, thereby undercutting religious freedom for everyone.

Thus, the wind pushing America forward is not just religion; it's religious freedom. What unites us is not a shared conception of God but rather a shared commitment to the idea that a search for God must be unobstructed.

The devoutly religious can show a little more confidence in God. Madison decried the "unchristian timidity" of those Protestants who wanted government support to prop up their church. Believers need to embrace the idea that in a free arena, their faith will triumph or at least reach the right people, even if it does not have the help of an assistant principal leading schoolchildren in prayer. Those who focus on small symbols of public piety—for instance whether people are saying "Merry Christmas" or "Happy Holidays" at the shopping mall—inadvertently convey an image of a faith that is petty and a God who is insecure. As the eighteenth-century Baptist leader Isaac Backus put it, "God's truth is great, and in the end He will allow it to prevail."[22] *That* is religious self-confidence.

Religious freedom does not mean that faiths have to give up the competition for souls. It just means that the state should not help in the effort. If you win people over, it will be because of the power of your teachings and the example of your behavior, not because you forced them to read a few lines of your sacred text on their way into a courthouse. John Adams put it well: "I am, therefore, of the opinion that men ought (after they have examined with unbiased judgments every system of religion, and chosen one system, on their own authority, for themselves), to avow their opinions and defend them with boldness."[23] The founders believed that such a freewheeling system, rather than forced uniformity, would lead not only to comity but also to truth.

Fragmentation and immigration will continue to strengthen religious freedom. Madison's vision of checks and balances for religion has worked. Now that America truly is a nation composed of religious minorities—many of which had been previously persecuted—it's easier than ever to embrace the concept. Fragmentation means no religion can dictate the rules for others. Each Hindu that arrives therefore strengthens the religious rights of Catholics.

This might seem like a difficult pill to swallow for those of you who believe that America is a Christian nation in a semi-official sense. I'm not sure if this will make you feel better or worse, but . . . the "Christian America" that you want back never existed. In the early days of the Republic, there had been a cultural consensus for two or three types of

Protestantism—which most certainly did not include Catholicism or a variety of other dissenting Protestant denominations, including evangelicals. The idea that the nation grew from a shared Christianity—or, to use the more recent lingo, a Judeo-Christian heritage—is an ex post facto revision of history.

While it never feels good to become a smaller part of a bigger system, in the case of religious freedom, evangelicals can thrive under the new reality. By surrendering their desire to "win" and embracing the religious freedom compact, they will benefit from its protections. The same decisions that once helped Jehovah's Witnesses now provide the legal underpinnings for the efforts of religious conservatives seeking to maintain their opposition to abortion and same-sex marriage. It's also possible that if religious minorities know that they are no longer in danger of being stomped out, they might become less adamant about keeping religion out of public spaces.

The nature of public religion must continue to change. For most of American history, we have sought a common denominator language to express our thanks to God in public spaces and during communal efforts (presidential speeches, public meetings, high school graduations, etc.). At this point, "In God We Trust" is pretty much all we can agree upon, and even that sentiment may someday lose support as America becomes populated by millions who either don't believe in God or do not believe in a distinct deity. "Public religion" gets harder to pull off by the day, in part because it would be unfair to treat secularists, atheists, ethical humanists, polytheists, and skeptics as second-class citizens.

We must continue to adapt, embracing pluralistic piety rather than generic Christianity. Oddly enough, our best model is the United States Congress. It begins each session with a prayer but invites a wide variety of guest clergy to deliver it. The government *can* be the protector of religious exertion so long as it doesn't favor one faith over another. Instead of being the anchor-tenant department store at the shopping mall, government has to be the shopping mall itself—expressing support for American spirituality by giving it a space in which to flourish.[24] Public religion is no longer primarily the art of finding a common message but rather the duty to provide a platform for a variety of messages, and for the singular idea of religious freedom.

When it comes to making accommodations for the religious, there is now no choice but to be pluralistic. If you want Christian bakers to be able to skip same-sex weddings, you'd better allow Muslim women to have Sharia-compliant swim times. If you want tax credits for Catholic schools—and that's a big if—you'll have to accept tax credits for madrassas.

The alternative is a secular public square. In some cases, this may well be fine. (In fact, it's probably what Madison would have desired.) But it is neither preferable nor inevitable. If we look at this challenge through a pluralistic lens, we can often retain an important religious dimension to our public and civic life.

America's democratic values should occasionally alter the DNA of even ancient religions. This young country has a way of putting its stamp on everything, even on religions that have been around for thousands of years. American Catholics changed the Church's approach to religious freedom. American Muslims have elevated the role of women in their faith. In each generation, a bloc of Americans has feared that immigrants would pollute our national culture. Instead, America's values have altered the religions.

Evangelical Christians should regain their position of moral leadership. Throughout American history, evangelicals have done more to advance religious liberty than any other group. They provided the intellectual framework and the political muscle for religious liberty's most significant early triumphs, including what became the First Amendment. The Second Great Awakening, an evangelical outpouring, helped destroy the regressive state religious establishments. It was as part of a divine plan that Representative John Bingham pushed through the Fourteenth Amendment.

But many modern evangelical leaders have redefined religious freedom downward, making it small and self-centered. It's now mostly about the freedom to oppose homosexual rights without suffering mockery. Or it's about churches being able to get tax-exempt donations while endorsing political campaigns. In addition, many Christians joined the aggressive attack on religious freedom by demonizing American Muslims.[25] They undercut another group's liberties at precisely the moment when they ask the rest of the nation to respect their own. The great champions of religious freedom have switched to the wrong side of history.

If they instead led the way in defending Muslims, they would become important voices in the history of religious freedom again. They have the credibility of having been in positions of both strength and weakness and having suffered persecution themselves. They have a theology that emphasizes a direct relationship with God. They have a history of driving righteous causes such as abolitionism. Nothing would strengthen religious freedom more than if twenty-first-century evangelicals embraced the philosophy of the eighteenth-century evangelicals and provided a model for others to emulate.

The press needs to better understand its critical role in preserving religious freedom. When some media outlets promote misinformation or delegitimize certain groups of religious Americans, they undermine religious freedom. When they casually conflate Muslim American grocers with extremist Muslim terrorists, they light a fuse that can destroy one of America's most sacred and hard-earned liberties. Those who benefit from one part of the First Amendment should try not to ruin the other parts.

Though we don't have to love our neighbors, Americans should feel morally obliged to understand them. Just as we ought to check the veracity of a Facebook post before sharing it, we should commit to conscientious caution when hearing about religious groups from ideological sources. Many (though not all) of the attacks on religious minorities have been facilitated by ignorance. The most common failure, of course, has been when any practitioner of a particular faith was ascribed the worst characteristics of that religion. Baptists were ignorant. Catholics were disloyal. Jews were greedy. Mormons were lowlifes. Jehovah's Witnesses were un-American. Christians are bigots. Muslims are terrorists. In each generation, toxic generalizations have been applied. In each generation, too many of us have forgotten our own history.

By the way, this does not mean that we have to refrain from criticizing other religions. We can't very well have a free market of faith if we muzzle ourselves. But we cannot undermine the core legitimacy of another person's faith by saying that it's not really a religion. We cannot cast people of other faiths as fundamentally alien and un-American or lay the groundwork for depriving them of their basic rights.

One anticipated response to this book's comparisons of the treatment of Muslims today and the persecution of Mormons, Catholics, Jews, Native Americans, and Jehovah's Witnesses in the past might be this: *Those other religions were just trying to practice their faith. The Muslims are trying to kill us.* Saying that Muslims are trying to kill us is, of course, a false generalization—just as it was to say that Catholics wanted the pope to run our country. Just as important, we've also seen in these pages that those earlier true believers in those minority faiths were not always angels either. Some Mormons *did* massacre a wagon train of innocent settlers, including women and children. Several popes *did* explicitly reject American notions of democracy and religious freedom. Jehovah's Witnesses spewed vile rhetoric against people of other faiths, on their blocks and in their homes. Yet despite that, what was done to the Mormons, Catholics, and Jehovah's Witnesses was wrong. We have to be able to see past the worst elements of any given faith—and to see the log in our own eye—if religious freedom is to remain strong.

We should remember that just because certain actions are constitutional, that doesn't mean they advance religious liberty. So many church-state fights focus on who has the right to do what. But religious freedom has grown in part because of informal social compacts. Those suing to take down the 9/11 "cross" certainly had the right to do so, but they showed contempt for people who were gaining comfort from that symbol. One can follow the Constitution and still be a jerk. FOX News certainly has the constitutional right to air views suggesting that American Muslims are terrorists in waiting. But it's irresponsible, un-American, and not journalism. Supporters of LGBT rights have the right to lambaste "bakers of conscience," but it's most likely counterproductive.

In other cases, policy actions may be *constitutional but unwise.* For instance, allowing houses of worship to endorse political candidates and still receive tax-exempt contributions may well be constitutional. But Madison and the early evangelicals would have vehemently opposed it because of the corrupting influence it would almost certainly have had on the churches themselves. The courts might also find that voucher programs providing money to private religious schools can be constitutional if they support a wide range of faiths. But it's worth nonetheless reflecting on Madison's argument, that taxpayer funds flowing into religious institutions will inevitably entangle them in the state, inviting more government oversight and reducing the church's credibility.

Secularists need to compromise as well. Nonbelievers benefit when believers are protected. Most of the worst persecution of atheists around the world comes in countries that also harass and imprison religious minorities. Just as religionists should not impose their vision on secular people, the "nones" should accept that religious language and symbolism must exist outside the walls of the church or home. Religion needs some space too. Religious people need the freedom not only to worship privately but also to express themselves publicly and to associate with like-minded Americans. Just as mainstream Christians had to accept the unorthodox views of Jehovah's Witnesses and Mormons, secularists cannot attempt to criminalize religious beliefs they find repugnant. For instance, labeling anti-gay statements as hate speech, and then attempting to ban such speech, would violate the First Amendment and endanger the very system that protects secular people as well as religious minorities.

LGBT rights advocates should drop the assumption that anyone who opposes same-sex marriage is a bigot. Their attacks on those Christians who want to avoid same-sex marriage ceremonies is both entirely understandable and potentially counterproductive. It's understandable because for two millennia organized religion has been the leading force in marginalizing, criminalizing, and destroying the lives of LGBT people. It would require an extraordinary sense of graciousness (and realpolitik) to now afford those conservative believers much leeway. Yet that's the approach advocated by Andrew Sullivan, one of the intellectual forefathers of the same-sex marriage movement.

> I would never want to coerce any fundamentalist to provide services for my wedding—or anything else for that matter—if it made them in any way uncomfortable. The idea of suing these businesses to force them to provide services they are clearly uncomfortable providing is anathema to me. I think it should be repellent to the gay rights movement as well.
>
> The truth is: we're winning this argument. We've made the compelling moral case that gay citizens should be treated no differently by their government than straight citizens. And the world has shifted dramatically in our direction. Inevitably, many fundamentalist Christians and Orthodox Jews and many Muslims feel threatened and bewildered by such change and feel that it inchoately affects their religious convictions. I think they're mistaken—but we're not talking logic here. We're talking religious conviction. My view is that in a free and live-and-let-live society, we should give them space.[26]

Note that Sullivan's argument is not about the Constitution; it's about tactics. LGBT advocates in Utah recently took a similar approach, joining together with leaders of the Mormon Church to forge the "Utah Compromise." In exchange for rules to protect gays in the workplace, LGBT leaders agreed that employees could not be fired for expressing their religious views, even if they were anti-gay.[27] Professor Chai Feldblum, an Obama-appointed member of the Equal Employment Opportunity Commission, brought a unique perspective to the issue. She's a prominent LGBT activist who was raised as an Orthodox Jew.[28] She wants all same-sex couples to be treated respectfully, but, she says, "Perhaps because of my upbringing as an Orthodox Jew, I can well understand the feeling that if God decides your actions have made you complicit in sin, that is all that matters." She suggests that if we discard the winner-take-all mentality and embrace nuance, we can sensibly balance the rights of LGBT families and religious believers. The key is really quite simple: make the effort. See if there is a way to accommodate believers. If there isn't, Feldblum says, by no means compromise on core principles—such as the right for LGBT people to marry. But don't start with the premise that any accommodation is a capitulation to bigotry. Instead, "acknowledge the full and complex reality of those who are different from us and then find the generosity of spirit to reach across divides."[29]

American Muslims must continue to lead. They have already gone far beyond merely cooperating with the police in fingering would-be terrorists and have begun building a new theology that merges core elements of Islam with American notions of pluralism, democracy, and women's rights. They will need to continue to fight the very real toxic elements in Islam, especially within the United States. They might echo the righteous anger of W. D. Mohammed, who declared that American Muslims will not find hope by looking to the Muslim-dominated countries around the world. Just as American Catholics changed the Catholic Church's approach to religious freedom, and American Jews used their experience to help strengthen American freedom, American Muslims can demonstrate to the world the compatibility of Islamic practice and democratic values.

We all should develop a sense of perspective. This is hard. You've just read a whole book about the importance of fighting for religious freedom and the dire consequences of neglecting it. But we also need to be clearheaded about what is a genuine assault on religious freedom and what is not. We have come a long way. We should recognize that. Most of our modern fights over religious freedom are minor skirmishes compared with the battles that were fought earlier.

Here's what's strange: the culture wars rage, but, with the exception of the attack on Muslims, most remaining controversies involve the balancing of two worthy goals in conflict rather than good versus evil. In legal terms, we now focus mostly on the hardest dilemmas—the grays rather than the blacks and whites. How do we provide extra accommodations to religious people without undermining the ability of society to enforce universally applicable secular laws? What kind of religious expression should be allowed in the public square? Even Madison warned that "it may not be easy, in every possible case, to trace the line of separation, between the rights of Religion & the Civil authority, with such distinctness, as to avoid collisions & doubts on unessential points."[30] We have the luxury of facing these difficult questions because we have vanquished the more brutal attempts to undermine liberty.

At the same time, we must remain vigilant, as it is clear the consensus can unravel rapidly. We should appreciate our unusual achievement and what our ancestors had to sacrifice. Let's not squander it. Indeed, as the world becomes more interconnected, America has something great to offer: a paradigm for how religious difference—so often the source of violent division—can be harnessed or even turned into strength. John Winthrop thought America would be a city upon a hill because it would show how purified religion could create a righteous society. Going forward, we should instead embrace the idea that our status as that inspiring model will come not from religion alone but from religious freedom—not so much from our unique status as a providentially favored nation as from our unique status as the champions of this sacred liberty. In the future, the world can benefit from what America has learned, if we manage not to forget it ourselves.

Acknowledgments

I want to first thank the historians. This book is built on the superb work of scholars who toiled for years to understand particular periods and themes. Every chapter was built on the foundation of their research. I think of each endnote as a little thank-you note. The ones I relied on most heavily are Steven K. Green, Mark Noll, Kevin Schultz, Kathleen Flake, Edward Shapiro, John Witte, Frank Lambert, Kevin Seamus Hasson, Daniel Dreisbach, Ralph Ketcham, Roger Finke, Rodney Stark, Katie Oxx, George Marlin, John T. McGreevy, John Pinheiro, Albert J. Raboteau, Sylviane Diouf, Kambiz GhaneaBassiri, Richard Aynes, Matthew Bowman, David Bigler, Spencer Fluhman, Sarah Barringer Gordon, Karen Watembach, Paul Prucha, Rani-Henrik Andersson, Heather Cox Richardson, Lloyd Jorgenson, David Manwaring, Leonard Dinnerstein, Roger Daniels, Barry Hudock, Daniel K. Williams, Nadia Marzouki, Jon Reyhner, David Wallace Adams, and Shawn Francis Peters.

I am lucky to have uncommonly literate friends and neighbors. The Goldwag family was invaluable. Nathan Goldwag, my talented research assistant, wrestled to the ground more than 1,300 endnotes, with great attention to detail, accuracy, and organization. His father, Arthur Goldwag, was an early reader and skillful copy editor. Only the Goldwag cat failed to contribute. (Next time, Ziggy.)

Special thanks go to my friends and family members who were subjected to this book's earliest incarnations, as well as those who helped me think through the project, including Paul Glastris; John Zimmerman; Richard Mouw; my wife, Amy; and my parents, Martin and Sandra Waldman. Mom and Dad also instilled in me a love of language (Ma still, at eighty-five, copyedits restaurant menus) and an ability to see any piece of writing through someone else's eyes. Writing is not for the writer but for the reader. Amy fearlessly told me which parts made her fall asleep and which made her want to kiss me. My young adult sons Gordon and Joe offered shrewd comments on key chapters and the remarkably precise copy editing.

Then, once the drafts were a bit further along, a large team of readers sprang into action. Each one had valuable contributions of fact or insight. Together they made this book far more nuanced and accurate. Thank you, Michael Waldman, Deal Hudson, Michael Wolfe, Craig Parshall, Kevin Schultz, Nicholas Miller, John Witte, Jonathan Curiel, Chai Feldblum, Shawn Francis Peters, Ingrid Mattson, Daisy Khan, Muhammad Rahim, Matthew Cooper, Kathleen Flake, and Peggy Fletcher Stack.

My agent, Rafe Sagalyn, and my editors, Mickey Maudlin, Anna Paustenbach, and Mark Tauber, had the vision to see how this piece of history has deep relevance to the cultural moment in which we now find ourselves. I particularly appreciated Mickey's insights about how to balance the needs for briskly paced narrative and explication of important ideas and trends.

Finally, I want to thank the freedom fighters themselves. So many ordinary men, women, and, yes, quite a few children took courageous steps to demand their rights. At this historic and momentous juncture, it's worth noting that the valiant true believers (whose views admittedly may differ from our own) never sought fame or money. Indeed, many were considered losers in their time. Yet collectively they earned and built religious freedom.

Notes

Introduction

1. Little, *Imprisoned Preachers*, p. 229.
2. Little, *Imprisoned Preachers*, p. 520.
3. Little, *Imprisoned Preachers*, p. 163.
4. G. Hugh Wamble, "Virginia Baptists and Religious Liberty, 1765 to 1802," *Journal of Baptist Studies* 1 (2007): 40–41.
5. Letter from James Madison to William Bradford, January 24, 1774. I added a little bit of punctuation to this quote for clarity. The way Madison wrote it: That diabolical Hell conceived principle of persecution rages among some and to their eternal Infamy the Clergy can furnish their Quota of Imps for such business. This vexes me the most of any thing whatever.
6. Jennifer Dobner and Glen Johnson, "Polygamy Was Prominent in Romney's Family Tree," *Deseret News*, February 25, 2007.
7. Matthew Burton Bowman, *The Mormon People: The Making of an American Faith* (New York: Random House, 2012), p. xix.
8. Mark Hensch, "Anti-Defamation League CEO: I'll 'Register as a Muslim' if Trump Makes Database," TheHill.com, November 18, 2016; Holly Yan and Eric Levenson, "Empathy and Action: Muslims Unite to Help Fix Vandalized Jewish Cemeteries," CNN.com, March 1, 2017.
9. Hartford Institute for Religion Research, "Fast Facts About American Religion," accessed online July 16, 2018.
10. "Religious Landscape Study: Frequency of Prayer," Pew Research Center, 2014.
11. *See figure on following page.* "Why do levels of religious observance vary by age and country?," Pew Research Center, June 13, 2018. To be precise, the Y axis was percentage of adults who say they pray daily. The X axis was 2015 per capita gross domestic product (adjusted for purchasing power parity).
12. Letter from Thomas Jefferson to Thomas Wittemore, June 5, 1822.
13. Ian Johnson, "Who Killed More: Hitler, Stalin, or Mao?," *New York Review of Books*, February 5, 2018.
14. "Global Uptick in Government Restrictions on Religion in 2016: Nationalist Parties and Organizations Played an Increasing Role in Harassment of Religious Minorities, Especially in Europe," Pew Research Center, June 21, 2018.
15. David Masci, "Key Facts About Government-Favored Religion Around the World," Pew Research Center, October 3, 2017.
16. Gabriel Samuels, "Muslim Woman Told to Remove Hijab by Police on French Beach Before Being Racially Abused," *Independent* (UK ed.), September 24, 2016.
17. Is religious freedom really America's *greatest* invention? Clearly such an award would be subjective, and I did not, in truth, spend much of this book comparing religious freedom with other contenders—including the internet, the light bulb, and freedom of press. And there are certainly days when it's hard to imagine life without

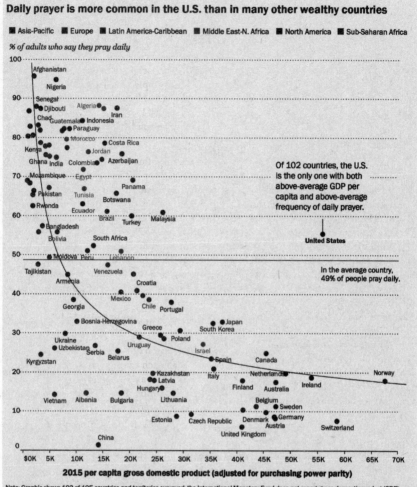

Daily prayer is more common in the U.S. than in many other wealthy countries

■ Asia-Pacific   ■ Europe   ■ Latin America-Caribbean   ■ Middle East-N. Africa   ■ North America   ■ Sub-Saharan Africa

% of adults who say they pray daily

Of 102 countries, the U.S. is the only one with both above-average GDP per capita and above-average frequency of daily prayer.

United States

In the average country, 49% of people pray daily.

2015 per capita gross domestic product (adjusted for purchasing power parity)

Note: Graphic shows 102 of 105 countries and territories surveyed; the International Monetary Fund does not report gross domestic product (GDP) figures for Kosovo, Palestinian territories or Puerto Rico.
Source: Pew Research Center surveys, 2008-2017. GDP data from the International Monetary Fund World Economic Outlook Database, October 2015. "The Age Gap in Religion Around the World"

the zipper or the hearing aid. The argument of this book would be unaffected if you concluded that religious freedom was not the *most* important invention. The key point is that what we have done is unique, profoundly important, and under threat.

But, since I did use that wording, I'd like lay out the case for why it's true. Let's look at the three key words, "America's," "greatest," and "invention."

"America's"?

America did not invent the concept of religious freedom. Some say Cyrus the Great, the Zoroastrian leader of around 500 BC, has first claim, as he allowed different faiths to worship unhindered and allowed the Hebrews to return from their Babylonian exile. Ashoka the Great, a Buddhist leader of the third century BC, established religious freedom in ancient India. He decreed, "All religions should reside everywhere, for all of them desire self-control and purity of heart," and

"Contact [between religions] is good. One should listen to and respect the doctrines professed by others. Beloved-Servant-of-the-Gods, King Piyadasi, desires that all should be well-learned in the good doctrines of other religions." The Ottomans were known for treating Jews and other religious minorities well.

Perhaps the most surprising one to give Madison a run for his money was Genghis Khan. In *Genghis Khan and the Quest for God*, Jack Weatherford argues that because the Mongol leader conquered such a broad empire—which included people who were Taoists, Confucianists, Muslims, Buddhists, Hindus, and others—he allowed religious freedom as a way of developing local loyalty. And as for the advantage of having a variety of sects, well, Madison couldn't have said it better himself:

> Genghis Khan deliberately limited the potential influence of any single religion by employing rivals of different sects and ethnicities and granting them overlapping responsibilities. These included Jews and Christians as well as a large variety of Muslims from normally contentious groups. He forced Sunnis and Shias to work together, alongside Zoroastrians and Sufis. The tensions between them kept any one person from achieving too much power. Their personal animosities were so strong that they often suppressed negative attitudes toward the Mongols. (Jack Weatherford, *Genghis Khan and the Quest for God: How the World's Greatest Conqueror Gave Us Religious Freedom* (New York: Penguin Books, 2016), p. 205.)

Of course, he also frequently slaughtered local populations, so it's hard to hold him up as a model of liberty. Madison had to figure out a way to create tolerance within a democracy. These earlier enlightened despots viewed religious tolerance as a means of social control. How does a small population of conquerors impose order on a vast multiethnic, multireligious empire? Turn each religious community into its own fiefdom that pays homage and tribute to the ruler and is responsible for law and order. Finally, innovation of religion—the literal creation of new ones—is built into the Madisonian system and seen as a good. That was certainly not the case in these earlier empires.

"Greatest"?

What about the other contenders for greatest invention? Contrary to popular opinion, we did not invent democracy. And while the US Constitution has certainly been emulated here and there, it is not even the most popular model of republican government (that honor goes to the parliamentary system). A strong case can be made for the American approach to freedom of the press. While other nations have a free press, few have quite the protections offered here. But that is very new—having become truly enshrined in 1971 in *New York Times Co. v. United States (the Pentagon Papers case)*—fragile, and not much copied.

Another contender would be the American approach to immigration—the idea of welcoming people from other nations and then both pushing them to adopt American values and allowing them to retain, and share, their own traditions. Eric Foner has made the case for birthright citizenship as one of our great inventions— the idea that just being here is enough to earn the right to full rights, without having to be of a certain ethnicity or lineage.

One could make a case for penicillin and antibiotics, but alas, they were invented by the French. Electricity has many inventors, including lightning. The idea of plumbing has probably saved more lives than anything else, but America can't claim credit. The internet really was an American invention for the most part (funded by the US government). But it may prove to be more like the discovery of how to split the atom—where it will take thousands of years before we know whether the benefits outweigh the harms. In any event, the internet is a tool that can be used for ill or good—depending in part on how people treat each other. That will be determined in part by the prevalence of the American model of religious freedom.

"Invention"?

I have to admit there is one thing misleading about the word "invention." It makes it seem sudden. The development of religious freedom has been quite gradual, with many hands helping to shape the final (or latest) sculpture. But many inventions actually were built on the work of previous women and men. In that sense, religious freedom qualifies nicely.

18. I refer to the eighteenth-century Baptists as evangelicals, even though that was not the commonly used term then. But religious historians agree that Baptists and other similar Protestant dissidents shared the key characteristics of those who would later be called evangelicals, including a focus on having a personal relationship with God, the centrality of the Bible, an emotional worship style, and an emphasis on salvation. Spiritually, the eighteenth-century Baptists were the direct forefathers of modern evangelicals.

19. Andrew Sullivan, one of the intellectual forefathers of the same sex-marriage movement, explained, "Unquestionably, the belief in the quality and dignity of gay people is completely inextricable from my faith." Interview with the author, November 27, 2018.

20. Brian J. Grim, "God's Economy: Religious Freedom and Socioeconomic Well-Being," in *Religious Freedom in the World*, ed. Paul A. Marshall (Lanham, MD: Rowman & Littlefield, 2008), p. 44. Rodney Stark has also argued that Americans who are more religious are less likely to commit crimes and more likely to donate blood, give to charity, and have greater mental health. Rodney Stark, *America's Blessings: How Religion Benefits Everyone, Including Atheists* (West Conshohocken, PA: Templeton Press, 2012). Meanwhile, other studies have shown that within the United States, religious people are more likely to volunteer, give to charity, and be civically involved in the community. Robert D. Putnam and David E. Campbell, *American Grace: How Religion Divides and Unites Us* (New York: Simon & Schuster, 2010), p. 444, Kindle.

21. Kathleen Flake, *The Politics of American Religious Identity: The Seating of Senator Reed Smoot, Mormon Apostle* (Chapel Hill: Univ. of North Carolina Press, 2004), p. 20, citing "The Smoot Case," *Kalamazoo Telegraph*, April 22, 1904.

22. Greg Miller, "An Army officer, years on, still a lightning rod," *Washington Post*, January 23, 2012. Boykin made the statement in a video for the Oak Initiative.

23. Little, *Imprisoned Preachers*, p. vii.

CHAPTER ONE

Failed Experiments

1. John Winthrop, *Winthrop's Journal: History of New England, 1630–1649*, ed. James Kendall Hosmer, vol. 1 (New York: Charles Scribner's Sons, 1908), p. 267.

2. Edward Johnson, *Johnson's Wonder-Working Providence, 1628–1651*, ed. J. Franklin Jameson (New York: Charles Scribner's Sons, 1910), p. 187.

3. George Bishop, *New England Judged, Not by Man's, but the Spirit of the Lord, etc.* (London: Printed for Robert Wilson, 1661), p. 52.

4. George Bishop, *New England Judged by the Spirit of the Lord: In Two Parts* (London: T. Sowle, 1703), 120.

5. There is some discrepancy about the actual location of the executions; many sources place them as happening on Boston Commons, but others say that they took place upon the Boston Neck. Some confusion may have been engendered by the fact that the land to the south of the Boston Neck was, at the time, "common land."

6. Horatio Rogers, *Mary Dyer of Rhode Island: The Quaker Martyr That Was Hanged on Boston Common, June 1, 1660* (Providence: Preston and Rounds, 1896), p. 60.

7. Thomas J. Curry, *The First Freedoms: Church and State in America to the Passage of the First Amendment* (New York: Oxford Univ. Press, 1986), p. 4.

8. Samuel Mather, "The Second Sermon Witnessing More Particularly Against the Ceremonies of the Church of England," Evans Early American Imprint Collection.

9. Kevin Seamus Hasson, *The Right to be Wrong: Ending the Culture War over Religion in America* (New York: Image, 2012), pp. 22–23.

10. Bruce C. Daniels, *Puritans at Play: Leisure and Recreation in Colonial New England* (New York: St. Martin's Press, 1995), p. 89; Cotton Mather, *Winter Meditations: Directions How to Employ the Leisures of Winter for the Glory of God* (Boston: Benjamin Harris, 1693), p. 8.

11. Heather Tourgee, "How the Puritans Banned Christmas," *New England Today*, December 7, 2016.

12. Daniels, *Puritans at Play*, p. 91.

13. Rogers, *Mary Dyer of Rhode Island*, pp. 18–19.

14. Edmund S. Morgan, *Visible Saints: The History of a Puritan Idea* (Ithaca: Cornell Univ. Press, 1965), p. 114.

15. Frank Lambert, *The Founding Fathers and the Place of Religion in America* (Princeton: Princeton Univ. Press, 2003), p. 96.

16. Kevin Seamus Hasson, *The Right to Be Wrong: Ending the Culture War over Religion in America* (New York: Crown, 2012), p. 42, Kindle.

17. John Cotton, *A Discourse About Civil Government in a New Plantation Whose Design Is Religion* (Cambridge: Samuel Green and Marmaduke Johnson, 1663), p. 14.

18. Martin E. Marty, *Pilgrims in Their Own Land: 500 Years of Religion in America* (New York: Penguin Books, 1984), p. 56.

19. They dropped the practice in 1661, possibly anticipating that the English monarchy would intervene to stop it. Carla Gardina Pestana, "The Quaker Executions as Myth and History," *Journal of American History* 80, no. 2 (September 1993): 441–69.

20. Evarts B. Greene, *Religion and the State: The Making and Testing of an American Tradition* (Ithaca: Cornell Univ. Press, 1941), p. 34.

21. Steven K. Green, *The Second Disestablishment: Church and State in Nineteenth-Century America* (New York: Oxford Univ. Press, 2010), loc. 1646–48, Kindle.

22. Lyman Beecher, *Autobiography, Correspondence, etc., of Lyman Beecher*, ed. Charles Beecher, vol. 1 (New York: Harper & Brothers, 1865), p. 259.

23. "Persecution of Catholics," The Pluralism Project, Harvard University, accessed online April 4, 2018.

24. John Tracy Ellis, *Catholics in Colonial America* (Baltimore: North Central, 1965), pp. 345–47.

25. Steven Mintz, "Winning the Vote: A History of Voting Rights," Gilder Lehrman Institute of American History, Fall 2004, accessed August 15, 2018.

26. Derek H. Davis, *Religion and the Continental Congress, 1774–1789: Contributions to Original Intent* (New York: Oxford Univ. Press, 2000), p. 153.

27. John Adams, "A Dissertation on the Canon and the Feudal Law," No. 1, August 12, 1765, Adams Papers, Massachusetts Historical Society.

28. Letter from John Adams to Thomas Jefferson, February 3, 1821.

29. Letter from John Adams to Abigail Adams, October 9, 1774.

30. "Spanish Requirement of 1513," *World Heritage Encyclopedia*.

31. Francis Drake, ed., *The Indian Tribes of the United States* (Philadelphia: J. B. Lippincott, 1884), p. 17.

32. Roger Williams, *The Correspondence of Roger Williams*, ed. Glenn W. LaFantasie, vol. 1 (Univ. Press of New England, 1988), pp. 12–23.

33. Roger Williams, *The Bloudy Tenent of Persecution for Cause of Conscience*, ed. Samuel L. Caldwell (1644; reprint, Providence: Narragansett Club, 1867), p. 3.

34. "Origins: First Jews in Newport," Touro Synagogue National Historic Site, accessed online April 9, 2018.

35. Alonzo Lewis, *The History of Lynn, Including Nahant* (Boston: Samuel N. Dickenson, 1844), p. 116.

36. "Lady Deborah Moody, a Dangerous Woman, Comes to New England," New England Historical Society, accessed online August 7, 2018.

37. James W. Gerard, *Lady Deborah Moody: A Discourse Delivered Before the New York Historical Society* (New York: Douglas Taylor, 1880), p. 27.

38. Evan Haefeli, *New Netherland and the Dutch Origins of American Religious Liberty* (Philadelphia: Univ. of Pennsylvania Press, 2013), p. 170.

39. Haefeli, *New Netherland*.

40. J. William Frost, *A Perfect Freedom: Religious Liberty in Pennsylvania* (University Park: Pennsylvania State Univ. Press, 1990), p. 5.

41. Edwin S. Gaustad, *A Religious History of America* (New York: Harper & Row, 1966), p. 99.

42. Benjamin Franklin, *Benjamin Franklin: His Autobiography, 1706–1757*, ed. Charles W. Eliot (New York: P. F. Collier & Son, 1909), chap. 8.

43. Letter from John Adams to Dr. Jedidiah Morse, December 2, 1815.

44. Carl Bridenbaugh, *Mitre and Sceptre: Transatlantic Faiths, Ideas, Personalities, and Politics, 1689–1775* (New York: Oxford Univ. Press, 1962), p. 222.

45. Bridenbaugh, *Mitre and Sceptre*, p. 226.

46. Samuel Adams, *Boston Gazette*, April 4, 1768.

47. Alexander Hamilton, "A Full Vindication," December 15, 1774, in *The Works of Alexander Hamilton* (federal ed.), ed. Henry Cabot Lodge (New York: G. P. Putnam's Sons, 1904).

48. *Pennsylvania Gazette*, October 12, 1774, quoted in Charles Metzger, *Catholics and the American Revolution: A Study in Religious Climate* (Chicago: Loyola Univ. Press, 1962), p. 32.

49. Alan Heimert, *Religion and the American Mind: From the Great Awakening to the Revolution* (Eugene, OR: Wipf & Stock, 2006), p. 389.

50. Ambrose Serle to Lord Dartmouth, November 8, 1776, in *B. F. Stevens's Facsimiles of Manuscripts in European Archives Relating to America, 1773–1783, with Descriptions, Editorial Notes, Collations, References and Translations*, ed. Benjamin F. Stevens, vol. 24 (1898; reprint, Wilmington: Mellifont Press, 1970), p. 2045, cited in Richard Gardiner, "The Presbyterian Rebellion?," *Journal of the American Revolution*, September 5, 2013.

51. Mark A. Noll, Nathan O. Hatch, and George M. Marsden, *The Search for Christian America* (Colorado Springs: Helmers & Howard, 1989), p. 55.

52. That statistic may mean less than it seems because many churches tried to limit their congregations to the chosen, but the consensus among historians is that the country was less religious then than it is now. Roger Finke and Rodney Stark, *The Churching of America, 1776–2005: Winners and Losers in Our Religious Economy* (New Brunswick: Rutgers Univ. Press, 2005), p. 16.

53. Orders issued November 5, 1775, quoted in Paul F. Boller, "George Washington and Religious Liberty," in *George Washington: A Profile*, ed. James Morton Smith (New York: Hill and Wang, 1969), p. 169.

54. Hasson, *The Right to Be Wrong* (New York: Image, 2012), pp. 50–51.

55. Davis, *Religion and the Continental Congress*, p. 163.

56. John Adams, letter to Abigail Adams, quoted in Metzger, *Catholics and the American Revolution*, p. 64.

57. Joseph M. Flynn, *The Story of a Parish, 1847–1892: The First Catholic Church in Morristown, N.J.* (New York: Columbus Press, 1892), pp. 16–17, citing Ebenezer Hazard to Rev. Jeremy Belknap, June 27, 1780, Belknap Papers, pp. 61–62, Massachusetts Historical Society Collection.

CHAPTER TWO
Madison's Model

1. William Meade, *Old Churches, Ministers, and Families of Virginia*, vol. 2 (Philadelphia: J. B. Lippincott, 1910), p. 99.

2. Lynne Cheney, *James Madison: A Life Reconsidered* (New York: Viking, 2014), pp. 31–32.

3. It was led by Rev. John Witherspoon, who believed that all men had the "right to private judgment" on matters of faith, meaning they could interpret the Bible themselves. Ralph Ketcham, *James Madison: A Biography* (Charlottesville: Univ. of Virginia Press, 1990), p. 43.

4. John A. Ragosta, *Wellspring of Liberty: How Virginia's Religious Dissenters Helped Win the American Revolution and Secured Religious Liberty* (New York: Oxford Univ. Press, 2010), p. 32.

5. In a brief autobiography he wrote in 1830, Madison described how a young Madison followed the "duty prescribed by his conscience," which had thereby "obtained for him a lasting place in the favour of that particular sect." Library of Congress.

6. Letter from James Madison to William Bradford, January 24, 1774.

7. Porter C. Bliss, *Johnson's (Revised) Universal Cyclopaedia: A Scientific and Popular Treasury of Useful Knowledge*, vol. 5 (New York: A. J. Johnson, 1889).

8. Lewis Peyton Little, *Imprisoned Preachers and Religious Liberty in Virginia* (Lynchburg: J. P. Bell, 1938), pp. 135–36.

9. Little, *Imprisoned Preachers*, p. 147.

10. One minister was arrested for presiding at a wedding, since by law marriages were valid only if an Anglican clergyman was present. Little, *Imprisoned Preachers*, p. 260.

11. Little, *Imprisoned Preachers*, p. 207.

12. Douglass Adair, "James Madison's Autobiography," *William and Mary Quarterly* 2, no. 2 (April 1945): 194.

13. He also offered a far narrower set of caveats than did Mason: states could not punish dissenters for disturbing the peace but rather only if their actions "manifestly endangered" the "existence of the State." "Madison's Amendments to the Declaration of Rights [29 May–12 June, 1776]," *Founders Online*, National Archives.

14. Robert A. Rutland, "James Madison's Dream: A Secular Republic," in *James Madison on Religious Liberty*, ed. Robert S. Alley (Amherst, NY: Prometheus Books, 1985), p. 201.

15. He even eventually stipulated that those who didn't want to support religion could target education more broadly.

16. Letter from Richard Henry Lee to James Madison, November 26, 1784.

17. Alley, *Madison on Religious Liberty*, p. 54.

18. Nicholas Miller presents a fascinating and persuasive argument that this part of the dissenting Protestant theology was a key ingredient drawing Americans toward disestablishment and a new approach to religious freedom. Nicholas P. Miller, *The*

Religious Roots of the First Amendment: Dissenting Protestants and the Separation of Church and State (New York: Oxford Univ. Press, 2012).

19. Charles Fenton James, *Documentary History of the Struggle for Religious Liberty in Virginia* (Lynchburg, VA: J. P. Bell, 1900), p. 126.

20. Letter from Thomas Jefferson to James Madison, December 8, 1784.

21. Letter from James Madison to Thomas Jefferson, August 20, 1785, in *The Republic of Letters: The Correspondence Between Thomas Jefferson and James Madison, 1776–1826*, ed. James Morton Smith, vol. 1 (New York: W. W. Norton, 1995), p. 374.

22. James Madison, "Memorial and Remonstrance Against Religious Assessments," 1784.

23. Letter from James Madison to Thomas Jefferson, August 20, 1785.

24. Little, *Imprisoned Preachers*, p. 487.

25. H. J. Eckenrode, *Separation of Church and State in Virginia: A Study in the Development of the Revolution*, Special Report of the Department of Archives and History, Virginia State Library (Richmond: D. Bottom, 1910), p. 108.

26. William Lee Miller, *The First Liberty: Religion and the American Republic* (St. Paul: Paragon House, 1988), p. 39.

27. James Madison, "Monopolies Perpetuities Corporations Ecclesiastical Endowments," quoted in Alley, *Madison on Religious Liberty*, p. 89.

28. James Madison, "The Debates in the Convention of 1787," Avalon Project.

29. Charles C. Haynes, "History of Religious Freedom in America: Overview," First Amendment Center, December 26, 2002.

30. John C. Van Horne, librarian, Library Company of Philadelphia, "The Federal Procession of 1788," talk delivered to the quarterly meeting of the Carpenters' Company, July 20, 1987, accessed May 2007, www.ushistory.org/carpentershall/history/procession.htm.

31. Isaac Kramnick and R. Laurence Moore, *The Godless Constitution: The Case Against Religious Correctness* (New York: W. W. Norton, 1997), p. 33.

32. Kramnick and Moore, *Godless Constitution*, p. 36.

33. Thomas J. Curry, *The First Freedoms: Church and State in America to the Passage of the First Amendment* (New York: Oxford Univ. Press, 1985), p. 195.

34. Kramnick and Moore, *Godless Constitution*, p. 33.

35. In North Carolina, James Iredell articulated the theory: "Is there any power given Congress in matters of religion? If any future Congress should pass an act concerning the religion of the country, it would be an act which they are not authorized to pass, by the Constitution, and which the people would not obey." "Debate in North Carolina Ratifying Convention, 30 July 1788," in *The Founders' Constitution*, ed. Philip B. Kurland and Ralph Lerner, vol. 5, Amend. 1 (religion), doc. 52.

36. L. H. Butterfield, "Elder John Leland, Jeffersonian Itinerant," *Proceedings of the American Antiquarian Society*, p. 160, citing John Leland, *The Writings of John Leland*, ed. L. F. Greene (New York, 1845), p. 188.

37. This part of the account is admittedly secondhand. G. N. Briggs, the governor of Massachusetts, described in writing a long meeting he'd had with John Leland during which they discussed his role in helping to secure ratification. In Briggs's account, Madison and Leland met privately and then again squared off publicly. But there are some inconsistencies in the account and some question of whether Leland stood up and announced his switch on the spot. The most detailed analysis of the impact of Leland is in Mark S. Scarberry, "John Leland and James Madison: Religious Influence on the Ratification of the Constitution and on the Proposal of the Bill of Rights," Pepperdine University Legal Studies Research Paper Series, April 2009, Paper Number 2009/6, pp. 767–68. One fascinating detail in the Briggs account: "For candour, integrity, and

intelligence, he placed Mr. Madison before any of our statesmen whom he had ever known. As a public debater, he said he had one trait which he had never witnessed in any other man—after stating, in the clearest manner, the positions and arguments of his opponent, if that opponent had omitted any thing that would strengthen his side of the case, he would add it, and then proceed to meet and answer the whole." William B. Sprague, *Annals of the American Baptist Pulpit* (New York: Robert Carter & Brothers, 1860), p. 180.

38. The vote tally was listed in a manuscript by Eugene Bucklin Bowen of Cheshire, Massachusetts. Joseph Martin Dawson, *Baptists and the American Republic* (Nashville: Broadman Press, 1956), p. 109.

39. Scarberry, "John Leland and James Madison," p. 776.

40. Patrick Henry, Virginia Ratifying Convention, June 12, 1788 in in *The Founders' Constitution*, ed. Philip B. Kurland and Ralph Lerner, document 50.

41. Ketcham, *James Madison: A Biography*, p. 263.

42. "James Madison, Virginia Ratifying Convention, 12 June 1788," in *Founders' Constitution*, vol. 5, Amend. 1 (religion), doc. 49.

43. Letter from James Madison to Thomas Jefferson, October 17, 1788.

44. Letter from Thomas Jefferson to James Madison, December 20, 1787.

45. Thomas Jefferson, "Notes on the State of Virginia," 1784, query 17.

46. "James Madison's Autobiography," p. 199.

47. Richard Labunski, *James Madison and the Struggle for the Bill of Rights* (New York: Oxford Univ. Press, 2008), p. 144.

48. Letter from James Madison to George Eve, January 2, 1789.

49. Letter from James Madison to George Eve, January 2, 1789.

50. Letter from Benjamin Johnson to James Madison, January 19, 1789.

51. Labunski, *Madison and the Struggle for the Bill of Rights*, p. 175.

52. Letter from Thomas Jefferson to William Baldwin (Draft), January 19, 1810, *Founders Online*, National Archives.

53. Letter from Thomas Jefferson to William Short, August 4, 1820.

54. Letter from Thomas Jefferson to William Short, April 13, 1820.

55. Letter from Thomas Jefferson to Francis Adrian Van der Kemp, July 30, 1816.

56. Letter from Thomas Jefferson to James Smith, December 8, 1822.

57. Letter from Thomas Jefferson to John Adams, April 11, 1823.

58. Letter from Thomas Jefferson to Salma Hale, July 26, 1818.

59. Because of his hostility to organized religion, and his emphasis on rationalism, Jefferson is often cast as a Deist. That's not quite right. He believed in a God who intervened in history. In his first inaugural address, Jefferson declared that we should be "acknowledging and adoring an overruling Providence, which by all its dispensations proves that it delights in the happiness of man here and his greater happiness hereafter." In his first message to Congress, in 1801, he thanked the "beneficent Being" who instilled in the warring politicians a (temporary) "spirit of conciliation and forgiveness." In his second message, he credited the "smiles of Providence" for economic prosperity, peace abroad, and even good relations with the Indians.

60. Letter from Thomas Jefferson to Benjamin Rush, September 23, 1800.

61. In *The Religious Roots of the First Amendment*, Nicholas Miller argues that "right of private judgment" was a key theological thrust brought to the colonies by dissenting Protestants. He quotes Isaac Backus, for instance, who wrote that "nothing can be true religion but a voluntary obedience unto his revealed will, of which each rational soul has an equal right to judge for itself." Nicholas P. Miller, *The Religious Roots of the First Amendment: Dissenting Protestants and the Separation of Church and State* (New York: Oxford Univ. Press, 2012), p. 107.

62. Letter from John Adams to Benjamin Rush, January 21, 1810.

63. Alvah Hovey, *A Memoir of the Life and Times of the Rev. Isaac Backus, A. M.* (Boston: Gould and Lincoln, 1859), p. 213.

64. Inaugural Address of John Adams, March 4, 1797.

65. Edward J. Larson, *A Magnificent Catastrophe: The Tumultuous Election of 1800, America's First Presidential Campaign* (New York: Free Press, 2007).

66. Washington's Farewell Address, 1796.

67. Letter from William White to Hugh Mercer, August 15, 1835, cited in Paul F. Boller, *George Washington and Religion* (University Park, TX: Southern Methodist Univ. Press, 1963), p. 35.

68. Consider the Continental Congress that had adopted the Declaration. Jefferson had in that very session voiced his "objections to Christianity" (only to be bailed out by Adams, who assured the other members that Jefferson was not "an enemy to Christianity"). In the almost Deist caucus, Jefferson was joined by Benjamin Franklin, who, while praising the "System of Morals" presented by Jesus, privately expressed "some Doubts as to his Divinity." But the Continental Congress also included more orthodox believers, such as John Hancock, who had presided over the Massachusetts congress when it declared that "it becomes us, as Men and Christians," to rely on "that GOD who rules in the Armies of Heaven." Another member of Congress, Rev. John Witherspoon, the president of Princeton when James Madison attended, had called for a day of fasting: "I entreat you in the most earnest manner to believe in Jesus Christ."

69. Jefferson's "original Rough draft," *The Papers of Thomas Jefferson,* ed. Julian P. Boyd, vol. 1, 1760–1776, (Princeton: Princeton Univ. Press, 1950), pp. 243–47.

70. Pauline Maier, *American Scripture: Making the Declaration of Independence* (New York: Alfred A. Knopf, 1997).

71. *Annals of Congress,* House of Representatives, 1st Cong., 1st sess., June 8, 1789, pp. 451–53 (Washington, DC: Gales and Seaton, 1834).

72. *Annals of Congress,* House of Representatives, 1st Cong., 1st sess., August 15, 1789, pp. 758–76.

73. *Annals of Congress,* House of Representatives, 1st Cong., 1st sess., August 15, 1789, pp. 758–76.

74. Gerard V. Bradley, "The No Religious Test Clause and the Constitution of Religious Liberty: A Machine That Has Gone of Itself," *Case Western Reserve Law Review* 37, no. 4 (1987): 683.

75. Leo Pfeffer, "Church and State: Something Less than Separation," *University of Chicago Law Review* 19, no. 1 (Autumn 1951): 1–29.

76. New Hampshire Constitution of 1784, Part 6.

77. "Congress shall make no law establishing religion, or to prevent the free exercise thereof, or to infringe the rights of conscience."

78. One senator suggested prohibiting Congress from "establishing one religious sect or society in preference to others." As long as it didn't favor one religion over another, Congress could legislate about religion. The motion was defeated. Another forbade Congress from establishing "any particular denomination of religion in preference to another." It would allow Congress to intermeddle (to use Madison's word) as long as it didn't select a particular state denomination to be an official state religion. This was rejected too.

79. "Senate Amendments, September 9, 1789," in Helen E. Veit, Kenneth R. Bowling, and Charlene Bangs Bickford, eds., *Creating the Bill of Rights: The Documentary Record from the First Federal Congress* (Baltimore: John Hopkins Univ. Press, 1991), p. 45.

80. Paine Wingate to John Langdon, September 17, 1789, quoted in Veit, Bowling, and Bickford, *Creating the Bill of Rights,* p. 297.

81. Senator William Grayson to Patrick Henry, September 29, 1789, quoted in Veit, Bowling, and Bickford, *Creating the Bill of Rights*, p. 45.

82. Anson Phelps Stokes and Leo Pfeffer, *Church and State in the United States* (New York: Joanna Cotler Books, 1964), p. 100.

83. Michael Waldman, *The Second Amendment: A Biography* (New York: Simon & Schuster, 2014).

84. United States Congress, Amendments to the Constitution, June–Sept 1789, House Debate, June 8, 1789, *Annals* 1:434–36, 440–43.

85. James Madison, "Detached Memoranda," 1817, quoted in Robert S. Alley, ed., *James Madison on Religious Liberty* (Amherst, NY: Prometheus Books, 1985).

86. Madison, "Detached Memoranda."

87. Vincent Phillip Muñoz, "James Madison's Principle of Religious Liberty," *American Political Science Review* 97, no. 1 (February 2003): 17–32; Jeffrey Sikkenga, "Government Has No 'Religious Agency': James Madison's Fundamental Principle of Religious Liberty," *American Journal of Political Science* 56, no. 3 (July 2012): 745–56.

88. James Madison, "Veto Message to Congress," February 28, 1811, in Hunt, *Writings of James Madison*, vol. 8, p. 133.

89. United States Supreme Court, *Town of Greece v. Galloway*, 572 US ____ (2014).

CHAPTER THREE

The Startup Boom

1. Letter from James Madison to Robert Walsh Jr., March 2, 1819.

2. Zephaniah Swift, *A System of the Laws of the State of Connecticut* (1795; reprint, New York: Arno Press, 1972), 1:13 6, 146, cited in Steven K. Green, *The Second Disestablishment* (New York: Oxford Univ. Press, 2010), loc. 1678, Kindle.

3. John Leland, *The Rights of Conscience Inalienable, and Therefore Religious Opinions Not Cognizable by Law or, the High-Flying Churchman Stripped of His Legal Robes Appears a Yahoo* (New London, CT: F. Green & Son, 1791), in Green, *Second Disestablishment*, loc. 1642.

4. John Leland, *The Writings of John Leland*, ed. L. F. Greene (New York, 1845), p. 71, cited in L. H. Butterfield, "Elder John Leland, Jeffersonian Itinerant," *Proceedings of the American Antiquarian Society*, p. 160.

5. Letter from the Danbury Baptist Association to Thomas Jefferson, October 7, 1801.

6. It is often assumed that Jefferson got the phrase from Roger Williams, who called for "a wall of separation between the garden of the church and the wilderness of the world." They did have different emphases, though. Williams's emphasis, in that quote, was about protecting the church from the contaminants of society, while Jefferson was more focused on blocking the nefarious priesthood tyrannizing the secular sphere.

7. "Jefferson's Letter to the Danbury Baptists: The Draft and Recently Discovered Text," Library of Congress Information Bulletin, June 1998, vol. 57, no. 6.

8. Final draft of Jefferson's letter to the Danbury Baptists, January 1, 1802.

9. Green, *Second Disestablishment*, loc. 1633.

10. Lyman Beecher, *Autobiography* (New York: Harper & Brothers, 1863).

11. Anson Phelps Stokes, *Church and State in the United States*, vol. 1 (New York: Harper & Brothers, 1950), p. 424, citing Jacob C. Meyer, *Church and State in Massachusetts from 1740 to 1833: A Chapter in the History of the Development of Individual Freedom* (Cleveland: Western Reserve Univ. Press, 1930), p. 8.

12. Chester James Antieau et al., *Freedom from Federal Establishment* (Milwaukee: Bruce, 1964), p. 168.

13. Antieau et al., *Freedom from Federal Establishment*, p. 170; Joseph Francis Thorning, *Religious Liberty in Transition* (New York: Benziger Brothers, 1931), p. 52.

14. Green, *Second Disestablishment*, loc. 661, citing *Independent Ledger*, May 15, 1780, p. 4; *Boston Gazette*, July 3, 1780, p. 1.

15. John Leland, *A Blow at the Roots* (Bennington, VT: Anthony Haswell, 1801), pp. 26–27, cited in Carl H. Esbeck, "Dissent and Disestablishment: The Church-State Settlement in the Early American Republic," *Brigham Young University Law Review*, 2004, p. 1517.

16. The journal *Agricultural History* in 1944 provided a marvelous explanation of how this all happened: "Many advance preparations were required for carrying out this design. A census had to be taken of the cow population of Cheshire and of the quantity of curds that might be expected from their milk on the date specified. When this had been determined, it was necessary to calculate the size of the hoop in which to press the estimated amount of curds. Directions had to be given to housewives respecting the preparation of the curds in order to secure the highest degree of uniformity and the necessary protection in the home and during transportation against contamination, especially from insects. The farm of Elisha Brown, Jr., which was centrally located and where there was a large cider press, was selected as the place of manufacture. Elisha's nephew, Darius Brown, the engineering genius of Cheshire, attended to all the mechanical details and looked after the construction of the huge cheese hoop, 4 feet in diameter and 18 inches deep, which were the dimensions calculated by him for holding the pressed curds from the milk of Cheshire's cows for a single day's milking. To surmount this immense hoop, which was strengthened with iron bands, a detachable rim or flange was, no doubt, constructed for holding the heaped up curds as they were being pressed constantly down into the hoop. On the appointed July 20, which was a holiday for Cheshire, the whole farming population of the township proceeded on foot, horseback, or in conveyance to the farm of Elisha Brown Jr., where their contributions of curds, after careful inspection by the ladies in charge, were seasoned with salt and spicy herbs, thoroughly mixed to secure uniformity of texture, and then emptied into the large hoop with its lining of cheesecloth. After repeated squeezings to fill the hoop to its utmost capacity, the ponderous screw of the press was turned down. As the escaping whey gushed out in foaming streams, the Elder rose and, invoking a blessing, dedicated the cheese to the honor and fame of the country's illustrious President, Thomas Jefferson." C. A. Browne, "Elder John Leland and the Mammoth Cheshire Cheese," *Agricultural History* 18, no. 4 (October 1944): 147.

17. Butterfield, "Elder John Leland," p. 220.

18. Butterfield, "Elder John Leland," p. 221.

19. Butterfield, "Elder John Leland," p. 224.

20. Butterfield, "Elder John Leland," p. 225.

21. Esbeck, "Dissent and Disestablishment," p. 1458.

22. Edward McCrady, *The History of South Carolina in the Revolution, 1775–1780* (New York: Macmillan, 1902), p. 211.

23. Francis Thorpe, *The Federal and State Constitutions*, vol. 5 (Washington, DC: Government Printing Office, 1909), pp. 2597–98.

24. Stokes, *Church and State in the United States*, p. 435.

25. Stokes, *Church and State in the United States*, pp. 428–29; Thorpe, *Federal and State Constitutions*, vol. 4, p. 2448.

26. Antieau et al., *Freedom from Federal Establishment*, p. 170.

27. Thorning, *Religious Liberty in Transition*, p. 165, cited in Antieau et al., *Freedom from Federal Establishment*, p. 170.

28. Stokes, *Church and State in the United States*, vol. 1, p. 431.

29. Maryland Constitution of 1851, in *The Federal and State Constitutions, Colonial Charters, and Other Organic Laws of the States, Territories, and Colonies Now or Heretofore*

Forming the United States of America (Washington, DC: Government Printing Office, 1909), pp. 1712–15, cited in Esbeck, "Dissent and Disestablishment," p. 1491.

30. "Thomas Kennedy: Maryland Legislator Who Made a Difference," Maryland State Archives for the State House Trust, Maryland.gov, accessed March 13, 2018.

31. Stokes, *Church and State in the United States*, vol. 1, p. 439.

32. *Torcaso v. Watkins*, 367 US 488 (1961).

33. Thorpe, *Federal and State Constitutions*, vol. 1, pp. 568, 582, 601, cited in Stokes, *Church and State in the United States*, vol. 1, p. 437.

34. Thorpe, *Federal and State Constitutions*, vol. 6, pp. 3255–57, cited in Stokes, *Church and State in the United States*, vol. 1, p. 432.

35. Antieau et al., *Freedom from Federal Establishment*, p. 165.

36. Thorpe, *Federal and State Constitutions*, vol. 5, p. 3100, cited in Stokes, *Church and State in the United States*, vol. 1, p. 439.

37. *Pennsylvania Statutes at Large, 1683–1801*, vol. 15, p. 111, cited in Antieau et al., *Freedom from Federal Establishment*, p. 184.

38. *People v. Ruggles*, 8 Johns. 295 (N.Y. 1811).

39. Antieau et al., *Freedom from Federal Establishment*, p. 172.

40. Green, *Second Disestablishment*, loc. 1035–37.

41. Esbeck, "Dissent and Disestablishment," p. 1503, citing John Leland and L. F. Greene, eds., *The Writings of the Late Elder John Leland* (New York: G. W. Wood, 1845), pp. 182–83.

42. Letter from James Madison to Edward Livingston, July 10, 1822.

43. Nathan O. Hatch, *The Democratization of American Christianity* (New Haven: Yale Univ. Press, 1991), p. 4.

44. Mark A. Noll, *America's God* (New York: Oxford Univ. Press, 2002), p. 174.

45. Noll, *America's God*, p. 166.

46. Lyman Beecher, *Autobiography, Correspondence, etc., of Lyman Beecher*, ed. Charles Beecher (New York: Harper & Brothers, 1865), p. 344.

47. Mark Noll puts the number at 85 percent. Richard Carwardine estimates 35 percent. Richard J. Carwardine, "Lincoln, Evangelical Religion, and American Political Culture in the Era of the Civil War," *Journal of the Abraham Lincoln Association* 18, no. 1 (Winter 1997): 27–55.

48. Noll summarized the approach: "Evangelicals called people to acknowledge their sin before God, to look upon Jesus Christ (crucified—dead—resurrected) as God's means of redemption, and to exercise faith in this Redeemer as the way of reconciliation with God and orientation for life in the world." Noll, *America's God*, p. 171.

49. Roger Finke and Rodney Stark, *The Churching of America, 1776–1990: Winners and Losers in Our Religious Economy* (New Brunswick: Rutgers Univ. Press, 2000), p. 56.

50. Noll, *America's God*, p. 181.

51. Finke and Stark, *Churching of America, 1776–1990*, p. 63.

52. Finke and Stark, *Churching of America, 1776–1990*, p. 76.

53. Finke and Stark, *Churching of America, 1776–1990*, p. 77.

54. Finke and Stark, *Churching of America, 1776–1990*, p. 78.

55. Thomas Bremer, *Formed from This Soil: An Introduction to the Diverse History of Religion in America* (Chichester, West Sussex: John Wiley & Sons, 2015), p. 173.

56. In 1776, Congregationalists had 20 percent of the adherents. By 1850, it was down to 4 percent. Episcopalians fell from 15.7 percent to 2.5 percent. Presbyterians dropped from 19 percent to 11.6 percent.

57. Finke and Stark, *Churching of America, 1776–1990*, p. 55.

58. Finke and Stark, *Churching of America, 1776–1990*, p. 103.

59. Post offices: 18,417; churches: 34,476. Noll, *America's God*, pp. 200–201.

60. Edwin Gaustad and Leigh Schmidt, *The Religious History of America: The Heart*

of the American Story from Colonial Times to Today (San Francisco: HarperOne, 2004), p. 141, Kindle.

61. John G. West, "Evangelical Reform in Early Nineteenth Century America," in *Building a Healthy Culture: Strategies for an American Renaissance*, ed. Don Eberly (Grand Rapids: Eerdmans, 2001), pp. 181–99.

62. Gaustad and Schmidt, *Religious History of America*, pp. 140–41.

63. Gaustad and Schmidt, *Religious History of America*, p. 144.

64. Ernest H. Cherrington, *The Evolution of Prohibition in the United States of America* (Westerville, OH: American Issue Press, 1920), p. 93.

65. "Charles Grandison Finney: Did You Know?," *Christianity Today*, no. 20, 1988.

66. John Coutts, "The Booths' American Mentors," Christian History Institute, accessed online March 20, 2018.

67. Tim Stafford, "The Abolitionists," *Christianity Today*, no. 33, 1992.

68. Catherine A. Brekus, "Female Preaching in Early Nineteenth-Century America," 2009, p. 20, The Center for Christian Ethics at Baylor University, accessed online March 16, 2018.

69. Brekus, "Female Preaching," p. 25.

70. Leslie M. Alexander and Walter C. Rucker Jr., eds., *Encyclopedia of African American History* (Santa Barbara: ABC-CLIO, 2010), p. 397.

71. Brekus, "Female Preaching," p. 25.

72. Zilpha Elaw, *Ministerial Travels and Labours of Mrs. Zilpha Elaw* (London, 1846), p. 61.

73. Elaw, *Ministerial Travels*, p. 63.

74. Letter from Thomas Jefferson to Thomas Cooper, March 13, 1820.

75. Thomas Dreisbach, *Thomas Jefferson and the Wall of Separation Between Church and State* (New York: New York Univ. Press, 2003), p. 22.

76. Letter from James Madison to Reverend Jasper Adams, 1832.

77. Letter from James Madison to Reverend Jasper Adams, 1832.

CHAPTER FOUR

The Romish Threat

1. Nancy Lusignan Schultz, *Fire and Roses: The Burning of the Charlestown Covenant, 1834* (Boston: Northeastern Univ. Press, 2002), p. 161.

2. Lyman Beecher, *A Plea for the West* (Cincinnati: Truman & Smith, 1835), p. 37.

3. Schultz, *Fire and Roses*, p. 7.

4. Investigators subsequently inspected the building, which was found to not resemble the descriptions in the book. Her mother swore an affidavit that the girl was mentally ill and prone to making things up. The convent was well respected for assisting the community during a cholera epidemic. "Affidavit of Maria Monk's Mother," Archive.org, October 24, 1835.

5. Maria Monk, *Awful Disclosures of the Hotel Dieu Nunnery* (1836; reprint, Laconia, 2017), loc. 1973–78, Kindle.

6. The author described what happened to a pair of twins: "They were then taken, one after another, by one of the old nuns, in the presence of us all. She pressed her hand upon the mouth and nose of the first, so tight that it could not breathe, and in a few minutes, when the hand was removed, it was dead. She then took the other and treated it in the same way. No sound was heard, and both the children were corpses." Monk, *Awful Disclosures*, loc. 1708–12.

7. In "The Paranoid Style in American Politics," Richard Hofstadter wrote, "Probably the most widely read contemporary book in the United States before

Uncle Tom's Cabin was a work supposedly written by one Maria Monk, entitled *Awful Disclosures*, which appeared in 1836." Richard Hofstadter, "The Paranoid Style in American Politics," *Harper's Weekly*, November 1964, pp. 80–81.

8. About 3.6 million people lived in the United States, according to the 1790 census. M. H. Carroll, *The Religious Forces of the United States*, vol. 1, American Church History Series (New York: Scribner, 1893), p. Iviii.

9. Ira M. Leonard and Robert D. Parmet, *American Nativism, 1830–1860* (New York: Van Nostrand Reinhold, 1971), p. 33.

10. Immigration from Ireland grew from 52,000 in the 1820s to 170,000 in the 1830s. In the 1840s, 656,000 Irish arrived, and more than 1 million arrived in the 1850s. George J. Marlin, *The American Catholic Voter* (South Bend, IN: St. Augustine's Press, 2004), p. 62.

11. Leonard and Parmet, *American Nativism, 1830–1860*, p. 33.

12. Samuel Morse, *Imminent Dangers to the Free Institutions of the United States Through Foreign Immigration and the Present State of the Naturalization Laws* (New York: E. B. Clayton, 1835), p. 25.

13. Morse, *Imminent Dangers*, p. 24.

14. Morse, *Imminent Dangers*, p. 13.

15. Samuel Morse, *Foreign Conspiracy Against the Liberties of the United States* (New York: Leavitt, Lord, 1835), p. 59.

16. Morse, *Imminent Dangers*, p. 25.

17. Morse, *Imminent Dangers*, p. 11.

18. *Home Missionary* 12, August 1839, p. 73, cited in Ray Allen Billington, *The Protestant Crusade, 1800–1860: A Study of the Origins of American Nativism* (Chicago: Quadrangle Books, 1938), p. 129.

19. Beecher, *Plea for the West*, p. 49.

20. Katie Oxx, *The Nativist Movement in America: Religious Conflict in the Nineteenth Century* (New York: Routledge, 2013), p. 91, Kindle, citing "American Citizens! We Appeal to You in All Calmness. Is It Not Time to Pause? . . . A Paper Entitled the American Patriot," advertisement (Boston: J. E. Farwell, 1852).

21. Morse, *Foreign Conspiracy*, p. 118.

22. American Baptist Home Mission Society, *Proceedings of the Convention Held in the City of New-York, on the 27th of April, 1832, for the Formation of the American Baptist Home Mission Society* (New York: A.B.H.M.S., 1832), p. 31.

23. Vincent P. Lannie and Bernard C. Diethorn, "For the Honor and Glory of God: The Philadelphia Bible Riots of 1840," *History of Education Quarterly* 8, no. 1 (1968): 44–45.

24. Oxx, *Nativist Movement in America*, p. 61, citing *Catholic Herald*, November 25, 1841.

25. Lannie and Diethorn, "For the Honor and Glory of God," p. 55.

26. Marlin, *American Catholic Voter*, p. 52.

27. Lannie and Diethorn, "For the Honor and Glory of God," p. 55.

28. Marlin, *American Catholic Voter*, p. 42.

29. Lannie and Diethorn, "For the Honor and Glory of God," p. 59, citing *Presbyterian*, January 21, 1843.

30. Tracy Fessenden, "The Nineteenth-Century Bible Wars and the Separation of Church and State," *Church History* 74, no. 4 (December 2005): 793; *Catholic Herald*, June 2, 1842.

31. *Address of the Board of Managers of the American Protestant Association; with the Constitution and Organization of the Association* (Philadelphia: James C. Haswell, 1843), pp. 5, 7–9, 18–19.

32. Lannie and Diethorn, "For the Honor and Glory of God," p. 61.

33. Lannie and Diethorn, "For the Honor and Glory of God," pp. 65–67, citing *Episcopal Recorder*, March 9, 1844.

34. Lannie and Diethorn, "For the Honor and Glory of God," pp. 68–70.

35. Lannie and Diethorn, "For the Honor and Glory of God," p. 74, citing *Native American*, May 7, 1844.

36. Oxx, *Nativist Movement in America*, p. 68.

37. Lannie and Diethorn, "For the Honor and Glory of God," p. 76.

38. Marlin, *American Catholic Voter*, p. 54, citing James F. Connelly, *The History of the Archdiocese of Philadelphia* (Philadelphia: Archdiocese of Philadelphia, 1976), p. 170.

39. Lannie and Diethorn, "For the Honor and Glory of God," p. 76.

40. Lannie and Diethorn, "For the Honor and Glory of God," p. 82.

41. Oxx, *Nativist Movement in America*, p. 54.

42. John T. McGreevy, *Catholicism and American Freedom* (New York: W. W. Norton, 2003), p. 40.

43. McGreevy, *Catholicism and American Freedom*, pp. 7–8.

44. Fessenden, "Nineteenth-Century Bible Wars," p. 798; George Campbell, *A Sermon . . . at the Ordination of Rev. George H. Atkinson* (Newbury, VT: L. J. McIndoe, 1847), pp. 20–21.

45. Roger Finke and Rodney Stark, *The Churching of America, 1776–1990* (New Brunswick: Rutgers Univ. Press, 2000), p. 135.

46. Finke and Stark, *Churching of America, 1776–1990*, p. 141.

47. Finke and Stark, *Churching of America, 1776–1990*, p. 123.

48. Edwin Gaustad and Leigh Schmidt, *The Religious History of America: The Heart of the American Story from Colonial Times to Today* (San Francisco: HarperOne, 2004), p. 144, Kindle.

49. Another, smaller organization, the Leopold Association in Austria, didn't provide as much money but got more attention because of the demagoguery of Samuel Morse, who viewed the organization as the center of the "Papal Plot." Ray Allen Billington, *The Protestant Crusade, 1800–1860* (Chicago: Quadrangle Books, 1938), p. 121.

50. "Missouri Home Missionary Society," *Home Missionary* 16, May 1843, p. 37.

51. Billington, *Protestant Crusade*, p. 278; *Proceedings of the Public Meeting of the Society for the Promotion of Collegiate and Theological Education at the West, etc.* (New York, 1845), p. 10, cited in Billington, *Protestant Crusade*, p. 278.

52. Billington, *Protestant Crusade*, p. 278, citing E. N. Kirk, *The Church and the College* (Boston, 1856), p. 29.

53. "Rev. Mr. Kirk's Address," in *History of the Formation of the Ladies' Society for the Promotion of Education at the West* (Boston: Henry Mason, 1846), p. 16.

54. John C. Pinheiro, *Missionaries of Republicanism: A Religious History of the Mexican-American War* (New York: Oxford Univ. Press, 2014), p. 129.

55. *Congressional Globe*, 29th Cong., 2nd sess., app., 130 cited in Pinheiro, *Missionaries of Republicanism*, p. 88.

56. Pinheiro, *Missionaries of Republicanism*, p. 95, citing *New York Journal of Commerce*, June 2, 30, 1847.

57. Pinheiro, *Missionaries of Republicanism*, p. 133, citing *Baptist Banner and Western Pioneer*, April 30, 1846.

58. Pinheiro, *Missionaries of Republicanism*, pp. 71–72, citing *The Rough and Ready Songster* (New York: Nafis and Cornish, 1848), p. 20.

59. A soldier from Missouri, for instance, described a service he attended as "a pompous unmeaning show, & a gross mockery of the pure religion of the meek and humble Jesus whom they pretend to serve." American soldiers were appalled when they saw priests playing cards or smoking or drinking on Sundays. Pinheiro, *Missionaries of Republicanism*, p. 117; William Elsey Connelley, *Doniphan's Expedition and the Conquest of New Mexico and California* (Kansas City: Bryant & Douglas, 1907), p. 69.

60. Pinheiro, *Missionaries of Republicanism*, p. 121, citing *U.S. Catholic Magazine*, March 1848, 157.

61. Pinheiro, *Missionaries of Republicanism*, p. 103, citing Antonio López de Santa Anna, "Mexicans to Catholic Irishmen," *New Orleans Daily Picayune*, October 7, 1847; *New York Herald*, October 17, 1847.

62. Marlin, *American Catholic Voter*, pp. 58–59.

63. Pinheiro, *Missionaries of Republicanism*, p. 75.

64. United States House of Representatives, "A Proclamation: By the General Commanding the Army of the United States of America," *House Documents*, vol. 33 (Washington, DC: Government Printing Office, 1847), p. 16.

65. Louis Clinton Hatch, *Maine: A History*, vol. 1 (New York: American Historical Society, 1919), p. 305.

66. Tyler Anbinder, *Nativism and Slavery* (New York: Oxford Univ. Press, 1994), pp. 75–102.

67. An exact number is hard to find, as the Know-Nothing coalition was fairly loosely organized. Some sources give numbers as high as one hundred, while others place the number at around fifty. Roger Daniels, *Guarding the Golden Door: American Immigration Policy and Immigrants Since 1882* (New York: Farrar, Straus and Giroux, 2005), p. 10; "Party Divisions of the House of Representatives, 1789–Present," History, Art, and Archives, United States House of Representatives, accessed online May 2, 2018.

68. Marlin, *American Catholic Voter*, p. 68.

69. Oxx, *Nativist Movement in America*, p. 95, citing *Philadelphia Public Ledger*, March 9, 1852.

70. Oxx, *Nativist Movement in America*, p. 96, citing John F. Weishampel, *The Pope's Stratagem: "Rome to America"* (Philadelphia, 1852), p. 7.

71. Oxx, *Nativist Movement in America*, pp. 98–99.

72. John Higham, *Strangers in the Land: Patterns of American Nativism, 1860–1925* (New York: Atheneum, 1969), p. 13.

73. Abraham Lincoln, *Collected Works of Abraham Lincoln*, vol. 1 (New Brunswick: Rutgers Univ. Press, 1953), p. 338.

74. Fessenden, "Nineteenth-Century Bible Wars," pp. 792–93.

CHAPTER FIVE

The Religious Freedom of Slaves

1. Jon Butler, *Awash in a Sea of Faith: Christianizing the American People* (Cambridge: Harvard Univ. Press, 1990), p. 153.

2. Albert J. Raboteau, *Slave Religion: The "Invisible Institution" in the Antebellum South* (New York: Oxford Univ. Press, 2004), p. 86.

3. Raboteau, *Slave Religion*, p. 8.

4. Raboteau, *Slave Religion*, pp. 12–15.

5. Butler, *Awash in a Sea of Faith*, p. 157.

6. Sylviane A. Diouf, *Servants of Allah: African Muslims Enslaved in the Americas* (New York: New York Univ. Press, 2013), p. 70; R. Kevin Jaques and Donna L. Meigs-Jaques, "Islam," in *Encyclopedia of Religion in the South*, ed. Samuel S. Hill, Charles H. Lippy, and Charles Reagan Wilson, 2nd ed. (Macon, GA: Mercer Univ. Press, 2005).

7. Peter Manseau, *One Nation, Under Gods: A New American History* (New York: Little, Brown, 2015), p. 234.

8. Kambiz GhaneaBassiri, *A History of Islam in America: From the New World to the New World Order* (New York: Cambridge Univ. Press, 2010), p. 17.

9. Boubacar Barry, *Senegambia and the Atlantic Slave Trade* (Cambridge: Cambridge Univ. Press, 1998), p. 34.

10. *CIA World Fact Book*, September 2018.

11. GhaneaBassiri, *History of Islam in America*, p. 14.

12. Diouf, *Servants of Allah*, p. 159; Michael Johnson, "Runaway Slaves and the Slave Communities in South Carolina, 1799 to 1830," *William and Mary Quarterly* 38, no. 3 (July 1981): 437, cited in Diouf, *Servants of Allah*, p. 159.

13. Denise A. Spellberg, *Thomas Jefferson's Qur'an: Islam and the Founders* (New York: Alfred A. Knopf, 2013), p. 7.

14. Edward E. Curtis IV, *Muslims in America: A Short History* (New York: Oxford Univ. Press, 2009), p. 20.

15. The actual transcription is "lill mat tuh kneel on." Diouf, *Servants of Allah*, p. 90; Works Project Administration, Savannah Unit, Georgia's Writers Project, *Drums and Shadows: Survival Studies Among the Georgia Coastal Negroes* (1940; reprint, Athens: Univ. of Georgia Press, 1986), p. 179.

16. Curtis, *Muslims in America*, p. 17.

17. The precise transcription was "bow uh head down tree time an she say 'Ameen, Ameen, Ameen.'" Diouf, *Servants of Allah*, p. 88; Works Project Administration, *Drums and Shadows*, p. 121.

18. GhaneaBassiri, *History of Islam in America*, p. 43.

19. Diouf, *Servants of Allah*, p. 83, citing Omar Ibn Said, "The Life of Omar Ibn Said, Written by Himself," in *A Muslim American Slave: The Life of Omar Ibn Said*, trans. and ed. Ala Alryyes (Madison: Univ. of Wisconsin Press, 2011), p. 51.

20. Diouf, *Servants of Allah*, p. 83; Charles Colcock Jones, *The Religious Instruction of the Negroes in the Southern States* (Philadelphia: Presbyterian Board of Publication, 1847), p. 51, cited in Diouf, *Servants of Allah*, p. 83.

21. Diouf, *Servants of Allah*, p. 120; Edward Teas, "A Trading Trip to Natchez and New Orleans in 1822: Diary of Thomas Teas," *Journal of Southern History* 7 (August 1941): 388, cited in Diouf, *Servants of Allah*, p. 120.

22. Diouf, *Servants of Allah*, p. 252.

23. Manseau, *One Nation, Under Gods*, p. 235.

24. John Thompson, *The Life of John Thompson, a Fugitive Slave* (Worcester, 1856), pp. 18–19, cited in Raboteau, *Slave Religion*, p. 133.

25. Raboteau, *Slave Religion*, p. 179.

26. Raboteau, *Slave Religion*, p. 175.

27. Raboteau, *Slave Religion*, p. 131.

28. Raboteau, *Slave Religion*, p. 176.

29. Raboteau, *Slave Religion*, p. 215, citing John B. Cade, "Out of the Mouths of Ex-Slaves," *Journal of Negro History* 20 (July 1935): 330–31.

30. Raboteau, *Slave Religion*, p. 217, citing Peter Randolph, *Sketches of Slave Life, or Illustrations of the Peculiar Institution* (Boston, 1855), pp. 30–31.

31. Raboteau, *Slave Religion*, p. 219, citing George P. Rawick, ed., *The American Slave: A Composite Autobiography*, vol. 13, *Georgia Narratives* (Westport, CT: Greenwood, 1972), p. 192.

32. Thomas Wentworth Higginson, *Army Life in a Black Regiment*, cited in Raboteau, *Slave Religion*, p. 261. See also Thomas Wentworth Higginson, *Army Life in a Black Regiment* (Boston, 1869; reprint, Boston: Beacon Press, 1962), p. 203.

33. Randolph, *Sketches of Slave Life*, p. 24.

34. Raboteau, *Slave Religion*, p. 214, citing Rawick, *American Slave: A Composite Autobiography*, vol. 7, *Mississippi Narratives*, p. 24.

35. Raboteau, *Slave Religion*, p. 306, citing G. W. Offley, *A Narrative of the Life and Labors of Rev. G. W. Offley* (Hartford, 1860), reprinted in Arna Bontemps, ed., *Five Black*

Lives: The Autobiographies of Venture Smith, James Mars, William Grimes, the Rev. G. W. Offley, and James L. Smith (Middletown, CT: Wesleyan Univ. Press, 1971), pp. 134–35.

36. Thomas R. Gray, *The Confessions of Nat Turner* (Richmond: T. H. White, 1832), pp. 8–10.

37. Gray, *Confessions of Nat Turner*, p. 22.

38. Jakobi Williams, "Nat Turner: The Complexity and Dynamic of His Religious Background," *Journal of Pan African Studies* 4, no. 9 (January 2012): 123, citing John Floyd, "Governor Floyd's Diary & Correspondence: Letters Pertaining to the Revolt Between 24 August 1831 and 19 November 1831," in *The Southampton Slave Revolt of 1831: A Compilation of Source Material*, ed. Henry Irving Tragle (Amherst: Univ. of Massachusetts Press, 1971), pp. 275–76.

39. Recently some doubt has been raised about whether there really was a rebellion being planned. The plot may have been fabricated as part of a power struggle between two white politicians. Jack Hitt, "History Returns to Charleston," *New Yorker*, June 19, 2015; Nicholas May, "Holy Rebellion: Religious Assembly Laws in Antebellum South Carolina and Virginia," *American Journal of Legal History* 49, no. 3 (July 2007): 249.

40. Maurie McInnis, "The First Attack on Charleston's AME Church," University of Virginia, June 23, 2015, accessed online August 7, 2018.

41. May, "Holy Rebellion," p. 244.

42. Hitt, "History Returns to Charleston."

43. Williams, "Nat Turner," p. 123.

44. John W. Cromwell, "The Aftermath of Nat Turner's Insurrection," *Journal of Negro History* 5, no. 2 (April 1920): 232 (published by the Association for the Study of African American Life and History).

45. Kurt T. Lash, "The Second Adoption of the Free Exercise Clause: Religious Exemptions Under the Fourteenth Amendment," Legal Studies Paper No. 2008-10, Loyola Law School, Los Angeles, 1994, p. 1134.

46. Frederick Douglass, *The Collected Works of Frederick Douglass: Autobiographies, 50+ Speeches, Articles & Letters: The Future of the Colored Race, Reconstruction, My Bondage . . . The Color Line, The Church and Prejudice . . .* (Musaicum Books, 2018), loc. 8417–19, Kindle.

47. Frederick Douglass, "Slavery in the Pulpit of the Evangelical Alliance: An Address Delivered in London, England, on September 14, 1846," *London Inquirer*, September 19, 1846, and *London Patriot*, September 17, 1846, cited in John Blassingame et al., eds., *The Frederick Douglass Papers, Series One: Speeches, Debates, and Interviews*, vol. 1, *1841–1846* (New Haven: Yale Univ. Press, 1979), p. 407.

CHAPTER SIX

The Divine Plan

1. Erving E. Beauregard, *Bingham of the Hills: Politician and Diplomat Extraordinary* (New York: Peter Lang, 1989), p. 4, citing Walter Gaston Shotwell, *Driftwood: Being Papers on Old-Time American Towns and Some Old People* (Longmans, Green, 1927; reprint, Freeport, NY: Books for Libraries Press, 1966), pp. 175–233.

2. Richard L. Aynes, "The Antislavery and Abolitionist Background of John A. Bingham," *Catholic University Law Review* 37, no. 4 (Summer 1988): 931, citing Howard Jay Graham, "The 'Conspiracy Theory' of the Fourteenth Amendment," pts. 1 and 2, *Yale Law Journal* 47 (1938): 610–22.

3. Beauregard, *Bingham of the Hills*, p. 48.

4. *Permoli v. Municipality No. 1 of the City of New Orleans*, 44 US 589 (1845).

5. Aynes, "Background of John A. Bingham," p. 886. Bingham was raised by a devout

Calvinist mother; his father was an elder in the Associate Reformed Presbyterian Church, a sharply anti-slavery congregation.

6. Aynes, "Background of John A. Bingham," p. 906, citing Shotwell, *Driftwood*, p. 137.

7. Erving E. Beauregard, "John A. Bingham and the Fourteenth Amendment," *Historian* 50, no. 1 (November 1987): 69, citing John Bingham's conversation with John N. Haverfield, Cadiz, Ohio, August 16, 1866, in John N. Haverfield, "Reminiscences," (unpublished, n.d.), p. 232, Campbell Collection, Cadiz, Ohio.

8. *Congressional Globe*, 34th Cong., 3rd sess., app., 137 (1857), "Statement of Rep. Bingham," cited in Gerard N. Magliocca, *American Founding Son: John Bingham and the Invention of the Fourteenth Amendment* (New York: New York Univ. Press, 2013), p. 46.

9. *Congressional Globe*, "Statement of Rep. Bingham," cited in Magliocca, *American Founding Son*, p. 46.

10. Noble J. Tolbert, "Daniel Worth: Tar Heel Abolitionist," *North Carolina Historical Review* 39, no. 3 (July 1962): 294, citing; *Daily Progress* (New Bern, NC), January 3, 1860.

11. Kurt T. Lash, "The Second Adoption of the Establishment Clause: The Rise of the Non-Establishment Principle," *Arizona State Law Journal* 27, no. 1085 (1995); Loyola Law School, Los Angeles, Legal Studies Paper no. 2008-16, p. 1138.

12. Lash, "Second Adoption of the Establishment Clause," p. 1133.

13. "The Constitutional Amendment, Discussed by Its Author: Speech of Hon. John A. Bingham at Bowerston, Harrison County, O.," *Cincinnati Commercial*, collected in *Speeches of the Campaign of 1866 in the States of Ohio, Indiana, and Kentucky* (Cincinnati: Cincinnati Commercial, 1866), p. 19.

14. Lash, "Second Adoption of the Establishment Clause," p. 1142, citing *The Reconstruction Amendment's Debates: The Legislative History and Contemporary Debates in Congress on the 13th, 14th, and 15th Amendments* (Richmond: Virginia Commission on Constitutional Government, 1967), January 27, 29, 1866.

15. Lash, "Second Adoption of the Establishment Clause," p. 1142, citing *Reconstruction Amendment's Debates*, p. 81.

16. "An Act to Provide for the Punishment of Persons for Tampering with, Persuading or Enticing Away, Harboring, Feeding, or Secreting Laborers, Servants, or Apprentices," December 20, 1865, *Acts of Louisiana*, extra sess. 24, cited in Paul Finkelman, "John Bingham and the Background to the Fourteenth Amendment," *Akron Law Review* 36, no. 671 (2003): 681–82.

17. "Before I would see this Government destroyed, I would see every negro back in Africa, and Africa disintegrated and blotted out of space," Andrew Johnson said. Andrew Johnson and Samuel F. Carey, "The Great Union Meeting, Held at Indianapolis, February 26th, 1863: Speeches of Andrew Johnson, of Tennessee, Gen. Samuel F. Carey, of Ohio, and Others," 1863, p. 7.

18. "The Row among Representatives—The Floor as Seen from the Gallery," *New York Times*, January 13, 1860, p. 1.

19. Beauregard, *Bingham of the Hills*, p. 98, citing John A. Bingham, letter to Andrew F. Ross, Washington, DC, February 27, 1866, John S. Campbell Collection, Cadiz, Ohio.

20. Beauregard, *Bingham of the Hills*, p. 99, citing John A. Bingham, letter to Rev. Titus Basfield, Washington, DC, March 3, 1866, Martin Collection, Portsmouth, Ohio.

21. That Bingham did not imagine the courts as a protector of rights likely stemmed from his experience with the Supreme Court in the years before the war, when the 1857 *Dred Scott v. Sandford* decision and others like it had convinced Republicans that the third branch of government would not protect liberty. Indeed, in 1867, Bingham proposed abolishing the Supreme Court! Beauregard, *Bingham of the Hills*, p. 106.

22. Magliocca, *American Founding Son*, p. 126, citing *New Hampshire Statesman*, August 24, 1866.

23. Beauregard, *Bingham of the Hills*, p. 108, citing Bingham letter to Andrew F. Ross.

24. Beauregard, *Bingham of the Hills*, p. 108, citing Bingham letter to Rev. Titus Basfield, Washington, DC, June 16, 1866, in Haverfield, "Reminiscences," p. 232.

25. Beauregard, *Bingham of the Hills*, p. 109, citing Bingham, conversation with Dr. John W. Comly, Cadiz, Ohio, 1866, in John W. Comly, "Talks with Honorable John A. Bingham," p. 138.

CHAPTER SEVEN

The Mormon Challenge

1. Alicia Purdy, "Mormons Serving in the House of Representatives (112th Congress)," *Deseret News*, July 9, 2012.

2. "Facts and Statistics: Worldwide Church," Church of Jesus Christ of Latter-day Saints Newsroom, accessed online July 26, 2018.

3. "Mass Meeting at Warsaw," in *History of the Church of Jesus Christ of Latter-day Saints*, vol. 6, BYU Studies Quarterly, chap. 22.

4. Alex Beam, *American Crucifixion: The Murder of Joseph Smith and the Fate of the Mormon Church* (New York: Public Affairs, 2014), pp. 181–82.

5. Douglas O. Linder, "Meet the Defendants in the Carthage Conspiracy Trial," University of Missouri, Famous Trials, accessed online February 11, 2018.

6. "History, Circa Summer 1832," p. 3, Joseph Smith Papers.

7. "History, Circa June 1839–Circa 1841 [Draft 2]," p. 3, Joseph Smith Papers.

8. "The Annual Report of the Church, July 1972," Church of Jesus Christ of Latter-day Saints.

9. Jonathan Baldwin Turner, *Mormonism in All Ages* (New York: Platt & Peter, 1842), pp. 3–4.

10. J. Spencer Fluhman, *"A Peculiar People": Anti-Mormonism and the Making of Religion in Nineteenth-Century America* (Chapel Hill: Univ. of North Carolina Press, 2012), pp. 68, 72, citing La Roy Sunderland, *Mormonism Exposed and Refuted* (New York: Piercy & Reed, 1838).

11. Matthew Bowman, *The Mormon People: The Making of an American Faith* (New York: Random House, 2012), p. 54.

12. Amos Hayden, *Early History of the Disciples in the Western Reserve, Ohio* (Cincinnati: Chase and Hall, 1876), p. 221, cited in Bowman, *Mormon People*, p. 55.

13. Fawn M. Brodie, *No Man Knows My History: The Life of Joseph Smith* (New York: Vintage Books, 1995), p. 131.

14. Beam, *American Crucifixion*, p. xiii.

15. *The Doctrine and Covenants of the Church of Jesus Christ of Latter-day Saints* (Salt Lake City: Church of Jesus Christ of Latter-day Saints, 2013), sec. 124.

16. Letter from General John C. Bennett, *New York Herald*, June 17, 1842.

17. Arnold K. Garr, "Joseph Smith," Church of Jesus Christ of Latter-day Saints, February 2009, accessed online February 5, 2018.

18. Joseph Smith, "The Globe," *Times and Seasons* 5, no. 8 (April 15, 1844): 510.

19. Gerrit J. Dirkmaat, "A New Voice from the Past: The Council of Fifty Minutes," *BYU Religious Education Review*, Winter 2017.

20. Council of Fifty, "Record," April 11, 1844, vol. 1, pp. 116–121, Church History

Library, in *Joseph Smith Papers, Administrative Records, Council of Fifty, Minutes, March 1844–January 1846*, pp. 97–101.

21. Gerrit Dirkmaat, "Op-ed: Joseph Smith Was a Champion of Religious Liberty," *Deseret News*, November 17, 2017; Michael De Groote, "Cylinders Preserve the First Recording of a Prophet," *Deseret News*, June 3, 2010.

22. Heman C. Smith et al., *Journal of History* 1, no. 1 (1908): 137 (published by Herald, Lamoni, IA, for the Reorganized Church of Jesus Christ of Latter-day Saints).

23. Beam, *American Crucifixion*, p. 55; Marvin S. Hill, "Carthage Conspiracy Reconsidered: A Second Look at the Murder of Joseph and Hyrum Smith," *Journal of the Illinois State Historical Society* 97, no. 2 (Summer 2004): 123.

24. "Letter from Citizens of Daviess and Livingston Counties to Governor Boggs, Jefferson City, Missouri, September 12, 1838," Mormon War Papers, 1837–1841, Missouri State Archives.

25. "Expulsion of the Saints from De Witt, Carroll County, Missouri," *History of the Church*, vol. 1, chaps. 1–5, *BYU Studies Quarterly*.

26. Beam, *American Crucifixion*, p. 253.

27. Journal History, LDS Church Historian's Office, Salt Lake City, August 6, 1838, images 175–77.

28. Brodie, *No Man Knows My History*, p. 132, citing *The Evening and the Morning Star* 2 (July 1833): 218–19, 221.

29. Lester E. Bush Jr., "Mormonism's Negro Doctrine: An Historical Overview," *Dialogue: A Journal of Mormon Thought* 8, no. 1 (Spring 1973): 12–13.

30. In 1844, during his race for the presidency, Smith shifted gears and did indeed become anti-slavery—"Some two or three millions of people are held as slaves for life, because the spirit in them is covered with a darker skin than ours." Joseph Smith, *General Smith's Views of the Powers and Policy of the Government of the United States* (Nauvoo, IL: John Taylor, 1844).

31. That was most likely not true, but the Mormons did have a unique attitude toward the Indians. The Book of Mormon is to some degree a tale about Native Americans being a remnant of the lost tribe of Israel. God cursed one subset of settlers, the Lamanites, by turning their skin dark. But the Book of Mormon also taught that Native Americans would rejoin the covenant in end times, and so early Mormons sometimes treated Native Americans as targets of proselytizing. For more information on this topic, see Ronald W. Walker, "Seeking the 'Remnant': The Native American During the Joseph Smith Period," *Journal of Mormon History* 19, no. 1 (1993): 1, as well as Ronald W. Walker, "Toward a Reconstruction of Mormon and Indian Relations, 1847–1877," *BYU Studies Quarterly* 29, no. 4 (Fall 1989): 23–42.

32. Letter from Daniel Dunklin, City of Jefferson, July 18, 1836, in *History of Joseph Smith, the Prophet, by Himself*, ed. B. H. Roberts, vol. 2 (Salt Lake City: Deseret News, 1902–12), pp. 461–62.

33. Juanita Brooks, *The Mountain Meadows Massacre* (Norman: Univ. of Oklahoma Press, 1991), p. 7.

34. Peter Crawley and Richard L. Anderson, "The Political and Social Realities of Zion's Camp," *BYU Studies Quarterly* 14, no. 4 (Summer 1974): 420; *Missouri Intelligencer*, June 28, 1843.

35. Brodie, *No Man Knows My History*, p. 158.

36. *History of the Church of Jesus Christ of Latter-day Saints, Period I: History of Joseph Smith, the Prophet, by Himself*, ed. B. H. Roberts, vol. 3 (Salt Lake City: Deseret News, 1905), pp. 180–81.

37. *History of the Church of Jesus Christ of Latter-day Saints, Period I: History of Joseph Smith, the Prophet, by Himself*, ed. B. H. Roberts, vol. 2 (Salt Lake City: Deseret News, 1904), pp. 157–65.

38. Affidavit of Thomas B. Marsh, October 24, 1838, in Joseph Smith, "History of the Church" (Salt Lake City, 1902), *BYU Studies Quarterly* 3, chap. 12.

39. "Highly Important from the Mormon Empire—Wonderful Progress of Joe Smith, the Modern Mahomet—Spread of the Mormon Faith and a New Religious Revolution at Hand," *New York Herald*, June 17, 1842, p. 2.

40. Church of Jesus Christ of Latter-day Saints, *Doctrine and Covenants and Church History* (1997), the Extermination Order, pp. 174–79; Stephen C. LeSueur, *The 1838 Mormon War in Missouri* (Columbia: Univ. of Missouri Press, 1987), pp. 143–44.

41. "The Missouri Mormon War Executive Orders," Missouri State Archives, accessed online February 12, 2018.

42. Beth Shumway Moore, *Bones in the Well: The Haun's Mill Massacre, 1838* (Norman: Univ. of Oklahoma Press, 2012), p. 129.

43. Moore, *Bones in the Well*, p. 64.

44. Bowman, *Mormon People*, p. xix; Brigham Young, "Epistle to the Brethren of the Church of Jesus Christ of Latter-day Saints, Scattered Abroad Through the United States of America," in *History of the Church of Jesus Christ of Latter-day Saints, Period II: From the Manuscript History of Brigham Young and Other Original Documents*, ed. B. H. Roberts, vol. 7 (Salt Lake City: Deseret News, 1932), p. 479.

45. David L. Bigler, *Forgotten Kingdom: The Mormon Theocracy in the American West, 1847–1896* (Logan: Utah State Univ. Press, 1998), p. 146.

46. "Whilst Governor Young has been both governor and superintendent of Indian affairs throughout this period, he has been at the same time the head of the church called the Latter-Day Saints, and professes to govern its members and dispose of their property by direct inspiration and authority from the Almighty. His power has been, therefore, absolute over both church and State. The people of Utah, almost exclusively belong to this church, and believing with a fanatical spirit that he is governor of the Territory by divine appointment, they obey his commands as if these were direct revelations from Heaven. If, therefore, he chooses that his government shall come into collision with the government of the United States, the members of the Mormon church will yield implicit to his will. Unfortunately, existing facts leave but little doubt that such is his determination." "First Annual Message by President James Buchanan, December 8, 1857," in James Buchanan, *The Works of James Buchanan*, ed. John Bassett Moore (Philadelphia: J. B. Lippincott, 1908), p. 152.

47. Mathias F. Cowley, *Wilford Woodruff: History of His Life and Labors* (Salt Lake City: Bookcraft, 1964), p. 391.

48. Exod. 22:16, AV.

49. Beam, *American Crucifixion*, p. 91.

50. Sermon by Parley Pratt, in *Deseret News, Extra*, September 14, 1852, cited in Richard S. Van Wagoner, *Mormon Polygamy: A History* (Salt Lake City: Signature Books, 1989), p. 85.

51. "Great Indignation Meeting of the Ladies of Salt Lake City, to Protest Against the Passage of Cullom's Bill," *Deseret Evening News*, January 14, 1870, p. 2, cited in Fluhman, "A Peculiar People," p. 117.

52. Fluhman, "A Peculiar People," p. 122, citing B. Carmon Hardy, *Doing the Works of Abraham: Mormon Polygamy* (Norman, UT: Arthur H. Clark, 2007), pp. 151–52.

53. Richard Corliss, "10 Memorable Depictions of Mormons in Pop Culture," *TIME*, April 25, 2011.

54. Alfreda Eva Bell, *Boadicea: The Mormon Wife* (Baltimore: Arthur R. Orton, 1855), pp. 54, 34, cited in Sarah Barringer Gordon, *The Mormon Question* (Chapel Hill: Univ. of North Carolina Press, 2002), p. 47.

55. Gordon, *Mormon Question*, p. 49.

56. Kathleen Flake, *The Politics of American Religious Identity: The Seating of Senator Reed Smoot, Mormon Apostle* (Chapel Hill: Univ. of North Carolina Press, 2004), p. 21.

57. Fluhman, *"A Peculiar People,"* p. 108, citing Caleb Lyon, "No Government Bounty to Polygamy: Speech of Hon. Caleb Lyon, of Lyonsdale, New York, in the House of Representatives, May 4, 1854," Congressional Globe Office, 1854, pp. 1–2.

58. Political scientist Francis Lieber equated monogamy with civilization and whiteness. "It is one of the elementary distinctions—historical and actual—between European and Asiatic humanity. . . . Strike it out, and you destroy our very being." See also Nancy Cott, *Public Vows: A History of Marriage and the Nation* (Cambridge: Harvard Univ. Press, 2008), pp. 114–15.

59. Wagoner, *Mormon Polygamy*, p. 106, citing Samuel A. Cartwright and C. G. Forshey, "Effects and Tendencies of Mormon Polygamy in the Territories of Utah," Anthony W. Ivins Collection, Utah State Historical Society Library, p. 238.

60. *Times and Seasons*, November 1, 1845, p. 1012, cited in Fluhman, *"A Peculiar People,"* p. 112.

61. Justin S. Morrill, "Speech of Hon. Justin S. Morrill, of Vermont, on Utah Territory and Its Law—Polygamy and Its License," February 24, 1857, *Appendix to the Congressional Globe*, 34th Cong., 3rd sess. (Washington, DC: Office of John C. Rives, 1857), p. 288.

62. Colfax went on to point out that Mormonism originally viewed polygamy as reprehensible. Schuyler Colfax and John Taylor, "The Mormon Question," originally in the *New York Independent*, later collected in *Deseret News*, 1870, pp. 4, 6.

63. Taylor continued: "This not our religion? You do not see things as we do. You marry for time only, 'until death does you part.' We have eternal covenants, eternal unions, eternal associations." Colfax and Taylor, "Mormon Question," pp. 4, 6.

64. Grant Underwood, "Early Mormon Millenarianism: Another Look," *Church History* 54, no. 2 (1985): 215.

65. Bigler, *Forgotten Kingdom*, p. 54.

66. Bigler, *Forgotten Kingdom*, p. 135.

67. Bigler, *Forgotten Kingdom*, p. 263.

68. Brigham Young, *Journal of Discourses*, vol. 2 (London: F. D. Richards, 1855), p. 311.

69. Brooks, *Mountain Meadows Massacre*, p. 52, citing *Cedar City Ward Record Book*, 1857, Archives of the LDS Church Historian, Salt Lake City.

70. "The Smoot Case," *Kalamazoo Telegraph*, April 22, 1904, cited in Flake, *Politics*, p. 20.

71. Fluhman, *"A Peculiar People,"* p. 142.

72. Fluhman, *"A Peculiar People,"* p. 109, citing Justin S. Morrill, "Speech of Hon. Justin S. Morrill, of Vermont, on Utah Territory and Its Law—Polygamy and Its License," February 23, 1857 (Washington, DC: Office of the Congressional Globe, 1857), pp. 12–14.

73. "Brigham Young Arrested," *New York Times*, October 3, 1871.

74. *Reynolds v. United States*, 98 US 145 (1878).

75. *Davis v. Beason*, 133 US 333 (1890).

76. Wilford Woodruff, "Epistle of the Elder Wilford Woodruff," *Latter-Day Saints' Millennial Star* 41, 1879, p. 242.

77. Flake, *Politics*, p. 66, citing Jessie Embray, *Mormon Polygamous Families: Life in the Principle* (Sandy, UT: Greg Kofford Books, 2008), p. 22.

78. Flake, *Politics*, p. 66, citing Annie Clark Tanner, *Mormon Mother: An Autobiography* (Salt Lake City: Signature Books, 1983), pp. 75–76.

79. John Kincaid, *Publius* 33, no. 1 (Winter 2003): 75–92.

80. Wagoner, *Mormon Polygamy*, p. 135, citing Wilford Woodruff to William Atkin, March 18, 1889, Woodruff Letterbooks Collection, LDS Archives.

81. Wagoner, *Mormon Polygamy*, p. 125.

Notes 349

82. "The Annual Report of the Church: July 1972," Church of Jesus Christ of Latter-day Saints.

83. The first Republican platform declared that it was "both the right and the imperative duty of Congress to prohibit in the Territories those twin relics of barbarism—Polygamy, and Slavery." "Republican Platform of 1856," USHistory.org.

84. Fluhman, *"A Particular People,"* p. 145. See also Edward Leo Lyman, *Political Deliverance: The Mormon Quest for Utah Statehood* (Urbana: Univ. of Illinois Press, 1986), p. 235.

85. Frank J. Cannon and Harvey J. Higgins, *Under the Prophet in Utah* (Boston: G. M. Clark, 1911), pp. 96–98.

86. B. H. Roberts, *Defense of the Faith and the Saints*, vol. 1 (Salt Lake City: Deseret News, 1907), pp. 123–24, cited in Flake, *Politics*, p. 14.

87. Murat Halstead, foreword to J. H. Beadle, *Polygamy* (Philadelphia: National, 1900), p. xvi; Flake, *Politics*, p. 15.

88. Flake, *Politics*, p. 21, citing US Senate, *Congressional Record*, 58th Cong., special sess., 1903, p. 37, pt. 2:96.

89. Flake, *Politics*, p. 87, citing W. J. McConnell to Joseph F. Smith, January 24, 1904, Reed Smoot Collection, L. Tom Perry Special Collection, Harold B. Lee Library, Brigham Young University.

90. Flake, *Politics*, p. 156, citing. US Senate, *Congressional Record*, 59th Cong., 2nd sess., 1907, p. 41, pt. 4:3412.

91. Flake, *Politics*, p. 146, citing Orvin Malmquist, *The First 100 Years: A History of the Salt Lake Tribune, 1871–1971* (Salt Lake City: Utah State Historical Society, 1971), p. 229.

92. Flake, *Politics*, p. 157.

CHAPTER EIGHT

Kill the Indian, Christianize the Man

1. William T. Sherman, letter to John Sherman, September 23, 25, 1868, cited in Michael Fellman, *Citizen Sherman: A Life of William Tecumseh Sherman* (New York: Random House, 1995), loc. 5050–51, Kindle.

2. "'Kill the Indian, and Save the Man': Capt. Richard H. Pratt on the Education of Native Americans," History Matters, George Mason University, accessed online January 17, 2018.

3. R. Pierce Beaver, *Church, State, and the American Indians* (St. Louis: Concordia, 1966), p. 186, citing *American Missionary* 37, no. 4 (April 1883): 105.

4. Ulysses S. Grant to Julia Dent Grant, March 19, 1853, in John Y. Simon, ed., *The Papers of Ulysses S. Grant*, vol. 1, *1837–1861* (Carbondale: Southern Illinois Univ. Press, 1967), p. 296.

5. Ulysses S. Grant to Major Osborn Cross, July 25, 1853, in Simon, *Papers of Ulysses S. Grant*, p. 310.

6. Francis Paul Prucha, *American Indian Policy in Crisis: Christian Reformers and the Indian, 1865–1900* (Norman: Univ. of Oklahoma Press, 1976), p. 53.

7. Robert M. Mardock, *The Reformers and the American Indian* (Columbia: Univ. of Missouri Press, 1971), p. 88, citing *Bulletin* (Leavenworth, KS), June 4, 1869, in *Western Observer* (Washington, KS), June 17, 1869.

8. Mardock, *Reformers and the American Indian*, p. 88, citing *Junction City (KS) Weekly Union*, June 19, 1869.

9. Prucha, *American Indian Policy in Crisis*, p. 161, citing *Lake Mohonk Conference Proceedings*, 1893, p. 12.

10. David Wallace Adams, *Education for Extinction: American Indians and the Boarding School Experience, 1875–1928* (Lawrence: Univ. Press of Kansas, 1995), 165.

11. Charles A. Eastman, *The Soul of the Indian*, Project Gutenberg e-book.

12. Adams, *Education for Extinction*, p. 165.

13. Ward Churchill, *Kill the Indian, Save the Man: The Genocidal Impact of American Indian Residential Schools* (San Francisco: City Lights Books, 2004), p. 12, citing Francis E. Leupp, *The Indian and His Problem* (New York: Scribner's, 1910), p. 93.

14. "Reports of Agents in Dakota," *Annual Report of the Commissioner of Indian Affairs to the Secretary of the Interior for the Year 1887* (Washington, DC: Government Printing Office, 1887), p. 61.

15. Karen Watembach, "The History of the Catechesis of the Catholic Church on the Crow Reservation" (master's thesis, Montana State University, Bozeman, August 1983), p. 57, citing Edwardo Griva, "Catechism of Christian Doctrine in the Crow Language," n.d., Oregon Province Archives of the Society of Jesus, Museum of Native American Culture, Spokane, Washington, p. 42, no. 8.

16. Jon Reyhner and Jeanne Eder, *American Indian Education: A History* (Norman: Univ. of Oklahoma Press, 2004), 105.

17. L. B. Palladino, *Education for the Indian* (New York: Benziger Brothers, 1892), p. 5, citing Senator George Vest, May 12, 1884).

18. Prucha, *American Indian Policy in Crisis*, p. 275, citing Richard Henry Pratt, *Battlefield and Classroom: An Autobiography by Richard Henry Pratt*, ed. Robert M. Utley (New Haven: Yale Univ. Press, 1964), p. 335.

19. Zitkála-Šá, *My Life* (Middletown: CreateSpace, 2014), p. 27.

20. Luther Standing Bear, *My People, the Sioux* (Lincoln: Univ. of Nebraska Press, 1975), p. 141.

21. Watembach, "History of the Catechesis," p. 44.

22. Adams, *Education for Extinction*, p. 110.

23. Adams, *Education for Extinction*, p. 122, citing Broderick Johnson, ed., "Myrtle Begay," in *Stories of Traditional Navajo Life and Culture* (Tsaile, AZ: Navajo Community College Press, 1977), p. 63.

24. Mary Crow Dog and Richard Erdoes, *Lakota Woman* (New York: Grove Press, 2014), p. 32.

25. Reyhner and Eder, *American Indian Education*, p. 187.

26. Adams, *Education for Extinction*, p. 322, citing Edmund Nequatewa, *Born a Chief* (Tucson: Univ. of Arizona Press, 1992), pp. 91–92.

27. K. Tsianina Lomawaima, *They Called It Prairie Light: The Story of Chilocco Indian School* (Lincoln: Univ. of Nebraska Press, 1995), p. 23.

28. John S. Milloy, *A National Crime: The Canadian Government and the Residential School System, 1879 to 1986* (Winnipeg: Univ. of Manitoba Press, 1999).

29. Adams, *Education for Extinction*, pp. 224–25, citing Minnie Braithewaite Jenkins, *Girl from Williamsburg* (Richmond: Dietz Press, 1951), p. 283.

30. Charles Alexander Eastman, *From the Deep Woods to Civilization* (1916; reprint, Amazon Digital Services, 2016), loc. 300–302, Kindle.

31. Reyhner and Eder, *American Indian Education*, p. 195.

32. Adams, *Education for Extinction*, p. 217.

33. Coleman, *American Indian Children*, p. 163, citing "Report of Agent for Fort Apache Agency," *Annual Report of the Commissioner of Indian Affairs*, 1902, House Document no. 5, 57th Cong., 2nd sess., serial 4458, p. 149.

34. Adams, *Education for Extinction*, p. 214, citing Robert H. Ruby and John A. Brown, *The Spokane Indians: Children of the Sun* (Norman: Univ. of Oklahoma Press, 1970), pp. 216–18.

35. Adams, *Education for Extinction*, p. 211; *Annual Report of the Commissioner of Indian Affairs* (Washington, DC: Government Printing Office, 1886), p. 417.

36. Adams, *Education for Extinction*, p. 216; *Annual Report of the Commissioner*, 1886, p. 150.

37. Wendy Holliday, "Hopi Prisoners on the Rock," National Park Service, accessed online February 27, 2015.

38. "Address of Hon. William A. Jones, Commissioner of Indian Affairs," *Proceedings of the Fourteenth Annual Lake Mohonk Conference of the Friends of the Indian, 1896*, Lake Mohonk Conference, 1897, p. 86.

39. Heather Cox Richardson, *Wounded Knee: Party Politics and the Road to an American Massacre* (New York: Basic Books, 2010), p. 74, citing George E. Hyde, *A Sioux Chronicle* (1965; reprint, Norman: Univ. of Oklahoma Press, 1993), pp. 53–58.

40. Reyhner and Eder, *American Indian Education*, p. 195; Albert H. Kneale, *Indian Agent* (Caldwell, ID: Caxton, 1950), p. 490.

41. Watembach, "History of the Catechesis," p. 71.

42. Watembach, "History of the Catechesis," p. 63.

43. Watembach, "History of the Catechesis," p. 36.

44. Watembach, "History of the Catechesis," p. 45.

45. Watembach, "History of the Catechesis," pp. 48–49, citing "With the Crow Indians," *Catholic Sentinel*, March 8, 1891, Archives of the Diocese of Helena, Helena, MT.

46. Zitkála-Šá, *My Life*, pp. 30–31.

47. Watembach, "History of the Catechesis," pp. 31–32.

48. Crow Dog and Erdoes, *Lakota Woman*, p. 32.

49. Prucha, *American Indian Policy in Crisis*, p. 312.

50. Estelle Reel, "Report of the Superintendent of Indian Schools," Washington, DC, 1899, pp. 438–41.

51. Students at the boarding schools rarely had the opportunity to learn the rituals that would have been important had they been with their families. For instance, the schools prohibited the *hanblecheyapi*, a Sioux vision quest that had been an important part of a boy's coming-of-age ritual. In this ritual, adolescent boys would first spend time in a sweat lodge as holy men summoned the spirits. They would then go to an isolated place and fast for several days in the hope of connecting with the Great Spirit. Suffice it to say, that ritual was not allowed at boarding school. Nor would the schools have allowed a coming-of-age ritual called the "throwing ceremony," also known as the Buffalo Rites, that adolescent girls had traditionally undertaken. Steve Talbot, "Spiritual Genocide: The Denial of American Indian Religious Freedom, from Conquest to 1934," *Wicazo Sa Review* 21, no. 2 (Autumn 2006): 15.

52. Adams, *Education for Extinction*, p. 192, citing *Red Man*, Carlisle Indian Industrial School, November–December 1892, p. 3.

53. Adams, *Education for Extinction*, pp. 128–29, citing letter from Richard H. Pratt to White Thunder, December 15, 1880, Pratt Papers, Beinecke Rare Book and Manuscript Library, Yale University.

54. Prucha, *American Indian Policy in Crisis*, p. 58; *Address to the Catholic Clergy of the Province of Oregon* (Portland, OR: Catholic Sentinel, 1874), p. 12.

55. Reyhner and Eder, *American Indian Education*, p. 85.

56. Francis Paul Prucha, *The Churches and the Indian Schools, 1888–1912* (Lincoln: Univ. of Nebraska Press, 1979), p. 3, citing letter from J. A. Stephan to Katharine Drexel, June 11, 1885, Archives of the Sisters of the Blessed Sacrament, Bensalem, Pennsylvania.

57. Reyhner and Eder, *American Indian Education*, p. 88.

58. Thomas Jefferson Morgan, *Roman Catholics and Indian Education: An Address* (Boston: American Citizen, 1893).

59. Prucha, *American Indian Policy in Crisis*, p. 312, citing *Report of the Board of Indian Commissioners*, 1893, pp. 112–15.

60. Reyhner and Eder, *American Indian Education*, p. 87, citing *Annual Report of the Commissioner of Indian Affairs for the Year 1892* (Washington, DC: Government Printing Office, 1892), p. 156.

61. Prucha, *Churches and the Indian Schools*, p. 50, citing letter from Ketcham to Gibbons, October 5, 1901, Bureau of Catholic Indian Missions Records, Washington, DC, 1901.

62. Prucha, *American Indian Policy in Crisis*, p. 317, citing *Catholic Herald*, December 3, 1892.

63. Prucha, *American Indian Policy in Crisis*, p. 318.

64. Coleman, *American Indian Children*, p. 122, citing Jason Betzinez and Wilbur Sturtevant Nye, *I Fought with Geronimo* (Lincoln, NE: Bison Books, 1987), p. 153.

65. Coleman, *American Indian Children*, p. 117, citing Thomas Wildcat Alford, *Civilization, and the Story of the Absentee Shawnees, as Told to Florence Drake* (Norman: Univ. of Oklahoma Press, 1936).

66. Adams, *Education for Extinction*, p. 212.

67. US Department of the Interior, Office of Indian Affairs, *Regulations of the Indian Department: With an Appendix Containing the Forms Used* (Washington, DC: Government Printing Office, 1884), p. 89; "Rules for Indian Courts, August 27, 1892," in Francis Paul Prucha, ed., *Documents of United States Indian Policy* (Lincoln: Univ. of Nebraska Press, 1975), p. 185.

68. "Reports of Agents in Dakota," in US Department of the Interior, Office of Indian Affairs, *Annual Report of the Commissioner of Indian Affairs, for the Year 1888* (Washington, DC: Government Printing Office, 1888), p. 65.

69. Federal Indian commissioner Charles H. Burke informed the Indians that "no good comes from your 'give away' custom at dances" and eliminating the practice would "foster a competitive, individualistic economic mentality and a Christian faith." Charles H. Burke, "A Letter to All Indians," US Bureau of Indian Affairs, 1923); Crow Dog and Erdoes, *Lakota Woman*.

70. "Therefore the child must early learn the beauty of generosity. . . . Public giving is a part of every important ceremony. It properly belongs to the celebration of birth, marriage, and death, and is observed whenever it is desired to do special honor to any person or event. Upon such occasions it is common to give to the point of utter impoverishment. The Indian in his simplicity literally gives away all that he has, to relatives, to guests of another tribe or clan, but above all to the poor and the aged, from whom he can hope for no return. Finally, the gift to the 'Great Mystery,' the religious offering, may be of little value in itself, but to the giver's own thought it should carry the meaning and reward of true sacrifice." Eastman, *Soul of the Indian*, p. 40.

71. "Reports of Agents in Dakota," p. 65.

72. Clyde Holler, *Black Elk's Religion: The Sun Dance and Lakota Catholicism* (Syracuse: Syracuse Univ. Press, 1995), p. 122, citing Julia B. McGillycuddy, *McGillycuddy, Agent: A Biography of Dr. Valentine T. McGillycuddy* (Palo Alto: Stanford Univ. Press, 1941), p. 40.

73. Allison M. Dussias, "Ghost Dance and Holy Ghost: The Echoes of Nineteenth-Century Christianization Policy in Twentieth-Century Native American Free Exercise Cases," *Stanford Law Review* 49, no. 4 (April 1997): 793, citing Robert M. Utley, *The Last Days of the Sioux Nation* (New Haven: Yale Univ. Press, 1963), p. 13.

74. Holler, *Black Elk's Religion*, pp. 123–24; *Annual Report of the Commissioner of Indian Affairs for the Year 1884* (Washington, DC: Government Printing Office, 1889), p. 54.

75. J. W. Powell, ed., *Fourteenth Annual Report of the Bureau of American Ethnology to the Secretary of the Smithsonian Institution, 1892–1893* (Washington, DC: Government Printing Office, 1896), p. 784.

76. Rani-Henrik Andersson, *The Lakota Ghost Dance of 1890* (Lincoln: Univ. of Nebraska Press, 2008), p. 28.

77. Andersson, *Lakota Ghost Dance of 1890*, p. 55.

78. Andersson, *Lakota Ghost Dance of 1890*, p. 69.

79. Andersson, *Lakota Ghost Dance of 1890*, p. 57.

80. James Mooney, *The Ghost Dance Religion and Wounded Knee* (New York: Dover, 1973), p. 772.

81. Andersson, *Lakota Ghost Dance of 1890*, p. 53, citing *Illustrated American*, January 17, 1891, p. 332.

82. Andersson, *Lakota Ghost Dance of 1890*, p. 175, citing *Word Carrier*, November 1890, p. 29.

83. Andersson, *Lakota Ghost Dance of 1890*, p. 169, citing Digman Papers, Marquette University Archives, Bureau of Catholic Indian Missions, September 30, 1890.

84. Mooney, *Ghost Dance Religion*, p. 827.

85. Richardson, *Wounded Knee*, p. 172.

86. Richardson, *Wounded Knee*, p. 175, citing *Daily Inter Ocean*, October 19, 1890, p. 30, from *Rapid City Republican*.

87. Richardson, *Wounded Knee*, p. 177, citing letter from Royer to Morgan, November 8, 1890, in "Reports and Correspondence Relating to the Army Investigation of the Battle at Wounded Knee and to the Sioux Campaign of 1890–1891," in *Records of the Adjutant General's Office*, microfilm M-983 (Washington, DC: National Archives and Records Administration).

88. Andersson, *Lakota Ghost Dance of 1890*, p. 110.

89. Richardson, *Wounded Knee*, p. 201, citing letter from Royer to Commissioner of Indian Affairs, November 15, 1890, in "J. M. Schofield to Major Miles," series 1, BH Mss. Schofield to Miles, November 17, 1890, *Records of the Adjutant General's Office*.

90. Andersson, *Lakota Ghost Dance of 1890*, p. 67.

91. Andersson, *Lakota Ghost Dance of 1890*, p. 197, citing *Chicago Tribune*, September 26, 1890, p. 1; *Washington Post*, September 27, 1890, p. 1.

92. *New York Times*, November 22, 1890, pp. 1–2, cited in Andersson, *Lakota Ghost Dance of 1890*, p. 205.

93. Gregory E. Smoak, "The Mormons and the Ghost Dance of 1890," *South Dakota History* 16 (1986): 269–94.

94. Andersson, *Lakota Ghost Dance of 1890*, p. 202.

95. Richardson, *Wounded Knee*, p. 9.

96. Mooney, *Ghost Dance Religion*, p. 869.

97. Mooney, *Ghost Dance Religion*, p. 885.

98. Richardson, *Wounded Knee*, p. 270, citing George A. Stannard, in Richard E. Jensen, ed., *The Settler and Soldier Interviews of Eli S. Ricker, 1903–1919* (Lincoln: Univ. of Nebraska Press, 2005), p. 39.

99. Louis S. Warren, *God's Red Son: The Ghost Dance Religion and the Making of Modern America* (New York: Basic Books, 2017), p. 8.

100. Richardson, *Wounded Knee*, p. 278, citing Elaine Goodale Eastman, *Sister to the Sioux: The Memoirs of Elaine Goodale Eastman, 1885–91*, ed. Kay Graber (Lincoln: Univ. of Nebraska Press, 1978), p. 166.

101. Mooney, *Ghost Dance Religion*, p. 878.

102. Amber L. McDonald, "Secularizing the Sacrosanct: Defining 'Sacred' for Native American Sacred Sites Protection Legislation," *Hofstra Law Review* 33, no. 2, art. 9 (2004): 754.

103. Robert Charles Ward, "The Spirits Will Leave: Preventing the Desecration and Destruction of Native American Sacred Sites on Federal Land," *Ecology Law Quarterly* 19, no. 4 (September 1992): 802.

104. Scholar Robert Charles Ward wrote, "The religion—and culture—of most indigenous Americans cannot be divorced from well-defined relationships with specific lands. Under Native American teleology, peoples are placed on the Earth in precisely the proper places; each tribe must live symbiotically with the other creatures, the plants, the rocks and soil, the air and water, and the spirits or gods that share those places." Ward, "Spirits Will Leave," p. 801; "Smohalla and His Doctrine," in *Fourteenth Annual Report of the Bureau of American Ethnology to the Secretary of the Smithsonian Institution, 1892–1893*, ed. J. W. Powell (Washington, DC: Government Printing Office, 1896), p. 721; "The Ghost-Dance Religion and the Sioux Outbreak of 1890," in *Fourteenth Annual Report of the Bureau of American Ethnology to the Secretary of the Smithsonian Institution, 1892–1893*, H.R. Doc. 230, 54th Cong., 2nd sess., 721 (1892–93) (quoting Shahaptian chief Smohalla, "You ask me to plow the ground! Shall I take a knife and tear my mother's bosom?").

105. Frederick E. Hoxie, *A Final Promise: The Campaign to Assimilate the Indians, 1880–1920* (Lincoln: Univ. of Nebraska Press, 1984), p. 24, citing letter from Powell to Henry Teller, March 34, 1880, Manuscript no. 3751, National Anthropological Archives.

106. Palladino, *Education for the Indian*, p. 17, citing *Congressional Record*, 51st Cong., 1st sess., vol. 21, July 25, 1890.

107. Tisa Wenger, "Indian Dances and the Politics of Religious Freedom, 1870–1930," *Journal of the American Academy of Religion* 79, no. 4 (December 2011): 856–57, citing *Annual Report of the Commissioner of Indian Affairs, for the Year 1889* (Washington, DC: Government Printing Office, 1889), p. 274.

108. Wenger, "Indian Dances," p. 865, citing Wolf Tail to Edgar Bradley, June 9, 1917, BIA Central Classified Files, 1907–1939, Series B: Indian Customs, Blackfeet, Records of the Bureau of Indian Affairs, Record Group 75, National Archives and Records Administration, Washington, DC.

109. Wenger, "Indian Dances," p. 866, citing Chippewa Indians to the Honorable Commissioner of Indian Affairs, August 30, 1916, BIA Central Classified Files, 1907–1939, Series B: Indian Customs, Red Lake, Records of the Bureau of Indian Affairs, Record Group 75, National Archives and Records Administration, Washington, DC.

110. Wenger, "Indian Dances," p. 866.

111. Talbot, "Spiritual Genocide," p. 28, citing Kenneth R. Philip, *John Collier's Crusade for Indian Reform, 1920–1954* (Tucson: Univ. of Arizona Press, 1977), p. 68.

112. "Indian Religious Freedom and Indian Culture," Bureau of Indian Affairs Circular no. 2970, January 3, 1934.

CHAPTER NINE

The KKK, Al Smith, and the Fight for Public Schools

1. Michael Jacobs, "Co-Opting Christian Chorales: Songs of the Ku Klux Klan," *American Music* 28, no. 3 (Fall 2010): 370.

2. Jacobs, "Co-Opting Christian Chorales," p. 370; Danny O. Crew, *Ku Klux Klan Sheet Music* (Jefferson, NC: McFarland, 2003), p. 207.

3. Elizabeth Dorsey Hatle and Nancy M. Vaillancourt, "One Flag, One School, One Language: Minnesota's Ku Klux Klan in the 1920s," *Minnesota History* 61, no. 8 (Winter 2009–10): 364; *Call of the North*, November 14, 1923, p. 5.

4. "Klansman's Manual (1925)," Hanover College History Department, accessed online May 9, 2018.

5. George J. Marlin, *The American Catholic Voter: 200 Years of Political Impact* (South Bend, IN: St. Augustine's Press, 2004), p. 132.

6. Marlin, *American Catholic Voter*, p. 133.

7. Roger Finke and Rodney Stark, *The Churching of America, 1776–1990: Winners and Losers in Our Religious Economy* (New Brunswick: Rutgers Univ. Press, 2000), p. 114.

8. James M. O'Toole, *The Faithful: A History of Catholics in America* (Cambridge: Belknap Press, 2008), p. 101.

9. As a percentage of the Catholic population, their presence more than tripled. Finke and Stark, *Churching of America, 1776–1990*, p. 135.

10. Lloyd P. Jorgenson, *The State and the Non-Public School, 1825–1925* (Columbia: Univ. of Missouri Press, 1987), p. 121.

11. Jorgenson, *State and the Non-Public School*, p. 122.

12. *Wisconsin Journal of Education*, September 9, 1864, pp. 78–79, cited in Jorgenson, *State and the Non-Public School*, p. 59.

13. Given the modern distribution of religiosity, it's surprising that Bible reading in schools in 1850 was the most common in the Northeast and the least common in the South, Midwest, and West. R. Laurence Moore, "Bible Reading and Nonsectarian Schooling: The Failure of Religious Instruction in Nineteenth-Century Public Education," *Journal of American History* 86, no. 4 (March 2000): 1586.

14. Horace Mann explained: "A nonsectarian system earnestly inculcates all Christian morals; it founds its morals on the basis of religion; it welcomes the religion of the Bible; and, in receiving the Bible, it allows it to do what it is allowed to do in no other system, to speak for itself. But here it stops, not because it claims to have compassed all truth, but because it disclaims to act as an umpire between hostile religious opinions." Horace Mann, *Twelfth Annual Report of the Board of Education, Covering the Year 1848* (Boston: Dutton & Wentworth, 1849), pp. 116–17.

15. Horace Mann, "Lecture IV," in *Lectures and Annual Reports* (Boston: M. T. Mann, 1867), pp. 289–90, cited in Steven K. Green, *The Second Disestablishment: Church and State in Nineteenth-Century America* (New York: Oxford Univ. Press, 2010), loc. 3580, Kindle.

16. Ruth Miller Elson, *Guardians of Tradition: American Schoolbooks of the Nineteenth Century* (Lincoln: Univ. of Nebraska Press, 1964), p. 53.

17. Jorgenson, *State and the Non-Public School*, p. 61.

18. Laurence Sterne, *A Sentimental Journey Through France and Italy*, ed. Henry Morley (T. Becket and P. A. De Hondt, 1768), p. 561.

19. Jorgenson, *State and the Non-Public School*, p. 64; William Channing Woodbridge, *Rudiments of Geography on a New Plan* (Hartford: O. D. Cooke, 1828), p. 122.

20. Frederick Butler, *Sketches of Universal History, Sacred and Profane* (Hartford, 1823), p. iv, in Jorgenson, *State and the Non-Public School*, p. 66.

21. Jorgenson, *State and the Non-Public School*, p. 126.

22. Steven K. Green, *The Bible, the School, and the Constitution: The Clash That Shaped Modern Church-State Doctrine* (New York: Oxford Univ. Press, 2012), p. 182.

23. Jorgenson, *State and the Non-Public School*, p. 114.

24. Jorgenson, *State and the Non-Public School*, p. 118; John Tracy Ellis, ed., "Instructions of the Congregation of Propaganda de Fide Concerning Catholic Children Attending American Public Schools," in *Documents of American Catholic History* (Milwaukee: Bruce, 1956), pp. 416–20.

25. Jorgenson, *State and the Non-Public School*, p. 114.

26. Pope Pius IX, The Syllabus of Errors, December 8, 1864.

27. Pope Leo XIII, "*Longinqua*: Encyclical of Pope Leo XIII on Catholicism in the United States," Vatican.va, January 6, 1895.

28. Barry Hudock, *Struggle, Condemnation, Vindication: John Courtney Murray's Journey Toward Vatican II* (Collegeville, MN: Liturgical Press, 1996), p. 4; Pope Pius X,

"*Vehementer Nos*: Encyclical of Pope Pius X on the French Law of Separation," February 11, 1906.

29. John Ireland, *The Church and Modern Society: Lectures and Addresses* (Chicago: D. H. McBride, 1896), p. 64.

30. Zachary R. Calo, "The Indispensable Basis of Democracy: American Catholicism, the Church-State Debate, and the Soul of American Liberalism, 1920–1929," *Virginia Law Review* 91, no. 4 (June 2005): 1049, citing John A. Ryan, "Church, State, and Constitution," *Commonweal*, 1927, pp. 680–81.

31. John A. Ryan, "The Civic Loyalty of Catholics," *National Welfare Conference Bulletin*, November 1924, p. 28, Mullen Library, Catholic University of America, cited in Calo, "Indispensable Basis of Democracy," pp. 1055–56.

32. Michael Dooley, "Editorial Cartoonist Thomas Nast: Anti-Irish, Anti-Catholic Bigot?," Printmag.com, January 4, 2012, accessed May 12, 2018.

33. Deborah Rieselman, "The Cincinnati Bible War," *UC Magazine*, April 2004.

34. "The President's Speech at Des Moines," *Catholic World*, January 1876, pp. 434–35.

35. Green, *Bible, the School, and the Constitution*, p. 193.

36. James P. Boyd, *Life and Public Services of Hon. James G. Blaine* (Philadelphia: Publishers' Union, 1893), p. 353.

37. *Congressional Record*, 44th Cong., 1st sess., August 4, 1876, p. 5562.

38. In the 1884 presidential election, the politics shifted against Blaine. As the Republican nominee, Blaine was tarred by a comment from a Presbyterian minister, Samuel D. Burchard, that the Democratic Party was the home of "rum, Romanism and rebellion." Green, *Bible, the School, and the Constitution*, p. 230.

39. Moore, "Bible Reading and Nonsectarian Schooling," p. 1591.

40. Green, *Bible, the School, and the Constitution*, p. 209, cited in *The Index*, September 7, 1876, p. 426.

41. Michael F. Holt, *By One Vote: The Disputed Presidential Election of 1876* (Lawrence: Univ. Press of Kansas, 2008), pp. 139–41.

42. Thomas C. Hunt, "The Edgerton Bible Decision: The End of an Era," *Catholic Historical Review* 67, no. 4 (October 1981): 595–600.

43. Hunt, "Edgerton Bible Decision," pp. 613–14.

44. A similar dynamic played out in Ohio. The King James Version had long been taught in the Cincinnati public schools, but the demographics had changed: by 1869, the school board included ten Catholics and two Jews in addition to eighteen Protestants and ten "others." A plan to merge the public and Catholic schools forced them to grapple with the Bible question. Catholics would have preferred a system in which their Bible could have been read alongside the King James Version but concluded that if that wasn't possible, then public schools should be secular, leaving religion for the religious schools. The school board voted 22 to 15 (with all of the Catholics voting yes) to prohibit the reading of religious books. Protestants sued, arguing, bizarrely, that by deferring to the Catholic preference for secularism, Cincinnati had established the Catholic religion in the schools. The Ohio Superior Court sided with the Protestants, with Judge Bellamy Storer explaining that "revealed religion, as it is made known in the Holy Scriptures" was alone "recognized by our Constitution." (He did not cite which clause of the US Constitution did that.) But the Ohio supreme court then overturned the lower court ruling, giving the school board permission to exclude the Bible. The court took the Madisonian position that religion lies "outside the true and legitimate province of government." State courts would spend the next forty years trying to decide whether the Bible counted as sectarian. Tracy Fessenden, "The Nineteenth-Century Bible Wars and the Separation of Church and State," *Church History* 74, no. 4 (December 2005): 803; Green, *Bible, the School, and the Constitution*, p. 113.

45. Moore, "Bible Reading and Nonsectarian Schooling," p. 1592, citing John D. Minor, *The Bible in Public Schools* (New York, 1870; reprint, 1967), p. 211.

46. Green, *Bible, the School, and the Constitution*, p. 241.

47. Kevin Seamus Hasson, *The Right to be Wrong: Ending the Culture War over Religion in America* (New York: Image, 2012), 27.

48. Don Byrd, "Oklahoma Legislature Sends Ten Commandments Bill to Governor," Baptist Joint Committee for Religious Freedom, BJC Online, May 7, 2018.

49. Green, *Bible, the School, and the Constitution*, p. 236.

50. Jorgenson, *State and the Non-Public School*, p. 154.

51. Horace Mann, *Seventh Annual Report of the Board of Education* (Boston, 1844), pp. 180–81, cited in Moore, "Bible Reading and Nonsectarian Schooling," p. 1589.

52. T. W. Medhurst, "Is Romanism Christianity?," chap. 6 in *The Fundamentals: A Testimony to the Truth*, vol. 11 (Chicago: Testimony, 1910).

53. In Denver, according to Kenneth Jackson, Klan members claimed "state representatives, state senators, the mayor, city attorney, manager of public safety, police chief, police inspector, two deputy sheriffs, the secretary of state, at least four judges, two federal narcotics agents, and scores of policemen" and a future governor. Kenneth T. Jackson, *The Ku Klux Klan in the City: 1915–1930* (New York: Oxford Univ. Press, 1967), pp. 215–31; Rory McVeigh, "Power Devaluation, the Ku Klux Klan, and the Democratic National Convention of 1924," *Sociological Forum* 16, no. 1 (March 2001): 2.

54. William Rawlings, *The Second Coming of the Invisible Empire* (Macon, GA: Mercer Univ. Press, 2016), loc. 4599, Kindle; Terence McArdle, "The Day 30,000 White Supremacists in KKK Robes Marched in the Nation's Capital," *Washington Post*, August 11, 2017.

55. Linda Przybyszewski, "Review of *Cross Purposes:* Pierce v. Society of Sisters *and the Struggle over Compulsory Public Education* by Paula Abrams," *Journal of Law and Religion* 27, no. 1 (2011–12): 207.

56. Nicole Mandel, "The Quiet Bigotry of Oregon's Compulsory Public Education Act," April 26, 2012, *Young Historians Conference*, paper 6, p. 9; David A. Horowitz, ed., *Inside the Klavern: The Secret History of a Ku Klux Klan of the 1920s* (Carbondale: Southern Illinois Univ. Press, 1999), p. 61.

57. Mandel, "Quiet Bigotry."

58. William Vance Trollinger Jr., "Hearing the Silence: The University of Dayton, the Ku Klux Klan, and Catholic Universities and Colleges in the 1920s," *American Catholic Studies* 124, no. 1 (Spring 2013): 3.

59. Trollinger, "Hearing the Silence," p. 5.

60. Trollinger, "Hearing the Silence," p. 8.

61. Mark Paul Richard, "This Is Not a Catholic Nation: The Ku Klux Klan Confronts Franco-Americans in Maine," *New England Quarterly* 82, no. 2 (June 2009): 290, citing *Official Catholic Directory for the Year of Our Lord, 1921* (New York: P. J. Kenedy and Sons, 1921), p. 527.

62. Richard, "Not a Catholic Nation," p. 291, citing Frederick L. Collins, "Way Down East with the K.K.K.," *Collier's*, December 15, 1923, p. 29.

63. Robert Slayton, *Empire Statesman: The Rise and Redemption of Al Smith* (New York: Free Press, 2001), p. 203; *New York Times*, December 17, 1923.

64. Slayton, *Empire Statesman*, p. 204; *New York Times*, December 17, 1923.

65. "Klan Marchers Routed by Police with Drawn Guns," *Brooklyn Daily Eagle*, May 30, 1927.

66. Philip Bump, "In 1927, Donald Trump's Father Was Arrested After a Klan Riot in Queens," *Washington Post*, February 29, 2016.

67. "Warren Criticizes 'Class' Parades," *New York Times*, June 1, 1927, p. 16.

68. Matt Blum, "1927 News Report: Donald Trump's Dad Arrested in KKK Brawl with Cops," BoingBoing, October 9, 2015, accessed online May 14, 2018; "Two Fascisti Die in Bronx, Klansmen Riot in Queens, in Memorial Day Clashes," *New York Times*, May 31, 1927; "Warren Criticizes 'Class' Parades"; "Warren Ordered Police to Block Parade by Klan," *Brooklyn Daily Eagle*, May 31, 1927, https://bklyn.newspapers.com /image/57551947; Mike Pearl, "All the Evidence We Could Find About Fred Trump's Alleged Involvement with the KKK," Vice.com, March 10, 2016.

69. McVeigh, "Power Devaluation," p. 5.

70. Thomas J. Carty, *A Catholic in the White House?* (New York: Palgrave Macmillan, 2004), p. 28.

71. Slayton, *Empire Statesman*, p. 310.

72. Robert A. Slayton, "When a Catholic Terrified the Heartland," *New York Times*, December 10, 2011.

73. Slayton, *Empire Statesman*, p. 308; Donald Heath, "The Presidential Election of 1928: Protestants' Opposition to Alfred E. Smith as Reflected in Denominational Journals," Ph.D. diss., Vanderbilt University, 1973, p. 7.

74. Slayton, *Empire Statesman*, p. 311; Fellowship Forum, "Book of Horrors," Columbia University Rare Book Room.

75. Slayton, *Empire Statesman*, p. 308.

76. Slayton, "When a Catholic Terrified the Heartland."

77. Joseph Proskauer, *A Segment of My Times* (New York: Farrar, Straus, 1950), pp. 61–62.

78. "Heflin Tells Klan Smith Cannot Win; South Will Keep 'Popery Out of the White House,' He Says at Queens Gathering. Order Solicits Members Campaign Against Bigotry Being Pushed in Southern States by Governor's Supporters," *New York Times*, July 2, 1927.

79. Slayton, "When a Catholic Terrified the Heartland."

80. William B. Prendergast and Mary E. Prendergast, *The Catholic Voter in American Politics: The Passing of the Democratic Monolith* (Washington, DC: Georgetown Univ. Press, 1999), p. 108.

81. Slayton, *Empire Statesman*, p. 306, citing Lou Hoover to Edgar Rickard, October 4, 1928, Box 21, Personal Correspondence Files, Lou Hoover Papers, Hoover Institution.

82. Slayton, *Empire Statesman*, p. 311, citing John Ryan, "A Catholic View of the Election," *Current History* 29, December 1928, p. 379.

83. Slayton, *Empire Statesman*, p. 310.

84. Slayton, *Empire Statesman*, p. 308, citing Heath, "Presidential Election of 1928," p. 7.

85. Philip Hamburger, *Separation of Church and State* (Cambridge: Harvard Univ. Press, 2002), p. 204.

86. M. Edward Hughes, "Florida Preachers and the Election of 1928," *Florida Historical Quarterly* 67, no. 2 (October 1988): 138; *Florida Baptist Witness*, Jacksonville, November 1, 1928.

87. Marlin, *American Catholic Voter*, p. 186, citing David Burner, *The Politics of Provincialism* (Cambridge: Harvard Univ. Press, 1986), p. 202.

88. Slayton, *Empire Statesman*, p. 316.

89. Douglas C. Stange, "Al Smith and the Republican Party at Prayer: The Lutheran Vote, 1928," *Review of Politics* 32, no. 3 (July 1970): 347, citing *Washington Post*, September 23, 1928.

90. James Hennesey, "Roman Catholics and American Politics, 1900–1960: Altered Circumstances, Continuing Patterns," in Mark Noll, ed., *Religion and American Politics: From the Colonial Period to the 1980s* (New York: Oxford Univ. Press, 1990), cited in Calo, "Indispensable Basis of Democracy," p. 1049.

91. Charles C. Marshall, "An Open Letter to the Honorable Alfred E. Smith," *Atlantic*, April 1927.

92. Slayton, *Empire Statesman*, p. 303.

93. Alfred E. Smith, "Catholic and Patriot," *Atlantic*, May 1927.

94. Politicians at the time believed that Smith's religion played a major role in his defeat. In a survey of Democratic leaders, 55.5 percent pointed to his religion, while 33 percent listed prohibition and 2.4 percent listed economic prosperity as the dominant reasons for his loss. More recently, political scientist Allan Lichtman did a regression analysis comparing Smith's performance with that of previous and subsequent Democrats and concluded that his religion was a decisive factor: "Protestant opposition to Smith's religion was remarkably widespread, extending to all regions of the country, to city and country, to church members of unaffiliated Protestants." Allan J. Lichtman, *Prejudice and the Old Politics: The Presidential Election of 1928* (Chapel Hill: Univ. of North Carolina Press, 1979), p. 76.

95. Slayton, *Empire Statesman*, p. 325, citing Samuel Lubell, *The Future of American Politics* (Garden City: Doubleday, 1951), pp. 36–37.

96. Slayton, *Empire Statesman*, p. 325.

97. Marlin, *American Catholic Voter*, p. 187.

98. Carty, *Catholic in the White House?*, p. 38.

99. O'Toole, *Faithful*, p. 166.

CHAPTER TEN

The Witnesses

1. Shawn Francis Peters, *Judging Jehovah's Witnesses* (Lawrence: Univ. Press of Kansas, 2000), p. 86, citing *St. Louis Post-Dispatch*, June 17, 1940; *Chicago Tribune*, June 17, 1940; "Statement of Bob Fischer, 14 September, 1940," in American Civil Liberties Union, *The Persecution of Jehovah's Witnesses* (New York: American Civil Liberties Union, 1941), pp. 15–16. One participant complained, "Why, they wouldn't even salute the flag! We almost beat one guy to death to make him kiss the flag."

2. Paul Finkelman, ed., *Religion and American Law: An Encyclopedia* (New York: Garland, 2000), p. 245.

3. John E. Mulder and Marvin Comisky, "Jehovah's Witnesses and Constitutional Law," *Bill of Rights Review*, 1941–1942, p. 261.

4. Edward F. Waite, "The Debt of Constitutional Law to Jehovah's Witnesses," *Minnesota Law Review* 28, no. 4 (March 1944): 246.

5. Finkelman, *Religion and American Law*, p. 245.

6. Charles Taze Russell, *The Finished Mystery* (New York: International Bible Students Association, 1918), p. 247.

7. David A. Manwaring, *Render Unto Caesar: The Flag Salute Controversy* (Chicago: Univ. of Chicago Press, 1962), pp. 18–19, 24.

8. Linda Lou Steveson, "Bible Students and World War I: Conflict Between an Indigenous American Apocalyptic Movement and Governmental Authorities," master's thesis, University of Montana, 1973, *Graduate Student Theses, Dissertations, & Professional Papers*, 5240, p. 70, citing US Congress, Senate, Letter and Memorandum for Insertion, April 24, 1918, *Congressional Record* 56, 5542, May 4, 1918, 6051–52.

9. William Shepard McAninch, "A Catalyst for the Evolution of Constitutional Law: Jehovah's Witnesses in the Supreme Court," *University of Cincinnati Law Review* 55 (1986–87): 1010; *Congressional Record* 56, 6052.

10. Steveson, "Bible Students and World War I," p. 70; *New York Times*, May 9, 1918, p. 22.

11. "20 Years in Prison for Seven Russellites: Judge Howe Scores Men Who Give Aid to the Enemy Under the Guise of Religion," *New York Times*, June 22, 1918, p. 18, cited in David T. Smith, *Religious Persecution and Political Order in the United States* (New York: Cambridge Univ. Press, 2015), pp. 95–96.

12. J. F. Rutherford, *Enemies* (New York: Watchtower Bible and Tract Society, 1937), p. 328, cited in Manwaring, *Render Unto Caesar*, p. 25.

13. "Jehovah's Witnesses," pamphlet published by the United States Holocaust Memorial Museum.

14. The United States Holocaust Memorial Museum estimates that about 10,000 Jehovah's Witnesses were sentenced to prison or camps at one point or another, with about 2,500 ending up in concentration camps and the remainder serving terms between a month and four years. The death toll is estimated at around 1,650, counting German and non-German Witnesses who died in the camps and the 250 shot by military tribunals for draft-dodging. Holocaust Encyclopedia, United States Holocaust Memorial Museum.

15. "Jehovah's Witnesses Stand Firm Against NAZI Assault," Watchtower Bible and Tract Society of New York, 1996.

16. Joel P. Engardio, "'Jehovah's Witnesses' Untold Story of Resistance to Nazis," *Christian Science Monitor*, November 6, 1996.

17. J. F. Rutherford, *Salvation* (New York: Watchtower Bible and Tract Society, 1939), p. 260.

18. J. F. Rutherford, *Children: Their Training and Their Hope* (New York: Watchtower Bible and Tract Society, 1941), p. 214.

19. Joseph F. Rutherford, "Saluting a Flag," *Loyalty* 16 (1935).

20. Manwaring, *Render Unto Caesar*, pp. 2–3.

21. Peters, *Judging Jehovah's Witnesses*, p. 27.

22. Kevin Seamus Hasson, *Believers, Thinkers, and Founders: How We Came to Be One Nation Under God* (New York: Image, 2016), loc. 244, Kindle, citing Billy Gobitas, "Letter to the Schoolboard," November 5, 1935, in Claudia Isner, ed., *The Right to Free Speech* (New York: Rosen, 2001), p. 75.

23. Peters, *Judging Jehovah's Witnesses*, p. 42.

24. Manwaring, *Render Unto Caesar*, p. 98 citing Joint and Several Answers, *Gobitis v. Minersville School District*, 24 F. Supp. 271 (E.D. Pa. 1938), Record, pp. 92–93.

25. You might have noticed that the family name was spelled Gobitas, while the court case was spelled *Gobitis*. A court clerk made a spelling error that apparently could not be corrected once the decision had been published.

26. Peters, *Judging Jehovah's Witnesses*, p. 91, citing the statement of C. A. Cecil, July 8, 1940, *American Civil Liberties Union Papers*, vol. 2249; *Catlette v. United States*, 132 F.2d 902, 903–7 (4th Cir. 1943).

27. Peters, *Judging Jehovah's Witnesses*, p. 95, citing the statement of Albert Walkenhorst, August 28, 1940, *American Civil Liberties Union Papers*, vol. 2237.

28. Manwaring, *Render Unto Caesar*, pp. 165–66.

29. Manwaring, *Render Unto Caesar*, p. 166.

30. American Civil Liberties Union, *Persecution of Jehovah's Witnesses*, p. 6.

31. Manwaring, *Render Unto Caesar*, p. 167.

32. Smith, *Religious Persecution*, p. 89.

33. Smith, *Religious Persecution*, p. 109; *Chicago Daily Tribune*, September 11, 1940.

34. Smith, *Religious Persecution*, p. 119.

35. Manwaring, *Render Unto Caesar*, p. 174.

36. Peters, *Judging Jehovah's Witnesses*, p. 165.

37. Manwaring, *Render Unto Caesar*, p. 78.

38. Peters, *Judging Jehovah's Witnesses*, p. 167, citing *State ex rel. Bleich v. Board of Public Instruction for Hillsborough County*, 190 So. 815 (Fla. 1939).

39. Manwaring, *Render Unto Caesar*, pp. 18–20.

40. Manwaring, *Render Unto Caesar*, p. 27.

41. Finkelman, *Religion and American Law*, p. 245.

42. Manwaring, *Render Unto Caesar*, p. 177.

43. Peters, *Judging Jehovah's Witnesses*, p. 127.

44. *Cantwell v. Connecticut*, 310 US 296 (1940).

45. Manwaring, *Render Unto Caesar*, p. 6; Bessie Louise Pierce, *Citizens' Organizations and the Civic Training of Youth* (New York: Charles Scribner's Sons, 1933), p. 33.

46. Manwaring, *Render Unto Caesar*, p. 210.

47. Manwaring, *Render Unto Caesar*, pp. 223–24.

48. They, plus Harlan Stone (who had offered a well-regarded dissent the first time around), plus two new justices, made a majority.

49. *West Virginia State Board of Education v. Barnette*, 319 US 624 (1943).

50. *Cox v. New Hampshire*, 312 US 569 (1941).

51. Manwaring, *Render Unto Caesar*, p. 30.

CHAPTER ELEVEN

World War II and the Judeo-Christians

1. Edward S. Shapiro, *A Time for Healing: American Jewry Since World War II* (Baltimore: Johns Hopkins Univ. Press, 1992), p. 7.

2. The best account of the *Dorchester* comes from Dan Kurzman, *No Greater Glory: The Four Immortal Chaplains and the Sinking of the Dorchester in World War II* (New York: Random House, 2004). He based his book on personal interviews he conducted, video interviews collected by the Immortal Chaplains Foundation, and affidavits provided to the army by eyewitnesses.

3. Kevin M. Schultz, *Tri-Faith America: How Catholics and Jews Held Postwar America to Its Protestant Promise* (New York: Oxford Univ. Press, 2011), p. 3.

4. "White House Ceremony Marks Issuance of Interfaith Postage Stamp Honoring Chaplains," Jewish Telegraphic Agency, May 30, 1948.

5. Letter from George Washington to the Hebrew Congregation of Newport, August 18, 1790.

6. Jonathan D. Sarna, "When Shuls Were Banned in America," *Forward*, August 11, 2010.

7. Naomi W. Cohen, *Jews in Christian America* (New York: Oxford Univ. Press, 1992), p. 57.

8. Leonard Dinnerstein, *Anti-Semitism in America* (New York: Oxford Univ. Press, 1994), p. 18.

9. Anson Phelps Stokes, *Church and State in the United States*, vol. 1 (New York: Harper & Brothers, 1950), p. 444.

10. Dinnerstein, *Anti-Semitism in America*, p. 7.

11. Stokes, *Church and State*, p. 858.

12. Sarna, "When Shuls Were Banned."

13. Kevin Seamus Hasson, *The Right to be Wrong: Ending the Culture War over Religion in America* (New York: Image, 2012), p. 110.

14. "Vital Statistics: Jewish Population in the United States, Nationally," Jewish Virtual Library, accessed online February 23, 2018.

15. Robert Stockman, "U.S. Bahá'í Community Membership: 1894–1996," in *American Bahá'í*, November 23, 1996, p. 27.

16. Paul Johnson, *A History of the Jews* (New York: HarperPerennial, 1998), p. 366.

17. Joellyn Zollman, "Jewish Immigration to America: Three Waves," My Jewish Learning, accessed online March 6, 2018.

18. Dinnerstein, *Anti-Semitism in America*, p. 53; Alter F. Landesman, *Brownsville* (New York: Bloch, 1969), pp. 58–59.

19. Dinnerstein, *Anti-Semitism in America*, p. 71.

20. Dinnerstein, *Anti-Semitism in America*, p. 101.

21. *Emergency Immigration Legislation: Hearings Before the Committee on Immigration, United States Senate*, 66th Cong., 3rd sess., on H.R. 14461 (Washington, DC: Government Printing Office, 1921), p. 93.

22. *Emergency Immigration Legislation*, p. 12.

23. Dinnerstein, *Anti-Semitism in America*, p. 65, citing E. A. Ross, "The Hebrews of Eastern Europe in America," *The Century Magazine*, December 1914, pp. 788–91.

24. "Immigration to the United States, 1933–41," Holocaust Encyclopedia, United States Holocaust Memorial Museum, accessed online August 4, 2018.

25. "Immigration to the United States, 1933–41."

26. Shapiro, *A Time for Healing*, p. 3.

27. Rebecca Erbelding and Gertjan Broek, "German Bombs and US Bureaucrats: How Escape Lines from Europe Were Cut Off," the United States Holocaust Memorial Museum and the Anne Frank House in Amsterdam, July 6, 2018.

28. Erbelding and Broek, "German Bombs and US Bureaucrats."

29. Schultz, *Tri-Faith America*, p. 24, citing Claris Edwin Silcox and Galen M. Fisher, *Catholics, Jews, and Protestants: A Study of Relationships in the United States and Canada* (Westport, CT: Greenwood Press, 1934; reprint, 1979), p. 71.

30. Peter Jacobs, "Harvard Is Being Accused of Treating Asians the Same Way It Used to Treat Jews," *Business Insider*, December 4, 2014.

31. Dinnerstein, *Anti-Semitism in America*, p. 110; "Jews, Christians, and Democracy," *Christian Century* 53, May 13, 1936, p. 697.

32. Dinnerstein, *Anti-Semitism in America*, p. 81.

33. Dinnerstein, *Anti-Semitism in America*, p. 99.

34. Roper Fortune Survey, July 1939; Susan Welch, "American Opinion Toward Jews During the Nazi Era: Results from Quota Sample Polling During the 1930s and 1940s," Pennsylvania State University, p. 23; Peter A. Shulman, "How America's Response to Syrian and Jewish Refugees Is Eerily Similar," *Fortune*, November 21, 2015.

35. Dinnerstein, *Anti-Semitism in America*, p. 110, citing "Tolerance Is Not Enough!," *Christian Century* 53, July 1, 1936, p. 928.

36. "Anti-Semitism," FatherCoughlin.org., accessed February 26, 2018.

37. Dinnerstein, *Anti-Semitism in America*, p. 115.

38. Schultz, *Tri-Faith America*, p. 36.

39. Schultz, *Tri-Faith America*, pp. 40–41.

40. "Annual Message to the Congress, January 4, 1939," in Franklin D. Roosevelt, *The Public Papers and Addresses of Franklin D. Roosevelt* (Ann Arbor: Univ. of Michigan Library, 2005), pp. 1–2.

41. Robert Morgenthau told Leo Crowley that Roosevelt had said this to him. Michael R. Beschloss, *The Conquerors: Roosevelt, Truman, and the Destruction of Hitler's Germany, 1941–1945* (New York: Simon & Schuster, 2003).

42. Schultz, *Tri-Faith America*, p. 47, citing Chilton Bennett to Andrew Gottschall, reprinted in "Manual for Army Camp and Naval Station Program," January 1, 1943, Annual Reports, 1940–1949 folder, box 1, NCCJ Papers, 3.

43. Schultz, *Tri-Faith America*, p. 49.

44. Schultz, *Tri-Faith America*, p. 45.

45. Schultz, *Tri-Faith America*, p. 40.

46. Albert Maltz, *The House I Live In*, directed by Mervyn LeRoy (1945).

47. Schultz, *Tri-Faith America*, p. 67, citing "Three Pals," 1945, World War II Publications folder, box 11, NCCJ Papers.

48. Andrew Preston, *Sword of the Spirit, Shield of Faith* (New York: Anchor Books, 2012), p. 335, citing "Wallace Addresses 500 Presenting Petition for Help," *Washington Post*, October 7, 1943, p. 1.

49. Shapiro, *A Time for Healing*, p. 16.

50. Schultz, *Tri-Faith America*, p. 58, citing "Heir to Millions," Why We Fight Series, Pamphlet no. 3, World War II Publications folder, box 11, NCCJ Papers.

51. Kurzman, *No Greater Glory*.

52. Shapiro, *A Time for Healing*, pp. 17–18.

53. "Address at the Cornerstone Laying of the New York Avenue Presbyterian Church," April 3, 1951, *Public Papers of the Presidents of the United States: Truman, 1951*.

54. He intoned a thoroughly generic and nondenominational prayer: "By Thy bounty we have become rich and mighty among the nations of the world. O Lord, make us worthy of all Thy blessings, to the end that both leader and people may continue to find favor in Thine eyes, and so live and serve that Thy glory, Thy majesty and Thy power may abide with us forever."

55. Preston, *Sword of the Spirit*, pp. 418–19, citing Robert H. Ferrell, ed., *Off the Record: The Private Papers of Harry S. Truman* (Columbia: Univ. of Missouri Press, 1997), p. 247.

56. Harry S. Truman, *Mr. Citizen* (Independence: Independence Press, 1960), p. 119.

57. Schultz, *Tri-Faith America*, pp. 70–71.

58. Schultz, *Tri-Faith America*, p. 84.

59. Jonathan P. Herzog, *The Spiritual-Industrial Complex: America's Religious Battle Against Communism in the Early Cold War* (New York: Oxford Univ. Press, 2011), p. 82.

60. Shapiro, *A Time for Healing*, p. 10.

61. Shapiro, *A Time for Healing*, p. 16.

62. Gregg Ivers, *To Build a Wall: American Jews and the Separation of Church and State* (Charlottesville: Univ. of Virginia Press, 1995), p. 61.

63. Ivers, *To Build a Wall*, p. 32.

64. Shapiro, *A Time for Healing*, p. 2.

65. Harry S. Truman, *Memoirs*, vol. 1, *Year of Decisions* (New York: Doubleday, 1955), p. 69.

66. Dwight D. Eisenhower, Inaugural Address, January 20, 1953.

67. James David Fairbanks, "Religious Dimensions of Presidential Leadership: The Case of Dwight Eisenhower," *Presidential Studies Quarterly* 12, no. 2 (Spring 1982): 261.

68. Dwight D. Eisenhower, *Mandate for Change* (Garden City: Doubleday, 1963), p. 100.

69. T. Jeremy Gunn and Mounia Slighoua, "The Spiritual Factor: Eisenhower, Religion, and Foreign Policy," *Review of Faith and International Affairs* 9, no. 4 (2011): 41.

70. Dwight D. Eisenhower, "Statement by the President Upon Signing Bill to Include the Words 'Under God' in the Pledge to the Flag," June 14, 1954, The American Presidency Project, University of California at Santa Barbara.

71. Patrick Henry, "'And I Don't Care What It Is': The Tradition-History of a Civil Religion Proof-Text," *Journal of the American Academy of Religion* 49, no. 1 (March 1981): 35–49.

72. William Lee Miller, *Piety Along the Potomac* (Boston: Houghton Mifflin, 1964), p. 34. Adapted from *The Reporter* magazine, July 7, 1953.

73. Mark Silk, "Notes on the Judeo-Christian Tradition in America," *American Quarterly* 36, no. 1 (Spring 1984): 69.

74. Letter from General Dwight Eisenhower to General George C. Marshall, April 15, 1945.

75. Gerald Bergman, "The Influence of Religion on President Eisenhower's Upbringing," *Journal of American and Comparative Cultures*, March 22, 2004, p. 95.

76. Shapiro, *A Time for Healing*, p. 44.

77. Shapiro, *A Time for Healing*, p. 45; Seymour Martin Lipset, "Blacks and Jews: How Much Bias?," *Public Opinion* 10, no. 5 (July–August 1987): 57–58.

78. "Washington's Letter to the Hebrew Congregation of Newport."

CHAPTER TWELVE
Enter the Supreme Court

1. Stephen D. Solomon, *Ellery's Protest: How One Young Man Defied Tradition and Sparked the Battle over School Prayer* (Ann Arbor: Univ. of Michigan Press, 2007), p. 28.

2. Linda K. Wertheimer, "50 Years After *Abington v. Schempp*, a Dissenter Looks Back on School Prayer," *Atlantic*, June 17, 2013.

3. From the *Washington Evening Star*, June 18, 1963, "The Court Bars the Lord's Prayer," in Terry Eastland, ed., *Religious Liberty in the Supreme Court: The Cases That Define the Debate over Church and State* (Grand Rapids: William B. Eerdmans, 1995), p. 167.

4. David Barton, *America: To Pray? Or Not to Pray?* (Aledo, TX: WallBuilder Press, 1994), back cover.

5. John Witte Jr., *Religion and the American Constitutional Experiment*, 4th ed. (Boulder: Westview Press, 2005), p. 108.

6. Witte, *American Constitutional Experiment*, p. 108.

7. Some conservatives argued that it's logically impossible to incorporate the Establishment Clause. Since the Establishment Clause was a prohibition on a federal government behavior, it couldn't be applied to the states in the same way that a right is. The view that has prevailed, though, embraced the idea at a higher level of abstraction. The First Amendment prohibited one government from establishing religion, so the Fourteenth Amendment should apply that same spirit to state governments, since the general point of the Fourteenth Amendment was protecting citizens from the tyranny of local government.

8. William D. Graves, "Separation of Church and State: Historical Fact or Myth?," *Christian Faith in America*, accessed online June 12, 2018.

9. Letter from James Madison to Edward Livingston, July 10, 1822.

10. In his influential work *Separation of Church and State*, scholar Philip Hamburger explains how the opinion in *Everson*, which enshrined the principle of separation, was written by Hugo Black, a former Klansman with proven animus toward Catholics. Black did owe his political success to the Klan. And one of his most famous cases as a trial lawyer was defending a Protestant minister who murdered a Catholic priest for marrying his daughter to a Catholic Puerto Rican man. The case that *Everson* was *primarily* driven by anti-Catholicism is weak, though, as every justice, not just Black, endorsed the idea that the First Amendment backed separation. Philip Hamburger, *Separation of Church and State* (Cambridge: Harvard Univ. Press, 2002), pp. 422–34.

11. *Everson v. Board of Education*, 330 US 1 (1947).

12. *Engel v. Vitale*, 370 US 421 (1962).

13. This is where culture becomes as important as the rules. In 1952, the plaintiffs challenging a common program in schools called "released time"—in which students can voluntarily take time off to attend religious classes—claimed that the stigma was severe. One teacher told a Jewish student who had become ill "that she did not object

to looking at the vomit as much as she objected to looking at the student's face because he did not participate in the released time program." Another student said that her classmates called her "Christ killer" and "Dirty Jew." James E. Wood, ed., *Religion and the State: Essays in Honor of Leo Pfeffer* (Waco, TX: Baylor Univ. Press, 1985), p. 500.

14. Solomon, *Ellery's Protest*, p. 320, citing Leo Pfeffer, *God, Caesar, and the Constitution: The Court as Referee of Church-State Confrontation* (Boston: Beacon Press, 1975), pp. 209–10.

15. Gregg Ivers, *To Build a Wall: American Jews and the Separation of Church and State* (Charlottesville: Univ. of Virginia Press, 1995).

16. Peter Y. Medding, *The Transformation of American Jewish Politics* (New York: American Jewish Committee, 1989), p. 2.

17. Kevin M. Schultz, *Tri-Faith America: How Catholics and Jews Held Postwar America to Its Protestant Promise* (New York: Oxford Univ. Press, 2011), p. 84.

18. To help define that last phrase, Burger suggested that lawmakers consider "the character and purposes of the institutions that are benefited, the nature of the aid that the State provides, and the resulting relationship between the government and the religious authority." *Lemon v. Kurtzman*, 403 US 602 (1971).

19. Norman Dorsen and Thomas Viles, "The Lynch and Alleghany Religious Symbols Cases and the Decline of the Lemon Test," in Paul Finkelman, ed., *Religion and American Law: An Encyclopedia* (New York: Garland, 2000), p. 283.

20. Dorsen and Viles, "Lynch and Alleghany Religious Symbols," p. 289.

21. Solomon, *Ellery's Protest*, p. 276; argument of Philip H. Ward III, Supreme Court of the United States, February 28, 1963, *School District of Abington v. Schempp*, in Philip B. Kurland and Gerhard Casper, *Landmark Briefs and Arguments of the Supreme Court of the United States*, vol. 57 (Washington, DC: University Publications of America, 1975), p. 1019.

22. *McCreary County v. ACLU of Kentucky*, 545 US 844 (2005), discussed in Martha C. Nussbaum, *Liberty of Conscience: In Defense of America's Tradition of Religious Equality* (New York: Basic Books, 2008), p. 260.

23. After the *Schempp* ruling, the Lutheran Church thought so. It came out against the reading of the Lord's Prayer, declaring, "The more we attempt as Christians or Americans to insist on common denominator religious exercise or instruction in the public schools, the greater risk we run of diluting our faith and contributing to a vague religiosity which identifies religion with patriotism and becomes a national folk religion." As Kevin Hasson, founder of the Becket Fund for Religious Liberty, put it, "Stealing Easter and leaving behind 'Special Bunny Day' isn't just tasteless, it's dishonest. It lies about who we really are." Solomon, *Ellery's Protest*, p. 322, citing *Proposed Amendments to the Constitution Relating to Prayers and Bible Reading in the Public Schools: Hearings Before the House Committee on the Judiciary*, 88th Cong., 2nd sess., 1964, p. 443, Statement of the Executive Council of the Lutheran Church in America.

24. Nussbaum, *Liberty of Conscience*, p. 229.

25. *Zelman v. Simmons-Harris*, 536 US 639 (2002).

26. *Illinois ex rel. McCollum v. Board of Education of School District No. 71, Champaign County*, 333 US 203 (1948).

27. *Zorach v. Clauson*, 343 US 306 (1952).

28. Dahlia Lithwick, "Bible Belt Upside the Head: Why the Constitution Tries So Hard to Protect the Buddhist Kid," *Slate*, February 16, 2005.

29. Witte, *American Constitutional Experiment*, p. 219.

30. Letter from James Monroe to Thomas Rutter, November 13, 1816, The Gilder Lehrman Collection.

31. Nussbaum, *Liberty of Conscience*, p. 124.

32. J. Wilfrid Parson, "Rev. Anthony Kohlmann, S. J. (1771–1824)," *Catholic Historical Review* 4, no. 1 (April 1918): 10.

33. Michael McConnell, "The Origins and Historical Understanding of Free Exercise of Religion," *Harvard Law Review* 103 (1990): 1504.

34. *Sherbert v. Verner*, 374 US 398 (1963).

35. Roger Williams, *The Bloody Tenent Yet More Bloody* (London: Printed for Giles Calvert, 1652), p. 28.

36. "Christian Scientist Loses Supreme Court Case," *Washington Post*, June 24, 1989.

37. *United States v. Lee*, 455 US 252 (1982),

38. *Church of Lukumi Babalu Aye, Inc. v. City of Hialeah*, 508 US 520 (1993).

39. Carolyn N. Long, *Religious Freedom and Indian Rights: The Case of Oregon v. Smith* (Lawrence: Univ. Press of Kansas, 2000).

40. *The Religious Freedom Restoration Act: Hearing Before the Committee on the Judiciary, United States Senate, 102nd Congress, 2nd Session, on S. 2969: A Bill to Protect the Free Exercise of Religion, September 18, 1992* (Washington, DC: Government Printing Office, 1993), p. 5.

41. Orrin G. Hatch, "Religious Freedom at Home and Abroad: Reflections on Protecting This Fundamental Freedom," *Brigham Young University Law Review* 413 (2001).

42. Rob Osberg, "School Prayer and American Politics," in Finkelman, *Religion and American Law*, p. 450.

CHAPTER THIRTEEN

"Alien Blood"

1. "Hindu Prayer in Congress Criticized," Associated Press, September 21, 2000; B. A. Robinson, "Hindu Invocation in Congress," ReligiousTolerance.org, November 4, 2005, accessed January 27, 2018.

2. "Study Finds Orthodox Have Most Synagogues in U.S.," *J Weekly*, August 16, 2002, accessed online August 4, 2018.

3. "Rivers of Faith," The Pluralism Project, Harvard University, accessed online February 2, 2018.

4. "The Religious Affiliation of U.S. Immigrants: Majority Christian, Rising Share of Other Faiths," Pew Research Center, May 17, 2013.

5. "Rivers of Faith."

6. "Address to the Members of the Volunteer Association of Ireland, December 2, 1783," in John C. Fitzpatrick, ed., *The Writings of George Washington* (Washington, DC: Government Printing Office, 1931).

7. Roger Daniels, *Guarding the Golden Door: American Immigration Policy and Immigrants Since 1882* (New York: Farrar, Straus and Giroux, 2005), p. 18, Kindle, citing US Congress, Senate, *Report of the Joint Special Committee to Investigate Chinese Immigration*, Report 68 (Washington, DC: Government Printing Office, 1877), pp. iii–viii.

8. Sherally Munshi, "Immigration, Imperialism, and the Legacies of Indian Exclusion," *Yale Journal of Law & the Humanities* 28, no. 1, art. 2 (2015): 62.

9. William Paul Dillingham et al., "Immigrants in Industries," *United States Immigration Commission (1907–1910)* (Washington, DC: Government Printing Office, 1911), p. 26.

10. Munshi, "Immigration, Imperialism," p. 64.

11. One senator explained why they made up cryptic new terminology: "Instead of describing the excluded persons as 'Hindus,' the committee took the same people within geographic lines and excluded them." Munshi, "Immigration, Imperialism," p. 78, citing the statement of Rep. John Raker, *Congressional Record* 54, H1492–93, January 16, 1917.

12. Margaret Sands Orchowski, *The Law That Changed the Face of America* (Lanham, MD: Rowman & Littlefield, 2015), p. 25.

13. Orchowski, *Law That Changed the Face of America*, p. 27.

14. Calvin Coolidge, "Whose Country Is This?," *Good Housekeeping* 72, no. 2 (February 1921).

15. Martin E. Marty, *Modern American Religion*, vol. 2, *The Noise of Conflict, 1919–1941* (Chicago: Univ. of Chicago Press, 1997), p. 60.

16. *Whom We Shall Welcome: Report of the President's Commission on Immigration and Naturalization* (Washington, DC: Government Printing Office, 1953), p. 12.

17. Daniels, *Guarding the Golden Door*, p. 55.

18. Jane H. Hong, "The Repeal of Asian Exclusion," Oxford Research Encyclopedias, September 2015, accessed online January 27, 2018.

19. Daniels, *Guarding the Golden Door*, pp. 92–94.

20. It allowed private charitable organizations to help process immigrants, and, tellingly, most of them ended up being religious groups, including the National Catholic Welfare Council, the Church World Service, the National Lutheran Council, and the United Service for New Americans, a Jewish group. Daniels, *Guarding the Golden Door*, pp. 106–7.

21. Daniels, *Guarding the Golden Door*, pp. 115–16.

22. Orchowski, *Law That Changed the Face of America*, p. 42.

23. Orchowski, *Law That Changed the Face of America*, p. 47, citing *Congressional Quarterly Almanac* (CQ Press, 1965), p. 467.

24. Tom Gjelten, *A Nation of Nations* (New York: Simon & Schuster, 2015), p. 97.

25. To improve chances in the Senate, he tried to more directly connect it to the JFK legacy by tapping the new senator from Massachusetts, thirty-three-year-old Ted Kennedy, to lead the charge in the Senate. Lenny Ben-David, "LBJ, a 'Righteous Gentile'?," *Jerusalem Post*, September 9, 2008.

26. Orchowski, *Law That Changed the Face of America*, p. 67.

27. David S. FitzGerald and David Cook-Martin, "The Geopolitical Origins of the U.S. Immigration Act of 1965," *Migration Immigration Source*, February 5, 2015, accessed online January 27, 2018.

28. Kevin MacDonald, "Jewish Involvement in Shaping American Immigration Policy, 1881–1965: A Historical Review," *Population and Environment* 19, no. 4 (March 1998): 343.

29. Maria Mazzenga, "The Church of and for Immigrants," Catholics in Alliance for the Common Good, July 16, 2014, accessed online January 27, 2018.

30. MacDonald, "Jewish Involvement," p. 343.

31. Gjelten, *A Nation of Nations*, p. 126.

32. *Congressional Record*, August 25, 1965, p. 21812.

33. United States Department of Homeland Security, *Yearbook of Immigration Statistics: 2015* (Washington, DC: US Department of Homeland Security, Office of Immigration Statistics, 2016), p. 10.

34. This created an immigration chain effect. If one person becomes a citizen, he or she can bring in other families according to a ranking system of importance: (1) unmarried adult children of citizens; (2) spouses and unmarried children of permanent resident aliens; (3) married children of US citizens; and (4) brothers and sisters of US citizens over the age of twenty-one. One new citizen could bring in many relatives.

35. "History of Korean Immigration to America, from 1903 to Present," Boston University School of Theology, Boston Korean Diaspora Project, accessed online September 29, 2018; "Pity the Children," *Economist*, May 23, 2015.

36. Daniels, *Guarding the Golden Door*, p. 216.

37. United States Department of Homeland Security, *Immigration Statistics: 2015*, pp. 8–10.

38. United States Department of Homeland Security, *Immigration Statistics: 2015*, p. 32.

39. Jie Zong and Jeanne Batalova, "Indian Immigrants in the United States," Migration Policy Institute, August 31, 2017, accessed online January 27, 2018.

40. Erika Lee, "Legacies of the 1965 Immigration Act," South Asian American Digital Archive, October 1, 2015, accessed online January 28, 2018.

41. Neil G. Ruiz, "The Geography of Foreign Students in U.S. Higher Education: Origins and Destinations," Global Cities Initiative: A Joint Project of Brookings and JPMorgan Chase, August 2014, p. 17.

42. Ruiz, "Geography of Foreign Students," p. 10.

43. Julia Belluz and Sarah Frostenson, "How Trump's Travel Ban Threatens Health Care, in 3 Charts," Vox.com, June 26, 2018.

44. "Religious Affiliation of U.S. Immigrants."

45. Daniels, *Guarding the Golden Door*, pp. 148–49.

46. Steve Waldman, "The Most Spiritually Important Entertainer of Our Time," Beliefnet.

47. John C. Freed, "Dalai Lama Gets Top Rating in Survey on World Leaders," *New York Times*, November 27, 2008.

48. Jessica Ravitz, "Why Americans Love the Dalai Lama," CNN.com, February 22, 2010.

CHAPTER FOURTEEN

Political Bedfellows

1. Thomas J. Carty, *A Catholic in the White House?* (New York: Palgrave Macmillan, 2004), p. 93.

2. David A. Bositis, "Blacks and the 2012 Democratic National Convention," Joint Center for Political and Economic Studies, Washington, DC, 2012, p. 9.

3. Kennedy added another note in the exchange: "Well, we all have our fathers, don't we?" This was a reference to Joseph Kennedy, not known for his tolerance. Harris Wofford, interview with author, 2017.

4. Will Herberg, *"American Freedom and Catholic Power*, by Paul Blanshard," *Commentary*, August 1949.

5. Carty, *Catholic in the White House?*, p. 43.

6. John F. Kennedy's speech before the Greater Houston Ministerial Association, September 12, 1960.

7. "The Religion Issue (cont'd)," *TIME*, May 2, 1960, p. 13.

8. Paul Murray, "54 Miles to Freedom: Catholics Were Prominent in the 1965 Selma March," *National Catholic Reporter*, March 7, 2015.

9. Barry Hudock, *Struggle, Condemnation, Vindication: John Courtney Murray's Journey Toward Vatican II* (Collegeville, MN: Liturgical Press, 1996), p. 64, citing John Courtney Murray, "Leo XIII: Separation of Church and State," pp. 185–86, Woodstock Theological Library at Georgetown University.

10. Hudock, *Struggle, Condemnation, Vindication*, p. 16, citing Francis J. Connell, "Catholics and 'Interfaith' Groups," *American Ecclesiastical Review* 105 (November 1941): 337–53.

11. Hudock, *Struggle, Condemnation, Vindication*, p. 22.

12. Hudock, *Struggle, Condemnation, Vindication*, p. 74, citing Alfredo Ottaviani, "Church and State: Some Present Problems in Light of the Teaching of Pope Pius XII," *American Ecclesiastical Review* 128 (May 1943): 321–34.

13. Hudock, *Struggle, Condemnation, Vindication*, p. 98.

14. Hudock, *Struggle, Condemnation, Vindication*, p. 137.

15. Hudock, *Struggle, Condemnation, Vindication*, p. 153, citing Xavier Rynne, *The Second Session: The Debates and Decrees of Vatican II* (New York: Farrar, Straus, 1964), p. 463.

16. Pope Paul VII, "Declaration on Religious Freedom: *Dignitatis Humanae*," December 7, 1965.

17. George Weigel, "*Dignitatis Humanae*: Origins and Unexpected Consequences," *Communio International Catholic Review*, Summer–Fall 2013, p. 381.

18. Daniel K. Williams, *Defenders of the Unborn: The Pro-Life Movement Before Roe v. Wade* (New York: Oxford Univ. Press, 2016), p. 80, citing "Cardinal Condemns Abortion Legalization," *Wanderer*, June 22, 1967, p. 1.

19. Frank Schaeffer, *Crazy for God* (New York: Carroll & Graf, 2007), p. 266.

20. Randall Balmer, "The Real Origins of the Religious Right," *Politico*, May 27, 2014.

21. Williams, *Defenders of the Unborn*, p. 67, citing "A Protestant Affirmation on the Control of Human Reproduction," *Christianity Today*, November 8, 1968, p. 18.

22. Williams, *Defenders of the Unborn*, p. 80.

23. Tellingly, when Phyllis Schlafly—one of the founding mothers of the religious right—began talking about abortion around that time, she didn't cast it as murder but rather as evidence that the Equal Rights Amendment undermined morality. Abortion was less the grand evil than an illustration of the greater threat, feminism. Deal W. Hudson, *Onward, Christian Soldiers* (New York: Threshold Editions, 2008), p. 54.

24. Williams, *Defenders of the Unborn*, p. 212.

25. Williams, *Defenders of the Unborn*, p. 207, citing "Abortion and the Court," *Christianity Today*, February 16, 1973, pp. 32–33.

26. Linda Greenhouse and Reva B. Siegel, "Before (and After) *Roe v. Wade*: New Questions About Backlash," *Yale Law Journal* 120 (2011): 2054, citing Patrick J. Buchanan to the President, March 24, 1971, in *Hearings Before the Senate Select Committee on Presidential Campaign Activities*, 93rd Cong., 1973, p. 4150.

27. Greenhouse and Siegel, "Before (and After) *Roe v. Wade*," p. 2054.

28. Greenhouse and Siegel, "Before (and After) *Roe v. Wade*," p. 2055, citing Richard M. Nixon, "Statement About the Report of the Commission on Population Growth and the American Future," May 5, 1972.

29. Michele McKeegan, *Abortion Politics: Mutiny in the Ranks of the Right* (New York: Free Press, 1992), p. 140.

30. Hudson, *Onward, Christian Soldiers*, p. 13.

31. Barbara Matuswo, "The Conversion of Bob Novak," *Washingtonian*, June 1, 2003.

32. "The Religious Affiliation of Supreme Court Justice Clarence Thomas," Adherents.com, accessed May 21, 2018.

33. "How and Why I Became a Catholic," Sacred Heart Catholic Church, accessed online May 21, 2018.

34. Hudson, *Onward, Christian Soldiers*, p. 256.

35. "Pope John Paul II," Gallup, April 1–5, 2005.

36. "Pope John Paul II Dies," *People*, April 2, 2005.

37. Pope Paul VI, "Dogmatic Constitution on Divine Revelation: *Dei Verbum*," November 18, 1965.

38. Email exchange with Richard Mouw, August 4, 2017.

39. "Evangelicals and Catholics Together: The Christian Mission in the Third Millennium," *First Things*, May 1994.

CHAPTER FIFTEEN
The "War" on "Christianity"

1. Lauren Markoe, "Trump Promises to Protect Christians at Liberty Commencement Speech," Religious News Service, May 13, 2017.

2. Jenna Johnson, "Donald Trump Says IRS Audits Could Be Tied to Being a 'Strong Christian,'" *Washington Post*, February 26, 2016.

3. "I have a very great relationship with God, and I have a very great relationship with evangelicals." Kaitlyn Schallhorn, "Donald Trump: 'I Have a Great Relationship with God,'" *The Blaze*, January 17, 2016.

4. Nick Ring, "Religious Freedom Part II: War on Christianity," GlennBeck.com, March 22, 2016, accessed July 11, 2018.

5. Brian Tashman, "Tony Perkins: Obama and Gay Rights Movement Inspire ISIS to Murder Christians," Right Wing Watch, April 22, 2016, accessed online July 11, 2018.

6. Nick Gass, "Mike Huckabee: U.S. Moving Toward 'Criminalization of Christianity,'" *Politico*, April 24, 2015, accessed online July 9, 2018.

7. Nate Madden, "New Report: Attacks on Religious Freedom in US Double in 3 Years," *Conservative Review*, March 23, 2016, accessed online July 9, 2018.

8. Eugene Scott, "Rick Saccone's Accusation That the Left Hates God May Be More Alienating than Compelling," *Washington Post*, March 14, 2018.

9. Jaweed Kaleem, "Clergy Launch Campaign for Student Loan Forgiveness, Aim to Qualify for 'Public Service' Rule," *Huffington Post*, February 8, 2012, accessed online July 9, 2018.

10. Melinda Skea, "Texas Churches Damaged by Harvey Sue FEMA," Becket Fund for Religious Liberty, September 5, 2015, accessed on becketlaw.org, July 11, 2018.

11. "*American Atheists v. Port Authority of New Jersey and New York*," Becket Fund for Religious Liberty, accessed July 11, 2018.

12. "*Caplan v. Town of Acton, Massachusetts*," Becket Fund for Religious Liberty, accessed July 11, 2018.

13. "In Depth: Topics A to Z: Religion," Gallup Polls, accessed online July 11, 2018.

14. Daniel Cox and Robert P. Jones, "America's Changing Religious Identity," Public Religion Research Institute, September 6, 2017.

15. Also, only 23 percent of white evangelical Protestants are under the age of thirty-five, compared with 51 percent of American Muslims, 52 percent of Hindus, and 40 percent who are Buddhists. "Religious Landscape Study: Generational Cohort," Pew Research Center.

16. Betsy Cooper et al., "Exodus: Why Americans Are Leaving Religion—and Why They're Unlikely to Come Back," Public Religion Research Institute, September 22, 2016.

17. "America's Changing Religious Landscape," Pew Research Center, May 12, 2015.

18. David Limbaugh, *Persecution: How Liberals Are Waging War Against Christianity* (Washington, DC: Regnery, 2003), pp. 47–48.

19. Todd Starnes, "VA Hospital Refuses to Accept 'Merry Christmas' Cards," FOX News, December 25, 2013, accessed online July 11, 2018.

20. Alan Noble, "Todd Starnes Sold Us a War on Christianity. We Bought It," Patheos.com, December 31, 2013; Todd Starnes's Facebook page, December 25, 2013, accessed October 4, 2018; statement of Jeff Milligan, director of the Veterans Administration of North Texas, on the Facebook page of Senator John Cornyn.

21. Phyllis Schlafly and George Neumayr, *No Higher Power: Obama's War on Religious Freedom* (Washington, DC: Regnery, 2012), p. 37.

22. Alex Horton, "Addressing Reports on the Houston National Cemetery," *VAntage Point*, Veterans Administration, June 30, 2011, accessed online July 11, 2018.

23. "2016 Hate Crime Statistics: Table 1: Incidents, Offenses, Victims, and Known Offenders by Bias Motivation, 2016," FBI.gov, accessed July 13, 2018.

24. Daniel Cox and Robert P. Jones, "Majority of Americans Oppose Transgender Bathroom Restrictions," Public Religion Research Institute, March 10, 2017.

25. In 2013, the kids at Nichols Elementary School got a lesson in how rumors spread. A parent sent an email to other parents saying that for the upcoming holiday parties they should avoid references to Christmas or other religious holidays, as well as the colors green and white. FOX News and others reported this as being an official school decree. Some Christians protested. The school clarified that anyone was allowed to bring Christmas or any other kinds of decorations. Conservative activists declared victory.

26. John Gibson, *The War on Christmas: How the Liberal Plot to Ban the Sacred Christian Holiday Is Worse Than You Thought* (New York: Sentinel, 2015), p. xvii.

27. Some 66 percent believe Jesus was born to a virgin and 75 percent that he was laid in a manger. Michael Lipka and David Masci, "5 Facts About Christmas in America," Pew Research Center, December 18, 2017.

28. "Quick Tree Facts," National Christmas Tree Association, accessed online July 9, 2018.

29. For a time, Kwanzaa was part of the December holiday season, but African American celebration of the holiday has waned. Tomi Obaro, "Is Kwanzaa Dead?," Time Out Chicago, December 20, 2012, accessed online July 13, 2018.

30. In *Persecution*, Limbaugh repeatedly offers horror stories . . . followed by a notation that some local court or administrator had corrected the misunderstanding. Here are some examples.

An elementary school girl in New York named Kayla Broadus was punished by school officials for saying, at snack table, "God is good. God is great. Thank you, God, for my school." But the school district later admitted it was wrong.

LaDonna DeVore, a receptionist in the Highland Park schools in Dallas, was chastised for sending a prayer in a group email. After being sued, the school admitted it was wrong and changed its policy.

Administrators at Columbine High School, site of the school shooting, removed some painted tiles on a memorial mosaic because they had religious messages. Some families sued, and the courts found in their favor.

A study called "First Liberty: The Survey of Hostility to Religion in America" states in passing, "The good news is that the vast majority of the hostility to religion you will read in this survey is unlawful. It succeeds only because of its own bluff and the passivity of its victims." That's pretty significant. The problem isn't the law, or the courts; it's the way regular people attempt to implement the rules.

31. Jeffrey Campbell, "High School Teachers' Knowledge of Legal Parameters Regarding Church/State Issues," Ph.D. diss., Department of Teaching and Teacher Education, University of Arizona, 2002, p. 57.

32. For instance, they were asked whether a teacher could announce a prayer meeting around the flagpole and encourage students to participate. Most teachers said that would be fine, when actually that *would* be unconstitutional because the government-paid teacher would be urging a form of worship.

33. Schlafly and Neumayr, *No Higher Power*, p. 21.

34. Rachel Weiner, "Romney: Obama Waging 'War on Religion,'" *Washington Post*, August 9, 2012.

35. Graham Vyse, "Trump and the Republicans Are Redefining 'Religious Freedom' to Favor Christians," *New Republic*, February 16, 2017.

36. "Women's Preventive Services Coverage and Non-Profit Religious Organizations," Centers for Medicare and Medicaid Services, Center for Consumer Information and Insurance Oversight, accessed online July 12, 2018.

37. Richard Wolf, "Supreme Court Sends 'Contraceptive Mandate' Cases Back to Lower Courts," *USA Today*, May 16, 2016.

38. Jonathan M. Pitts, "Little Sisters of the Poor Approve Trump Order on Religion," *Baltimore Sun*, May 4, 2017.

39. Pitts, "Little Sisters of the Poor."

40. Billy Hallowell, "Why Many Churches Can't Endorse Political Candidates," *Deseret News*, July 20, 2016; Grant Williams, "Appeals Court Says IRS Was Right to Strip Church's Tax Exemption," *Chronicle of Philanthropy*, May 15, 2000.

41. John Wagner and Sarah Pulliam Bailey, "Trump Signs Order Seeking to Allow Churches to Engage in More Political Activity," *Washington Post*, May 4, 2017.

42. Andrew L. Whitehead, Samuel L. Perry, and Joseph O. Baker, "Make America Christian Again: Christian Nationalism and Voting for Donald Trump in the 2016 Presidential Election," *Sociology of Religion* 79, no. 2 (2018): 147–71.

43. Whitehead, Perry, and Baker, "Make America Christian Again."

44. Limbaugh, *Persecution*, p. 330.

45. Schlafly and Neumayr, *No Higher Power*, p. 42.

46. Limbaugh, *Persecution*, p. 107.

47. Limbaugh, *Persecution*, p. 229.

48. Michael Brown, "7 Signs That America Declared War on Christianity," *Christian Post*, May 2, 2016, accessed online July 11, 2018.

49. "Bill O'Reilly: The War on Christianity Getting Even Worse," FOX News, April 3, 2015, accessed online July 11, 2018.

50. Oral arguments before the US Supreme Court in *Obergefell v. Hodges*, April 28, 2015.

51. Sage, "Military to Chaplains—Resign or Conform to Acceptance of Homosexuality," CommandtheRaven.com, August 29, 2011, accessed July 13, 2018; Jean McCarthy, "'Get in Line' or 'Resign' Admiral Tells Military Chaplain," LifeSiteNews .com, June 20, 2012, accessed July 13, 2018.

52. Chaplain Alliance for Religious Liberty, Guidestar.org, accessed August 6, 2018.

53. Sean Fine, "Ontario Intervenes in Case of Proposed Trinity Western Law School's Ban on Sexual Activities," *Globe and Mail*, September 10, 2017.

54. "Indiana Pizzeria Forced to Close After Backlash for Refusal to Cater Gay Wedding," FOXNews.com, April 1, 2015.

55. Jill Disis, "$800,000 Raised for Indiana Pizza Shop," *USA Today*, April 3, 2015.

56. "Bill O'Reilly: War on Christianity."

57. In an interview with the author, Chai Feldblum, a leading LGBT scholar and a member of the US Equal Employment Opportunity Commission, acknowledged that promotion of LGBT rights does sometimes restrict religious beliefs. "Judges, legislators and the public should recognize that complying with a law prohibiting discrimination against LGBT people can be a burden on the religious beliefs of some individuals." For that reason, "it is important to consider in each circumstance whether that burden is justified. In most cases dealing with individuals in employment and in business, the burden will be justified because it is necessary to achieve the compelling purpose of equality for LGBT people in society. But that won't always be the case."

58. Cooper, "Exodus: Why Americans Are Leaving Religion," Public Religion Research Institute, September 22, 2016.

59. "Guidance on Constitutionally Protected Prayer in Public Elementary and Secondary Schools," US Department of Education, February 7, 2003, accessed online July 14, 2018.

60. Steven Waldman and the Working Group on Information Needs of Communities, "The Information Needs of Communities: The Changing Media Landscape in a Broadband Age," Federal Communications Commission, July 2011, p. 315.

61. "A $71 Billion Tax Break for Churches? Don't Think So," *Nonprofit Law Prof Blog*, November 30, 2012.

62. "$71 Billion Tax Break for Churches?"; Joseph B. Cordes, Marie Grantz, and Thomas Pollak, "What Is the Property-Tax Exemption Worth?," in Evelyn Brody, ed., *Property Tax Exemption for Charities* (Washington, DC: Urban Institute Press, 2002).

63. Marcus Owens, former head of the Tax Exempt and Government Entities division of the IRS, interview with the author.

64. Phil Zuckerman, "Why Americans Hate Atheists," *Psychology Today*, June 23, 2014.

65. Katha Pollitt, "Why It's Time to Repeal the Religious Freedom Restoration Act," *Nation*, July 30, 2014.

66. *Listecki v. Official Committee of Unsecured Creditors*, United States District Court, Eastern District of Wisconsin, July 29, 2013.

67. Frank Kummer, "Lancaster Nuns Sue Feds over Pipeline, Citing Religious Freedom," *Philadelphia Inquirer*, July 18, 2017.

68. Tom Jackman, "Heroin Dealer Cites Religious Freedom as His Defense. Court Says Yeah, but What About the Buyers?," *Washington Post*, May 4, 2017.

69. Paul Berger, "Rabbi Performs Controversial Metzitzah B'Peh Circumcision Rite—Law or No," Forward.com, March 27, 2014.

70. "Lawsuit Unites Jewish Groups," Community News Service, COLlive, October 24, 2012.

71. Marc Santora, "Suit Is Filed Over Move to Regulate Circumcision," *New York Times*, October 11, 2012.

CHAPTER SIXTEEN

All-American Islam

1. Will Herberg, *Protestant-Catholic-Jew* (New York: Doubleday, 1955), p. 274.

2. Sulayman S. Nyang, *Islam in the United States of America* (Chicago: ABC International Group, 1999), p. 88.

3. Sylvester A. Johnson and Steven Weitzman, eds., *The FBI and Religion: Faith and National Security Before and After 9/11* (Berkeley: Univ. of California Press, 2017), p. 58, citing Rhea Whitley to Director of FBI, Internal Memorandum, September 12, 1931, p. 3, FBI File 62-25889, "Moorish Science Temple of America," Part 1, US Department of Justice, FBI Records.

4. Don Terry, "W. Deen Mohammed: A Leap of Faith," *Chicago Tribune*, October 20, 2002.

5. Edward E. Curtis IV, *Muslims in America: A Short History* (New York: Oxford Univ. Press, 2009), p. 79. He changed the name of the organization to Al-Islam in the West and invited whites to join.

6. Nathaniel Sheppard Jr., "Islamic Leader Says Organization Is Taking a Turn Toward Patriotism," *New York Times*, May 25, 1978.

7. Victor Mather, "In the Ring He Was Ali, but in the Newspapers He Was Still Clay," *New York Times*, June 9, 2016.

8. Thomas Hauser, *Muhammad Ali: His Life and Times* (New York: Simon & Schuster, 1991), p. 294.

9. "Demographic Portrait of Muslim Americans," Pew Research Center, July 26, 2017.

10. Besheer Mohamed, "New Estimates Show U.S. Muslim Population Continues to Grow," Pew Research Center, January 3, 2018.

11. Peter Skerry, "America's Other Muslims," *Wilson Quarterly*, Autumn 2005.

12. Kareem Abdul-Jabbar and Peter Knobler, *Giant Steps: The Autobiography of Kareem Abdul-Jabbar* (New York: Bantam Books, 1983), p. 173.

13. Abdul-Jabbar and Knobler, *Giant Steps*, p. 177.

14. Over time, Abdul-Jabbar would part from Hamaas, who became unhinged after his family was massacred, likely by members of the Nation of Islam. Abdul-Jabbar and Knobler, *Giant Steps*, p. 177.

15. Laura Wagner, "Muhammad Ali Changed His Name in 1964: Newspapers Called Him Cassius Clay for Six More Years," Slate.com, June 10, 2016.

16. John Papanek, "A Different Drummer: Getting Inside the Mind of Kareem Abdul-Jabbar," *Sports Illustrated*, December 16, 2014.

17. Samuel G. Freedman, "North Dakota Mosque a Symbol of Muslims' Long Ties in America," *New York Times*, May 27, 2016; Cary Beckwith, "Of Mosques and Men," *New Republic*, January 31, 2016.

18. Curtis, *Muslims in America*, p. 79.

19. David S. Bowerman, "What's on Your Dog Tag?," US Army, April 1, 2014.

20. Philip Harsham, "Islam in Iowa," *Aramco World* 27, no. 6 (November–December 1976).

21. Jonathan Curiel, *Islam in America* (London: I. B. Tauris, 2015), p. xvi.

22. Curiel, *Islam in America*, p. 68.

23. Carol L. Stone, "Estimate of Muslims Living in America," in Yvonne Yazbeck Haddad, ed., *The Muslims of America* (New York: Oxford Univ. Press, 1991), pp. 27–28.

24. Curiel, *Islam in America*, p. 69.

25. Kambiz GhaneaBassiri, *A History of Islam in America: From the New World to the New World Order* (New York: Cambridge Univ. Press, 2010), p. 243.

26. Curiel, *Islam in America*, p. 80.

27. Seventy percent of American Muslims who were born abroad are now US citizens. Nadia Marzouki, *Islam: An American Religion* (New York: Columbia Univ. Press, 2013), p. 38.

28. Peter Skerry, "The Muslim-American Muddle," Brookings Institution, September 7, 2011.

29. Pew Research Center, *Muslim Americans: No Sign of Growth in Alienation or Support for Extremism* (Washington, DC: Pew Research Center, 2011), p. 6.

30. John Bilotta, "Salman Rushdie, Facing Death Threats from Iran, Apologized Saturday . . . ," United Press International, Archives, February 18, 1989.

31. "History: Highlights from 28 Years of Service," Muslim Public Affairs Council, December 2016, accessed online June 19, 2018.

32. Blaine Harden, "A Nation Challenged: American Muslims; Saudis Seek to Add U.S. Muslims to Their Sect," *New York Times*, October 20, 2001; Curiel, *Islam in America*, p. 69.

33. Harden, "A Nation Challenged."

34. A Saudi-financed book at a Los Angeles mosque declared, "Be dissociated from the infidels, hate them for their religion, leave them, never rely on them for support, do not admire them, and always oppose them in every way according to Islamic law." Freedom House, "Saudi Publications on Hate Ideology Invade American Mosques" (Washington, DC: Center for Religious Freedom, 2005), p. 11.

35. Barrett, *American Islam*, p. 140.

36. Skerry, "America's Other Muslims."

37. Muhammad Frazier-Rahim, interview with the author, October 12, 2017.

38. "Interview: Maher Hathout," *Frontline*, October 26, 2001.

39. Curiel, *Islam in America*, pp. 39–40.

40. Jane I. Smith, *Islam in America*, 2nd ed. (New York: Columbia Univ. Press, 2010), p. 135.

41. Smith, *Islam in America*, p. 136.

42. Yvonne Yazbeck Haddad, *Not Quite American? The Shaping of Arab and Muslim Identity in the United States* (Waco, TX: Baylor Univ. Press, 2004), p. 12.

43. Curiel, *Islam in America*, p. 44, citing Sheila Musaji, "Laleh Bakhtiar's Qur'an Translation Controversy over Verse 4:34," *American Muslim*, October 25, 2007.

44. Nick Street, "First All-Female Mosque Opens in Los Angeles," *Al Jazeera America*, February 3, 2015.

45. Elizabeth Dias, "For Rashida Tlaib, Palestinian Heritage Infuses a Detroit Sense of Community," *New York Times*, August 14, 2018. Just as American Catholic bishops had succeeded in influencing the Vatican, American Muslim women are beginning to have an influence in other countries. Daisy Khan, an American feminist, created the Women's Islamic Initiative in Spirituality and Equality, which formed an Islamic council of thought leaders, a *shura*, that has issued scripturally based position papers on controversial topics previously dominated by conservative, male-run Islamic institutions. A network of feminist Muslim leaders brought together globally got some practitioners of female genital mutilation in Egypt and Gambia to stop, trained traditional imams in Afghanistan to oppose the Taliban's barbaric Quranic interpretations, and thwarted an effort to exclude women from the most sacred spaces in Mecca.

46. "They have unprecedented freedom to experiment with forms and structures for the separation of religion and state away from the watchful eyes of wary governments and the criticism of traditionalists." Yvonne Yazbeck Haddad, ed., *The Muslims of America* (New York: Oxford Univ. Press, 1991), p. 5.

47. Curiel, *Islam in America*, p. 65.

48. Omar Sacirbey, "Shiite Muslims Quietly Establish a Foothold in U.S.," *Washington Post*, October 2, 2012; Ihsan Bagby, "The American Mosque 2011: Report Number 1 from the US Mosque Study 2011," Council on American-Islamic Relations, January 2012, p. 15.

49. David Frey, "Ahmadiyya Muslim Community Continues to Serve Despite Fears of Persecution in Frederick," *Frederick (MD) News-Post*, November 18, 2016.

50. Peter Skerry, "The American Exception: Why Muslims in the U.S. Aren't as Attracted to Jihad as Those in Europe," *TIME*, August 21, 2006.

51. *Islamic Center of Mississippi, Inc., et al., v. City of Starkville, Mississippi*, 840 F.2d 293, March 23, 1988.

52. Alan E. Brownstein and Ira C. Lupu, "Equal Protection Clause and the Free Exercise of Religion," in Paul Finkelman, ed., *Religion and American Law: An Encyclopedia* (New York: Garland, 2000), p. 161.

53. Billy Graham, interview with David Frost, 1977, cited in Callum Borchers, "The Media Savvy of Billy Graham," *Washington Post*, February 21, 2018.

54. Feisal Abdul Rauf, *What's Right with Islam Is What's Right with America* (New York: HarperOne, 2004), pp. 54–55.

55. Although there are also a few verses in the Quran that indicate hostility to other faiths, more of them praise tolerance to at least Christianity and Judaism: "Do not argue with the People of the Book except in the best way . . . and say [to them] We believe in that which was revealed to us as well as that which was revealed to you. Our God and your God is One and the same. We all submit to Him" (Quran 29:46).

56. Asma Gull Hasan, *American Muslims: The New Generation* (New York: Continuum, 2004), p. 159.

57. Curiel, *Islam in America*, p. 142; Brooks Jackson, "Muslim Stamp," FactCheck.org, September 14, 2009.

58. Tove Danovich, "Street Meat: The Rise of NYC's Halal Cart Culture," *Eater*, July 10, 2015.

59. Farr A. Curlin et al., "Religious Characteristics of U.S. Physicians," *Journal of General Internal Medicine* 20, no. 7 (July 2005): 629–34.

60. Geneive Abdo, "Strong Religious Beliefs Are Only One Part of Muslim American Identity," Pew Research Center, September 1, 2017.

61. Marzouki, *Islam: An American Religion*, p. 39.

62. "Ali-Led Family Day Parade Snubs His Ex-Wife, Khalilah," *Jet* 58, no. 19 (July 24, 1980): 46.

63. Skerry, "America's Other Muslims."

64. "Muslim Organizations Endorse George W. Bush for US President," Sound Vision, 2000; "American Muslim Group Endorses Bush," Beliefnet.com, November 2000.

65. Peter Beinart, "When Conservatives Oppose 'Religious Freedom,'" *Atlantic*, April 11, 2017.

66. Christopher Bail, *Terrified: How Anti-Muslim Fringe Organizations Became Mainstream* (Princeton: Princeton Univ. Press, 2015), p. 28.

67. Suhail A. Khan, "America's First Muslim President," *Foreign Policy*, August 23, 2010.

68. George W. Bush, Inaugural Address, January 20, 2001.

69. "'We Are All Sinners': In the Final Weeks of the 2000 Election, George W. Bush Discussed His Faith and Policies with Editor-in-Chief, Steve Waldman," Beliefnet, Fall 2000.

70. "Post September 11 Attitudes: Religion More Prominent; Muslim-Americans More Accepted," Pew Research Center, December 6, 2001.

71. Abigail Simon, "This Bush Cabinet Official Was Imprisoned in a Japanese Internment Camp. He Sees Troubling Parallels with Family Separations," *TIME*, June 21, 2018.

72. President George W. Bush, remarks on September 17, 2001 at the Islamic Center of Washington, DC; George W. Bush, *Decision Points* (New York: Crown, 2010); Samuel Freedman, "Six Days After 9/11, Another Anniversary Worth Honoring," *New York Times*, September 7, 2012.

73. President George W. Bush, address before Congress, September 22, 2001.

CHAPTER SEVENTEEN

"An Enemy Inside Our Perimeter"

1. Michael Schulson, "Why Do So Many Americans Believe That Islam Is a Political Ideology, Not a Religion?," *Washington Post*, February 3, 2017; Nick Natalicchio, "Robertson: 'Islam Is Not a Religion. It Is a Worldwide Political Movement Meant on Domination,'" Media Matters, June 12, 2007. He repeated the claim in 2015. Katherine Hafner, "Pat Robertson: Islam Is 'Not a Religion,'" *Virginian-Pilot*, December 9, 2015.

2. Hannah Wise, "Trump's Favorite General Doesn't View Him as a Republican or Islam as a Religion, He Says in Dallas," DallasNews.com, August 2016; Peter Beinart, "The Denationalization of American Muslims," *Atlantic*, March 19, 2017.

3. Greg Miller, *Washington Post*, January 23, 2012. Boykin made the statement in a video for the Oak Initiative. Republican congressman Jody Hice explained the implications. "It is a complete geo-political structure and," he said, "as such, does not deserve First Amendment protection."

4. "Survey Report: U.S. Image Still Poor," Pew Research Center, March 16, 2004.

5. "Nationalism in Asia, Islamic Extremism in Africa—the 2017 World Watch List," *World Watch Monitor*, January 11, 2017, accessed online June 29, 2018.

6. It did not, however, stop individual attacks on Muslims, and most Americans probably do not realize just how prevalent those were in 2001. While 28 hate crimes against Muslims were recorded by the FBI in 2000, that number rose to 481 in 2001, and a total of 2,064 between 2001 and 2014. Other estimates put the 2001 number at over 1,000. The good news is that the number dropped from 481 in 2001 to 155 the next year, and it stayed in that range until 2016. As a point of context, this still puts the raw numbers of anti-Muslim hate crimes below those against Jews or blacks.

7. Deborah Caldwell, "How Islam-Bashing Got Cool," Beliefnet, August 2002.

8. "Plurality Sees Islam as More Likely to Encourage Violence," Pew Research Center, September 9, 2004.

9. Nadia Marzouki, *Islam: An American Religion* (New York: Columbia Univ. Press, 2017), p. 87.

10. Chris McGreal, "Muslims in America Increasingly Alienated as Hatred Grows in Bible Belt," *Guardian* (US ed.), September 10, 2010.

11. Scott Broden and Doug Davis, "Mosque Expansion Proposal in Murfreesboro Spotlights Fear, Shame," *Tennessean*, June 21, 2010, accessed online August 12, 2012.

12. Annie Gowen, "Far from Ground Zero, Other Plans for Mosques Run into Vehement Opposition," *Washington Post*, August 23, 2010.

13. An earlier instance, in which a Muslim in Nashville had become radicalized in Yemen and shot a military recruiter in Tennessee, was cited as evidence that the state was a hotbed of Islamic radicalism. "Sen. Ketron Hands Out DVD to Support Terror Bill," Associated Press, May 13, 2011.

14. Erik Schelzig, "Tenn. Gov Hopeful Questions if Islam Is a 'Cult,'" AP Online, July 27, 2010, accessed July 3, 2018.

15. "Candidate Denounces Mosque Proposal," *Paris (TN) Post-Intelligencer*, June 25, 2010.

16. "Judge Rules Against Plaintiffs Trying to Stop Construction of Tennessee Mosque," *Kingsport (TN) Times News*, May 19, 2011.

17. Marzouki, *Islam: An American Religion*, p. 89; Christian Grantham, "Murfreesboro Mosque Opponents Appear in Chancery Court," *Murfreesboro (TN) Post*, September 27, 2010.

18. As the case moved into the federal courts, the US Department of Justice soon intervened, arguing that the county had violated the Religious Land Use and Institutionalized Persons Act. The local congresswoman, Republican Diane Black, responded, "Christians' rights to freedom of religion are violated frequently and the Obama Justice Department doesn't come rushing to our aid, but they will meddle in a local zoning matter to promote Islam."

19. Marie Kemph, "Appeals Court Overturns Mosque Ruling," *Murfreesboro (TN) Post*, May 30, 2013; Scott Broden, "Supreme Court Won't Hear Murfreesboro Mosque Case," *Tennessean*, June 2, 2014.

20. US Department of Justice, "Justice Department Files Brief in Support of Continued Construction of Murfreesboro, Tenn., Mosque," press release, October 18, 2010.

21. "Controversies over Mosques and Islamic Centers Across the U.S.," Pew Research Center, September 27, 2012.

22. Rory Linnane, "Brookfield Officials Grapple with Opposition to Proposed Mosque," *Brookfield Patch*, April 12, 2012.

23. Peter Beinart, "The Denationalization of American Muslims," *Atlantic*, March 19, 2017.

24. Mary Slosson, "Mosque Approval in Southern California: Bellwether for the Rest of the Country?," *Huffington Post*, February 10, 2011.

25. Beinart, "Denationalization of American Muslims."

26. Tim Barber, "Justice Department Files Suit over Blocked Mosque Construction in Culpeper," WJLA, December 12, 2016.

27. Denise Lavoie, "Backlash Greets Plans for Muslim Cemeteries Across US," Associated Press, April 25, 2016.

28. Scott Shane, "In Islamic Law, Gingrich Sees a Mortal Threat to U.S.," *New York Times*, December 21, 2011.

29. Nathan Lean, *The Islamophobia Industry* (London: Pluto Press, 2017), p. 150, Kindle.

30. Abigail Hauslohner, "How a Series of Fringe Anti-Muslim Conspiracy Theories Went Mainstream—via Donald Trump," *Washington Post*, November 6, 2016.

31. A report by one of the anti-Sharia groups that ostensibly provides six hundred pages of proof is mostly made up of such cases where courts decide whether religious contracts are valid. In not a single case did the courts throw American law out the window in order to kowtow to religious preferences, but the fact that the word "Sharia"—or, for that matter, "Halacha" or "Canon Law"—was uttered in the chambers enabled them to say, "Shariah law has entered into state court decisions." One commonly cited case involves a Muslim man who defended himself against spousal abuse charges by saying his religion countenanced punishing his wife. A lower court judge bought the argument, claiming that the man did not therefore have criminal intent. The ruling was overturned by the appellate court, which stated: "As the judge recognized, the case thus presents a conflict between the criminal law and religious precepts. In resolving this conflict, the judge determined to except defendant from the operation of the State's statutes as the result of his religious beliefs. In doing so, the judge was mistaken." Note that the judge's error was that he gave too much deference to the defendant's religious views. Eugene Volokh, "Cultural Defense Accepted as to Nonconsensual Sex in New Jersey Trial Court, Rejected on Appeal," *The Volokh Conspiracy*, July 23, 2010.

32. "The World's Muslims: Chapter 1: Beliefs About Sharia," Pew Research Center, April 30, 2013.

33. "The World's Muslims: Chapter 2: Religion and Politics," Pew Research Center, April 30, 2013.

34. For instance, 84 percent of Muslims in South Asia (Afghanistan, Pakistan, and Bangladesh) say Sharia should be the law of the land—and yet 64 percent say it should apply only to Muslims.

35. David Bier, "Muslims Rapidly Adopt U.S. Social Views," Cato Institute, October 13, 2016.

36. Magali Rheault and Dalia Mogahed, "Majorities See Religion and Democracy as Compatible," Gallup Polls, October 3, 2007.

37. Pew Research Center, *Muslim Americans: No Sign of Growth in Alienation or Support for Extremism* (Washington, DC: Pew Research Center, 2011).

38. Charles C. Marshall, "An Open Letter to the Honorable Alfred E. Smith," *Atlantic*, April 1927.

39. Hauslohner, "Fringe Anti-Muslim Conspiracy Theories."

40. Stop the Islamization of America rally, June 6, 2010, YouTube video, https://www.youtube.com/watch?v=GK5EEjozbso, accessed October 18, 2018.

41. Marzouki, *Islam: An American Religion*, p. 120, citing James C. McKinley Jr., "Oklahoma Surprise: Islam as an Election Issue," *New York Times*, November 14, 2010.

42. "Oklahoma's Sharia Law Ban Creates Controversy," Southern Poverty Law Center, February 23, 2011.

43. Alejandro Beutel and Saeed Khan, "Manufacturing Bigotry: A State-by-

State Legislative Effort to Pushback Against 2050 by Targeting Muslims and Other Minorities," Institute for Social Policy and Understanding, 2014, p. 3.

44. @ACTforAmerica, September 4, 2014.

45. Pamela Geller, "Stop the Islamization of America: Maryland Public Pools Enforce Sharia-Muslim Swim, Segregated Swimming," GellerReport.com, November 16, 2011.

46. Pamela Geller, "Happy Halal Thanksgiving," *American Thinker*, November 21, 2011.

47. Bryan Fischer, on his radio show *Focal Point*, November 2011.

48. Sarah Posner, "Welcome to the Shari'ah Conspiracy Theory Industry," Religion Dispatches, March 8, 2011.

49. "The Secure Freedom Strategy: A Plan for Victory over the Global Jihad Movement," Center for Security Policy, January 23, 2015, p. 15.

50. William G. Boykin et al., *Shariah: The Threat to America: An Exercise in Competitive Analysis* (Washington, DC: Center for Security Policy, 2010), p. 34.

51. Ron Kampeas, "Anti-Sharia Laws Stir Concerns That Halachah Could Be Next," Jewish Telegraphic Agency, April 28, 2011.

52. Hos. 13:16, NIV.

53. Ps. 137, NASB.

54. 2 Thess. 1:8, AV.

55. "Karadzic Defends Bosnian Serb 'Holy' Cause at Trial," BBC News, March 1, 2010.

56. *Richmond Enquirer*, February 15, 1820. The biblical defense of slavery was commonly used throughout the Missouri Controversy. For an elaborate defense from the Missouri territorial newspapers, see the *Franklin (MO) Intelligencer*, February 18, 1820; Larry R. Morrison, "The Religious Defense of American Slavery Before 1830," *Journal of Religious Thought* 37, no. 2 (Fall 1980–Winter 1981): 17.

57. Morrison, "Religious Defense of American Slavery," p. 17.

58. George Yancey, "Was Opposition to Interracial Marriage Motivated by Christianity?," Patheos, April 18, 2014.

59. W. Deen Mohammed, *Diversity in Al-Islam* (Calumet City, IL: WDM, 2016), p. 160.

60. Mohammed, *Diversity in Al-Islam*, p. 162.

61. Michael Wolfe, ed., *Taking Back Islam: American Muslims Reclaim Their Faith* (Emmaus, PA: Rodale and Beliefnet, 2002), p. xiii.

62. Geneive Abdo, "Like Most Americans, U.S. Muslims Concerned About Extremism in the Name of Islam," Pew Research Center, August 14, 2017.

63. Mariam Khan and Luis Martinez, "More than 5,000 Muslims Serving in US Military, Pentagon Says," ABCNews.com, December 8, 2015.

64. Daniel Bates, "Faces of the American Muslims Who Died Fighting for Their Country After 9/11 Revealed as Fallen Soldier's Father Tells Trump: 'You Have Sacrificed Nothing and No-One,'" *Daily Mail*, July 29, 2016.

65. Peter Beinart, "America's Most Prominent Anti-Muslim Activist Is Welcome at the White House," *Atlantic*, March 21, 2017.

66. Chip Berlet, "AFA's Fischer Tells 'Values' Crowd: Islam, Gays Threaten U.S.," Southern Poverty Law Center, October 10, 2011.

67. Ed O'Keefe, "John McCain Defends [Huma] Abedin Against Accusations She's Part of Conspiracy," *Washington Post*, July 18, 2012.

68. Wayne Madsen, "Exclusive: Khizr Khan Founded Islamic Journal to Defend Sharia Law," Infowars.com, August 3, 2016. In an article in the *Daily Caller*, Khan is quoted as saying, "It has to be admitted, however, that the Quran, being basically a book of religious guidance, is not an easy reference for legal studies. It is more particularly an appeal to faith and the human soul rather than a classification of legal prescriptions." Khan added that "the major portion of the Quran is, as with every Holy

Book, a code of divine exhortation and moral principles." Alex Pfeiffer, "Khizr Khan Has Written Extensively on Sharia Law," *Daily Caller*, August 1, 2016, accessed online July 2, 2018.

69. Amelia Thomson-DeVeaux, Public Religion Research Institute, December 19, 2011.

70. Josh Rogin, "Briefing Skipper: Ground Zero Mosque, Lebanon, Pakistan, Moscow, Wikileaks," ForeignPolicy.com, August 10, 2010.

71. "Robert Spencer," Southern Poverty Law Center, accessed online July 2, 2018.

72. *FOX & Friends*, August 16, 2010.

73. *The Sean Hannity Show*, FOX News, August 12, 2010.

74. *The Sean Hannity Show*, FOX News, May 20, 2010.

75. Another point of attack against Rauf was his statement that the United States was an "accessory" to the 9/11 attacks. Protest signs even used that phrase. But the full context is pretty clear: he was saying that American policies that have hurt Muslims in other countries have sown anger that has come back in the form of terrorism.

MR. ABDUL RAUF: Fanaticism and terrorism have no place in Islam. That's—that's just as absurd as associating Hitler with Christianity or—or David Koresh with Christianity. There are always people who will—who will do peculiar things and think that they are doing things in the name of their religion. But—but the Koran—you know, God says in the Koran that they think that they're doing right, but they're doing wrong. . . .

MR. BRADLEY (voiceover): And throughout the Muslim world, there is also strong opposition to America's foreign policy, particularly in the Middle East, because of its support of Israel and economic sanctions against Iraq.

MR. ABDUL RAUF: It is a reaction against the policies of the U.S. government, politically, where we espouse principles of democracy and human rights and where we ally ourselves with oppressive regimes in many of these countries.

MR. BRADLEY: Are—are—are you in any way suggesting that we in the United States deserved what happened?

MR. ABDUL RAUF: I wouldn't say that the United States deserved what happened, but the United States policies were an accessory to the crime that happened.

MR. BRADLEY: O.K. You say that we're an accessory?

MR. ABDUL RAUF: Yes.

MR. BRADLEY: How?

MR. ABDUL RAUF: Because we have been an accessory to a lot of—of innocent lives dying in the world. In fact, it—in the most direct sense, Osama bin Laden is made in the U.S.A. . . .

After the *60 Minutes* interview, the Cordoba Initiative elaborated: "The '60 Minutes' piece was completely incorrect, as the statement was edited out of context. In the full interview, Imam Feisal describes the mistake the C.I.A. made in the 1980s by financing Osama bin Laden and strengthening the Taliban. This view is widely shared within the U.S. and the U.S. government today, and Imam Feisal underlines the importance of not supporting 'friends of convenience' who may in the future become our enemies." A good review of Rauf's contested statements is Anne Barnard, "Parsing the Record of Feisal Abdul Rauf," *New York Times*, August 21, 2010.

76. Daisy Khan, *Born with Wings: The Spiritual Journey of a Modern Muslim Woman* (New York: Spiegel & Grau, 2018), p. 298.

77. Peter Skerry, "The Muslim-American Muddle," Brookings, September 7, 2011.

78. Jacob Engels, "Exposed: Islamic Supremacists of North America," Cold Stone Truth, August 7, 2017, accessed online August 7, 2018; "ISNA Endorser and Chaplains Respond to Negative Allegations," Islamic Society of North America, April 8, 2014, accessed online August 7, 2018.

79. Boykin et al., *Shariah: The Threat to America*, p. 34.

80. Viewing Liberty, "'Rise of Radical Islam'—Sean Hannity Special" YouTube video, 41:08, posted January 12, 2015.

81. Engy Abdelkader, "Special Report: When Islamophobia Turns Violent: The 2016 U.S. Presidential Elections," The Bridge Initiative, a Georgetown University Research Project, 2016, p. 48.

82. "Muslims Pray on Capitol Hill," the Ethics and Religious Liberty Commission of the Southern Baptist Convention, September 29, 2009.

83. Bail, *Terrified*, p. 55; "1425+ Muslim Leaders Condemn Terrorism—Over 200+ Condemnations," WiseUp, accessed online July 8, 2018.

84. Ingrid Mattson, "American Muslims' Special Obligation," in Wolfe, *Taking Back Islam*, pp. 2–3.

85. Jamie Grierson, "Donald Trump: Muslim Communities 'Not Reporting' Terror Suspects," *Guardian* (US ed.), March 23, 2016.

86. The director of the FBI at the time, Robert Mueller, testified in 2008 that "many of our cases are a result of the cooperation from the Muslim community in the United States." Charles Kurzman, "Muslim-American Terrorism Since 9/11: An Accounting," Triangle Center on Terrorism and Homeland Security, University of North Carolina, Chapel Hill, p. 6, February 2, 2011.

87. Boykin et al., *Shariah: The Threat to America*, p. 19.

88. Martin Peretz, "The *New York Times* Laments 'A Sadly Wary Misunderstanding of Muslim-Americans,' But Really Is It 'Sadly Wary' or a 'Misunderstanding' at All?," *New Republic*, September 4, 2010, accessed online June 29, 2018.

89. Beinart, "Denationalization of American Muslims."

90. Lean, *Islamophobia Industry*, p. 66; Sarah Griffiths, "289 Islamophobic Tweets Were Sent Every Hour in July," *Wired*, August 18, 2016.

91. Examples of Russian hacking were released by the Democrats on the House Intelligence Committee; see https://democrats-intelligence.house.gov/social-media -content/social-media-advertisements.htm and https://democrats-intelligence.house .gov/uploadedfiles/3_of_3_stop_ai__1163765713737743.pdf.

92. Claire Allbright, "A Russian Facebook Page Organized a Protest in Texas. A Different Russian Page Launched the Counterprotest," *Texas Tribune*, November 1, 2017.

93. Josh Harkinson, "Trump Campaign CEO Was a Big Promoter of Anti-Muslim Extremists," *Mother Jones*, September 15, 2016.

94. Beinart, "Denationalization of American Muslims."

95. Naomi A. Palk, "The Mass Incarceration of Japanese Americans Offers a Lesson for Muslims and Allies," *Chicago Reporter*, June 25, 2017.

96. Lean, *Islamophobia Industry*, p. 90.

97. Max Fisher, "It's Not Just Fox News: Islamophobia on Cable News Is Out of Control," Vox.com, January 13, 2015.

98. Chris Rovzar, "Brian Kilmeade on *Fox & Friends*: All Terrorists Are Muslims," NYMag.com, October 15, 2010.

99. "'We Need to Kill Them': Judge Jeanine Says It's Time to Stop Islamic Terror," FOX News, January 11, 2015, accessed online July 2, 2018.

100. Viewing Liberty, "'Rise of Radical Islam.'"

101. "Fox News Host: 'History of Islam' Shows a 'Bullet to the Head' Is 'Only Thing These People Understand,'" TheWeek.com, August 20, 2014.

102. Fisher, "It's Not Just Fox News."

103. "Top Talk Audiences," Talkers.com, accessed July 4, 2018.

104. Jeff Poor, "Limbaugh: 'Islam Is a Conquest Ideology—Not Even a Religion,'" Breitbart, December 24, 2015, accessed online July 4, 2018.

105. Rush Limbaugh, *The Rush Limbaugh Show*, July 23, 2012.

106. Julie Bosman, "Michael Savage to Write Two Thrillers," *New York Times*, November 22, 2010.

107. "Mark Levin: 'The Muslim Brotherhood Has Infiltrated Our Government, It's Called Barack Obama,'" Real Clear Politics, January 31, 2013.

108. Bill Carter and Brian Stelter, "Fox News Hires Glenn Beck Away from CNN," *New York Times*, October 16, 2008.

109. Glenn Beck, *It Is About Islam* (New York: Threshold Editions, 2015), p. 10.

110. Allum Bokhari and Milo Yiannopoulos, "The West vs. Islam Is the New Cold War—Here's How We Win," Breitbart, August 12, 2016, accessed online July 4, 2018.

111. Tom Tancredo, "Political Correctness Protects Muslim Rape Culture," Breitbart, January 2, 2016, accessed online July 4, 2018.

112. John Nolte, "6 Reasons Pamela Geller's Muhammad Cartoon Contest Is No Different Than Selma," Breitbart, May 6, 2016, accessed online July 5, 2016.

113. Dan Riehl, "Roger Stone: Huma Abedin 'Most Likely a Saudi Spy' with 'Deep, Inarguable Connections' to 'Global Terrorist Entity,'" Breitbart, June 15, 2016, accessed online July 5, 2018.

114. Cody Shepard, "Easton Official's Anti-Muslim Post Leads to Calls for Resignation," *Enterprise* (Brockton, MA), July 19, 2016.

115. Michael Tanenbaum, "Embattled N.J. School Board Member Steps Down over Anti-Muslim Facebook Posts," PhillyVoice.com, April 24, 2016.

116. Esme Cribb, "Minnesota GOPers Sorry for Post Calling Keith Ellison 'Muslim Goat Humper,'" Talking Points Memo, May 2, 2017.

117. Shawn Annarelli, "County Commissioner Posts Anti-Islamic Messages on Facebook," *Centre Daily Times* (State College, PA), August 20, 2016.

118. Rachel Revesz, "Trump Campaigner Says She Is Not Racist After Writing 'I Do Not Want Any Type of Muslims' on Facebook," *Independent*, November 23, 2016.

119. Robert P. Jones et al., "What It Means to Be American," Brookings Institution and Public Religion Research Institute, 2011, p. 13.

120. Laura Ingraham radio show, March 30, 2011; Kristine Phillips, "Trump Has Been Pushing Fake News for Years, Obama's Former Press Secretary Says," *Washington Post*, March 1, 2017.

121. Jenna Johnson and Sean Sullivan, "Trump and Rubio Question President Obama's Visit to a Mosque," *Washington Post*, February 3, 2016; Aaron Blake, "Why Obama's Mosque Visit Is Criticized—in a Way George W. Bush's Wasn't," *Washington Post*, February 4, 2016.

122. @realDonaldTrump, February 20, 2016.

123. Abdelkader, "When Islamophobia Turns Violent," p. 50.

124. Theodore Schleifer, "Donald Trump: 'I Think Islam Hates Us,'" CNN.com, March 10, 2016.

125. "Transcript of Republican Debate in Miami, Full Text," CNN.com, March 15, 2016.

126. The *Sean Hannity Show* on FOX News, June 15, 2016. This was rated "false" by PolitiFact.com: Louis Jacobson, "Donald Trump Wrong That 'There's No Real Assimilation' by U.S. Muslims," PolitiFact.com, June 18, 2016.

127. Lauren Carroll, "Fact-Checking Trump's Claim That Thousands in New Jersey

Cheered When World Trade Center Tumbled," PolitiFact.com, November 22, 2016, accessed July 2, 2018.

128. "Donald Trump Urges Muslims 'to Turn People In,'" BBC News, May 16, 2016.

129. Andrew Kaczynski, "Trump Repeats False Claim That Muslims Knew in Advance of San Bernardino Shooting," BuzzFeedNews.com, June 14, 2016.

130. Matt Hamilton, "Donald Trump Repeats False Claim That Neighbors Saw 'Bombs All Over' Before San Bernardino Attack," *Los Angeles Times*, October 9, 2016; "Fact Check: Trump's Terrorism Speech," *USA Today*, August 16, 2016.

131. This idea may have been inspired by the Baptist leader Franklin Graham, who had proposed such a ban six months earlier. Franklin Graham's Facebook page, July 17, 2015, accessed July 9, 2018, https://www.facebook.com/FranklinGraham /posts/967305353325646.

132. "Donald Trump Remarks in Manchester, New Hampshire," C-Span, June 13, 2016. On July 24, 2016, on NBC News, he defended the Muslim ban by saying this: "People were so upset when I used the word Muslim. 'Oh, you can't use the word Muslim,'" Trump said. ". . . But just remember this: Our Constitution is great, but it doesn't necessarily give us the right to commit suicide, okay? Now, we have a religious—you know, everybody wants to be protected. And that's great. And that's the wonderful part of our Constitution. I view it differently. Why are we committing suicide? Why are we doing that?"

133. Miriam Hernandez, "Trump Cites History to Defend Muslim Immigration Ban," ABC7.com, December 9, 2015.

134. Trip Gabriel, "Donald Trump Says He'd 'Absolutely' Require Muslims to Register," *New York Times*, November 20, 2015.

135. Nick Gass, "Trump: 'Absolutely No Choice' but to Close Mosques," Politico. com, November 18, 2015.

136. Louis Jacobson, "Donald Trump Says He Never Called for Profiling Muslims," PolitiFact.com, October 21, 2016, accessed August 7, 2018.

137. Hunter Walker, "Donald Trump Has Big Plans for 'Radical Islamic' Terrorists, 2016, and 'That Communist' Bernie Sanders," Yahoo News, November 19, 2015.

138. Michael Lipka, "Muslims and Islam: Key Findings in the U.S. and Around the World," Pew Research Center, August 9, 2017.

139. Peter Beinart, "When Conservatives Oppose 'Religious Freedom,'" *Atlantic*, April 11, 2017.

140. Andrew L. Whitehead, Samuel L. Perry, and Joseph O. Baker, "Make America Christian Again: Christian Nationalism and Voting for Donald Trump in the 2016 Presidential Election," *Sociology of Religion* 79, no. 2 (2018): 147–71.

141. Hannah Wise, "Trump's Favorite General Doesn't View Him as a Republican or Islam as a Religion, He Says in Dallas," DallasNews.com, August 10, 2016.

142. Beinart, "Denationalization of American Muslims."

143. Beinart, "Denationalization of American Muslims."

144. Christopher Mathias, "The Anti-Muslim Extremists Steve Bannon Thinks Are Experts on Islam," *Huffington Post*, November 15, 2016.

145. Anai Rhoads, "Muslim Groups Respond to False Claims by Congressman Pompeo," *Huffington Post*, June 13, 2013.

146. Michael W. Chapman, "DCI Pompeo After Boston Bombing: 'Silence Has Made These Islamic Leaders Across America Potentially Complicit,'" CNSNews.com (Media Research Center), January 24, 2017, accessed July 4, 2018.

147. Beinart, "Denationalization of American Muslims."

148. Andrew Kaczysnki, Nathan McDermott, and Chris Massie, "John Bolton Has Decade-Long Association with Anti-Islam Activist Pamela Geller," CNN.com, March 23, 2018.

149. Dion Nissenbaum, "John Bolton's Deputy Draws Ire of Jewish, Muslim Groups," *Wall Street Journal*, June 1, 2018.

150. Carson comments on *Meet the Press*, September 20, 2015.

151. Jeff Stein, "Trump Says His Ban Will Protect Christian Refugees. He Just Sent 6 Back to the Middle East," Vox.com, January 29, 2017.

152. Laurie Goodstein, "Christian Leaders Denounce Trump's Plan to Favor Christian Refugees," *New York Times*, January 29, 2017.

153. Interview with Christian Broadcasting Network, January 17, 2017.

154. Phillip Connor, "U.S. Admits Record Number of Muslim Refugees in 2016," Pew Research Center, October 5, 2016.

155. Andrew Griffin, "Donald Trump Retweets Britain First: What Is the Truth Behind Anti-Islam Tweets Shared by the President?," *Independent*, November 29, 2017.

156. Sam Knight, "Trump, Britain First, and the Purveyors of Racism and Bigotry," *New Yorker*, November 30, 2017.

157. Rudy Giuliani, interview with Maria Bartiromo on FOX News, August 20, 2018.

158. Lauren Gambino et al., "Thousands Protest Against Trump Travel Ban in Cities and Airports Nationwide," *Guardian* (US ed.), January 29, 2017.

159. Ray Gustini, "Utah Republican Stands Up for NYC 'Mosque,'" Atlantic.com, August 31, 2010.

160. Mark Hensch, "Anti-Defamation League CEO: I'll 'Register as a Muslim' If Trump Makes Database," TheHill.com, November 18, 2016; Holly Yan and Eric Levenson, "Empathy and Action: Muslims Unite to Help Fix Vandalized Jewish Cemeteries," CNN.com, March 1, 2017; Kate Smith, "Muslim-Led Fundraiser Nets $150,000 for Funeral Costs of Synagogue Shooting Victims," CBSNews.com, October 29, 2018.

161. American Sociological Association, "Sociologists Reflect on the 2016 Presidential Election," *ASA Footnotes* 44, no. 8 (December 2016).

162. "2014 Hate Crime Statistics: Incidents, Offenses, Victims, and Known Offenders by Bias Motivation, 2014," FBI: UCR, table 1; "2017 Hate Crime Statistics: Incidents, Offenses, Victims, and Known Offenders by Bias Motivation, 2017," FBI: UCR, table 1.

163. Abdelkader, "When Islamophobia Turns Violent," pp. 1–2.

164. Abdelkader, "When Islamophobia Turns Violent," p. 4.

165. Justin Carissimo, "Indiana University Student Expelled After Attacking Muslim Woman, Yelling 'White Power' and 'Kill Them All,'" *Independent*, October 19, 2015.

166. Abdelkader, "When Islamophobia Turns Violent," p. 53.

167. Glenn Marshall, Marc Fortier, and Michael Rosenfield, "Two Teens Accused of Spray Painting 'USA' on Massachusetts Mosque Arraigned," NECN, November 1, 2015.

168. Hannah Covington, "Guilty Plea Entered in Assault with Beer Mug on Muslim Woman at Coon Rapids Applebee's," *Star Tribune*, November 17, 2016.

169. Dave Altimari, "Mosque Shooter Gets 6 Months in Federal Prison; Judge Says Deterrence Needed," *Hartford Courant*, June 17, 2016.

170. "Feces, Torn Pages of Quran Thrown at Door of Texas Mosque," CBS News, November 16, 2015.

171. Caitlin Nolan, "Muslim Sixth Grader Allegedly Attacked by Schoolmates Who Called Her ISIS, Tore at Her Hijab," InsideEdition, December 7, 2015.

172. "Arrest in Shooting of Muslim Cab Driver on Thanksgiving," CrimeSider CBS, December 2, 2015.

173. Alexandra Sims, "'Bullet-Riddled' Quran Found Outside Islamic Clothing Shop in Southern California," *Independent*, December 3, 2015.

174. Malaika Fraley, "Castro Valley Woman Takes Plea Deal for Coffee Attack on Muslim Man," *East Bay Times*, September 9, 2016.

175. Dana Ford, "Pig's Head Left at Philadelphia Mosque," CNN.com, December 9, 2015.

176. Abdelkader, "When Islamophobia Turns Violent," p. 62.

177. Patrick Edgell, "Palm Desert Man Sentenced to 6 Years for Firebombing Coachella Mosque," KESQ News Channel 3, February 29, 2016.

178. Greg Toppo, "Police: Two Mosques Near L.A. Defaced," *USA Today*, December 13, 2015.

179. John Agar, "Robber Called Store Clerk 'Terrorist' Before Shooting Him in Face, Worker Says," MichiganLive, December 14, 2015.

180. Tasha Tsiaperas, "Murderer with Anti-Muslim Vendetta Convicted in Dallas Tire Shop Shooting," *Dallas News*, July 21, 2016.

181. Bates, "Faces of the American Muslims."

CHAPTER EIGHTEEN

Preserving Religious Freedom

1. Nina Shea, director of the Center for Religious Freedom, Hudson Institute, interview with the author, March 20, 2018.

2. Mario Kravchenko, "Inventing Extremists: The Impact of Russian Anti-Extremism Policies on Freedom of Religion or Belief," United States Commission on International Religious Freedom, January 2018, p. 15.

3. Kravchenko, "Inventing Extremists," p. 17.

4. Brian J. Grim and Roger Finke, *The Price of Freedom Denied: Religious Persecution and Conflict in the 21st Century* (New York: Cambridge Univ. Press, 2011), p. 146.

5. George J. Marlin, "The U.S. Should Pressure India to Curb Hindu Extremism," *National Review*, February 2, 2018, accessed online July 17, 2018.

6. "2017 Annual Report," United States Commission on International Religious Freedom, April 2017, p. 151.

7. "2017 Annual Report," p. 60.

8. In all, in 2014, 105 people were charged with blasphemy: 11 Ahmadis, 7 Christians, 5 Hindus, and 82 Muslims.

9. "Pakistan: On Fifth Anniversary of Shahbaz Bhatti Assassination, USCIRF Calls for Reform and Repeal of Blasphemy Law," United States Commission on International Religious Freedom, March 1, 2016.

10. "2017 Annual Report," p. 62.

11. Robert P. George and Hannah Rosenthal, "Rampant Religious Persecution Against Atheists," *USA Today*, May 3, 2016.

12. Sigal Samuel, "Banning Muslim Veils Tends to Backfire—Why Do Countries Keep Doing It?" *The Atlantic*, August 3, 2018. Robert Zeretsky, "How French Secularism Became Fundamentalist," *Foreign Policy*, April 7, 2016.

13. "Global Uptick in Government Restrictions on Religion in 2016: Nationalist Parties and Organizations Played an Increasing Role in Harassment of Religious Minorities, Especially in Europe," Pew Research Center, June 21, 2018.

14. What's more, modern research suggests that people who are more religious tend to respect authority more, which also makes them less open to dissent. Robert D. Putnam and David E. Campbell, *American Grace: How Religion Divides and Unites Us* (New York: Simon & Schuster, 2010), pp. 488–89, Kindle.

15. "Religious Landscape Study," Pew Research Center.

16. Caryle Murphy, "Interfaith Marriage Is Common in U.S., Particularly Among the Recently Wed," Pew Research Center, June 2, 2015.

17. Putnam and Campbell, *American Grace*, pp. 494–95.

18. Trump interview with Christian Broadcasting Network, David Brody and Jenna Browder, November 1, 2018.

19. To elaborate, besides his negative record on Muslim rights, what is Trump's record on other religious liberty issues?

The White House website on July 15, 2018, laid out the evidence that "President Donald J. Trump Stands Up for Religious Freedom in the United States." Examples included various elements championed by religious conservatives on abortion, same-sex marriage, the Johnson Amendment, and conscience exemptions:

He spoke at several prayer breakfasts.

He "declared several days of prayer, including a National Day of Prayer for the Victims of Hurricane Harvey and for America's National Response and Recovery Efforts."

He addressed the March for Life anti-abortion rally and thus "became the first President to address the March for Life rally live via satellite."

Mike Pence addressed the March for Life rally in 2017, becoming the first sitting vice president to do so in person.

He blocked foreign aid from going to organizations that perform abortions.

He made it easier for states to defund abortion clinics.

On October 13, 2017, President Trump spoke at the Values Voter Summit. (There, he declared victory in the "war on Christmas." "You know, we're getting near that beautiful Christmas season that people don't talk about anymore. They don't use the word 'Christmas' because it's not politically correct. You go to department stores, and they'll say, 'Happy New Year' and they'll say other things. And it will be red, they'll have it painted, but they don't say it. Well, guess what? We're saying 'Merry Christmas' again." "Remarks by President Trump at the 2017 Values Voter Summit," WhiteHouse.gov, October 13, 2017, accessed July 18, 2018, https://www.whitehouse.gov/briefings-statements /remarks-president-trump-2017-values-voter-summit/.)

Most of those either are not directly related to religious liberty (e.g., speaking at an anti-abortion rally), are symbolic (speaking at a prayer breakfast), or are damaging (perpetuating the "war on Christmas" myth).

He did also take some steps that, while minor, were positive. The administration created a Conscience and Religious Freedom Division in the Department of Health and Human Services. It is designed to better review complaints from doctors and other health-care professionals who feel they have not been able to fully take advantage of the numerous conscience exemptions already on the books, many of which deal with abortion. The *Washington Post* summarized: "Under that rule of the George W. Bush administration, which was rescinded and replaced by the Obama administration in 2011, covered institutions or groups could continue to receive federal funding by signing a certification that they were aware of existing legal protections. The new regulation would incorporate elements of the older rule but also would go further and require entities to post notices of the protections. Officials say they expect them to ensure that organization-wide safeguards are in place, update policies as needed and implement staff training." Sarah Pulliam Bailey, Ariana Eunjung Cha, and Juliet Eilperin, "HHS Releases New Rule on Health Workers' Religious, Moral Objections," *Washington Post*, January 19, 2018. It also gave states greater freedom to regulate or defund Planned Parenthood. "The new policy could allow states to receive millions in federal funding while banning abortion providers from participating in a family planning program for low-income women." The head of the new division, Roger Severino, said, "The regulations make clear and give notice to the public that we're in business on these statutes, and we'll give it the proper focus and energy they deserve because they've been ignored for too long."

Trump has also repeatedly claimed that he had eliminated the Johnson Amendment. "You've seen all the things that we've passed including the Johnson Amendment," Trump said in 2018. But the Johnson Amendment is a law and cannot be overturned by executive order. Congress as of the end of 2018 had not passed his proposal. He did issue an executive order telling the IRS not to punish churches for their political beliefs, "consistent with law," which experts on all sides of the issue said didn't have much substantive impact.

20. When he was still a general, he issued the notorious General Order No. 11, which ordered the expulsion of every Jew from Tennessee, Mississippi, and Kentucky (it was countermanded by Abraham Lincoln).

21. "Hindu Prayer in Congress Criticized," Associated Press, September 21, 2000; B. A. Robinson, "Hindu Invocation in Congress," ReligiousTolerance.org, November 4, 2015, accessed January 27, 2018.

22. Isaac Backus, *Truth Is Great and Will Prevail* (Boston, 1781).

23. Adams diary entry, March 7, 1756, quoted in Norman Cousins, *In God We Trust: The Religious Beliefs and Ideas of the American Founding Fathers* (New York: Harper and Brothers, 1958), p. 81.

24. This approach does have drawbacks. As society becomes ever more diverse, the practicalities of giving a platform to all the relevant religious groups become more challenging. At presidential inaugurations, it became cumbersome to include all faiths in the ceremony itself, but smaller religions were included in a second religious service the next day.

25. Andrew L. Whitehead, Samuel L. Perry, and Joseph O. Baker, "Make America Christian Again: Christian Nationalism and Voting for Donald Trump in the 2016 Presidential Election," *Sociology of Religion* 79, no. 2 (2018): 147–71.

26. Andrew Sullivan, "Erick Erickson Has a Point," The Daily Dish, February 24, 2014.

27. Michelle Boorstein, "LGBT, Mormon Groups Announce Compromise Anti-discrimination Measure in Utah," *Washington Post*, March 4, 2015.

28. Statement of Chai R. Feldblum, nominee for Commissioner, Equal Employment Opportunity Commission, before the Committee on Health, Education, Labor, and Pensions, US Senate, November 19, 2009.

29. Writing on August 1, 2018, Feldblum elaborated: "I hold strongly to the belief that we can work through the complexity of these issues. Respecting religious organizations and people, and respecting LGBT organizations and people (including religious LGBT organizations and people) will result in different answers in different circumstances, and the law should reflect that. When dealing with religious organizations, the government should work to ensure that such organizations can thrive and flourish even if they hold and teach views that others may find offensive. When dealing with individuals, the government should respect a statement by a religious person that complying with a non-discrimination law or some other law will place a burden on that person's religious beliefs, unless there is a good reason to believe that statement is false. If there is a way to accommodate the person and still achieve the compelling purpose of the law, the government should do that. If there is no way to accommodate the person, and still ensure that the compelling purpose of the law is achieved, then the accommodation should not be made. That is what nuance means. If one believes there is only a "win-lose" battle, then everyone must be painted as a radical advocate of one side or another. But that is not a constructive way forward. What we

need instead is to acknowledge the full and complex reality of those who are different from us and then find the generosity of spirit to reach across divides and come together in thoughtful and respectful dialogue. That is what our country needs and deserves." Chai Feldblum, "What I Really Believe About Religious Liberty and LGBT Rights," Medium.com, August 1, 2018.

30. Letter from James Madison to Jasper Adams, September 1833.

Captions, Permissions, and Credits

Cover: "Riot in Philadelphia." This contemporary lithograph depicts Nativists, wearing top hats, battling with state militias on July 7, 1844, in the Southwark neighborhood of Philadelphia during riots between Protestants and Catholics in Philadelphia in 1834. Artist unknown.

Chapter One: Mary Dyer being led to her execution on the Boston Common, June 1, 1660. Artist unknown, nineteenth century. Granger.

Chapter Two: James Madison, 1783. Bust portrait miniature, facing slightly right, by Charles Willson Peale (1741–1827). Library of Congress, Prints & Photographs Division.

Chapter Three: Depiction of a religious revival camp meeting, ca. 1830. Lithograph by Hugh Bridgeport (1794–ca. 1868). Library Company of Philadelphia / Bridgeman Images.

Chapter Four: "Destruction of the Ursuline Convent by Fire." Illustration by unknown artist from *Trial of John R. Buzzell, the Leader of the Convent Rioters, for Arson and Burglary* (Boston: Lemuel Gulliver, 1834). Hathi Trust.

Chapter Five: A slave in chains praying for freedom, n.d. Colored engraving by unknown artist, American School. Private collection / Peter Newark American Pictures / Bridgeman Images.

Chapter Six: "Hon. John A. Bingham of Ohio," ca. 1860–1875. Photograph by Mathew Brady (1822–1896). Brady-Handy photograph collection, Library of Congress, Prints & Photographs Division.

Chapter Seven: Mormon leaders in striped prison uniforms, including George Q. Cannon *(center, with cane)*, William Gimbert Saunders *(second from right)*, and William Morley Black *(to right of Cannon, with white beard)*, April 5, 1886. They were arrested for practicing polygamy. Photographed by C.R. (Charles Roscoe) Savage, 1832–1909; used by permission of Special Collections. J. Willard Marriott Library, University of Utah.

Chapter Eight: Timber Yellow Robe, Henry Standing Bear, and Wounded Yellow Robe in Native American dress, 1879. Wounded Yellow Robe, Henry Standing Bear, and Timber Yellow Robe in school uniforms, 1879. Photograph by John N. Choate, 1879; National Anthropological Archives, Smithsonian Institution, Photo Lot 81-12 06812700 & Photo Lot 81-2 06819400.

Chapter Nine: Ku Klux Klan members at a march in Washington, DC, August 9, 1925. Bettman / Getty Images.

Chapter Nine: "The American River Ganges. The Priests and the Children" / Thomas Nast, 1871.

Chapter Nine: "Don't Believe in That" / Thomas Nast, 1871.

Chapter Nine: "Church & State—Europe—United States" / Thomas Nast, 1870.

Chapter Nine: "'The Promised Land' as Seen from the Dome of Saint Peter's, Rome" / Thomas Nast, 1870.

Chapter Ten: Schoolchildren saluting the flag, Rochester, New York, 1943. Photographed by Ralph Amdursky. Farm Security Administration—Office of War Information photograph collection / Library of Congress, Prints & Photographs Division.

Chapter Eleven: The "These Immortal Chaplains" stamp, issued in 1948 by the US Postal Service. Personal collection of the author.

Chapter Twelve: Pennsylvania Amish men walking toward the Supreme Court building in Washington, DC, December 8, 1971. The Court heard the case of the State of Wisconsin versus the Wisconsin Amish school system. AP Photo / John Duricka.

Chapter Thirteen: A naturalization ceremony in Austin, Texas, Thursday, June 29, 2017. Jay Janner / Austin American-Statesman /AP.

Chapter Fourteen: President Ronald Reagan and Pope John Paul II, Fairbanks, Alaska, May 2, 1984. AP Photo / Scott Stewart.

Chapter Fifteen: A rally, organized in part by the Catholic Archdiocese of Philadelphia, in front of Independence Hall, Philadelphia, Friday, March 23, 2012. AP Photo / Alex Brandon.

Chapter Sixteen: W. Deen Mohammed, one of the nation's most prominent African American Muslim leaders, September 17, 2002. Alex Garcia / *Chicago Tribune* / AP.

Chapter Seventeen: Protesters opposing construction of an Islamic center near the former site of the World Trade Center, downtown New York, August 22, 2010. James Estrin / *The New York Times* / Redux.

Index